Valparaíso School / Open City Group

MASTERS OF LATIN AMERICAN ARCHITECTURE SERIES
An international joint project developed by Birkhäuser – Publishers for Architecture
Contrapunto, Logos, McGill-Queen's University Press and Tanais Ediciones
Part of the Biblioteca Iberoamericana de Arquitectura collection
BIENAL IBEROAMERICANA DE ARQUITECTURA E INGENIERÍA CIVIL
Ministerio de Fomento del Reino de España, Junta de Andalucía

Valparaíso School
Open City Group

Rodrigo Pérez de Arce
Fernando Pérez Oyarzun

Edited by Raúl Rispa

Birkhäuser – Publishers for Architecture
Basel · Boston · Berlin

Originally published in 2003 under the title
escuela de valparaíso / grupo ciudad abierta
by Tanais Ediciones s.a

Publisher *Raúl Rispa*
Executive Editor *Valeria Varas*
English Editor *Teresa Santiago*

Original Spanish version *Tanais Ediciones, s.a (Sevilla, Madrid)*
For Chile, Argentina, Uruguay and Paraguay *Contrapunto (Santiago de Chile)*
English edition *Birkhäuser — Publishers for Architecture (Basel)* and
McGill-Queen's University Press (Montreal)
Italian edition *Logos (Modena)*

Texts: Selected Works by *Fernando Pérez Oyarzún* (pages 20-31 and 36-55), *Rodrigo Pérez de Arce* (pages 32-35 and 56-133); Biography and Chronology by *Catholic University of Valparaíso School of Architecture, Corporación Amereida* and *Tanais Editorial Team*; Bibliography by *Tanais Editorial Team* and *Catholic University of Valparaíso School of Architecture.*
Original drawings, plans and photographs by *Institute of Architecture, Catholic University of Valparaíso School of Architecture, Corporación Amereida, Juan Purcell, Raúl Rispa et al.*: see page 167.
Documentation by *Catholic University of Valparaíso School of Architecture, Architecta Outsourcing 21, s.l., Tanais Editorial Team*
English translation by *Erica Witschey* and *Gavin Powell*
Text editing *Lettice Small*
Design and Layout by *Tanais Editorial Team*
Electronic Edition by *José Luis Casado, Belén Gómez*

A CIP catalogue record for this book is available from the Library of Congress, Washington D.C. USA

Bibliographic information published by Die Deutsche Bibliothek
Die Deutsche Bibliothek lists this publication in the Deutsche Nationalbibliographie; detailed bibliographic data is available in the Internet at <http://dnb.ddb.de>.

© Tanais Ediciones, s.a., 2003
© 2003 for this English edition:
Birkhäuser — Publishers for Architecture, P.O. Box 133
CH-4010 Basel, Switzerland

This work is subject to copyright. All rights are reserved, whether the whole or part of the material is concerned, specifically the rights of translation, reprinting, re-use of illustrations, recitation, broadcasting, reproduction on microfilms or in other ways, and storage in data banks. For any kind of use, permission of the copyright owner must be obtained.

Printed by Torreangulo arte gráfico, s.a., Madrid
Printed on acid-free paper produced from chlorine-free pulp. TCF ∞
Printed in Spain
ISBN: 3-7643-6994-9

Member of the BertelsmannSpringer Publishing Group
www.birkhauser.ch

9 8 7 6 5 4 3 2 1

8   The Valparaíso School
    Fernando Pérez Oyarzún
13 So far yet so near: the Open City and the *Travesías*
    Rodrigo Pérez de Arce

19 Selected Works

20 Achupallas Urban Development
24 Los Pajaritos Chapel
28 Naval Academy
32 Avenida del Mar
36 Benedictine Monastery of the Holy Trinity
42 Casa Cruz
48 Southern Churches
    50   Mother Church in Puerto Montt
    51   Church in Corral
    54   Church of Nuestra Señora de la Candelaria

56 Open City
66 Music Room
72 Palace of Dawn and Dusk
78 House of Names
86 Wanderer's Lodge
98 Henri Tronquoy Agora and Vestal
102 Double or Banquet Lodge
108 Temple, Cemetery and Gully
114 Prototype Workshop

122 Works in *Travesías*
    124 *Travesía* to Lake Titicaca
    126 *Travesía* to Caldera
    128 *Travesía* to the Plains of Curimahuida
    130 *Travesías* to Comau Huinay Fjord and the *Amereida* Vessel

135 Works and Designs
152 Biography and Chronology
161 Bibliography
166 Glossary

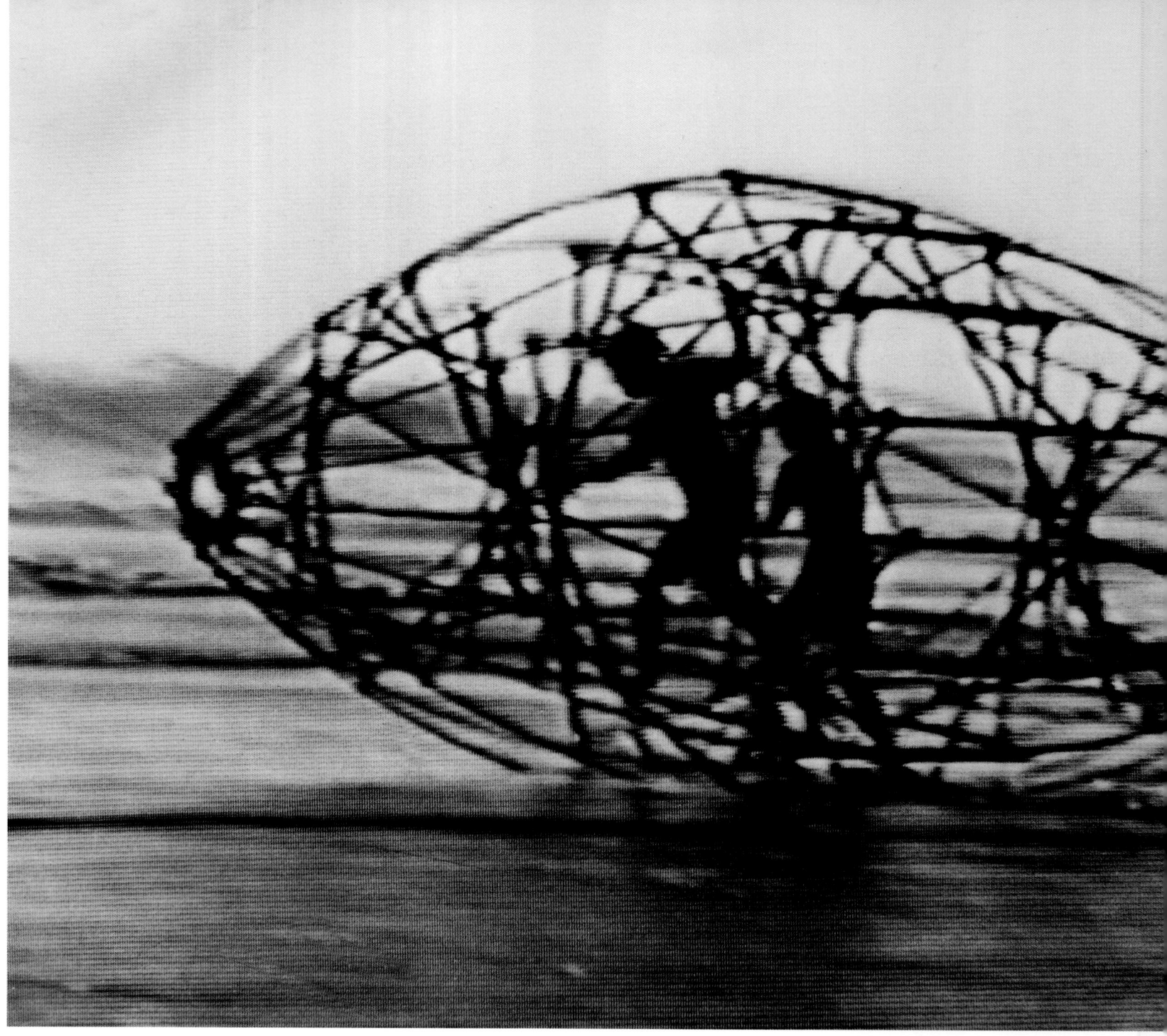

As poets, men inhabit the land
Heidegger

You have in your hands an exceptional book. It is exceptional, first and foremost because of its subject matter: the work and life of the Valparaíso group is somewhat polyhedral, with its multiple facets so intrinsically interrelated and hierarchically alike that it is by no means easy to place them within the context of the original format of words such as the book and the narrative. This volume seeks to transmit to the reader that polyhedral character of those four generations of men and women, so we recommend that you start reading the book at any point which immediately appeals to you, thereby creating your own roadmap. However, we believe that it would be useful to begin with the Biography and take a look at the basic dictionary of concepts, both of which are to be found at the end of the monograph. It is no coincidence that we refer you first to the words, because another exceptional feature of Alberto Cruz and his companions is their architecture sustained by the Word and co-generated with poetry, the ultimate distillate of the word. The word! What a contrast to the visual banality which surrounds us!

Let us pass from the power of the word to the shapes and forms of the architecture itself and the visual arts which flourish within the group; here you will find extremely modern and up-to-date formal language: diagonals, sloping planes, acute and obtuse angles, apparent examples of destructuring which can immediately be associated with the shapes and forms of deconstructivism. But these are not hollow, empty formulas, monotonous fashion of our times, a blurred, diffuse and unfocused Neo-Baroquism (such, perhaps, because it does not really have anything to say?); rather they are paths discovered by radical researchers who, on the periphery, are prepared to challenge everything and face the consequences, but always with the greatest mathematical, structural and analytical rigour.

For aesthetics and ethics, architectural discipline and individual and social life could not be more inextricably linked than in the case of these university teachers who make their models on a scale of 1:1 and live in them, thereby following in the footsteps of the Christian communities, humanism, the Jesuits and their missions in South America (including their work with the Araucan Indians), of Owens, the Bauhaus and Le Corbusier, of Torres-García and his proposition of the south as north, of Ulm, Tomás Maldonado, Utopia. . .

They revel in the splendour of poverty, the poverty of the materials used in their buildings, the transitory *hospederías* rather than privately-owned houses, the austerity of their way of life, the assumption of the ephemeral condition, the fragility and temporality—as an alternative to the Vitruvian firmitas; which all means divesting oneself of the non-essential. It refers us back to early Christianity, and then forward to the here and now, to a "return to not knowing", authentic deconstruction *avant la lettre*, a play of oppositions. . . We think you will love these people who, from outside the mainstream, propose a true radical alternative to architecture, and the way it is taught, researched and practised professionally. The publishers Birkhäuser, Logos, McGill-Queen's, Contrapunto, and Tanais, and the Ibero-American Biennial, have believed from Basel, Modena, Montreal, Santiago de Chile, Seville and Madrid that it is well worth learning about this group. To the people of Valparaíso who trusted us—soul companions in this *travesía*—to show their life and work in their first book open to the world, we offer our apologies if we do not succeed in arousing in you the same enthusiasm which they, and their telluric land of poets have aroused in us.

The Editor

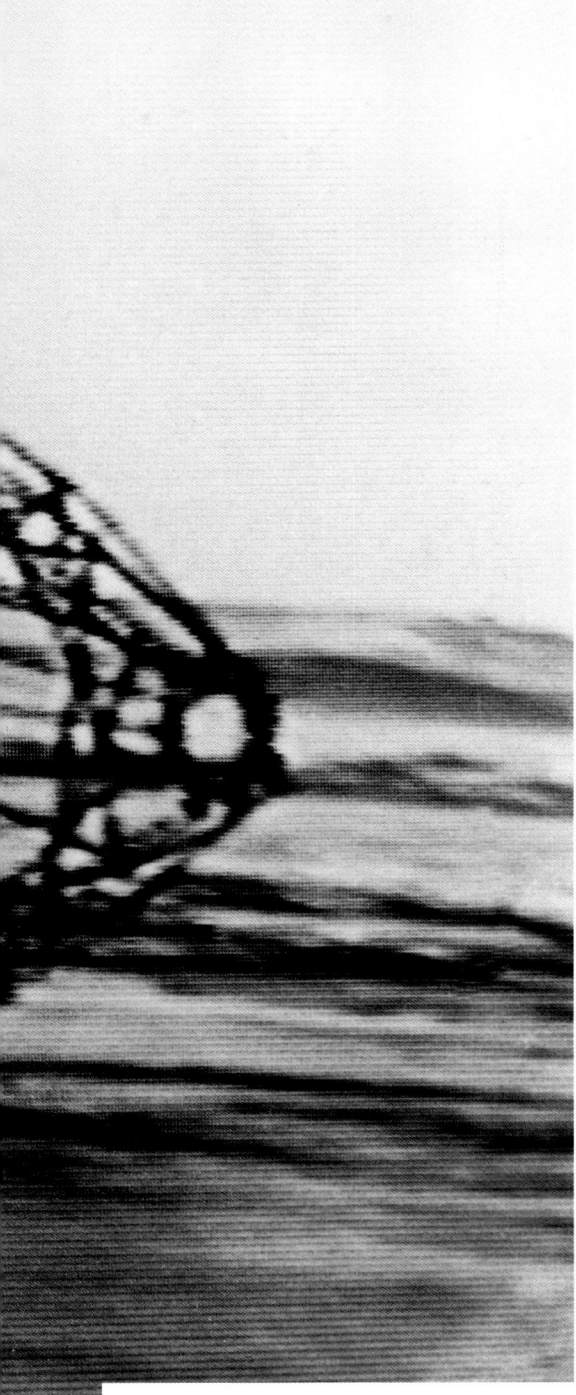

Luodo, games at Open City

The Valparaíso School

Fernando Pérez Oyarzún

In 1952, a group of young architects led by Alberto Cruz and the Argentine poet Godofredo Iommi moved from Santiago de Chile to the city of Viña del Mar, next to the port of Valparaíso. Having accepted contracts with the Catholic University of Valparaíso, they had come to teach at the School of Architecture founded some decades before. The Rector of the University, the Jesuit Jorge González, had initially invited Alberto Cruz, who had been teaching at the Catholic University of Chile, in Santiago. Cruz and Iommi, who had become friends and co-operated at an intellectual level for several years, decided to transfer as a group and made this a pre-condition for accepting the invitation.

A radical experience.

Born in 1917, Alberto Cruz studied architecture at the Catholic University of Santiago, and soon proved himself as a charismatic young professor, organizing an introductory course on architecture which was a departure from the traditional; he played a significant role in the movement to reform his School in 1949. However, Cruz afterwards gave up teaching and travelled to Europe. Iommi, also born in 1917, for his part did not complete his studies in Economics. He decided instead to dedicate his life to poetry, having come under the influence of the poet Vicente Huidobro, and settled in Chile.

The newly-arrived group moved into a collection of recently built dwellings in Cerro Castillo, in Viña del Mar. Overlooking the city, the houses, set in a *cul-de-sac*, offered the right conditions for the life of social and strong communal interaction which they intended to lead. The influence of the new teachers from Santiago was such that it completely dominated the School. Before long, the Valparaíso School, as it became known, acquired a reputation for its radical stance. Its teaching, compared with other schools, offered an experimental alternative. At the same time, the group also founded the Institute of Architecture, envisaged as a place for research and completion of architectural projects. Using various names and methods, this flank of research and practice, often experimental in nature, was to become one of the more permanent features of the group.

The school soon attracted other artists, such as the Argentine sculptor Claudio Girola who, together with Tomás Maldonado and others, formed a substantial art group in Buenos Aires linked to experiences such as that of Max Bill in Basilea and the Salon Realités Nouvelles in Paris. Contacts were also established with artists, thinkers and men of science, among them the Brazilian poet Thiago de Melo, the French philosopher Francois Fedier, the Chilean intellectuals Mario Góngora (historian), Jorge Eduardo Rivera (philosopher), and Juan de Dios Vial Correa (biologist). In this way the group affirmed, on the one hand, its universal vocation and, on the other, its intention of establishing a dialogue between different arts and disciplines around the innovative activity of teaching, research and creating which were being proposed by the school. At a certain distance, contacts were maintained with those who —albeit from different positions, such as Juan Borchers— shared the group's concern with the theoretical development of, and the search for, alternative ways of working professionally.

In addition to its unusual teaching activity, its projects and its participation in competitions, the group became known for staging poetic acts in public, which served to highlight both its alternative nature and its adherence to a poetic vision of culture and existence. The best known of these acts, which they called *phalènes*, consisted of an act of poetic creation performed on a collective basis and in public places. Iommi, inventor of the *phalènes* and of their poetic rules, travelled around Europe performing these acts.

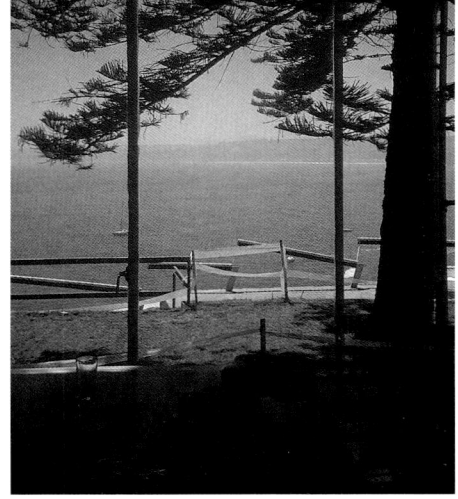

Terrace, Valparaíso School of Architecture, Recreo, Viña del Mar

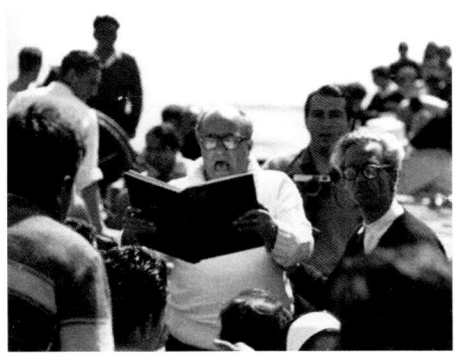

Alberto Cruz and Godofredo Iommi (reading) in a poetic act or *phalène* in Caleta Abarca

In 1965 members of the school, together with poets, philosophers and foreign guest painters, set off on a poetic journey from Punta Arenas, in Patagonia, to Bolivia, in the very centre of South America, staging a series of events and poetic acts while they travelled. The experience of the trip led to two publications, entitled *Amereida I* and *II*, which, the first especially, have played a significant inspirational role in the activity of the School. This first poetic journey marked a new stage in its history, which germinated, years later, in that pedagogical and creative proposal which went under the name of *travesías* (poetic voyages or crossings).

In 1967 the Valparaíso School, its students and professors, led a movement to reform the university. This movement was unable to maintain the momentum which Iommi and his group had started and finally ended up going the way of other university movements at the end of the Sixties. However, it acquired significant historical importance both as the initiator of a series of similar movements inside and outside the country, and for its theoretical content, expressed in various documents and manifestos.

From 1970 onwards the research and design activity, and a large proportion of the energy of the group, began to be focused on what became known as the Open City. Founded as a co-operative in Ritoque, a small coastal village to the north of Viña del Mar, it was conceived as a space of collective life and work which would bring together the disciplines cultivated by the School and was intended as an open site in the double sense that it was open to its destiny and had a vocation for hospitality. At the beginning of the 21st century, the Open City changed its legal status, becoming a foundation and seeking to open itself up to those who are interested in its ideas, thereby expanding outwards beyond the relatively small circle of its founders and owners.

The permanence and continuity of the Valparaíso School over a period spanning more than fifty years makes it, on that basis alone, rather exceptional in the architectural production of the world, and one of the most important cultural phenomena in the recent history of Latin America, transcending what might have been an atypical academic experience. Strictly speaking, it can be considered a "school" because of its collective nature, but above all, because it is a collective which is distinctive and recognizable. A school is recognized not only for sharing a set of ideas and beliefs, but also for its capacity to generate a characteristic iconography. In this case it does not restrict itself to architecture, but covers a set of formal options ranging from a way of drawing and writing to a way of speaking. There is a "Valparaíso line", a "Valparaíso lyric", a "Valparaíso rhetoric". Furthermore, sustained by its dedication to teaching, the group has joined in, creatively and unusually, with the university institution. Taking very much into account the role played by research in the contemporary university, the group has brought into being a remarkable foundation which could, indeed, be described as an institutional creation with a scope that goes beyond what is usual in a school of architecture.

The end of the First World War and the infectious enthusiasm which accompanied it had played an important role in disseminating the *avant garde* movements in Europe. With some exceptions, these ideas reached Chile ten or fifteen years later, on the eve of, or even during, the Second World War, at a time when they were beginning to be questioned in Europe. The reception of Modern architecture in Chile occurred at a time when the profession was going through a critical moment in its development. Therefore, the emergence of the Valparaíso School can be placed between this critical experience which arose

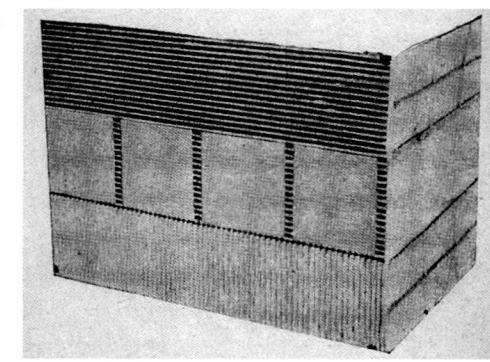

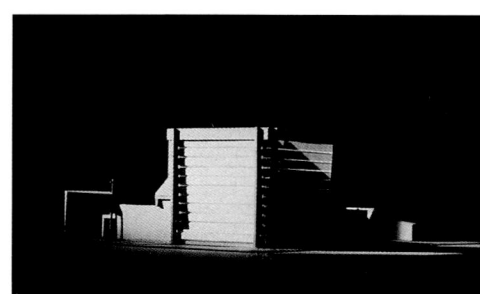

1 and 2 Works from Alberto Cruz's course on pre-architectural composition, published in *Plinto*, n° 1, 1947

3 Model of the church of Santa Clara, Santiago, first cubic version

from the Second World War and a certain cultural enthusiasm which existed in the country in the Fifties.

It is unlikely that the discussions taking place within the CIAM, which led to the emergence of Team X, and are expressive of a new vanguard, less trusting and more critical of the principles of modern architecture, were fully known in Chile at that time. However, something of that critical revision—not only of architecture but of modern culture itself, based as it was on the unlimited progress of technology—was present in the spirit of the refounders of the Valparaíso School. It was from this lack of confidence in a naively optimistic modernity, and at the same time from faith in radical modern poetics—perceived from an almost scatological perspective —that the fundamental tension which inspired the group surged. Its cultural attitude seemed to be closer to that critical spirit found among young European architects than to the orthodoxy of the modern masters who were at that time embarking upon their great works, from Le Corbusier's Unité to Mies van der Rohe's American sky-scrapers. Their interest in daily urban life as the inspiration for a specific architectural order was sufficient proof of this.

Furthermore, the Fifties in Chile were marked by highly significant cultural experiences and ventures, among them, the expansion of the university through the creation of new centres and institutes in several cities. Research came to be considered as a fundamental component of the activity of the university, and the traditional training provided by professional schools came under criticism. The arts found new niches for development within the university through orchestras, ballet, festivals and theatre groups. In short, a literary generation, known as the *Generation of 1950*, emerged in the country. Beyond any controversy which may have surrounded the Valparaíso School, it has essentially constituted an attempt to include architecture within that sphere of events and intentions. For its founders, the presence of architecture at the university had to be justified by research activity, but also by its capacity for dialogue with other arts and disciplines. This was to be a trend which would accompany the group throughout the whole of its development.

The collective dimension.

If a certain collective dimension is a characteristic of any school worthy of the name, with disciples gathering around one or more masters, this in the case of the Valparaíso School was one of its founding and permanent features. The condition laid down by Alberto Cruz that the invitation to teach would only be accepted as an invitation to the group was symbolic of the line which was to be followed by the school. Their arrival in Valparaíso as a group undoubtedly gave greater weight to the presence of the new teachers at the School. Beyond that, the intellectual force of the group arose from the variety of different talents offered by its members. In addition, the decision taken from the very beginning to share an experience of life, as well as of work and research, had a crucial impact on the culture of the School. What is more, both dimensions appear to be closely connected.

The foundation of collectives of artists who shared daily life in a climate conducive to work is a recurring motif, at least since the middle of the 19th century, and can be seen as a kind of poetic version of some of the social utopias which arose in that century. The well-known experiences of Tolstoy in Europe were emulated in various parts of the world. *The Group of Ten* in Chile at the beginning of the

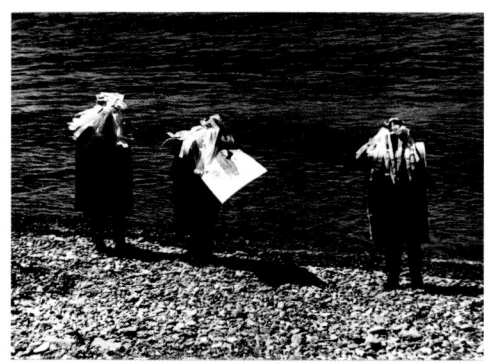
Phalène in Caleta Membrillo, Valparaíso

century brought together architects, painters and poets. Similar phenomena have to be taken into account by way of a backdrop to the Valparaíso experience. In fact, before settling in Chile, Godofredo Iommi had planned to organize colonies of poets in the Amazon and on the Island of Juan Fernández, but for various reasons these plans did not materialize. However, what was unusual about the Valparaíso experience was that it involved founding a working community and linking it to the university atmosphere: the group always maintained its own identity and its own objectives, while at the same time participating in the structure and regular activities of the university.

Moreover, architecture, like the cinema, has always, by its very nature, involved a collective dimension greater than that of the other arts. It is therefore understandable that the attempt to give shape to this collective condition has led to the emergence of very distinctive situations: from informal schools, such as that of Wright in Taliesin, to teams such as the TAC founded by Gropius, or the big corporate offices such as SOM where the dissolution of authorship and the collective realization of architectural design tasks arose more from the requirements of productive efficiency than from any bias towards social utopia. In the case of the Valparaíso School, the objective of collective work takes on greater scope and radicalism. And not only because of the weight of a community of interests which went beyond that of the work environment, but because, for the School, this collective dimension represented a value in itself: it formed part of a vision which transcended the boundaries of architecture to provide a glimpse of the possibility of an art made by all.

Although the initial designs of the School, such as the Chapel in Pajaritos and the urban development in Achupallas, have been attributed to Alberto Cruz in the school's publications, in reality they seem to have been the result of a collective production task involving the whole group. This paradigm of the workshop, as would occur later in the Botegha, appears to have had several versions in the history of the school and finds its theoretical conceptualization in what has more recently been called *trabajo en ronda* (work in a circle). This consisted of project co-operation which could manifest itself at several levels: from the possibility of contributing ideas or observations, in dialogue form, to working collectively on a project starting from relatively independent fragments developed by different architects. This way of working is not to be considered primarily as an efficient articulation of tasks, but as an attempt to clarify a problem of architecture—in the Wittgenstein sense of the term—or as an understanding of the work itself as a result of an architectural dialogue between relatively independent parties and architects. In this way, the usual individual authorship of works is relegated to a secondary level in the production of the Valparaíso School: its works are rarely signed works in the conventional sense. Within the group, the record of who was in charge or who assumed a more protagonistic role in each work is kept rather within the oral tradition and is not normally reflected in the public presentation of the works.

Art and life.

The idea of an art consistent with life, reflecting and representing it, of an art dissolved into life, transforming it into a deeper and richer experience, was one of the leitmotifs of the Valparaíso School. This was one of the constant concerns of Godofredo Iommi who, harking back to Rimbaud, talked of an art which rhymed with life. Perhaps in this relationship between art and life we can find a community of

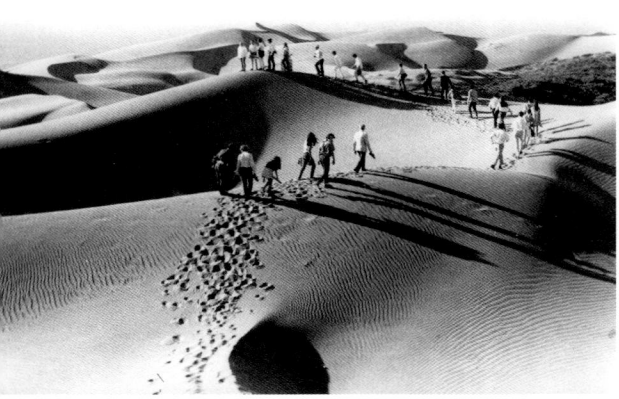

Opening ceremony of the site of the Open City in Ritoque, 1970

interests with certain versions of surrealism. And although this is not a suitable epithet for the school, it serves to throw some light upon that quest to insert art into the flow of everyday life. The very notion of life, such as it is understood within the group sphere, deserves special attention. It appears as something given, a gift in which everyday life and destiny are comprehended at one and the same time. Attention to the more ordinary realities, the object of both study and homage, never runs out. Everyday things are considered as the bearers of a destiny which, although manifested through them, transcends them.

The need for consistency in word and action, teaching and profession, appears to have been at the root of the formation of the Valparaíso group. Thus, the search for this consistency acquired a dimension in Valparaíso which was at the same time both ethical and disciplinary. Ethical, because what one said had to correspond with what one did. Disciplinary, because the existence of an explicit discourse which declared the "underlying principles" of a project became the essence of the design method.

The vision of the group concerning architecture, its practice and its teaching seemed to call for a certain style of life. This was why they organized a community as soon as they arrived in Valparaíso, which anticipated the later communal experience in the Open City. This decision stands as witness not only to a way of working but, above all, to the conviction that a specific professional activity, or even a series of theoretical convictions or aesthetic preferences, was not sufficient to carry forward the task which the group proposed. Just as Wittgenstein maintained with regard to philosophy, an authentic practice of architecture would call for a certain way of life.

In this context, teaching was perceived as being by way of example. The same strategies which the group put into practice in its first research about the city of Valparaíso, based on direct observation and on a certain way of recording impressions in sketches and notes, were implemented at the School, where they attained the status of method. This would become further enriched and varied over time. Partly indebted to Le Corbusier's travel sketches and Cruz's own experiences during his trip to Europe, this method manifested another facet of that attention to everyday life as a basis for architecture.

In the future, poetic acts and *travesías* would forge new links between art and everyday life which, once again, would translate into instruments of teaching or research. Thus, the foundation of the work ceased to be the life-based data understood in a naturalist perspective and became an act which interpreted and symbolically represented that life.

Finally, it was this very attention to life which provided the most explicit source of the trend towards the complexity of form demonstrated by many of the group's works. Frequently interpreted in an organicistic or even deconstructivist key, the road which led to these forms, and also the final result, had diverse origins. In any event, this primary bond with life understood simultaneously as a determinant and an illuminating gift, in the context of both its everyday and its mythical conditions, is essential for understanding the Valparaíso experience.

Incorporating a particular aspect of a formal organicism, resisting any conventional form of systematisation, always resorting to observation and to the case in question, in a kind of poetic empiricism, the reference to that everyday life understood in as a classical myth was a central element in the convictions of the school.

So far yet so near: the Open City and the Travesías

Rodrigo Pérez de Arce

1. The architectural projects undertaken by the Valparaíso group can be divided into three groups: professional commissions, the Open City, and *travesías*. The first adopted a more usual format, while those in the Open City have been undertaken by the community as a whole, with the roles of architect, client, and often inhabitant, coinciding. The *travesía* works, self-managed and self-constructed like those of the Open City, are spread throughout Chile and the American continent but were not intended for the use of the authors.

Each of these groups represented specific modes of relationship between author and work: the first group represents the conventional relationship between architect, builder and client, with the corresponding etiquette, documents and meetings; this is followed by the direct and more intimate experience of the Open City where these formalities were circumvented and exchanged for the physical effort of construction and also the knowledge acquired from the experience; finally, the *travesía* is a continuation of those conditions, albeit in a fleeting way. Thus, between the everyday intimacy of the Open City in Ritoque on the one hand, and the far-off destinations of so many *travesías* on the other, the experiences of the Valparaíso group became radically polarized, and finally separated by the breach which occurs between habit and memory: since 1970, the majority of the group's works have been seen either in the Open City, or in the destinations of the *travesías*, with all of them side-stepping the market and the channels it normally provides for typical professional practice.

2. Strongly influenced by Edmundo O'Gorman's vision of America, the Valparaíso group developed an Americanist discourse, searching for spatial keys and specific fields of application. They finally built their own text on a collective basis, the *Amereida*, with the participation of philosophers and poets, a kind of "poem in circle" about the continent, acknowledging its authority from the very beginning and becoming, after their own fashion, a "People of the Book". Of the three *Amereidas* published (with each edition having a limited print-run and intended for internal circulation only), it was the first which advanced most proposals; the second was above all a travel log and the third was a compilation of the *travesías* undertaken. The text of *Amereida I* was drawn up in the course of a journey made in 1965. Its name is an allusion to the *Aeneid*, a story of travel and foundation, an experience which assumes an epic stature (epic, from the Greek word for poem, "something worthy of being sung by poets, a feat, worthy of poetry").

Treatises are traditionally the most important texts in Architecture, documents equivalent to classical remains in their role as facilitators of a rapprochement with the arts of Antiquity. Their influence is as powerful as it is palpable in colonial America, a wasteland as far as its own models of architecture were concerned (at least for an eye trained according to the European canon) and too detached from the classical models. In the absence of the model, it is the text which has prevailed historically. Although not a treatise on architecture as such, the *Amereida* investigates the spatiality of the continent, opens a new and radical design dimension, and stimulates the realization of an architecture, in the words of Cruz, "co-generated with poetry". From the foundations of its exegesis arose the Open City and the program of *travesías*.

Amereida I was a journey or first *travesía* which followed an almost straight line over the southern part of Latin America from Cape Horn in Chilean Patagonia to Santa Cruz de la Sierra in Bolivia.

The journey was cut short in the vicinity of Caimiri owing to the activity nearby of Che Guevara's guerrillas and the ensuing political and military upheaval. The resulting poem, published in 1967, is indispensable as a key to appreciating the American vocation of the Valparaíso group and its interest in the vast stretches of territory of the American continent. Other studies of the territory dealt with the exploration of the American shores of the Pacific, or the archi-pelagos and marine territories of the last southern frontier to be colonized in Patagonia (at one extreme, this continental vision once again took up the view of Corbusier's work to place the city within its continental matrix and connected with Borchers' theoretical insistence on clarifying the logic of the Hispano-American city; yet another study encouraged the pioneering work of the architect and member of the group Jorge Sánchez in the creation of tourist guides from an almost total lack of previous documentation). As in *Amereida*, an impressive documentary and literary value is attributed to the Spanish chronicles: reading them was an obsession and fragments of them were incorporated literally into *Amereida*, thereby acknowledging them as a poetic work and asserting their pioneering quality. The fact that these ideas took root in the sphere of the School of Architecture was the most remarkable factor about them. Inherent to the value attributed to the poem as an instrument of proposition was the idea of architecture as art.

3. *Amereida I* used maps and star charts which subverted the conventions of mapmaking. Particularly remarkable are the inversion of the map of America (in accordance with the "thesis of our own north" (*tesis del propio norte*) and the superimposition of the Southern Cross (the constellation which guided navigators) onto the shape of the continent. Both of these operations sought to turn iconographic convention and its corresponding political and conceptual undertones upside down, to create a new way of approaching Latin America. The "own north" linked up with precedents such as that of Joaquín Torres García: his "because our north is the south ... that is why we turn the map around" (*porque nuestro norte es el sur ... por eso giramos el mapa*— 1935) asserted a system of references quite independent from the dominant northern cultures. The projection of the Southern Cross coincided approximately with the city of Santa Cruz de la Sierra, the continental meeting point of the Pampas and the Amazon jungle. As a result of this series of coincidence, which conjured up empirical and metaphorical facts, *Amereida* proclaimed the city to be the Poetic Capital of America: this is why it was designated as the destination for the 1965 itinerary.

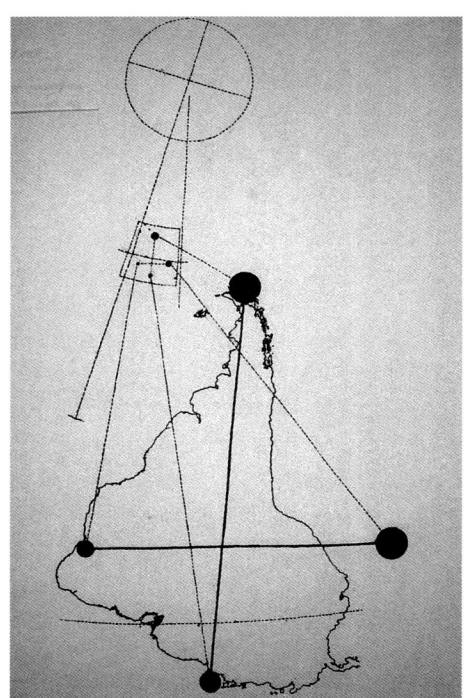

4. In its approach to the scale of the continent, the group investigated the significance of the structures of frontiers, political boundaries and delineations which shape the territory somewhat geometrically. Perhaps they attributed importance to those boundaries because they were the first approaches to dividing or arranging the territory: both inaugural signs and specific strategies of domination. Thus they drew up two models of territorial conceptualization (see adjacent drawing): the first, abstract and geometric, the *regios* or regular structures of the Spanish Empire under Charles V whose parallel and equidistant strips partitioned the territory systematically from ocean to ocean. The second, organic by nature, portrayed the political and territorial structures of the emerging independent republics of the 19th century, whose frontiers were generally drawn up along watersheds. The counterpoint between abstract vision and organic vision influenced the framework of reference of the School of Architecture. *Amereida I* encompassed these observations and underlined the importance of the continent's vast inland emptiness (citing the concept of Inland Sea: see drawing on p. 16), asserting it as the specific circumstances of South America and the coast-to-coast colonization of North America.

5. If words enclose oracular keys, these are particularly decisive in the initial stage of every undertaking, allocated in a kind of founding act, sometimes very brief, which transcribes the circumstances casting light on the architectural approach. In the words of Alberto Cruz: "... the work of the School of Architecture and of the Open City is... the passage between origin and generation". The inaugural ritual is collective and solemn, and "no work is realized without a founding act". The poet officiates as augur possessing, according to *Amereida*, "the gift of divining things, of clarifying... a way of merging with the land". Thus, the word acquires a specific and clairvoyant hierarchy as regards the relationship between work and place.

The project embodied the move, full of nuances and subjectivity, peculiar to the transition from the word to the work. *Amereida I* cites chronicles which recorded the adaptation of indigenous terms by the conquistadors, later giving rise to present day place-names, in a process as full of errors as of unexpected tones, when "... the Christians... understood that which they wished to understand... as if the indigenous people and they had spoken in Castillian Spanish".

Sustained by the conviction that while things (and places) remain unnamed they cannot be grasped, the architects of Valparaiso established that "...the poetic act... just like cattle branded with a red-hot iron... brings names to things."

Undoubtedly, the appeal to poetry connotes a particular predisposition towards randomness, and also a privilege of the intuition and the game. The role conferred upon the latter by the group is remarkable, both in terms of its continual reinvention and its collective practice—Claudio Girola cited extensively the *Homo Ludens* of Huizinga, and the concepts of the architect, professor and group member Manuel Casanueva are of particular interest.

6. The Open City came into being 18 years after the creation of the Institute of Architecture in Valparaiso, after a period which witnessed a variety of professional experiences. It was a city in a metaphorical sense and open because of the quality of its imprecise destiny and its commitment to hospitality. The chronicle of the founding stage is full of events, poetic acts and collective readings. Its extensive rural site was face to face with the loneliness of the Pacific Ocean and the unpopulated hinterland, in a kind of articulation of vast empty spaces. Together with the *travesías*, this was to be the most fruitful scene of collective works. As in the case of Wright's Taliesin West, the autonomy of the place facilitated freedom in construction.

Built up around *agoras* and meeting places, the ensemble included lodges (*hospederías*), a cemetery, an open-air chapel, halls and workshops, in accordance with the desire to unite life, study and work. Filled with dunes, the ground erased traces and vestiges in a remarkable similarity to the blackboard, the favourite teaching tool of the group, the repeated use of which extolled a testimonial and civic way of drawing. While time has destroyed the more precarious works, the cemetery has asserted itself as an impressive testimony to permanence. Diverse works have appeared on this stage, some more finite and complete than others, in a sequence of experiences which have enjoyed the relative autonomy of the laboratory experiment. But the Open City is also a meeting space, a place for parties, tournaments, games and events which transform and disguise the installation themselves. In contrast to the European city, and like the American city, its public events do not necessarily go hand in hand with massive and dense architectural forms but rather with light brushstrokes and forms. In this way the processes of the emergence of new forms alternate with situations of gradual destruction: certain traces evolve into stable forms. The outer shells of the buildings can be enlarged through fresh interventions; new works can absorb former remains, material can be recycled, while some pieces remain unscathed and finite. Deliberately lacking an overall plan, the ensemble unravels itself on the basis of impulses guided by collectively assumed principles underlying design and execution and by the circumstantial conditions of time and place. The space of the Open City is large enough to contain multiple experiences. And two propositions have existed side by side: one, in intimate relationship with its own locality, and another in relationship to territory in its widest sense, in its continental magnitude.

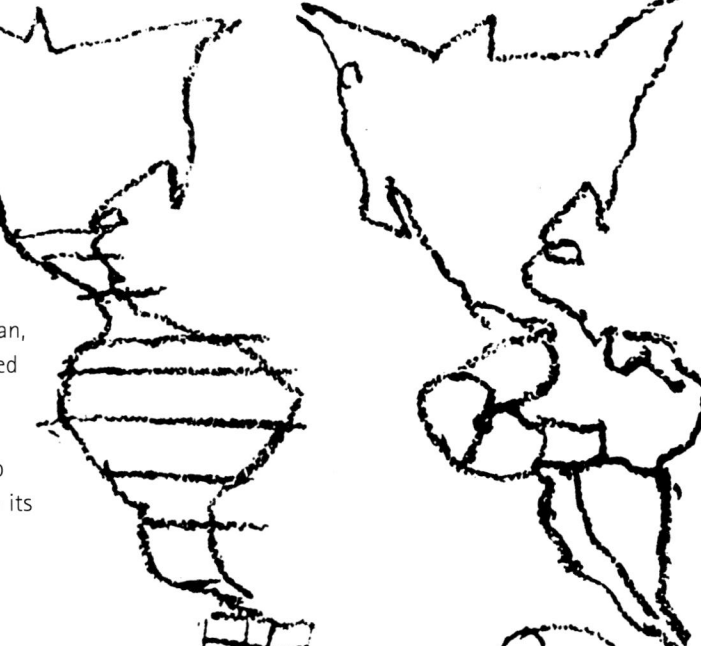

Previous page:
Amereida, projection of the Southern Cross onto the South American continent
This page:
On the left, the *regios* or territorial divisions of Carlos V, and *on the right* the borders of the republics

7. In 1984, 14 years after the foundation of the Open City, the Valparaíso School of Architecture, persuaded by the poet Godofredo Iommi, commenced the program of *travesías*, and has since then mobilized contingents of professors and students to produce works in a hundred consecutive itineraries through the Continent of America. In the words of the first travellers: "We have set off... for America with the spirit of beginners... there is... a passion which consists of looking to the beginning for a beginning... and it is this which makes a beginner."

The scope of the undertaking is varied. In the first place, the *travesías* are a new version of the *Amereida* voyage of 1965, alluding to the myth of the voyage of wandering and foundation. Then there is the operational dimension, giving rise to works and opening up fields of action which present an alternative to the professional format. Beyond that is its strategic dimension with regard to the privileged stimulus it provides for an oral tradition, in tune with the importance attributed by the group to the oral transmission of poetry as a method of participation which had existed prior to written transmission. Finally, there is its nomadic insistence, with regard to the reiteration of the questions about place and permanence in architecture, art of "substantial immobility", to use Juan Borchers' definition.

8. "The Amereida *travesías* belong to the founding, defining, recording and proclamation of that vision of America...; (in them) poetic acts..., works of sculpture, painting, design and architecture are performed which give shape to that which is the place..." Since 1984 there have been six *travesías* every year (see list on pages 148-151) in which architects, industrial and graphic designers, painters, sculptors and poets usually participate, thereby representing the disciplines with the greatest presence at the School.

Through the *travesías* the School reaches out to many places in America, inaugurating a radical academic strategy. As project workshop experiences, they belong to the curricular system, although they do not always lead to lasting or habitable projects. Occasionally they generate works which contradict the "brief and light" format which Alberto Cruz once described as characteristic of these constructions.

9. If the journey of the architect is understood in its dual sense of formative experience and a widening of knowledge, there are specific precedents within the discipline. One example is provided by the journey undertaken by the architects of the Renaissance to visit the remains of Antiquity and another by its sequel enshrined in the tradition of the Grand Tour, fruit of the Enlightenment. A more modern version can be found in the recurrent pilgrimages made by architects to the scenes of classical architecture. A particularly relevant example of this was the *Journey to the Orient* undertaken in 1911 by Charles Edouard Jeanneret, the title given to the work published posthumously. This experience, fragments of which were set down by Jeanneret in his main texts, constituted a precedent of double importance for Valparaíso, in that the group recognized him as a master, but also because it pointed to the primacy of direct observation as a way of confronting reality and the primacy of the travel log as a record. These tineraries were, in general, circular. Almost all the founders of the group travelled to Europe at some time in search of direct knowledge of the works and processes of Modernity.

10. The *travesías* are also circular voyages, considered wholly as a work, including all of the logistics of the undertaking. As with certain propositions of contemporary art, the whole of the experience is considered as a project. Likewise, it is in the documents which record the work, its itineraries and vicissitudes, where the experience persists in a tangible form. In general, as stated earlier, both architects and designers participate in the *travesías*, each being responsible for certain aspects

America's "inland sea" with air and land *travesías*
Opposite:
Travesía to Bahía Blanca, sketches of the layout

in accordance with the demarcation between specific fields of action, according to the logic which distinguishes furniture and objects from buildings.

11. For the works of each *travesía*—as with the majority of the works of the Open City—both the conception and realization of the project are managed by the same person, thereby dispensing with the multiplying network which normally surrounds the work of construction. How does this procedure compare with other more generalized processes? Any professional course of action gives rise to specific levels of control; even more, each architect tends to define his or her own. Between the obsessive control of a Gaudí, on the one hand, and the distant approach adopted by Le Corbusier for the Curruchet house in La Plata, on the other, there is a wide range of attitudes or levels of fidelity between work and design. Valparaíso opts for direct control, occasionally taken to an extreme. But at the same time it also accepts the possibilities of chance, improvization, construction "in a circle" and bricolage.

The everyday life of the architect in his or her design establishes a direct link to the work: this precise wedge between life and work can be understood in a way similar to the principle of "made-to-measure tailoring", as opposed to the idea of *prêt-à-porter*. Moving beyond the constructional roughness—which would call into question any notion of wedge or precision—the persistence of the Open City stimulates the continuous exercise of this dynamic adaptation of the work to the everyday impulses of life.

12. The fact that a project combines an extreme disparity of scales, including the vast dimensions of the territory, suggests an architectural property historically attributed to the sacred place whose true dimensions are linked to those of the cosmos. The Open City seeks to transfer this property to the sphere of a modern, secular architecture.

Carlos V's territorial divisions foretold the concordance of the lines of territory, the urban draughtboard and the constructions and sites according to the underlying principle of orthogonality, in a sequence of wedges regulated by the pattern—we must not forget that, as Cruz emphazises, the new Hispanic cities of the Indies are drawn up on a grid system. Perhaps the corollary of these concordant relationships offers a possible key to the relationship of dimensions, although, because they are inspired by the free forms of the modern movement, the works of the Valparaíso group dispense with singular or unitary geometric matrices. However, in spite of their apparent fortuitous nature, they seek simultaneously to include in their formal strategies both the immediate and the large magnitudes.

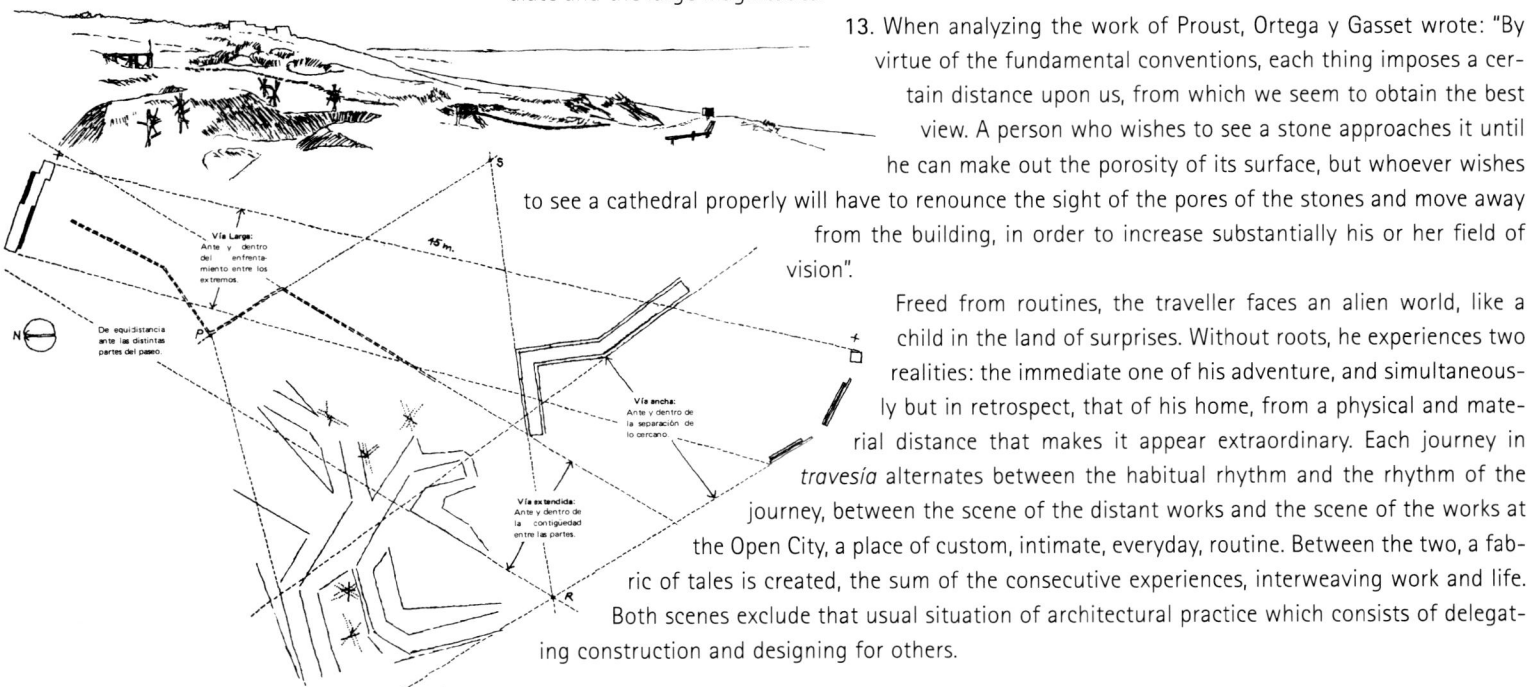

13. When analyzing the work of Proust, Ortega y Gasset wrote: "By virtue of the fundamental conventions, each thing imposes a certain distance upon us, from which we seem to obtain the best view. A person who wishes to see a stone approaches it until he can make out the porosity of its surface, but whoever wishes to see a cathedral properly will have to renounce the sight of the pores of the stones and move away from the building, in order to increase substantially his or her field of vision".

Freed from routines, the traveller faces an alien world, like a child in the land of surprises. Without roots, he experiences two realities: the immediate one of his adventure, and simultaneously but in retrospect, that of his home, from a physical and material distance that makes it appear extraordinary. Each journey in *travesía* alternates between the habitual rhythm and the rhythm of the journey, between the scene of the distant works and the scene of the works at the Open City, a place of custom, intimate, everyday, routine. Between the two, a fabric of tales is created, the sum of the consecutive experiences, interweaving work and life. Both scenes exclude that usual situation of architectural practice which consists of delegating construction and designing for others.

The works selected are presented in an order which is not strictly chronological but rather mixed. The first block contains the designs and works from the period prior to the creation of the Open City. The second block deals with the Open City itself and some of its main pieces. Finally, the third block is devoted to the works forming part of the *travesías*. As far as the photographs and other graphic materials are concerned, and in order to more faithfully reflect the work of the Valparaíso group, we have used original documents with the historical features and styles typical of those authors.

Selected Works

Achupallas Urban Development

Achupallas, Viña del Mar
Project
Alberto Cruz, Institute of Architecture
1954

The Achupallas estate, which covered around 1,000 hectares, was at the edge of Viña del Mar. Lying in the lower foothills of the coastal mountain chain which forms the geographical backbone of the city to the east, the site had been chosen for building a major ensemble of workers' housing. Sergio Larraín and Emilio Duhart were initially commissioned to do the work and together they drew up an ambitious urban design project. The Institute of Architecture of the Catholic University of Valparaíso offered them the possibility to prepare an alternative study. They would each develop their different perspectives for a project of such significance for the urban development of Viña del Mar. With the agreement of Sergio Larraín and the reluctant acquiescence of Duhart, the study went ahead, causing friction between the two teams and neither of the two designs was ever used.

Published together with the Los Pajaritos Chapel design in the first issue of *Annals* of the Catholic University of Valparaíso, the urban development project for Achupallas formed part of that duo of initial manifestos of the School. Presented in the form of a manuscript by Alberto Cruz and accompanied by a series of drawings, it showed for the first time the thinking of the school regarding the city of Valparaíso and modern urban development. Moving away from the dominant functionalism, Cruz stated emphatically that: "the town planner reveals the destiny of the city and places it in space so that the city and its inhabitants can live out their destiny whether this be gentle or hard, heroic or non heroic, but he

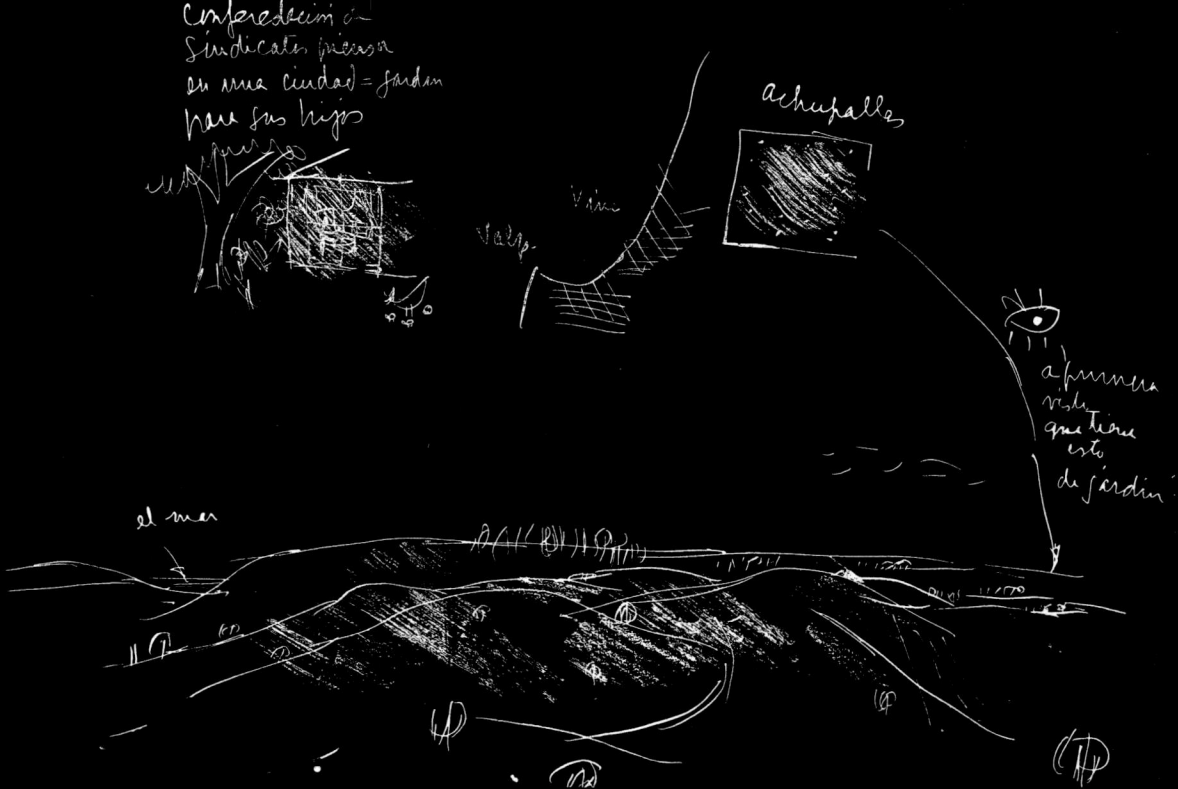

On both pages:
Sketch of Alberto Cruz with basics of Achupallas urban development.

doesn't go around looking for the means to make life pleasant for anybody". Thus, he rejected the garden city model, focused on itself and on a certain urban comfort. In its place he proposed making the far-off presence of the sea and the city of Valparaíso the dominant motif of the design. Not as objects of aesthetic pleasure but as participants in the destiny of a city, Valparaíso, whose geographic role, even when considered on a continental scale, he saw as the origin of the project. In its final section, the work took the shape of a threaded sequence of propositions. These underlined, once again, the importance of a founding discourse in the group's thinking. In essence, they described a straight road connecting Achupallas and Viña del Mar acting as the backbone of the design and forming part of a network of traffic routes between Valparaíso, Viña and the villages of the interior. A series of platforms, like those at a station, were erected next to this backbone, on which, it was supposed, the city would build itself in a relatively spontaneous way, although subject to a basic urban order. Thus, the new part of the city was not conceived as a large building, or even as a series of buildings. Anticipating viewpoints which would acquire relevance one or two decades later, the urban development of Achupallas was conceived as an urban order which could be built over time. This order expressed itself in the line of a road and movements of earth, which recognised the layout and vocation of the city, alongside which the buildings would be integrated insofar as possibilities and circumstances permitted.

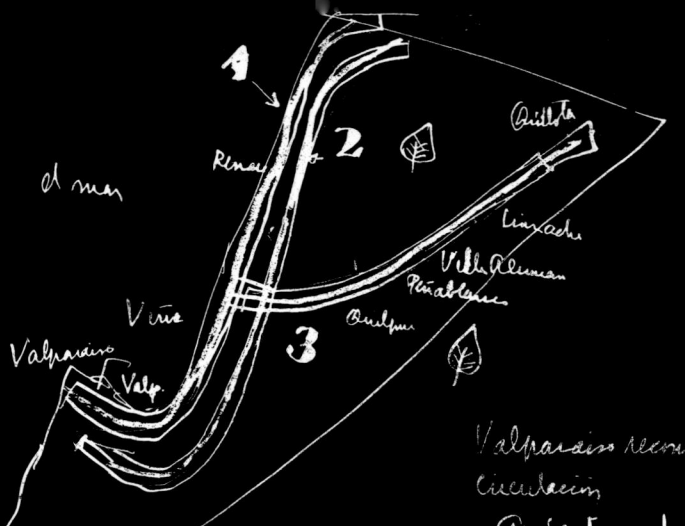

Urban development strategy, sketch and text by Alberto Cruz.
Final proposal with the principles of zoning

Valparaíso reconquista su destino por la
Circulación

① Se traza la avenida costanera al lado del
    mar
② Se traza la avenida "cerros" por las cum=
    bres de los cerros que miran en el mar
③ Se traza la avenida interior que a buscar el
    árbol.

Entre estas circulaciones que hagan lo que quieran
nosotros no sabemos que forma se derivarán de estas circulaciones ni podemos predecirlo
Quiza la misión de ellos será encontrar la vida en el estar.
Lo que es nosotros no podemos engañarnos en esto

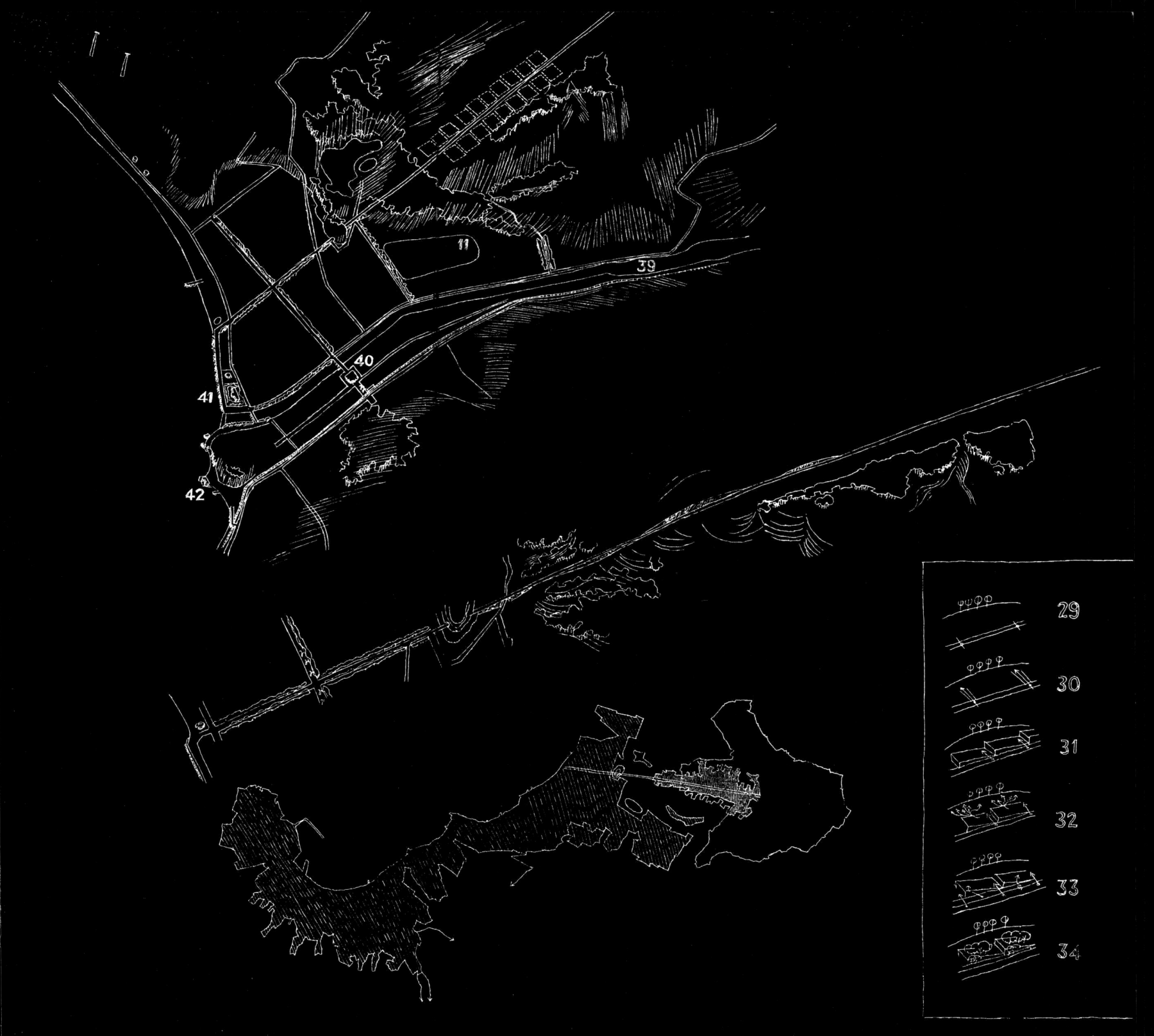

Los Pajaritos Chapel

Maipú, Santiago
Design
Alberto Cruz
1952-1953

Set in the Los Pajaritos estate to the west of the city of Santiago, this small memorial chapel, despite the fact it was never built, played a fundamental role in the architectural production and the body of ideas of the Valparaíso group. Initially commissioned to one of its members, it was adopted as a collective task in 1952. As stated previously, publication of its design, together with that of Achupallas urban development in the *Annals* of the Catholic University of Valparaíso in 1954, converted both into a kind of manifesto of the ideas of the school.

The land was at the entrance to a complex which included the house of the landowners, warehouse and other outbuildings. The project, following a rural tradition, included a small chapel with its sacristy, which could be extended outwards, and a small niche intended for an image of the Virgin.

Beyond the quality of the project, at the same time dense and unadorned, its importance lay in the discourse of underlying principles which accompanied its publication. Convinced that the work of architecture had to be the result of a process of searching, and that its form had to come about from a process of thinking, the chapel provided a unique opportunity to illustrate these convictions in a concrete form: architecture should not be the result of the choice of an option within a formal repertoire—the forms, in Cruz's own words—but rather a form, conceived as an expressive result of a way of considering a problem. Posing the radical question of

"what should the shape be like within which people pray?"

the text sought to answer on the basis of a series of observations on daily life, so putting to the test the working method it had been refining as a school. Thus, the discourse oscillated between the reference to situations of illuminating and general reflections on modern architecture, conceived as something other than the expression of technological progress, of the magic of efficiency or of beautiful construction forms.

The response was synthesized in the idea of the

cube of light, the church whose form reflects that which is absent.

What was proposed through this was the creation of an architectural form which was not perceived as an object, but as a basis for illuminating the "acts" which took place inside it. Observations about a table painted white, against which dishes and food stood out in high relief, provided an inspiration for the shape of the chapel, thus affirming the role of "acts" in the origin of the architecture.

The cube, stable by nature and one of the paradigmatic figures of modern architecture, provided the recurring formal motif of the project: from the larger cube of the chapel to the small ones of the bell tower and the side chapel. The atrium, in turn, constituted a kind of virtual exterior nave which duplicated the nave itself. The light, which streamed down from an upper skylight hidden by a hanging ceiling, dematerializing the forms, completed the idea of the cube of light.

Construction of the chapel would make use of the materials available, entrusting the powerful shape of the cube with the task of giving them homogeneity. Both this particular treatment of the light and the willingness to build with anything to hand would be recurring motifs in the later work of the Valparaíso School.

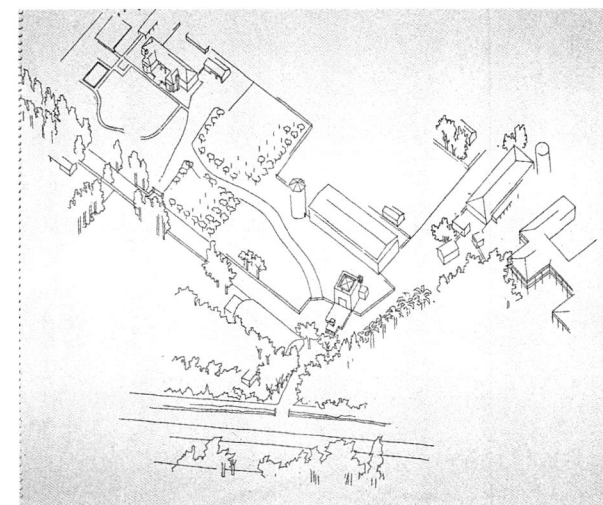

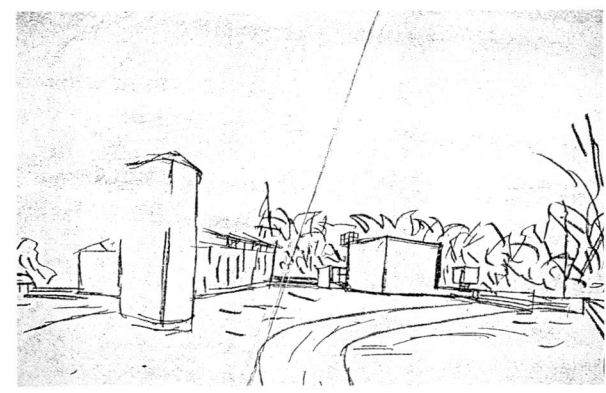

1 The chapel set among the rural constructions
2 Preliminary sketch, Alberto Cruz
3 Wire and paper model

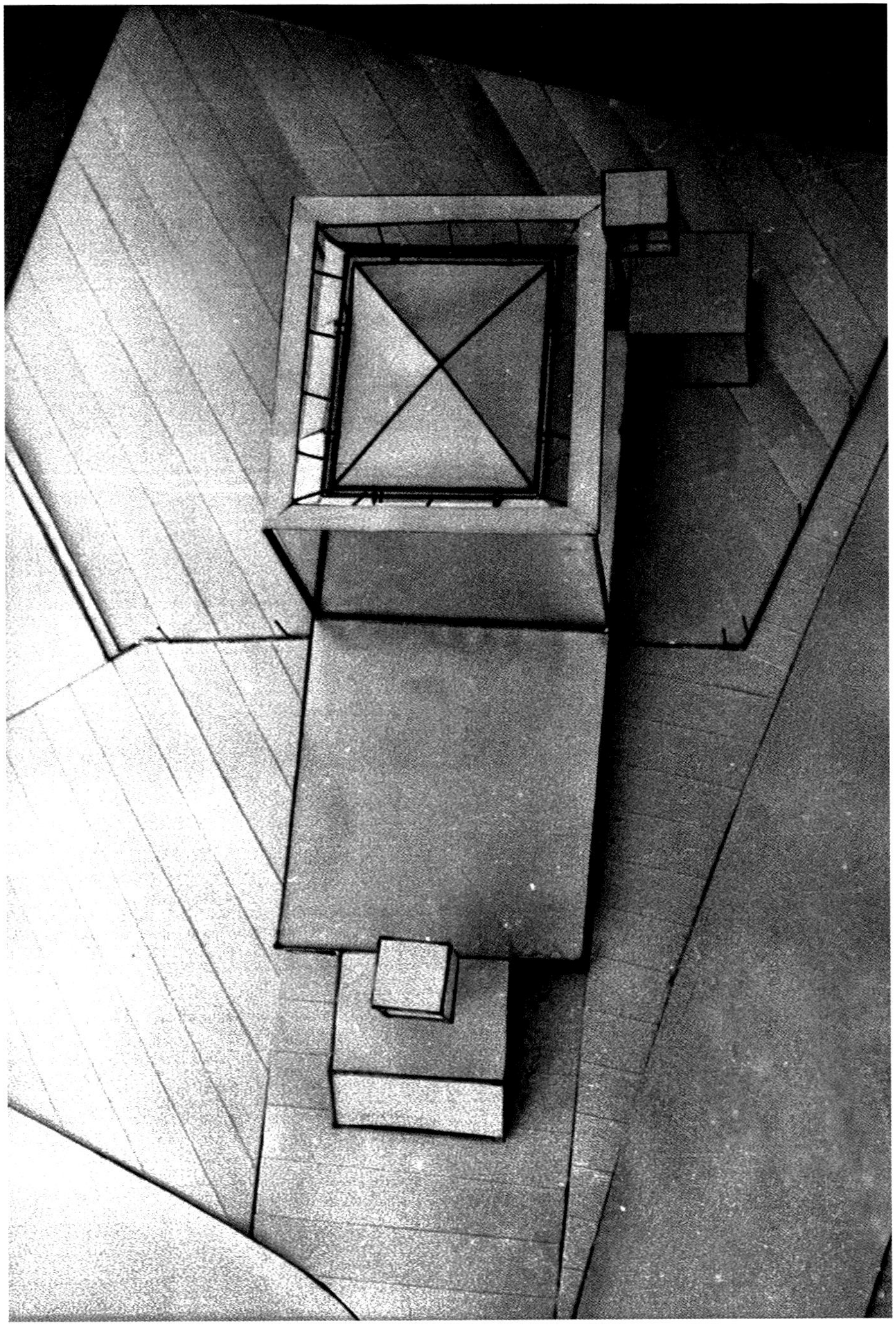

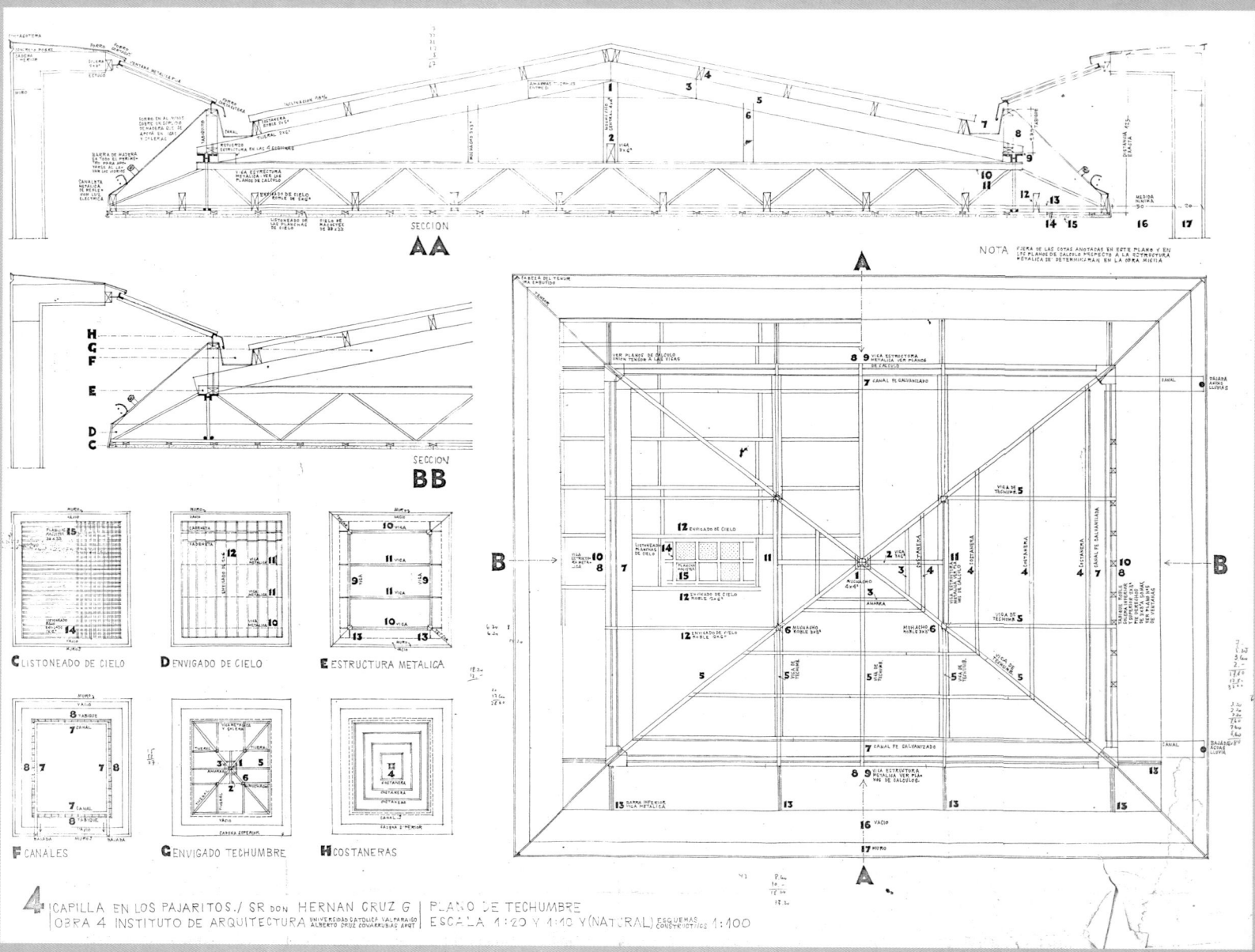

Previous page:
Structure and construction details of the hanging ceilings
This page:
Axonometric projection and sketch of the liturgical celebration, with a layout which was innovative for the period

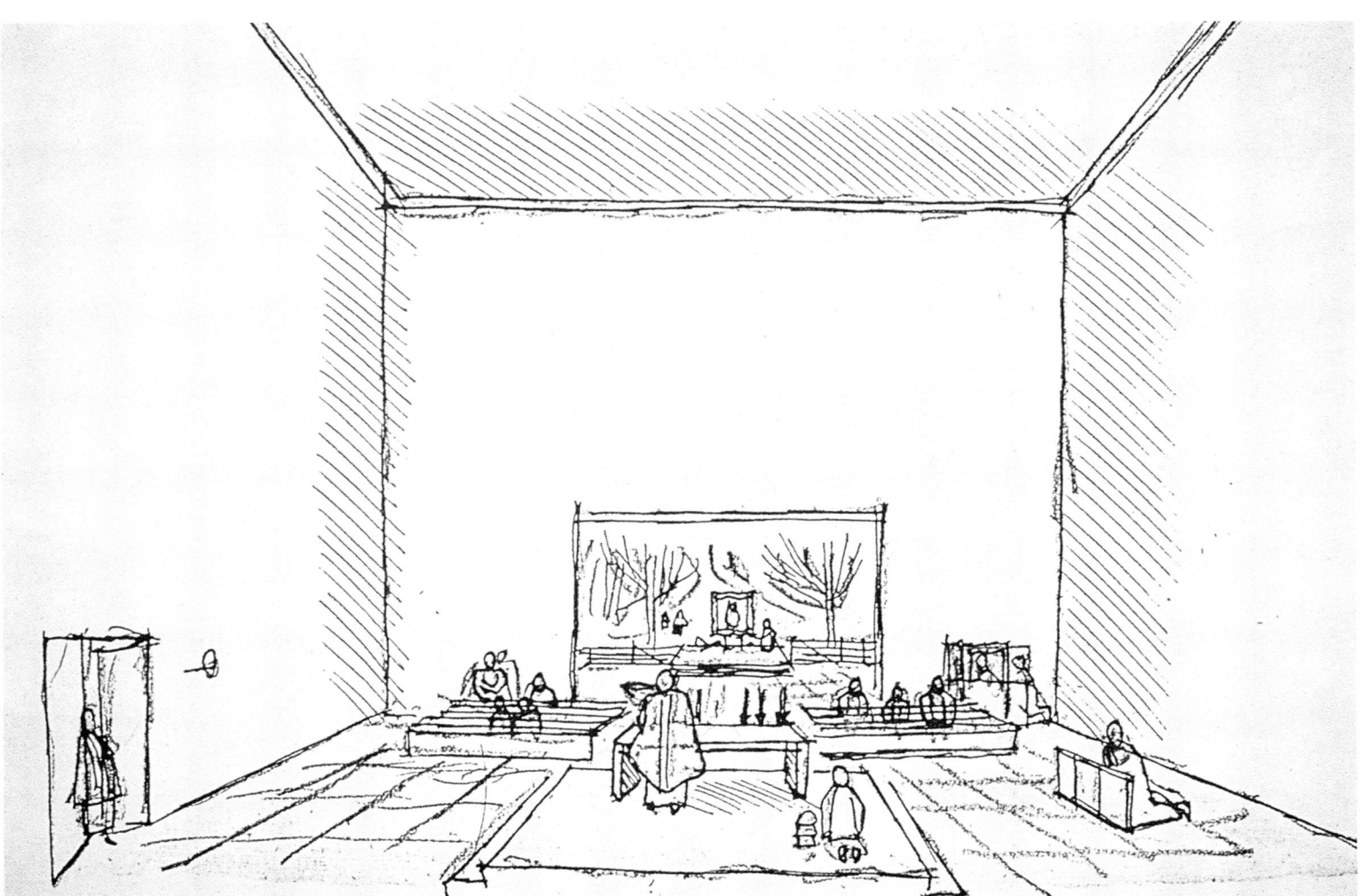

Naval Academy

Playa Ancha, Valparaíso
Competition design
Fourth prize in the competition
Francisco Méndez and the Institute
of Architecture
1956-1957

With the working and teaching methods of the School in Valparaíso now consolidated, at least in an initial phase, the competition for a new building for the Naval Academy, which would involve a change of location and increase capacity, presented the group with an excellent opportunity to enter the public arena and put its convictions into practice in the context of a major project. The architect Carlos Bresciani—partner in the distinguished firm Bresciani, Valdés, Castillo and Huidobro and appointed dean of the Faculty around the same time as the arrival of the group of new professors at the School—was a firm supporter of participation in the competition.

Led by the architect and professor Francisco Méndez, participation in the competition was tackled with enormous energy and passion. The entire School was involved in the project, including the students at some stages. It was a unique opportunity to demonstrate the links between architectural research and practice.

The routine of the cadet's daily life and the conditions of the site, located on a slope on the cliffs of Playa Ancha beach, dominating Valparaíso Bay from the south, formed the basis of the design. The site was carefully observed, even from the air. The topography and the presence of the wind, considered an integral part of the form of the site, were the basic elements studied. The intention of working architecturally with an intangible element like the wind—at Pajaritos it had been the light—was a characteristic feature of this design and of the concerns which prevailed at the School at that time. To this end a laboratory was set up which included a wind tunnel where the architectural intentions could be put to the test. The basic proposal involved creating public spaces in the lee of the wind, i.e. free from its presence. With this aim in mind, and using the model provided by aircraft (which some members of the School such as Miguel Eyquem knew a lot about), and by the bridges of ships, the main buildings, conceived as windbreaks, were endowed with slots which, like peculiar cornices, threw the wind upwards, creating an effect equivalent to the one which would have been generated if they had been much higher.

The series of long and curved volumes, placed freely on the ground, almost like horizontal slots, aimed at transforming the landscape, giving it a new rhythm but without actually changing it. The volumes act as boundaries which determine the fundamental areas of the design, supported by the structure of the topography. The aim of this was to create the maximum number of spatial situations, thereby enriching the daily life of the cadet, who would be constantly moving from one point of the Academy to another according to an established daily regime.

The project was one of the four selected to enter a second stage of the competition. However, because the group rejected the observations made by the jury and insisted on their own arguments, it came fourth. This relative failure in a professional incursion which had required such a significant investment on the part of the group was to feed their scepticism as regards their possibilities of practising the profession of architecture through the more usual channels.

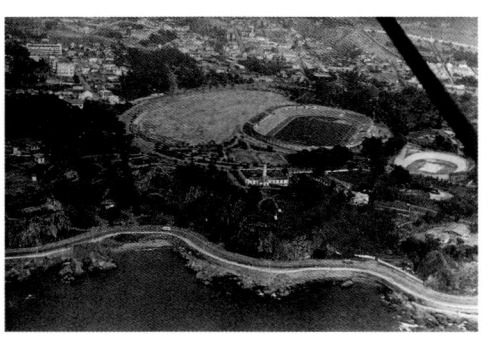

Left:
Aerial view of the lands proposed for the Academy at Playa Ancha, Valparaíso
Following page:
Sketches of traffic flows

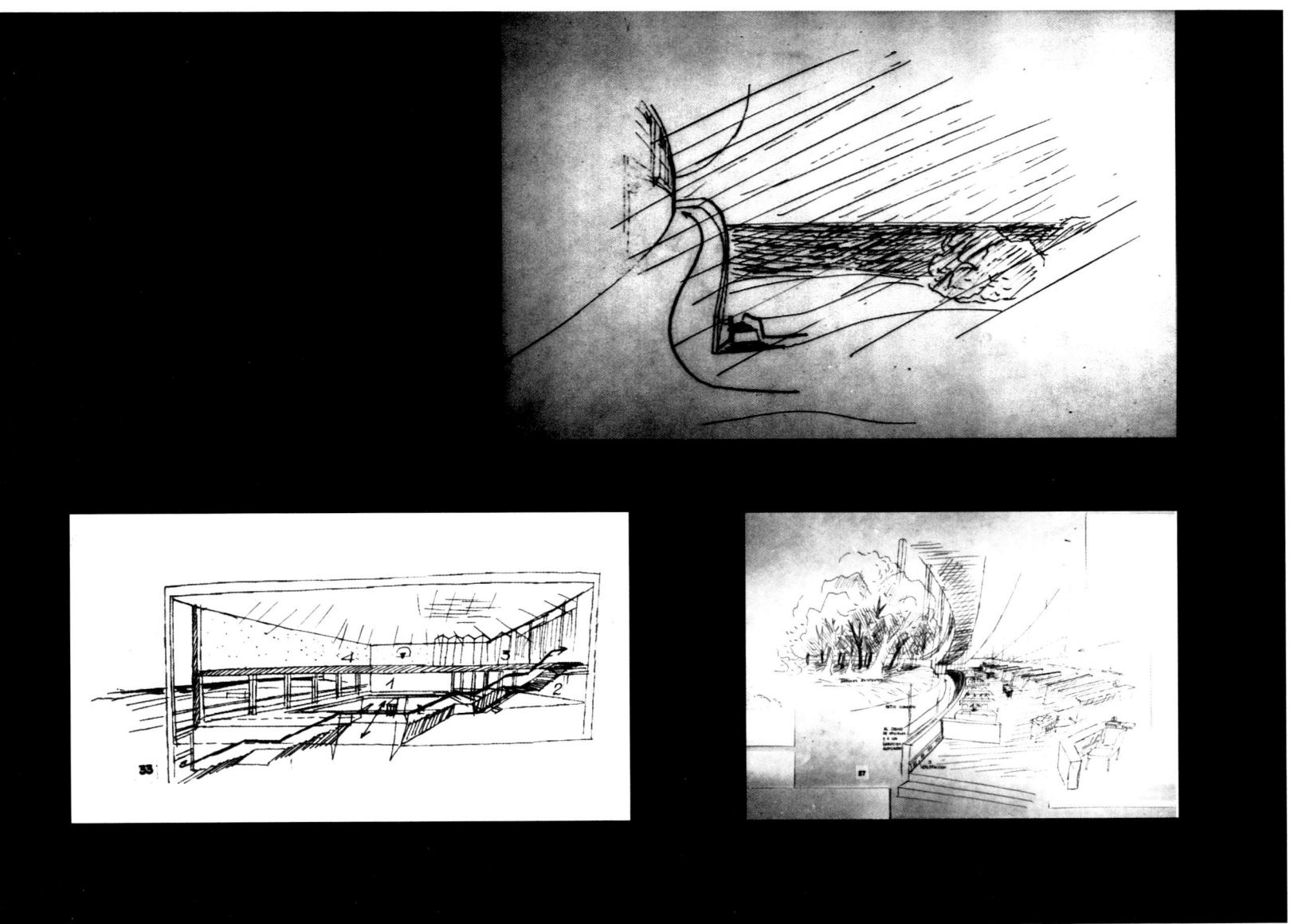

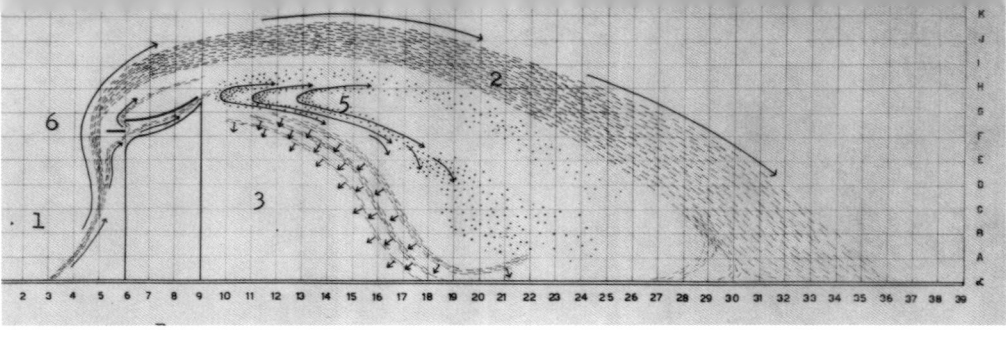
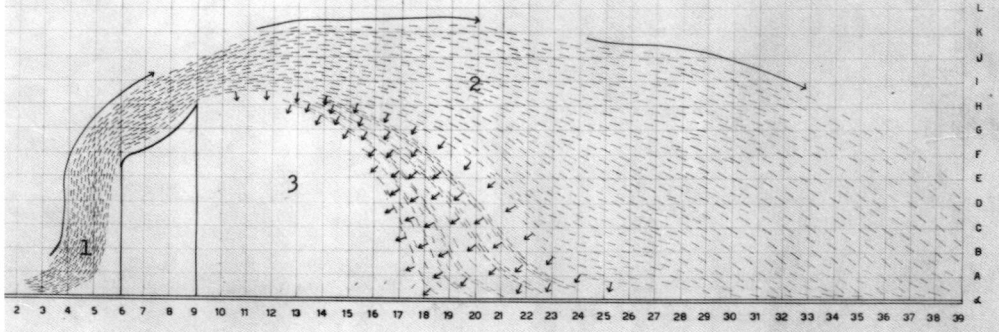
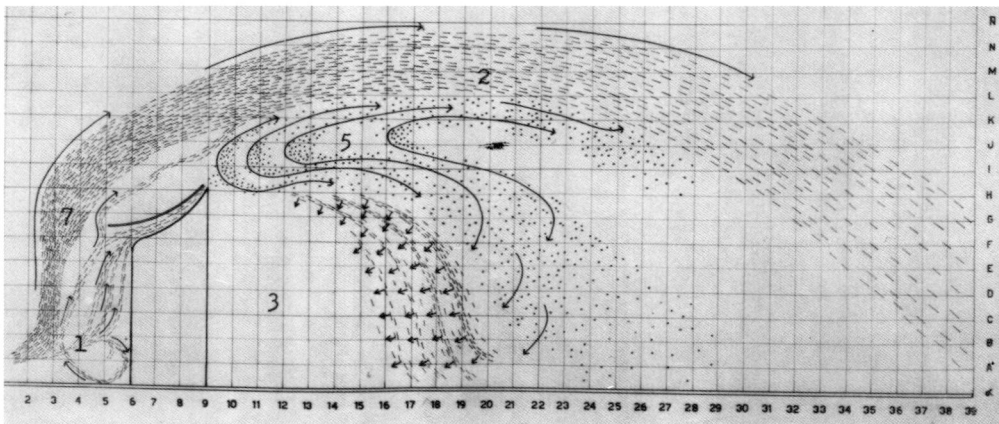
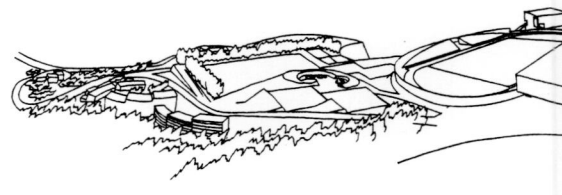
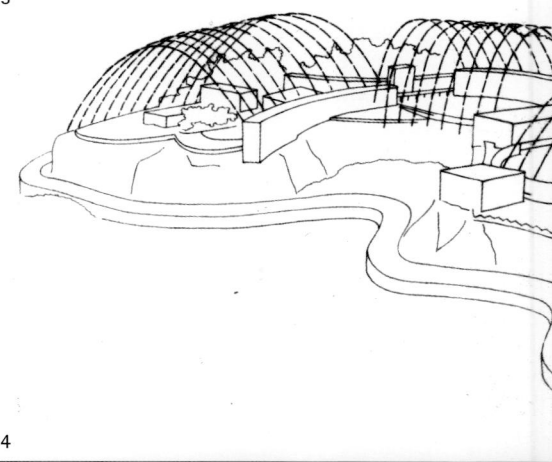

1 Studies of the wind carried out at the School's laboratory
2 Perspective of ensemble looking towards the sea
3 Graphics showing the wind cupolas created by the buildings
4 Detail of model of the project
5-6 Photomontages of the model on site

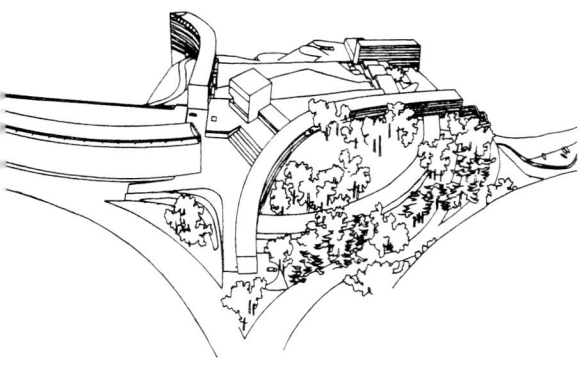

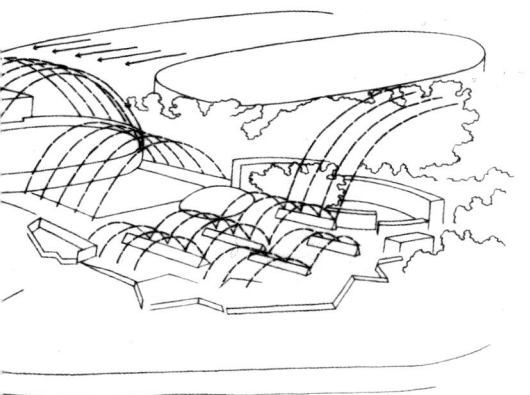

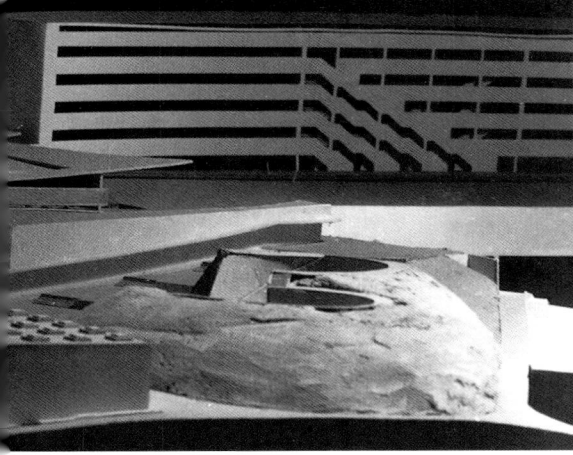

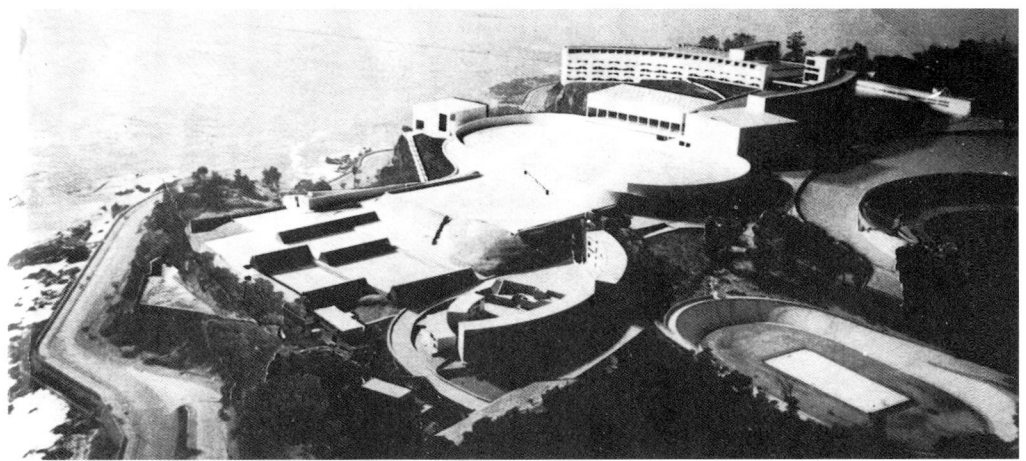

5

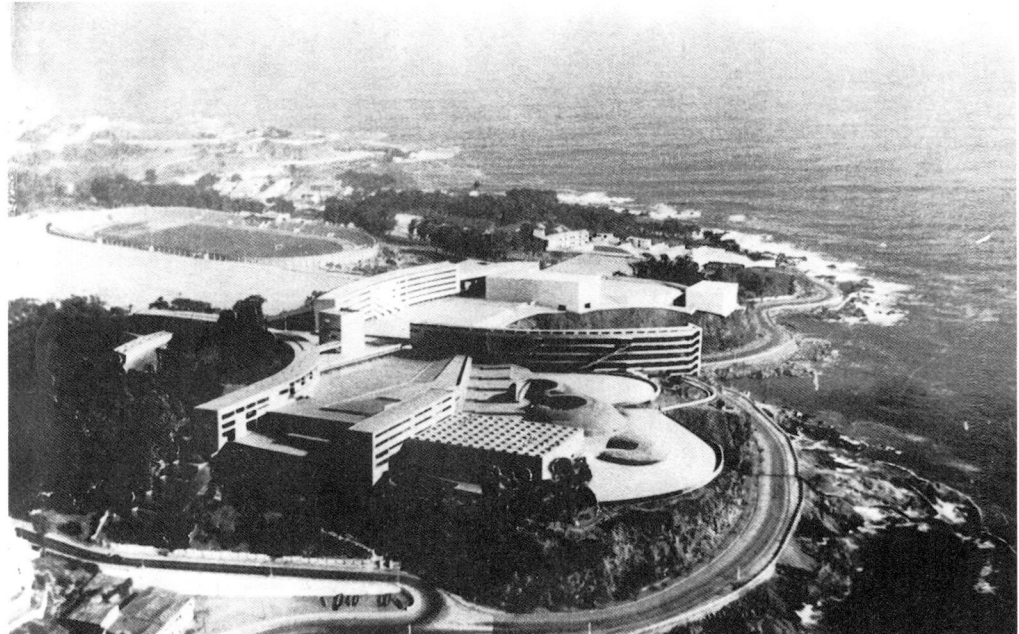

6

Avenida del Mar

Coast between Valparaíso and Viña del Mar
Urban development project with
public exhibitions and citizen's awareness
campaign
Arturo Baeza, Alberto Cruz, Institute of
Architecture
1969

This initiative came about as a counterproposal to the Ministry of Public Works' Via Elevada overpass project for a 4.5-km-long coastal viaduct to satisfy the demands of vehicular traffic in the Valparaíso-Viña del Mar conurbation, which would without doubt lead to an irreversible degradation of the urban coastline. In the face of this, the whole of the School became a Workshop with the specific objective of creating an alternative design constrained by the same budgetary limitations as the official project.

The Avenida del Mar was one of a series of large-scale works, such as the Achupallas urban development project (1954) and the Section Plan for the Viña del Mar estuary (1971). As with the designs for the Exagon Building (Cerro Castillo, Viña del Mar, 1955) and the Naval Academy (Valparaíso, 1956), this one also faced themes strongly linked to the particular topographical context of the coast, characterized by the relationship of shore and cliff. The location of the School of Architecture itself, on the brow of a cliff in the sector, coincided by chance with the siting of the Avenida del Mar design.

In contrast to the official motorway project, restricted by its exclusive criterion as a road infrastructure, the Avenida was conceived as a thoroughly urban work, a guarantor of the multiple transactions between the city and its seaboard, both with regard to its longitudinal connectivity and to its diverse and complex transversal relationships. It encompassed all means of travel, including pedestrian traffic. Backed by a detailed knowledge of the urban coast, its history and its social practices, the design sought to be faithful to the maritime destiny of the city, to protect its natural shores and to facilitate accessibility and public enjoyment of the beaches, rocks and fishing bays along the coast, defined in the underlying principles of the design as a complex shore. According to its authors, the approach was characterized by the following objectives:

1. To reclaim the shore for the inhabitants of the city by making use of the new banks of the spa resort.
2. To build today's complex mode of traffic flows which it considered as "going in activity, going at speed and going in contemplation".
3. To rearrange the hills between Barón and Caleta Abarca by connecting them via this vitalizing element, differentiating, according to their accessibility and function, the public modes of life of the spa-plaza/spa-club and the fishing bay, the place of the craftsmen of the sea. Consequently, to articulate the system of traffic flows with systems of transversal accesses, designed as the case may be as footbridges, bridge-stairways or routes which linked the city to its seaboard via access nodes to the high parts in the respective ravine mouths.

Longitudinally, traffic routes were established, differentiated according to this expected use and the speed of traffic. These were interwoven with the lines of the city railway, in a kind of three-stranded plait which articulated the "going for a walk" along the shore, "going at speed" along the fast lane and the railway, and "going about in [urban] activity", all winding their way to the hills.

The vision which inspired the design was consistent with the one enshrined in the writings of *Amereida* and the studies referring to the Pacific. For this reason the process included cartographies which linked the historical evolution of the territory of Chile, from 1540 to the present to the specific problem of this urban strip. The changing systems of frontiers evolved historically according to a linear trend, until they became consolidated in the present configuration of the territory, whose coastline is around 4,500 km long. As Chile's main port, Valparaíso naturally appears as the most effective urban link with the sea.

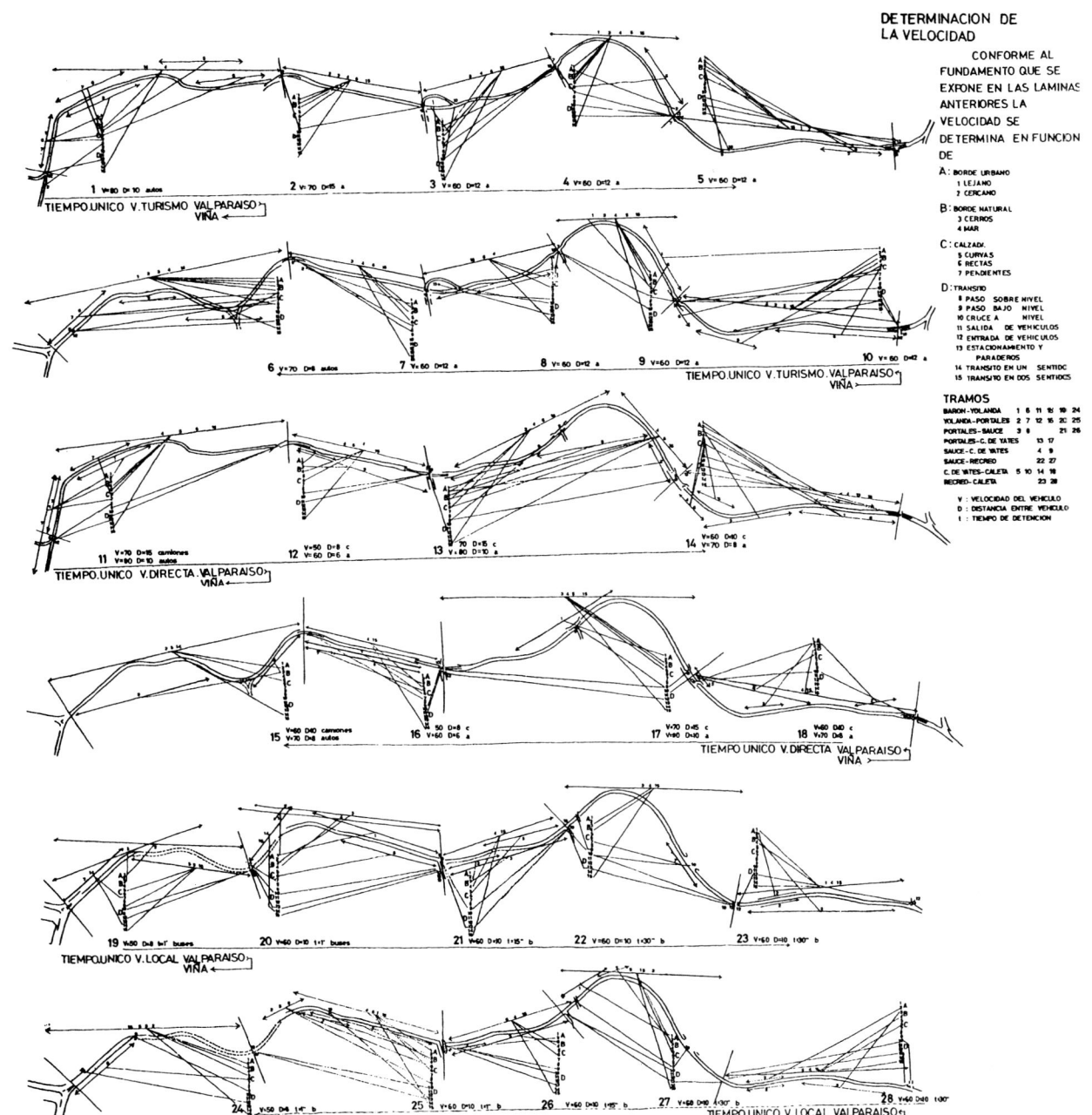

Flow and speed studies corresponding to the three rhythms established in the design

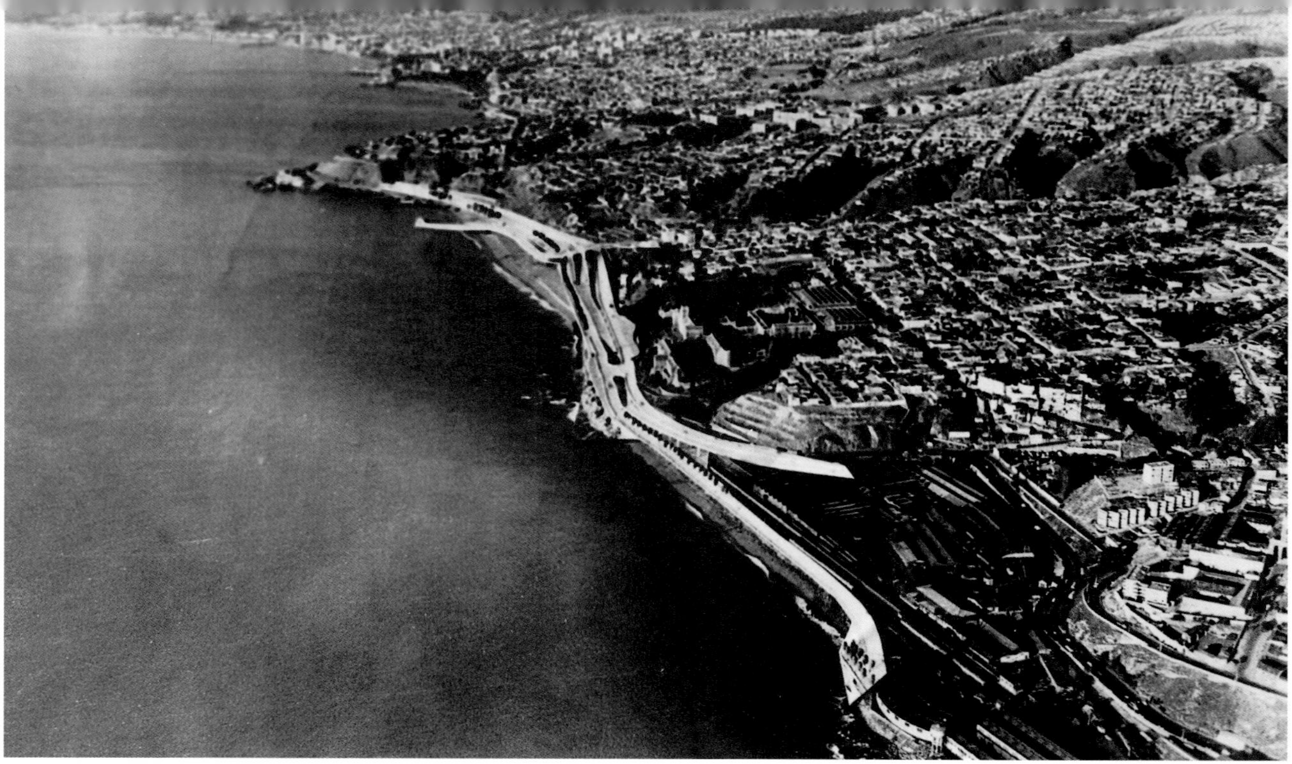

1

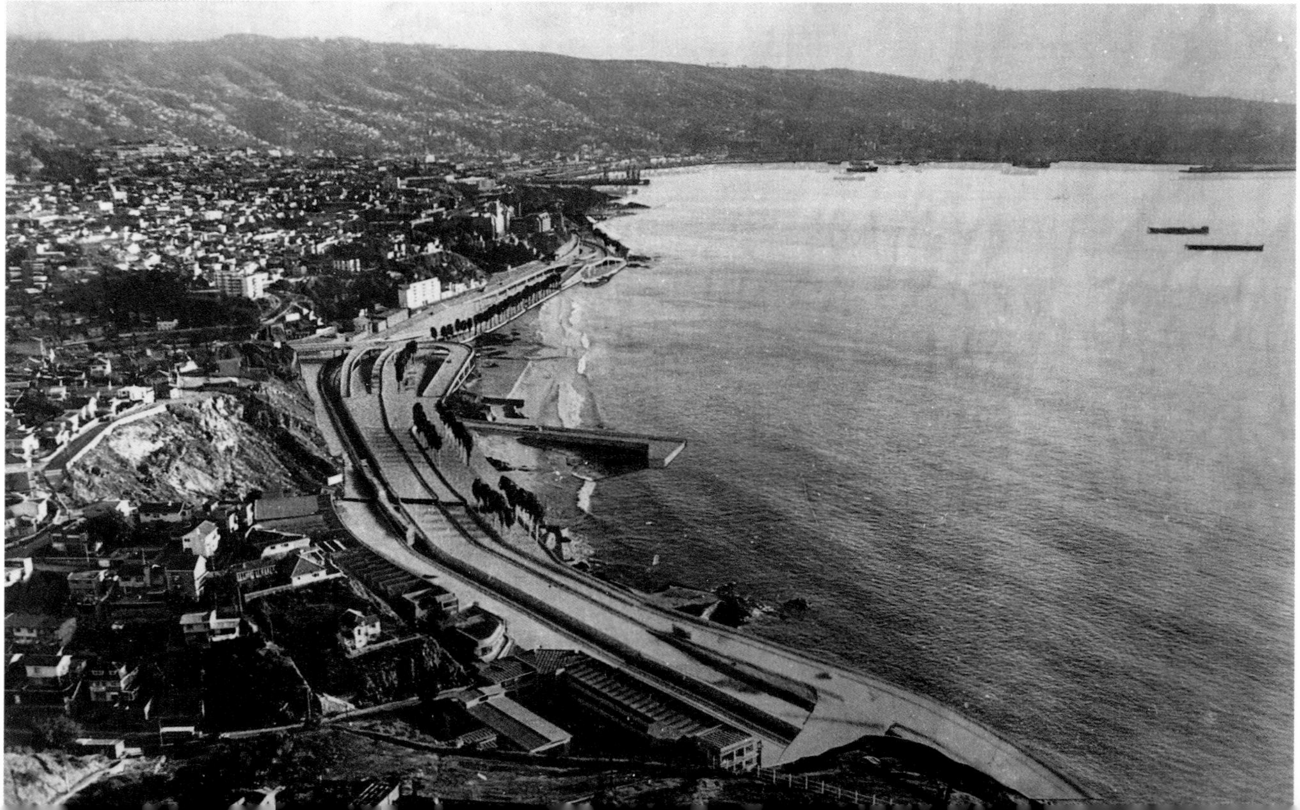

2

1 Avenida del Mar, view towards Viña del Mar
2 Avenida del Mar, view towards Valparaíso
3 The Placeres beach sector before the intervention
4 Public swimming pool and Recreo Beach, Viña del Mar
5 Pedestrian walkway and promenade, Caleta Portales beach

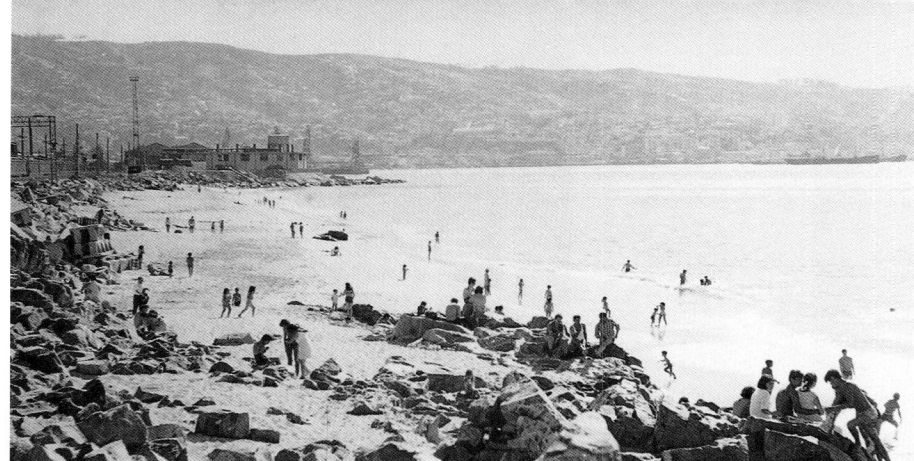

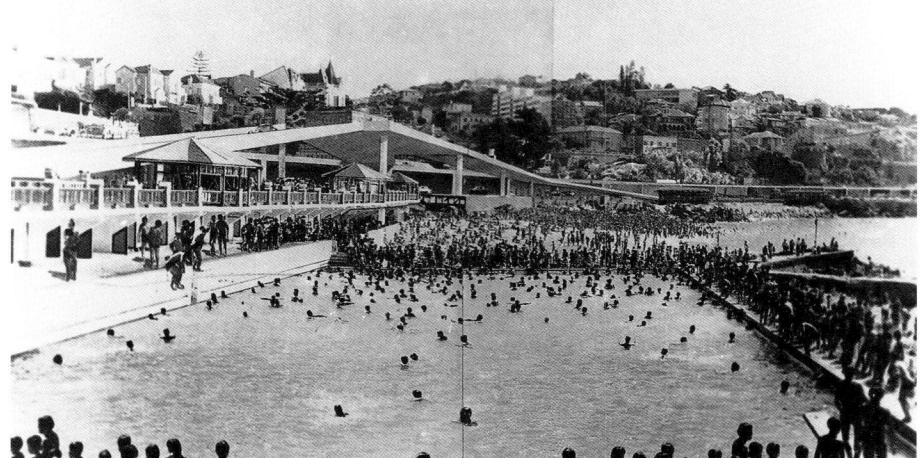

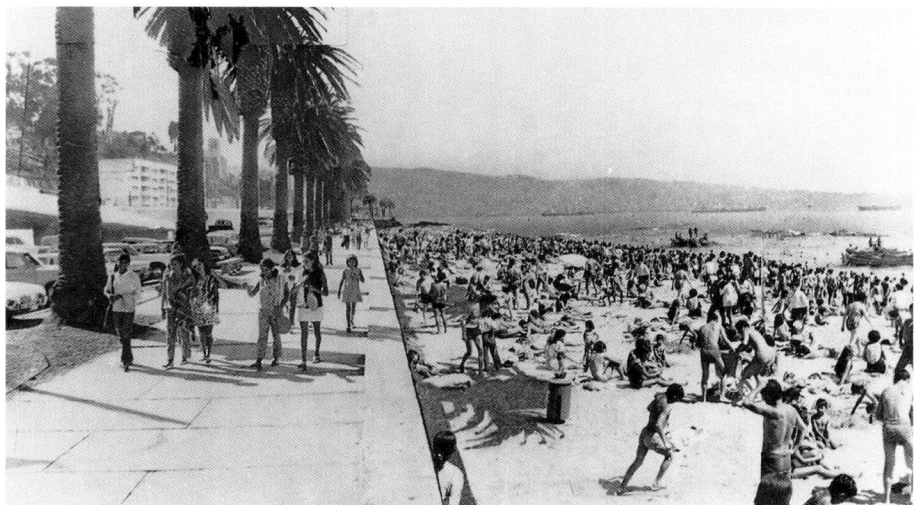

Benedictine Monastery of the Holy Trinity

Las Condes, Santiago
Jaime Bellalta, Esmee Cromie, Octavio Sotomayor, Fernando Mena, León Rodriguez
First design, 1954
Arturo Baeza, Alberto Cruz, José Vial, Institute of Architecture
Second design, 1960
Gabriel Guarda, Martín Correa, and Patricio Gross (collaborator)
Church, 1963-64
Jorge Swinburn, Raúl Irarrazával
Other pieces, 1972-1980

The history of this monastery has been linked with that of the Valparaíso School, in different ways and for various reasons. After a Benedictine community was founded in Chile, under the authority of the French community in Solesmes through Quarr Abbey in England, it settled provisionally in Las Condes, to the east of Santiago, next to the lower foothills of the Andes mountain chain. Once the community had acquired a plot of land on the nearby Los Piques hill on which to settle permanently, several offices were invited to take part in a private competition. This was won, in 1954, by Jaime Bellalta, a member of the first group of professors to have arrived at Valparaíso, in co-operation with his wife, the landscape artist Esmee Cromie, and a group of graduates from the Catholic University of Chile (Octavio Sotomayor, León Rodríguez and Fernando Mena) who, although they did not belong to the School, sympathized with its ideas.

Bellalta's project consisted of a modern reinterpretation of the traditional monastery: the volumes of cells, chapel, porter's lodge and other buildings would surround a complex and an articulated cloister, capable of adapting itself to the sloping terrain. Only the block of cells, reminiscent of the first Le Corbusier, and a provisional chapel were finally built under Bellalta's direction.

In 1960, with Jaime Bellalta in England, the project was commissioned to the Institute of Architecture of the Catholic University of Valparaíso. With the participation of Alberto Cruz, José Vial and Arturo Baeza, the Institute drew up a new plan which, while incorporating the building already constructed by Bellalta, gave a new direction to the ensemble as a whole.

This design, urban in ambition and scope, added a further series of broken volumes to the volume of existing cells. The original cloister, articulated around a patio, was now turned into a linear path which linked the vertexes of the volumes laid down in zigzag fashion. The church, which had never got beyond the drawing board stage, also acquired a new form and layout in the new project: two link-ed volumes, with varied access for light and a particular concern for acoustics, an important issue bear-ing in mind the requirements of the Gregorian chant. The shifting of the access from the east to the west of the monastery formed part of this second design which, in general terms, was never built.

In a third phase, the church was commissioned to the young architects Gabriel Guarda and Martín Correa, graduates of the Catholic University of Chile (Santiago) and recent entrants to the Order, with the collaboration of Patricio Gross. Although the commission was accepted with reluctance, within a couple of years they had produced what was one of the most valuable pieces of modern architecture not only in Chile but in the whole of Latin America. It is difficult to determine how much the new church owed to Bellalta's initial design and to the second design by the Institute of Architecture in Valparaíso. In any event, it seems to have been designed in tune with those earlier studies and some of their concerns. This opinion is supported by two intersected cubes and, more especially, by the remarkable treatment of the light which is in tune with the results of many of the searches of the Valparaíso School.

Other elements of the monastery, such as the porter's lodge and the library, were completed later, in a fourth stage, with the intervention of the architects Jorge Swinburn and Raúl Irarrazával.

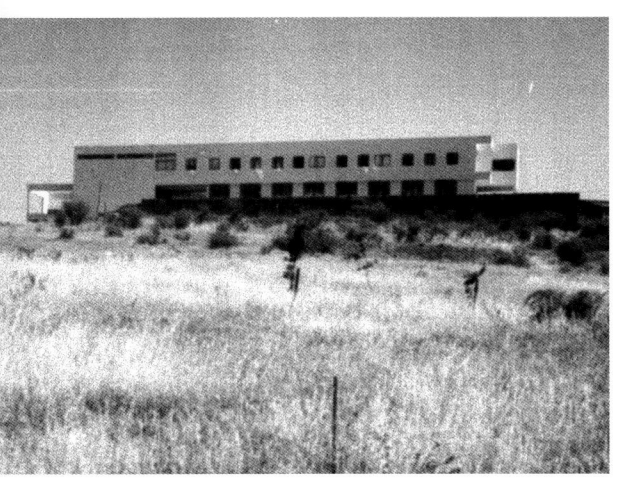

Left:
Block of cells designed by Jaime Bellalta and team
Following page:
Corridors and stairs on level 1 of the block of cells

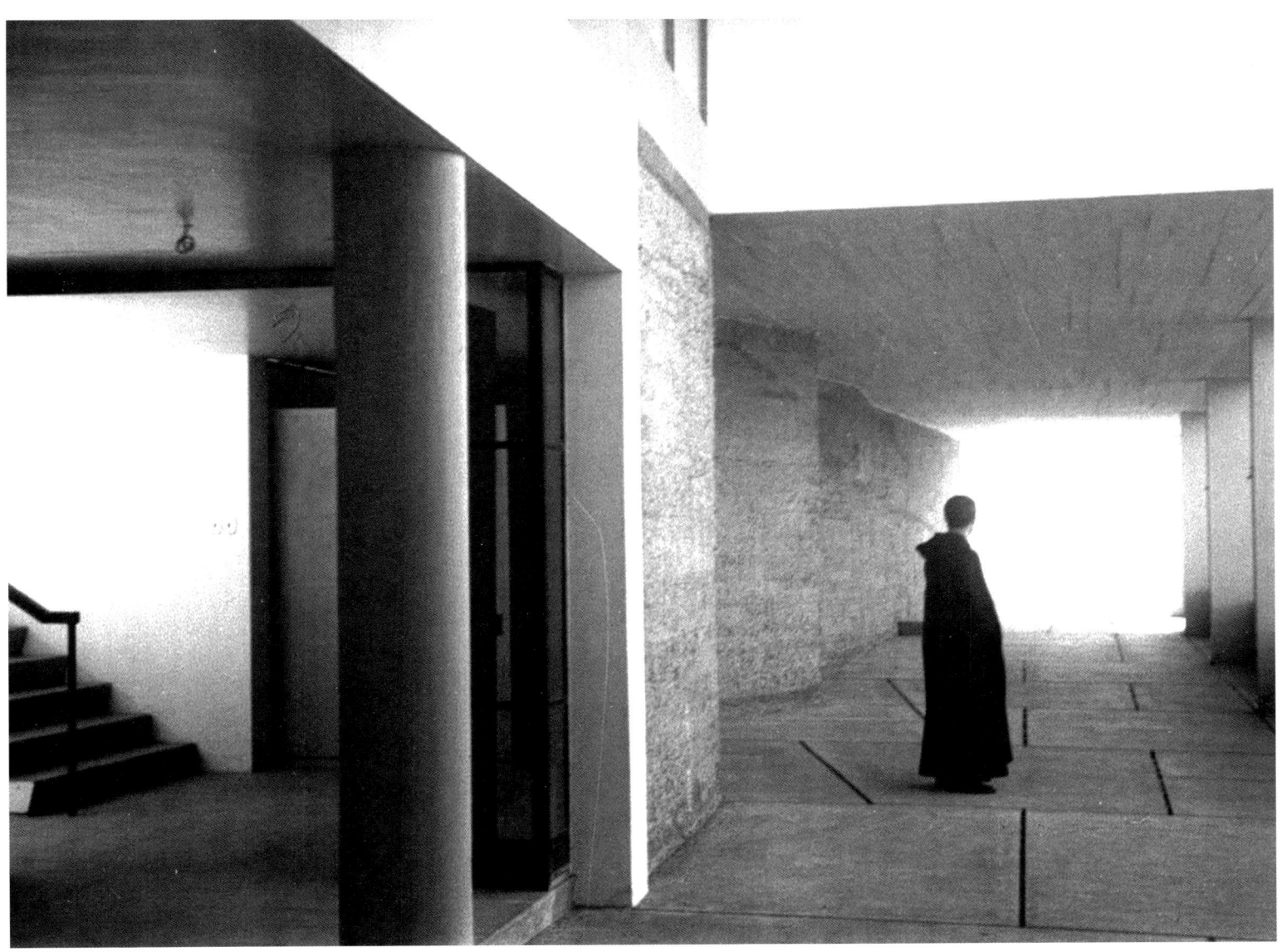

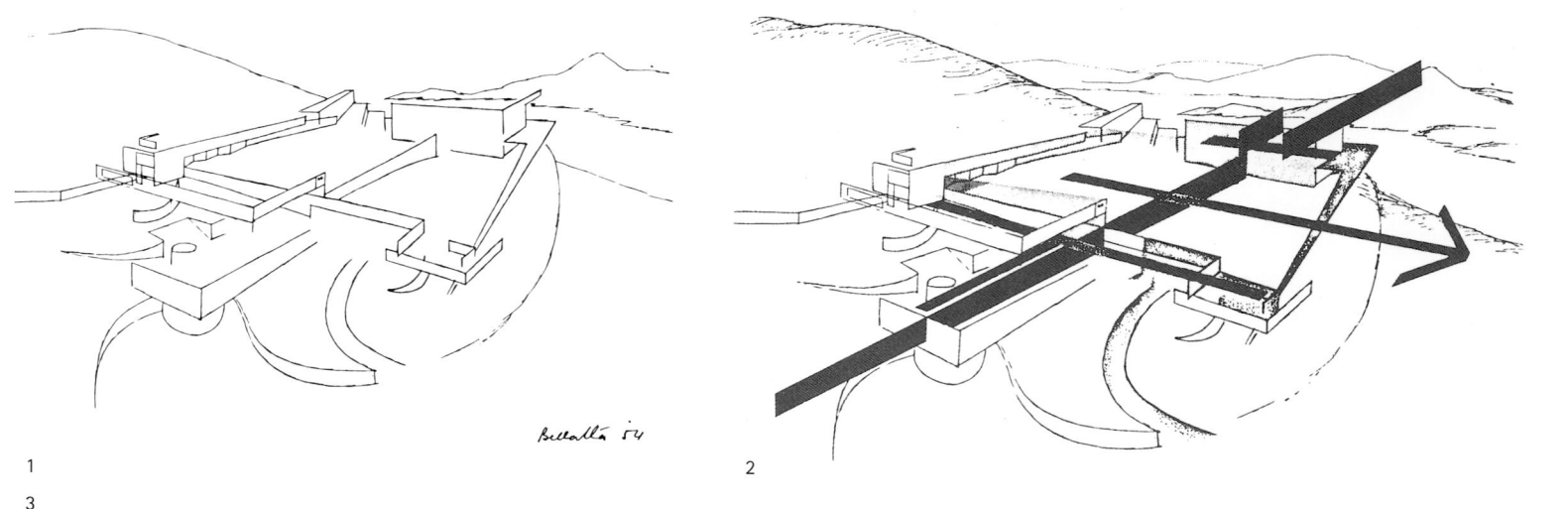

1
2
3

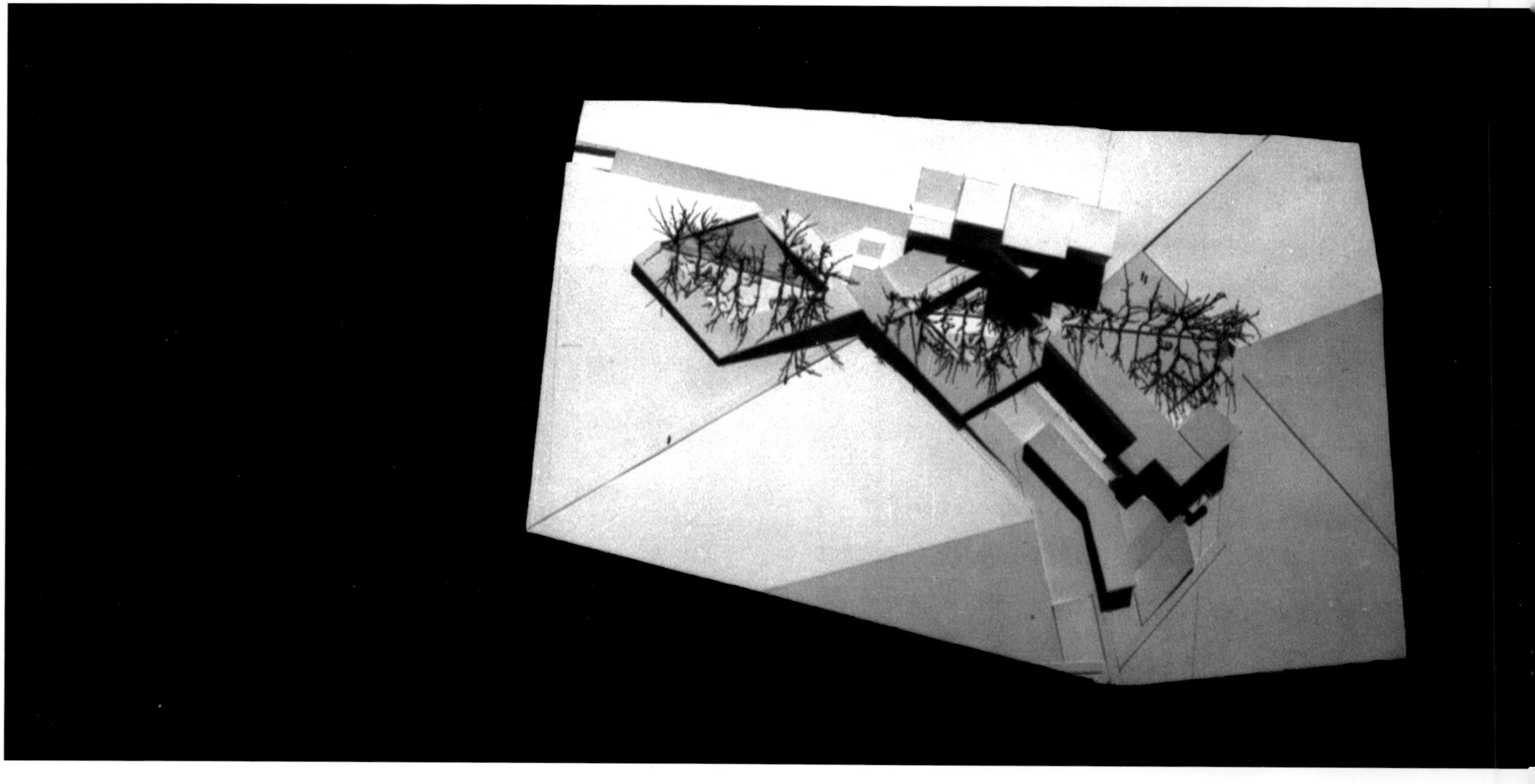

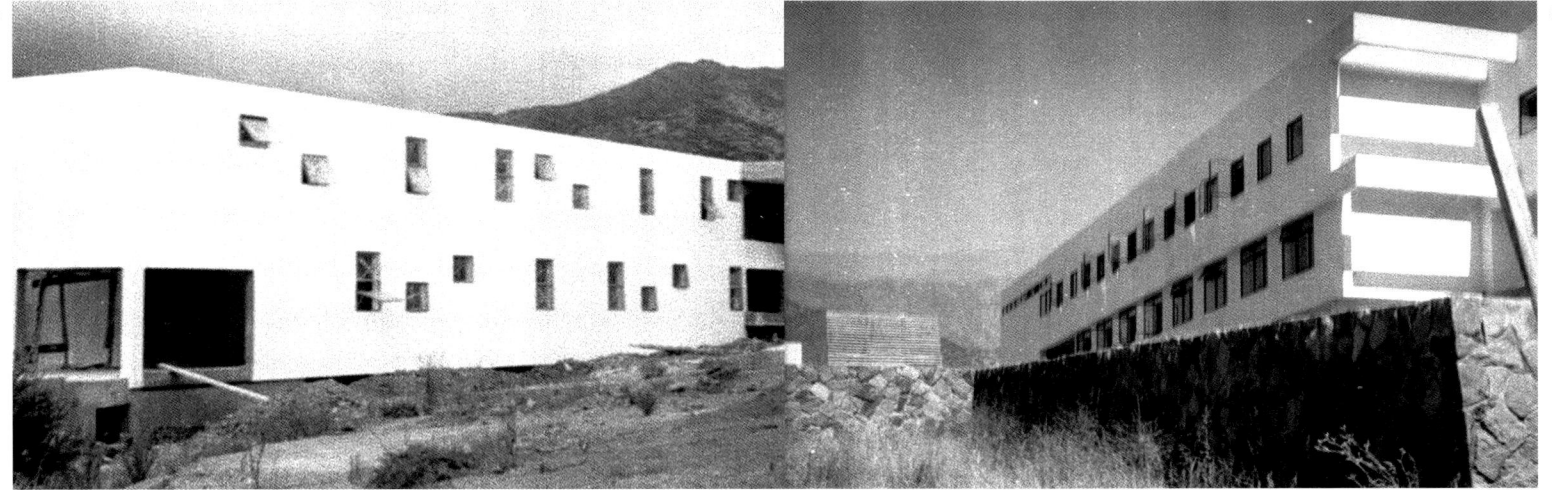

1 Sketch of Jaime Bellalta's competition design
2 Sketch with spatial directions of the initial project by Jaime Bellalta
3 Model of the proposal drawn up by the Institute of Architecture
4, 5 and 6 Block of cells: views before and after Bellalta's work

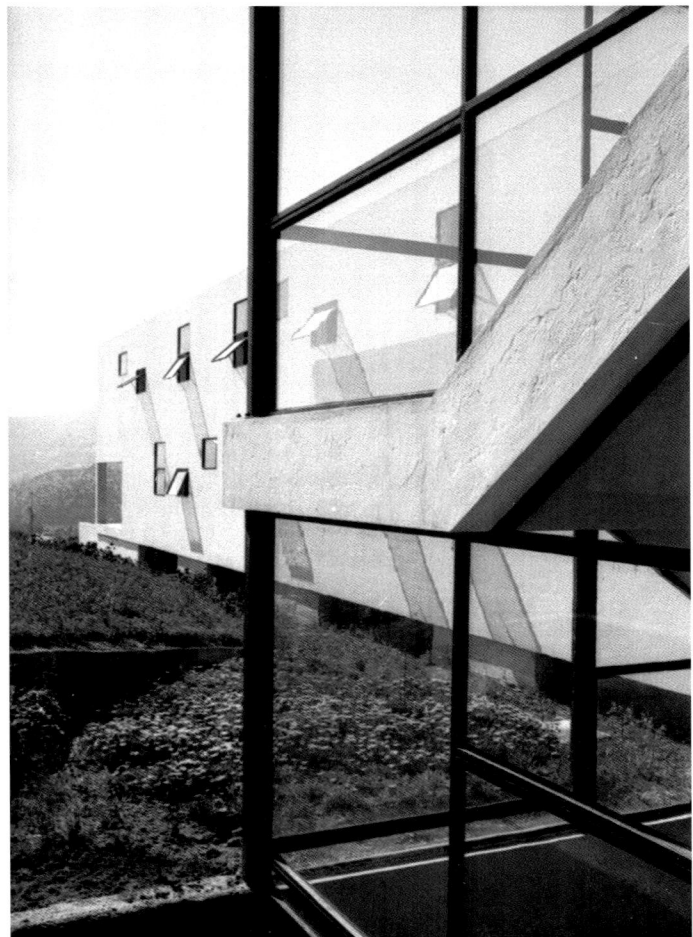

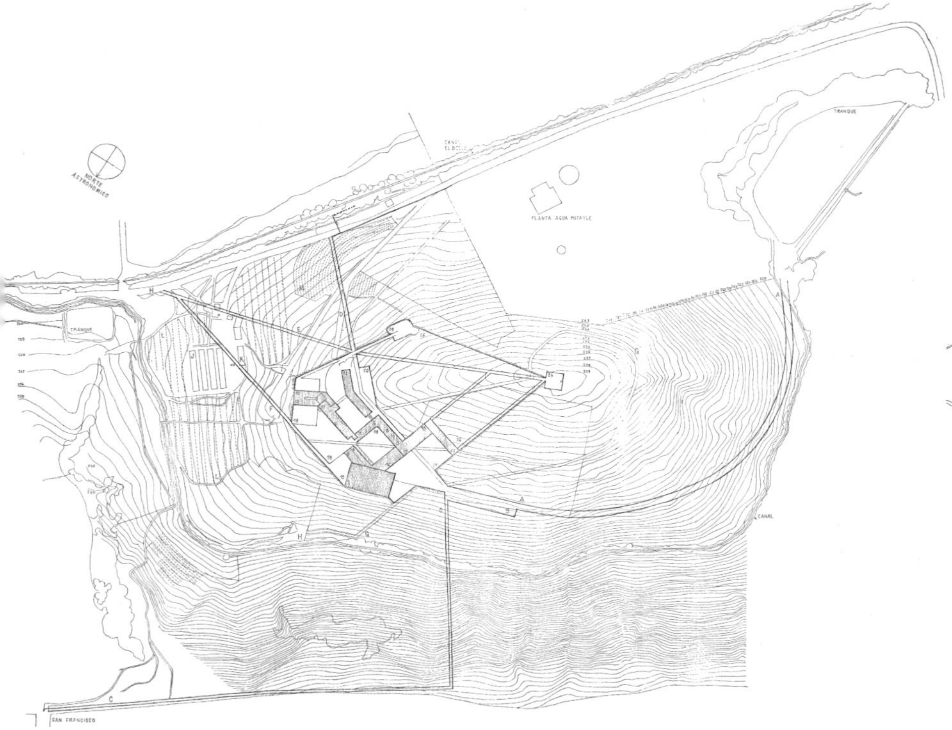

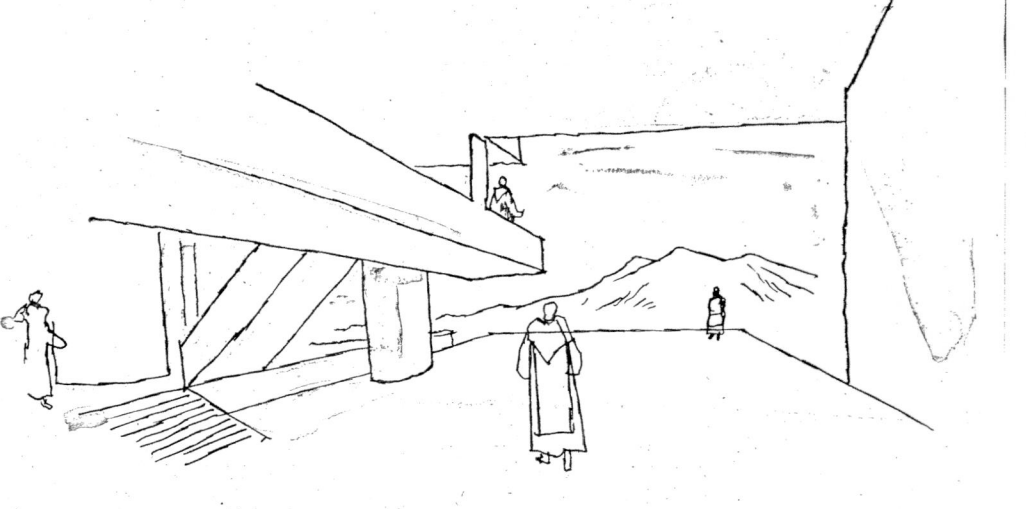

From the proposal by the Institute of Architecture:
1 Plan of the ensemble
2 Perspective
3 Sketch by Alberto Cruz and team

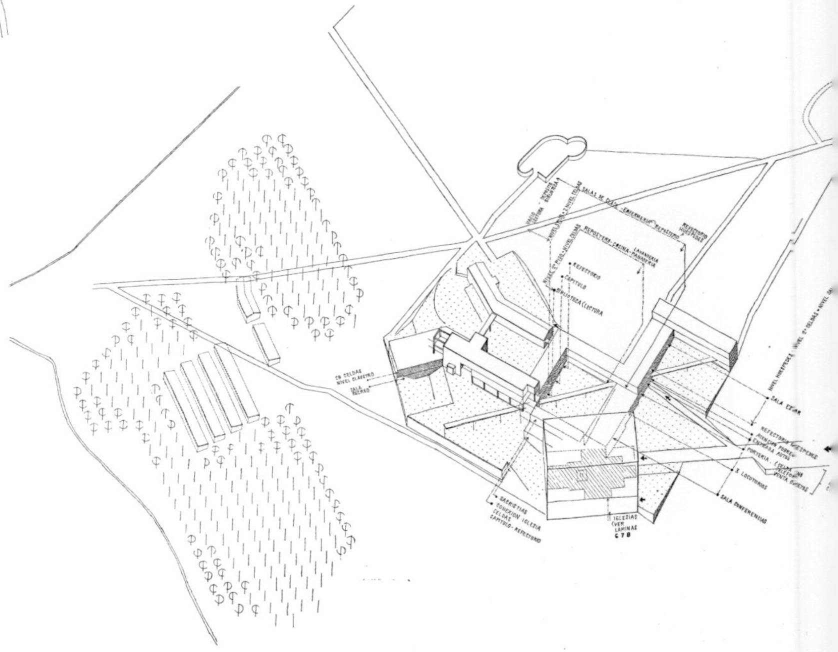

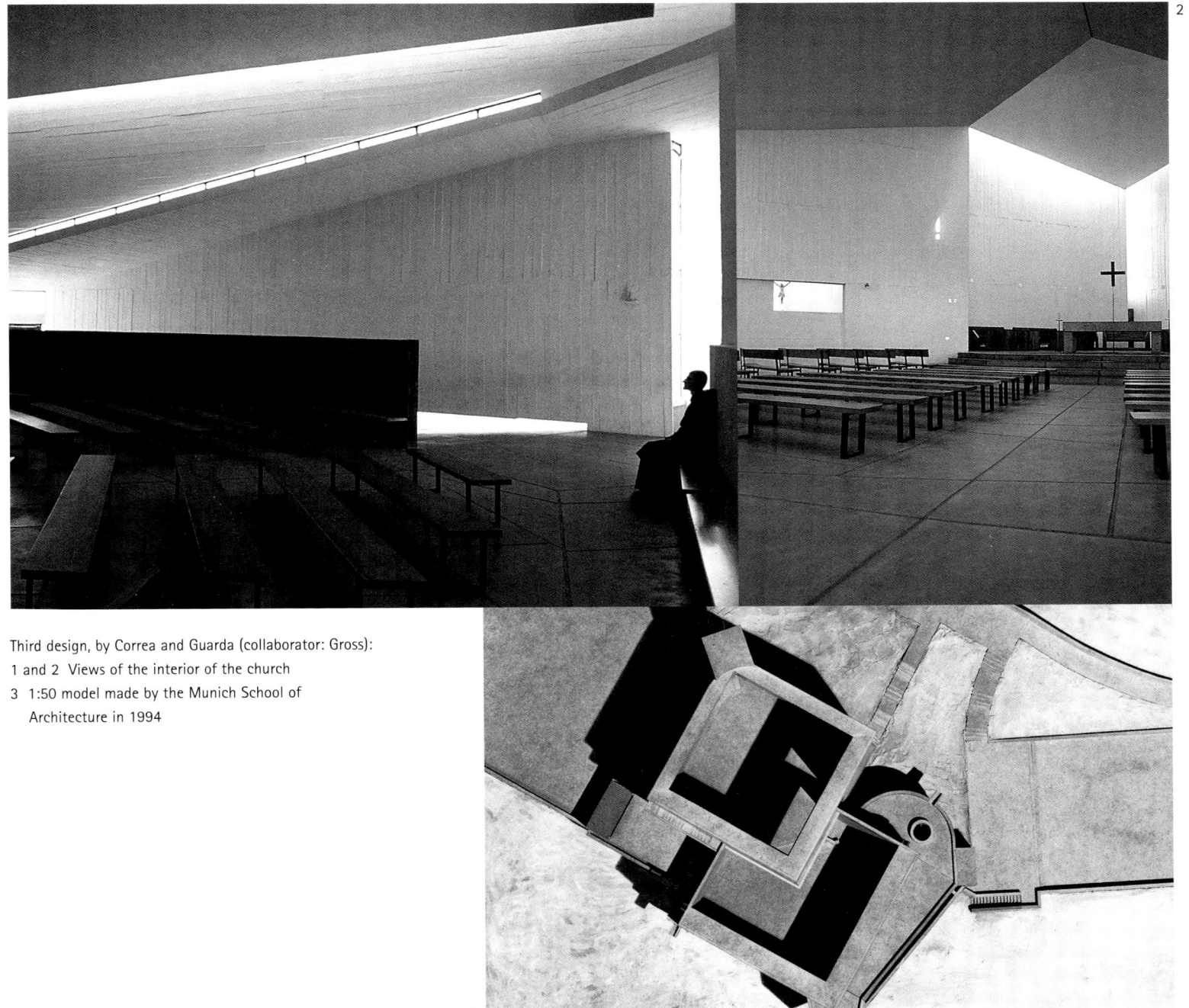

Third design, by Correa and Guarda (collaborator: Gross):
1 and 2 Views of the interior of the church
3 1:50 model made by the Munich School of Architecture in 1994

Casa Cruz

Calle Jean Mermoz, Santiago
Fabio Cruz, Institute of Architecture
First draft design
1956
Design and work
1958-1961

The house in Calle Jean Mermoz, in Santiago, was managed by Fabio Cruz, an architect belonging to the group which founded the School, as a commission for a relative. It was a significant work, not only because of its theoretical content and its undoubted interest in terms of form, but also because it was the first work in which members of the Valparaíso group participated to be actually built. The presence of graduates and later year students in the design and construction process made it an important precedent for what was to evolve as the school's way of doing things.

The plot was in a garden city suburb in a secondary street to the east of the city of Santiago. It is precisely the way the work was implanted into this urban context, and the process followed by the design and construction, which clarified its architectural content.

Avoiding the normal tendency to place isolated volumes in narrow plots of land, Fabio Cruz chose to place a roughly triangular-shaped volume against the western edge of the plot. This left more than half of the land free, in a single unbroken stretch, and highlighted its diagonals, i.e. its maximum dimensions, as the generating guidelines.

The process of conception and construction of the house was, in good part, responsible for its characteristics. There was no completed initial design but rather one which defined itself in a series of independent phases: once the structure was built a decision was taken as to the outer shells, and so on. During building, provisional plans were provided to the council. In this way the building process existed alongside the creative process, a feature which would be present in many of the group's works in the future.

In harmony with the shape chosen, governed as it was by the figure of the triangle, the volumetric and programmatic complexity was installed in a structure made up of modulated triangles which were reflected in the concrete structure. This was covered by a wooden skin to form floors, ceilings, windows and doors.

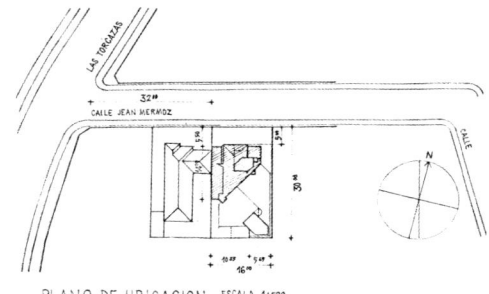

PLANO DE UBICACION

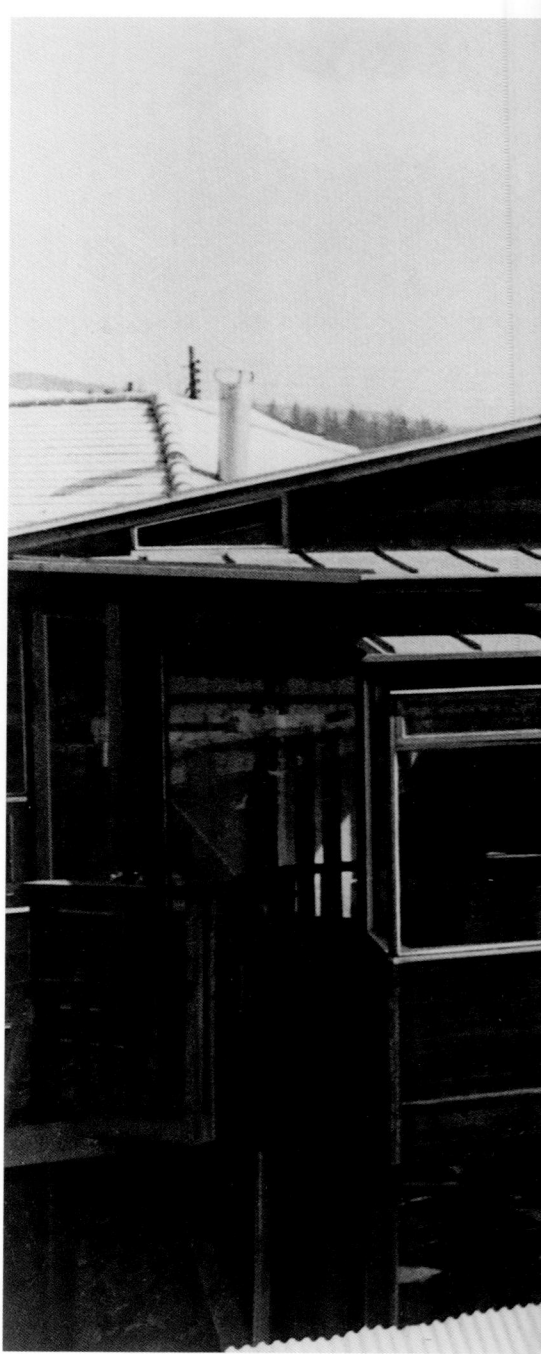

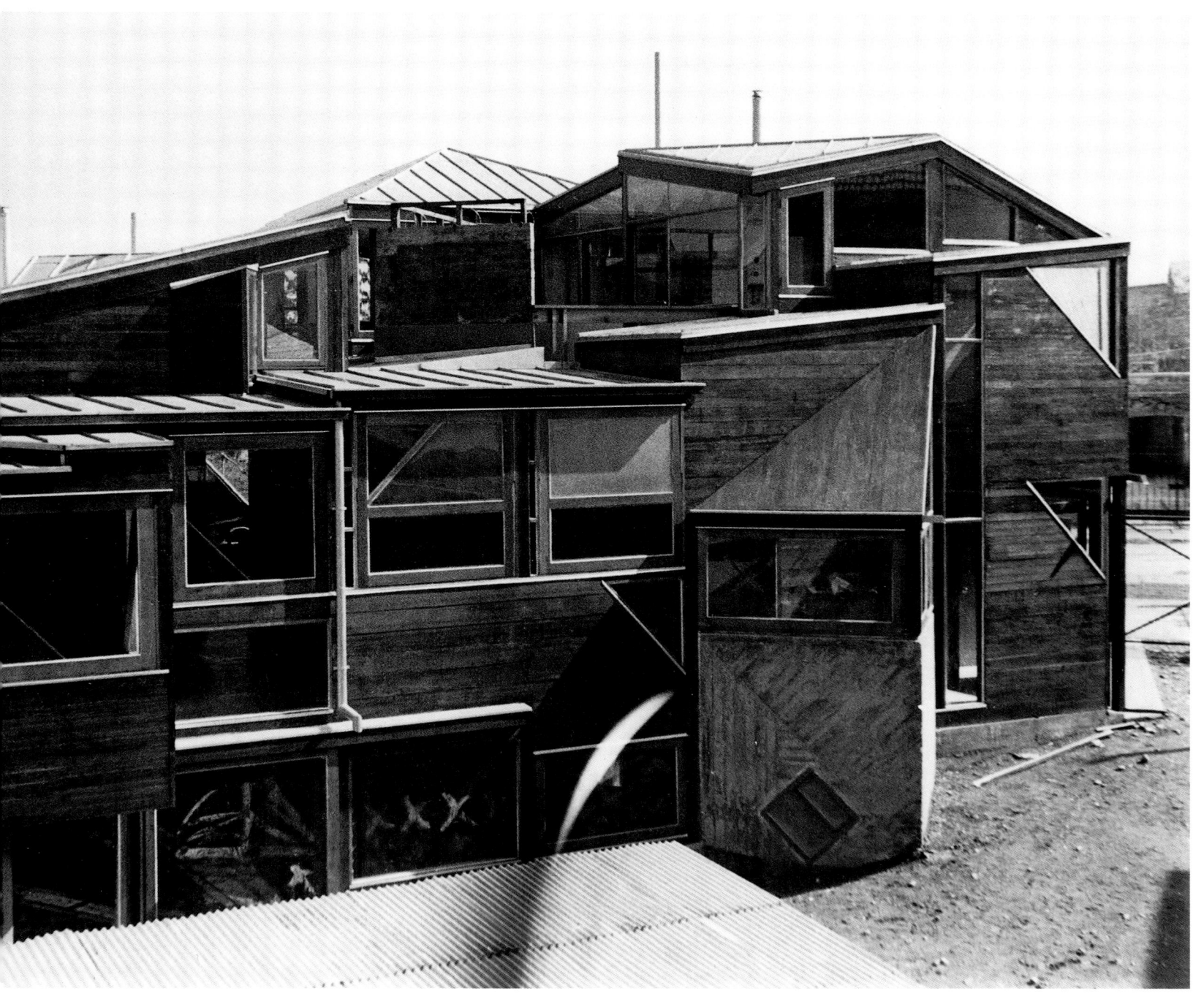

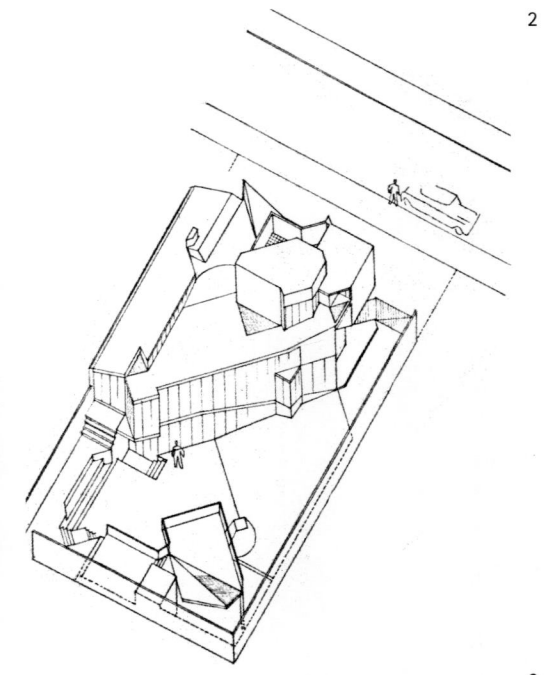
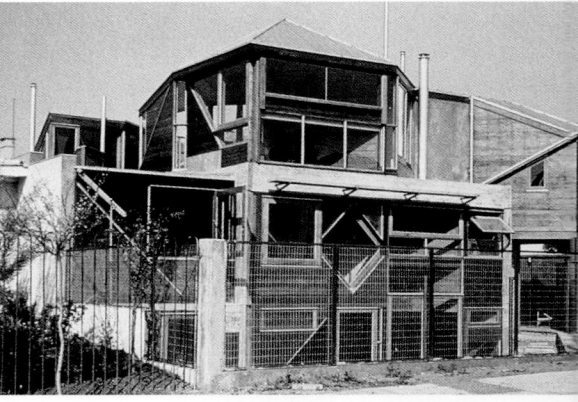

1 Process of deciding on the outer shell of the house
2 Schematic axonometric projection
3 View from the street
4, 5 and 6 Floor plans of level 1, 2 and 3
7 Interior passageway

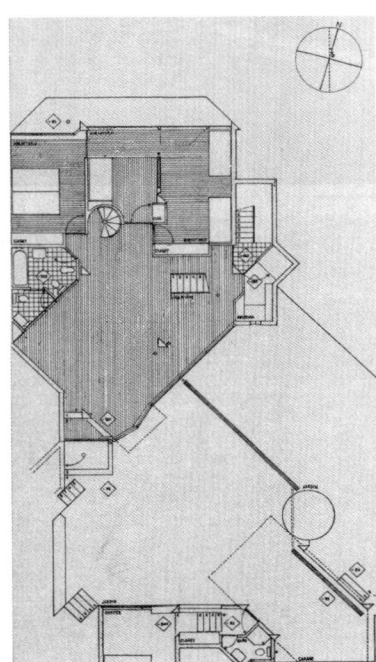

4

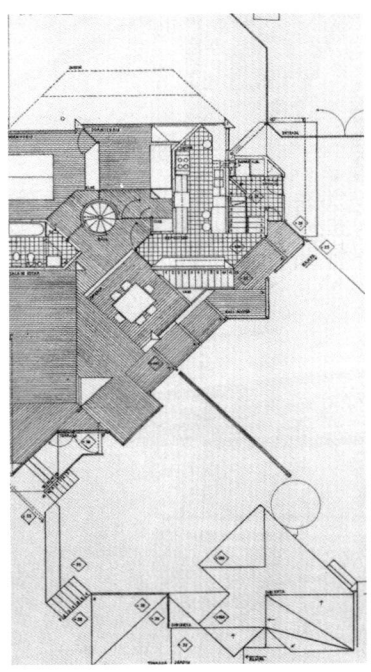

5

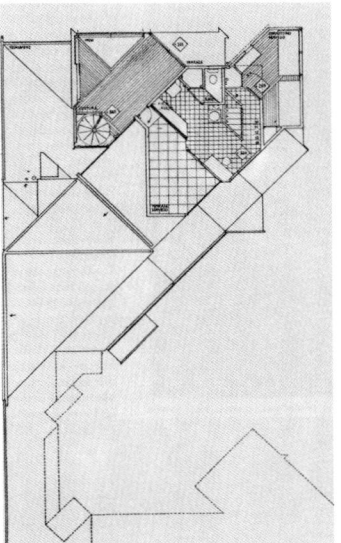

6

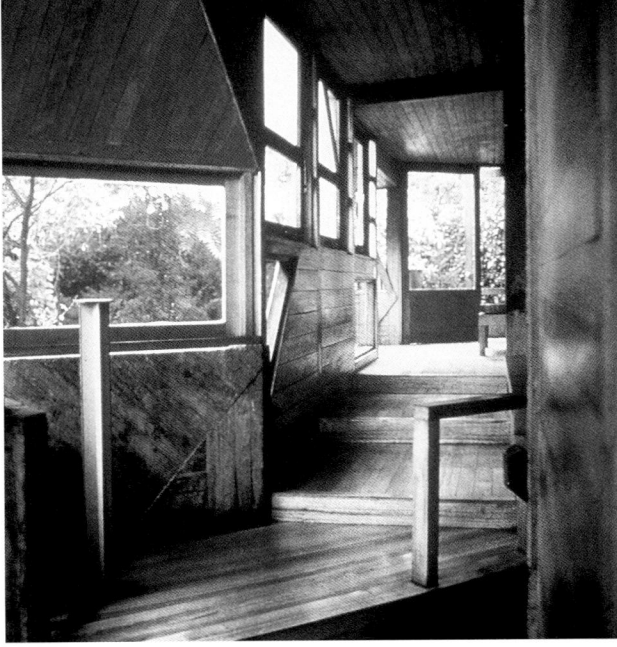

7

Even the roof was planned as independent pieces, and it was this last operation which gave the final shape to the rooms below it.

With regard to the circulation flows, the house was conceived as a spiral which, starting from the access gallery, led to the atelier, washroom and maid's room on the upper level. The children's playroom and bedrooms were on a lower, semi-sunk level. The living-dining room and kitchen, on the middle level. A straight stairway connected the access gallery directly with the lower level. A service stairway linked the kitchen with the washroom and maid's room. Finally, a remarkable wooden spiral staircase connected the three floors from the atelier to the children's playroom. The garage and the chauffeur's quarters were in an independent volume, at the rear of the plot.

The house, which has since been unfortunately and regrettably demolished, appeared as a porous volume of complex geometry and cubist features, in which interior and exterior, light and shadow, covered and uncovered spaces were interwoven.

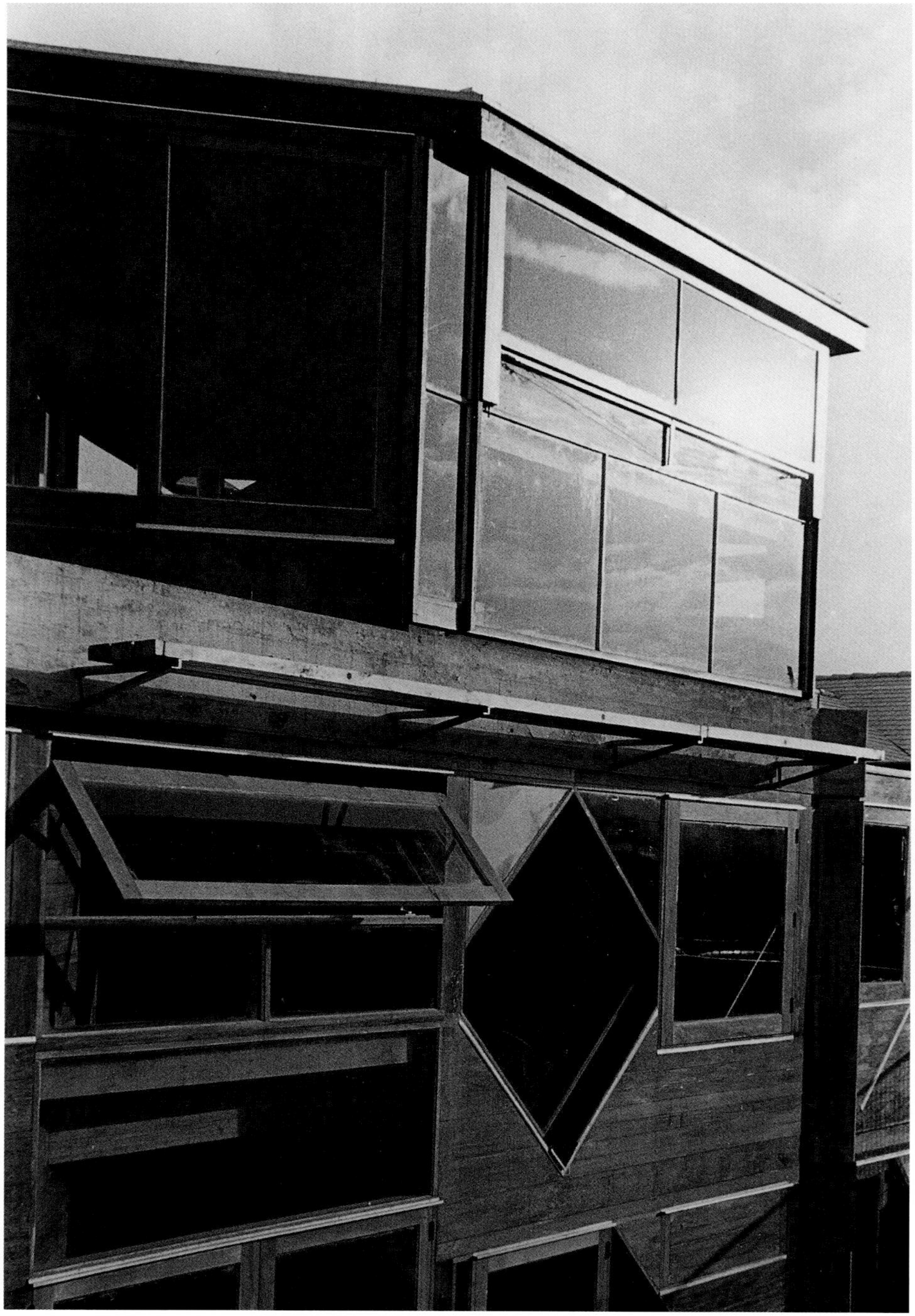

Detail of façade facing the street
Interior during building work

Following page:
North façade, seen from the street

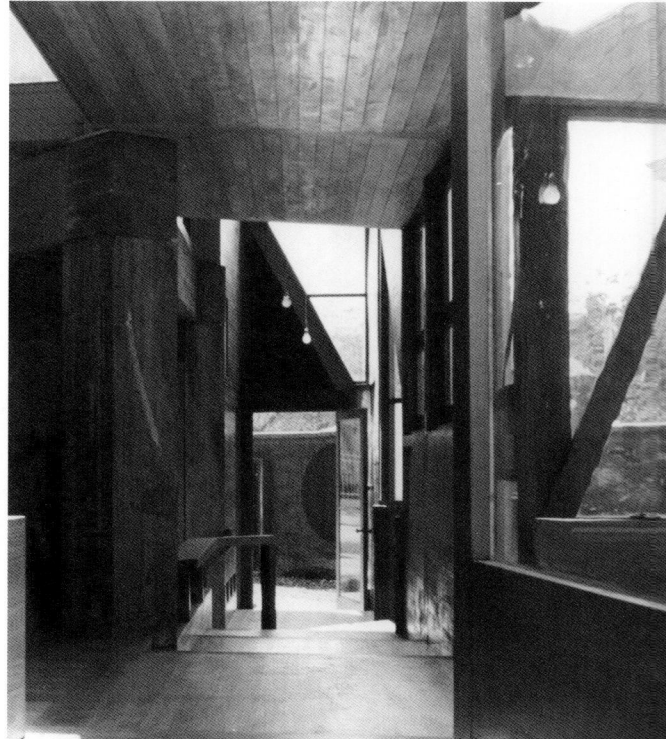

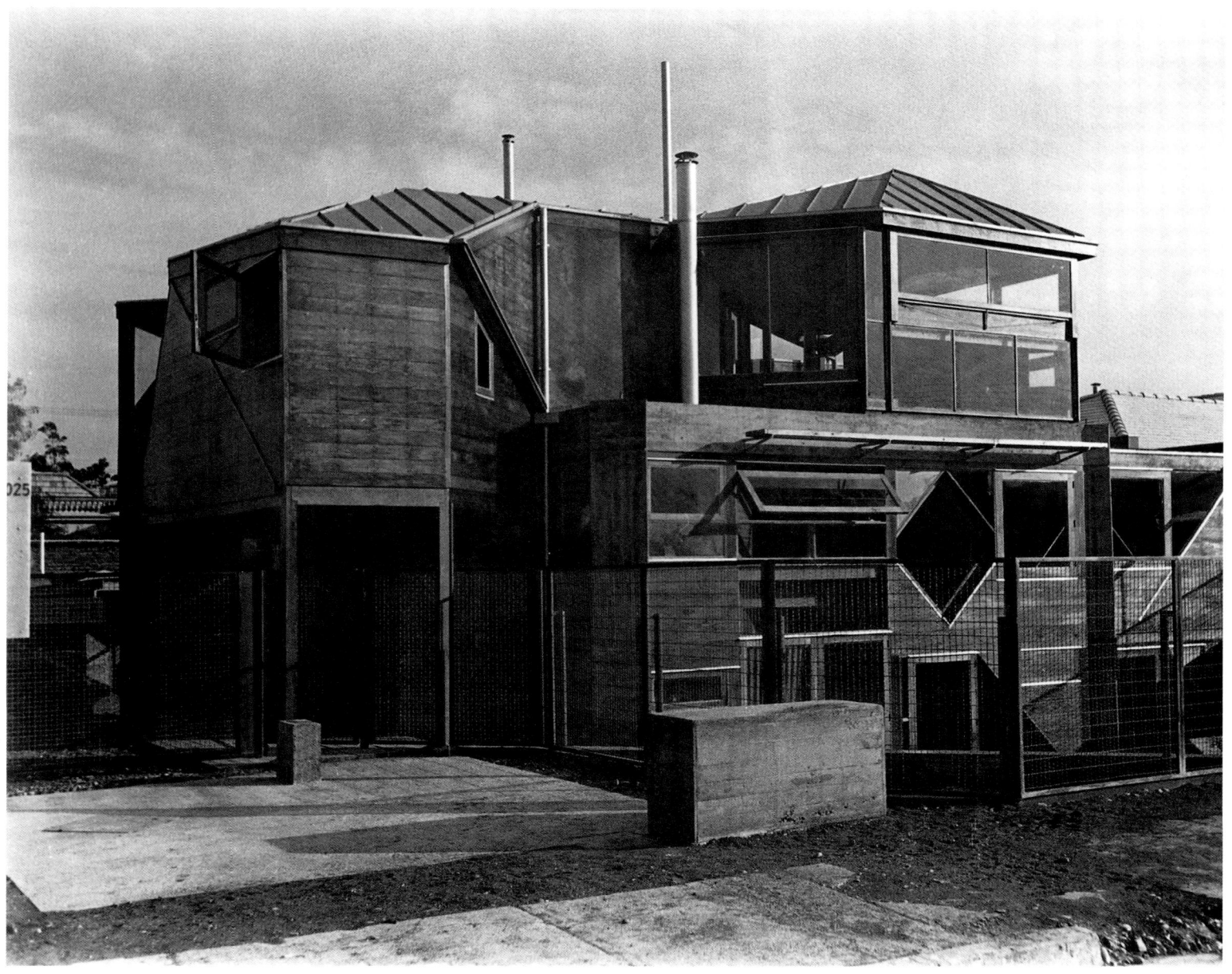

Southern Churches

Various towns in the south of Chile
—see inventory of Works and Designs on pages 138-141
1960-1965

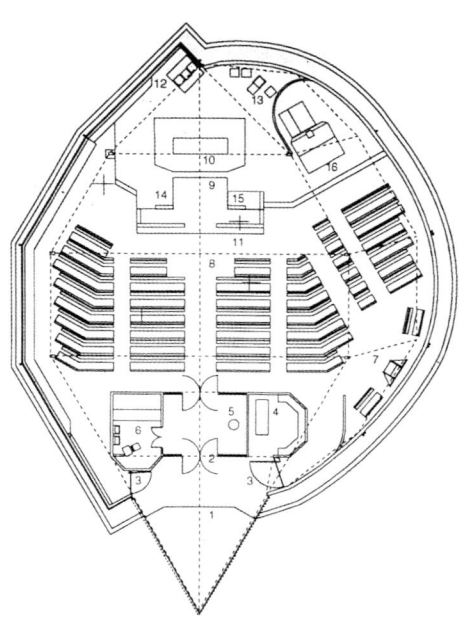
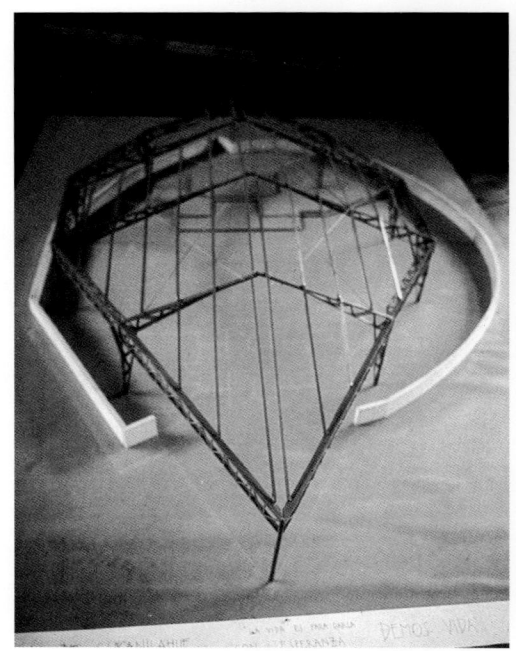

Earthquakes have marked the history of architecture in Chile. When the country was a colony, the weak constructions made of earth were frequently destroyed. Earthquakes were even regarded as historical milestones which signalled the end of one era and the beginning of a new one. In 1906 a severe earthquake destroyed Valparaíso. The earthquakes in Talca (1928) and Chillán (1939) not only caused death and destruction in the centre and south of the country, but forced a change in the technical standards which governed construction. In 1960, one of the most powerful earthquakes on record occurred, with the city of Valdivia in the south of Chile as its epicentre; it caused enormous damage between Concepción and Puerto Montt.

Together with other universities and social institutions, the Valparaíso School felt committed to show its solidarity with the affected area. An agreement with the Church authorities permitted the School to design a dozen churches between Concepción and Puerto Montt, providing it with the opportunity to confront issues which it had been reflecting upon in the preceding years, as well as new challenges presented by the completely new working conditions. Compared with what had become its method of working, the operation was to acquire very different dimensions. Not only professors were involved, but also students who were occasionally on site, sometimes in very tough conditions, to supervise the works. In this way a method of working on a collective basis took shape, which had been apparent in the Naval Academy project and which was to reappear in later activities; it linked the classroom to practical experience.

Work on these churches, in which Professors José Vial and Arturo Baeza seem to have played a particularly important role, had a considerable impact on the development of the ideas and methods of the

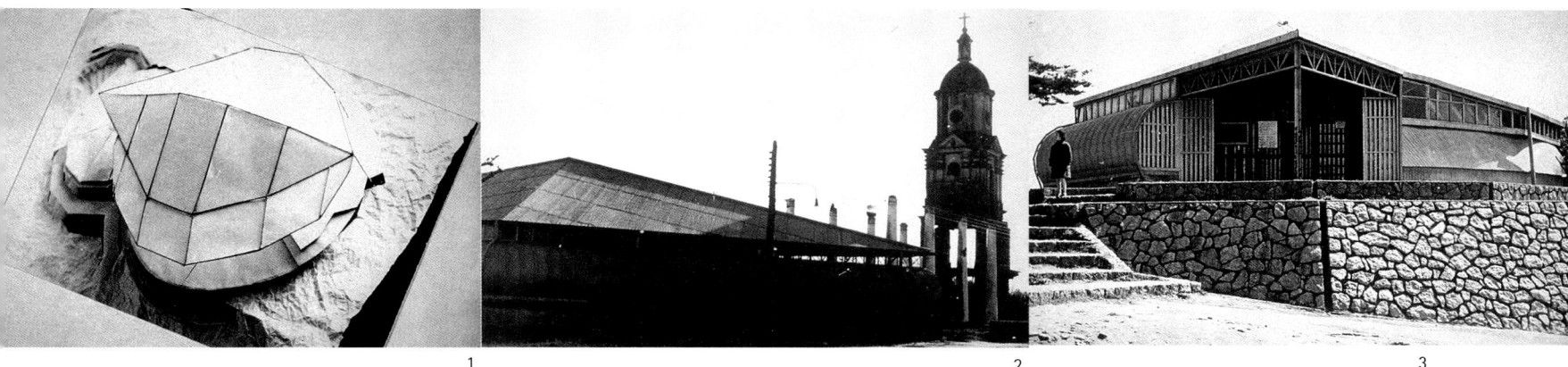

1 2 3

Previous page:
Floor plan and model of Curanilahue Parish Church

1 and 3 Church of La Florida, Santiago: paper and wire model and view of the entrance
2 Arauco Parish Church, with the tower which survived the earthquake

Next two pages:
4 Blackboard with sketch by Alberto Cruz of the church in Puerto Montt
5 Presbytery of the church in Puerto Montt
6 Paper and wire model of the structural outline of the church in Corral
7 Presbytery and side altar of the church in Corral

School. They created an opportunity for continuity in the area of religious architecture which had been a concern of the group since the studies for the Los Pajaritos Chapel, the first project for the Parish of Santa Clara, or Alberto Cruz's studies of parish territories. The conditions surrounding the commission itself and the maturity achieved through the architectural reflection involved meant that these churches marked the beginning of a new stage in the architecture of the school. This was to manifest itself in very diverse facets, from the forms employed to the role assumed by the school in construction and fieldwork.

The cases tackled included new churches, such as those of Florida, Curanilahue, Lebu and San Pedro; the reconstruction and transformation of old churches, such as those in Puerto Montt and Corral; and, finally, the coexistence of new buildings alongside the remains of old ones, as was the case in Arauco. At one time this was also proposed for the Cathedral in Osorno, though it was never put into effect.

In several cases—Florida, Curanilahue, Arauco and Lebu—lack of resources made it necessary to use industrial metallic structures donated to the Church. This gave rise to interesting manipulations of form, in which the same central nucleus—a kind of turtle shell created with the industrial structures—was adapted to different types of terrain and location by using a variable outer shell. This took the form of a wall which was concave towards the interior.

Of special importance in these churches was the concern with the requirements of a new liturgy which had been the subject of discussion in certain circles within the Catholic Church since the beginning of the century, though it acquired particular force after the Second World War. This new liturgy was later officially introduced with the encouragement of Juan XXIII and the II Vatican Council. This renewal

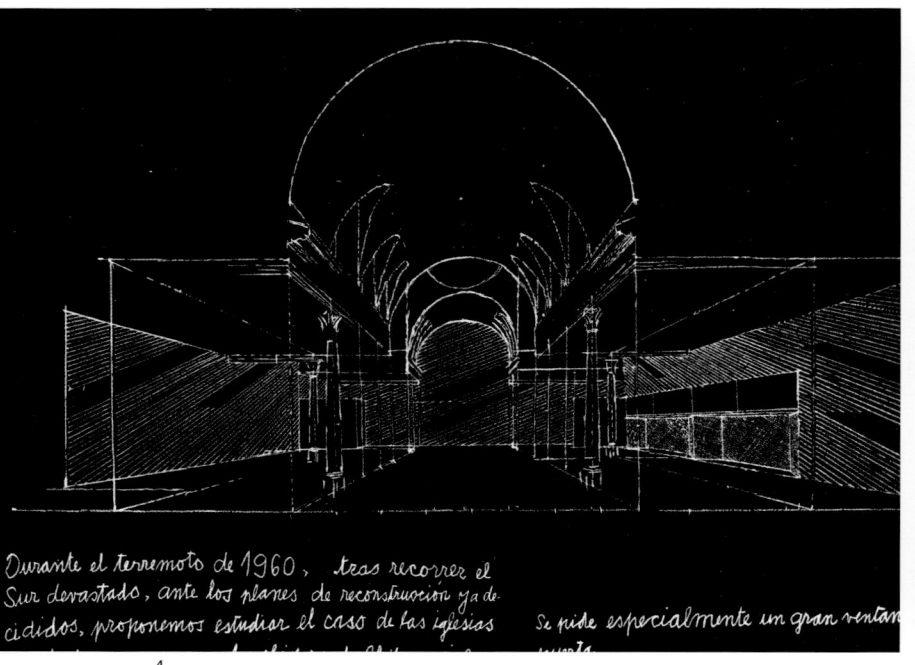

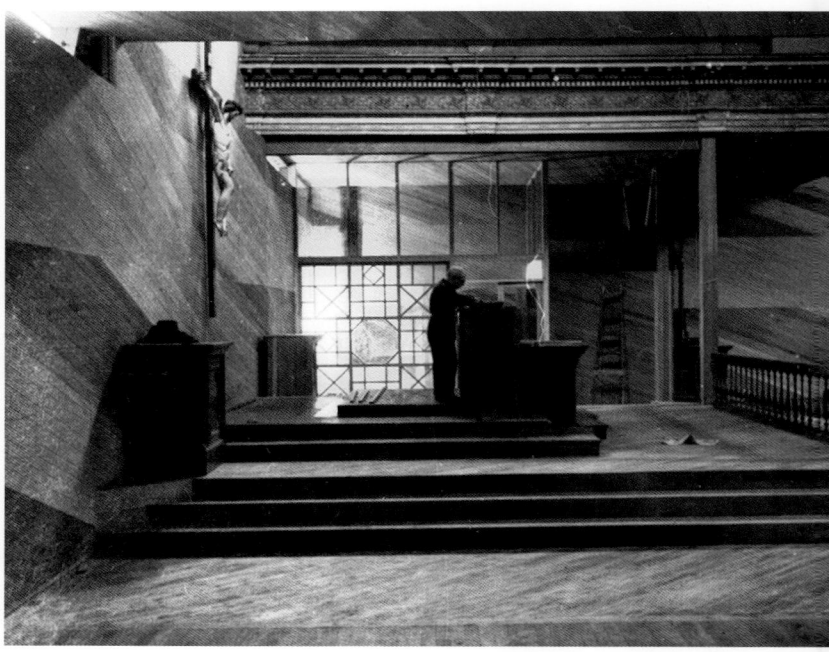

expressed itself in the shape and size of the presbyteries, the layout of the pews and in a multiplication of the focal points which freed these designs from an excessive centralism.

Mother Church in Puerto Montt
1961-1965

The Jesuit church in Puerto Montt was one of the most significant interventions of the overall project taken on by the Valparaíso School in the south of the country. Centrally located in the city, next to the school of the order of which it formed part, it was crowned by a tower which, as with so many churches in Chiloé, stood out as a particularly recognizable motif in the continuity of the urban façade. Inside, the lavishly decorated church had the traditional floorplan in the shape of a Latin cross, consisting of three naves and a long barrel vault. The earthquake of 1960 seriously damaged the church, affecting the structure and foundations, and the project involved restoring these. To this end, new concrete foundations were laid to support the existing columns, as were twelve structural bracing castles, which formed the new structure. These were built with pieces of timber, iron tensors and concrete connecting pieces; similar techniques to those used in the church in Corral were employed.

The floorplan of the church was extended, to eliminate some of the spaces which surrounded it. In this way it acquired the form of an almost regular rectangle of approximately 22x30 metres, with the old floorplan in the shape of a Latin cross inscribed within it. The decoration was conserved in columns, entablature, upper windows and vault. By contrast, the walls which marked the new perimeter of the nave were distinguished by the use of diagonal wooden panelling which, quite apart from its structural advantages, appeared as a series of delicate textured planes acting much like a backcloth, against which the conserved

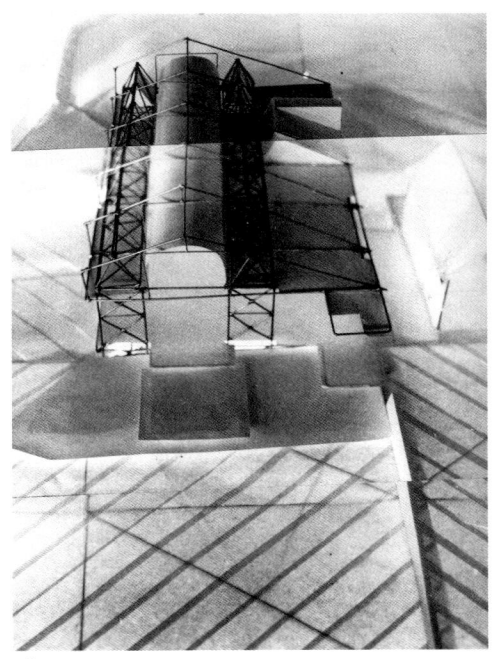
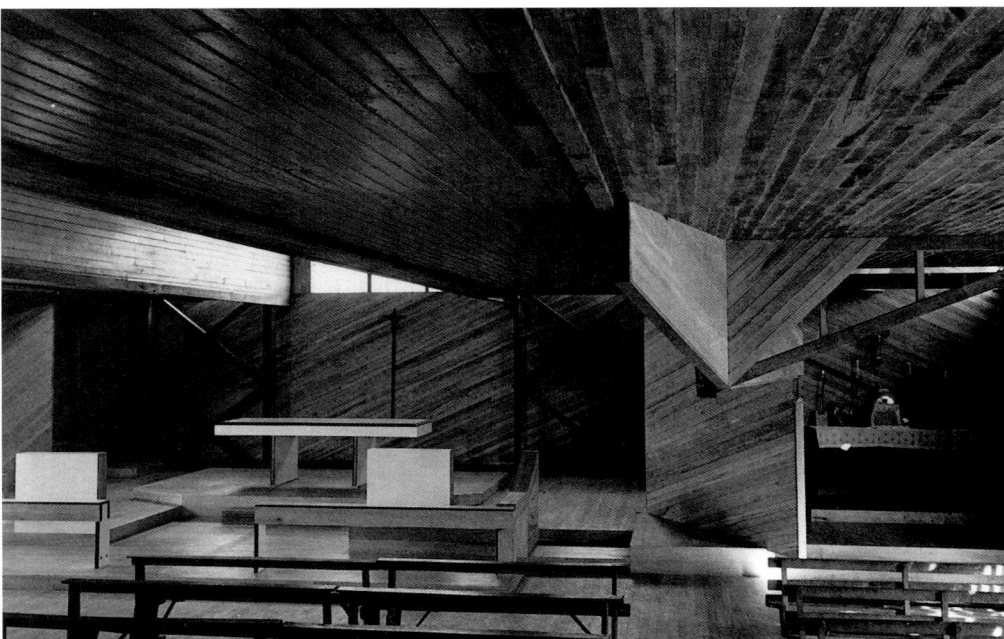

elements of the old church stood out. These conserved elements thus remained as a memory of the past, but, even beyond that, they acquired a new meaning by being integrated into the new proposal.

A small access enclosure, in the fashion of a narthex, constituted another of the elements which enriched the proposal. Next to it, a remarkable spiral staircase built from small pieces of wood led to the choir loft and was a forerunner of building methods which would be used years later in the Open City.

The meeting points of the new wooden walls and the structure of the old church provided a wonderful opportunity for generating new sources of light to modulate the interior brightness. To these sources was added the light entering from the façade which, at the request of the parish priest of the time, was planned as a large window connecting the nave with the urban exterior. Using principles similar to those employed in the nave, the tower kept its original form and decoration, while the lower part of the façade, today sadly changed, was redesigned as a skin of diagonal wood, perforated by five transparent doors which allowed the new profile of the nave to be visible.

Church in Corral
Corral, Valdivia
1960-1961

The town of Corral is on the southern bank of the River Valdivia and close to the mouth of the river, just a few kilometres from the city of the same name. Badly damaged in the 1960 earthquake, this small church, set on top of a hill overlooking the river, was rebuilt and radically transformed in the same operation.

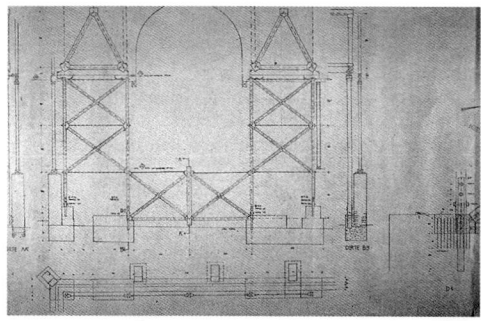
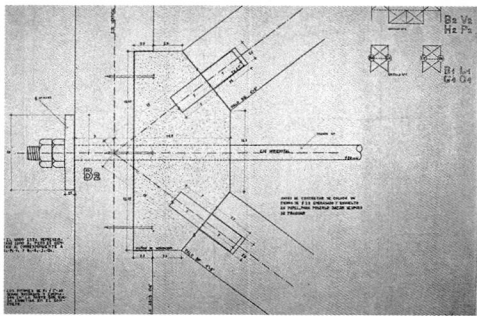
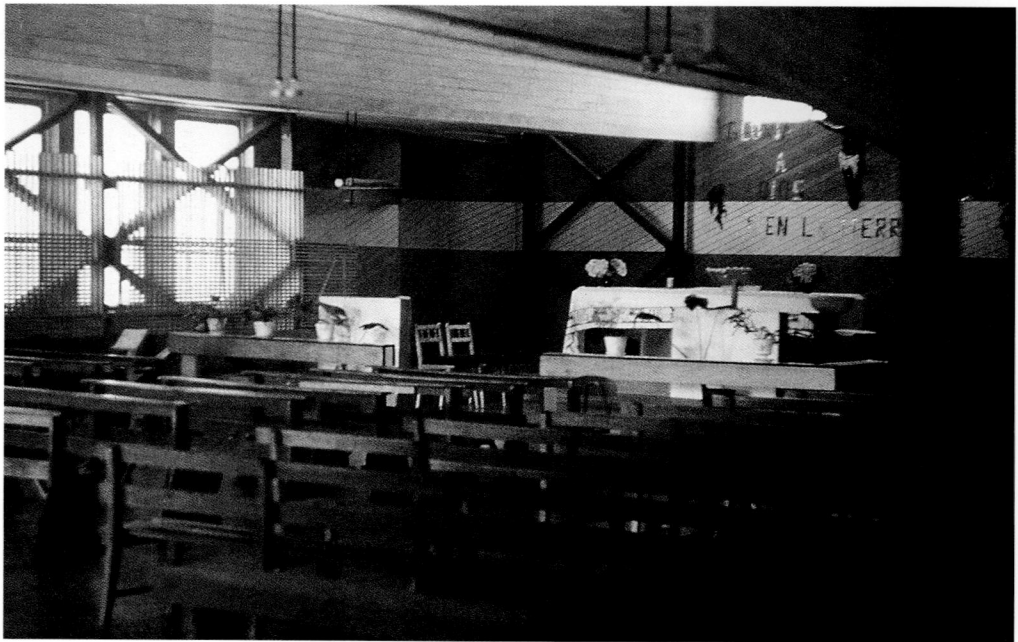

In order to do this, the floorplan was extended asymmetrically and the direction of the roof structure was changed. To extend the floorplan, an adjacent room on the west was annexed to the nave, thereby increasing considerably its width. As far as the structure was concerned, the old church had a traditional one of wood running crosswise. In the nave, originally included in a larger volume, a long narrow barrel vault was supported on five pairs of columns. In the project, this transversal structure was replaced by a longi-tudinal one. Four large reticular pillars, in the fashion of castles, placed at the four corners of the church, supported two beams, also reticular and triangular in section, which ran the length of the nave—approximately 20 metres. An unusual system of concrete connecting pieces was used in the wooden structures in order to resolve the problems arising from building such large structures without specialized personnel. These structural modifications also brought about a change in the roof: it became an asymmetric gable roof which reflected the changes wrought in the floorplan.

The result of these operations was a church with a rectangular nave and floorplan, capable of holding 180 worshippers. The absence of columns gave this interior space great continuity. The horizontal ceiling kept the inflexion of the old vault which remained as if floating above the nave. A secondary altar, to the west of the presbytery, together with a baptistery, in a small space next to the entrance, constitute focal points which enrich the interior space and free it from being exclusively dominated by the main altar. The arrangement of the pews in longitudinal rows allowed, on the one hand, areas to be differentiated—one linked to the main altar and another to the secondary—while at the same time integrating them into a single assembly. The presbytery was devised as a large and complex platform (especially when we con-

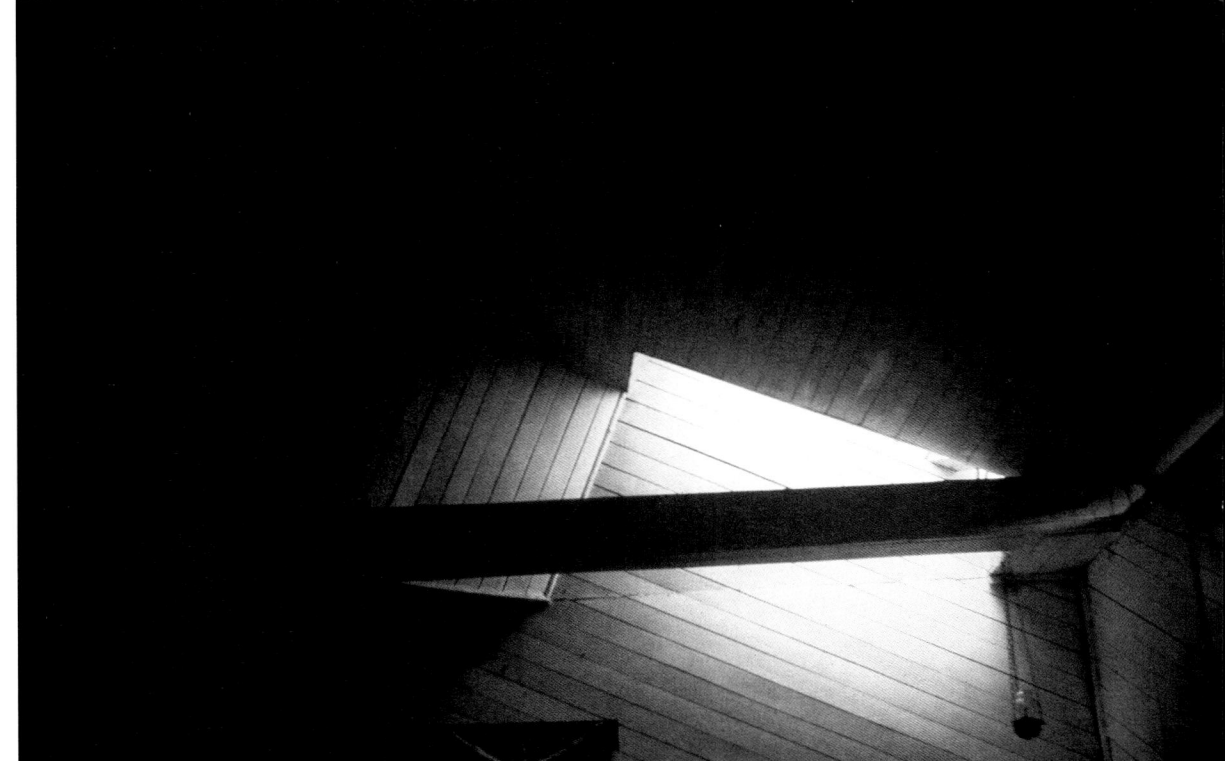

Previous page:
Structural details and view of the interior of the church in Corral

This page:
Details of the natural lighting in the church in Corral

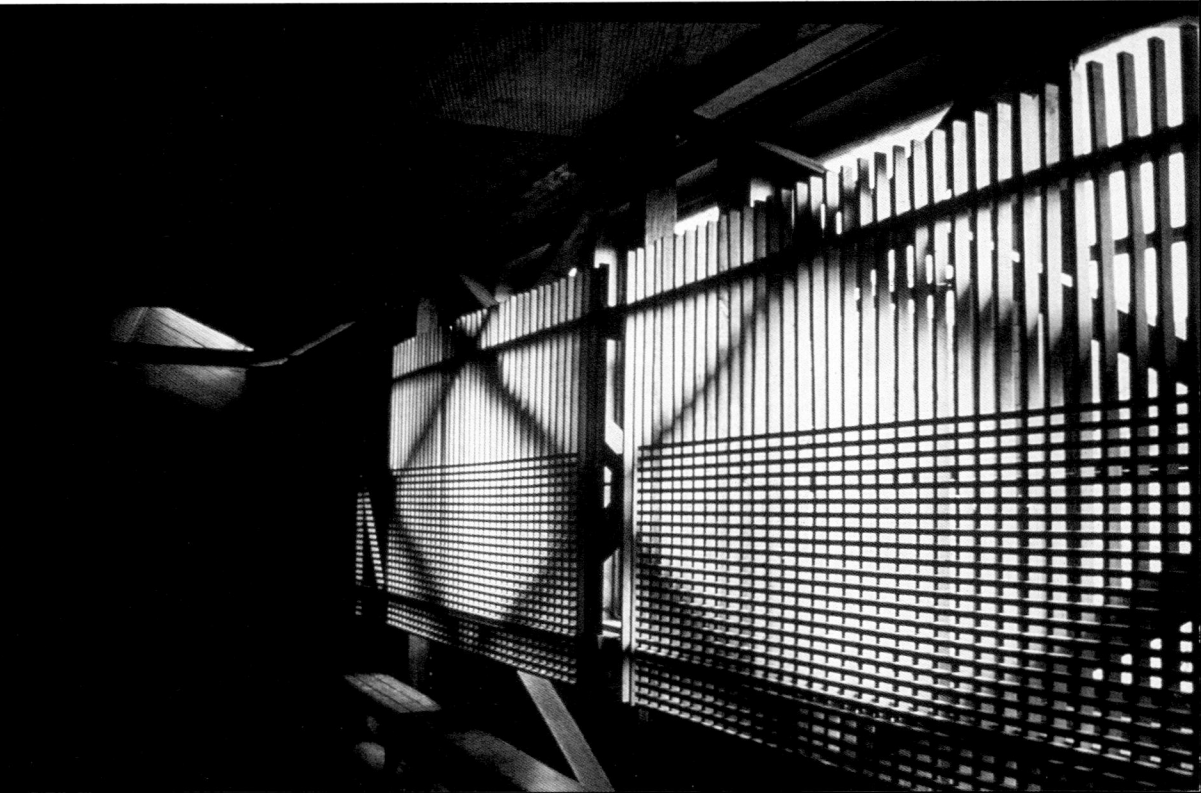

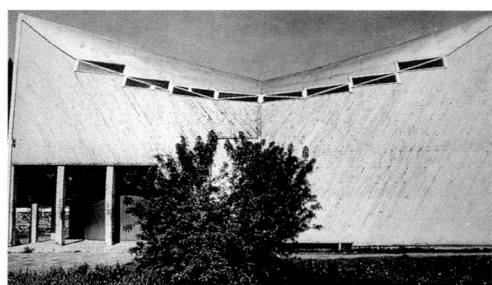
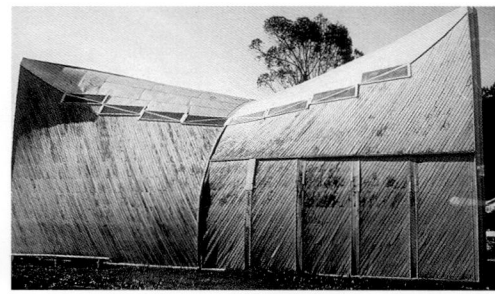
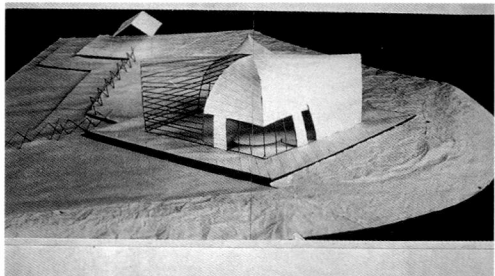
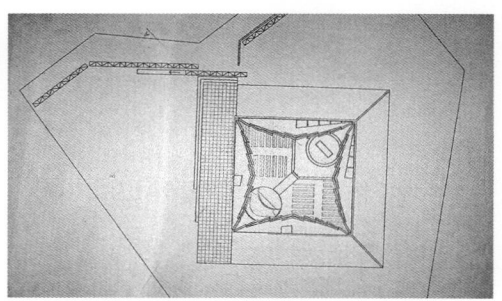

sider the small size of the church) which celebrated the ritual gestures and movements of the Eucharistic liturgy.

The light which penetrates from the west through a large window in the new area annexed to the nave is filtered by the wooden lattices of oriental delicacy. The exterior paintwork of the church, covered in metal sheets, forms part of the design. A series of geometric figures of differing colours, arising from the deterioration of those façades, presents an interplay in which the formal structure of the church is, simultaneously, both affirmed and negated.

Church of Nuestra Señora de la Candelaria
San Pedro
1960

Built on the outskirts of the city of Concepción, next to the southern bank of the River Bío-Bío, the church was meant to provide shelter for the pilgrims coming to worship Nuestra Señora de la Candelaria. It was a unique and remarkable case among the body of churches built by the Workshop of the Catholic University of Valparaíso after the 1960 earthquake. Its special nature manifested itself both in the forms—which differed from those of all the other churches—and in the way it related to its immediate environment. Basically, the fact that it was only necessary for the church to receive a large number of the faithful at certain times of the year led to the design for a small chapel—with a capacity for 150 people—but one which could be extended outwards.

Built in wood, the volume of the church arose from a rectangular square-shaped prism. However, this acquired a large degree of complexity owing to the formal treatment to which it was subjected. The floorplan of 15x15 metres was laid on the basis of its diagonal axes: the entrance was at the end of one of these axes and at the opposite end was the altar, thereby increasing the depth of the nave. The four ver-

Church in San Pedro:
Previous page:
1 and 2 access and rear entrance
3 and 4 model and floorplan
This page:
View from the southeast

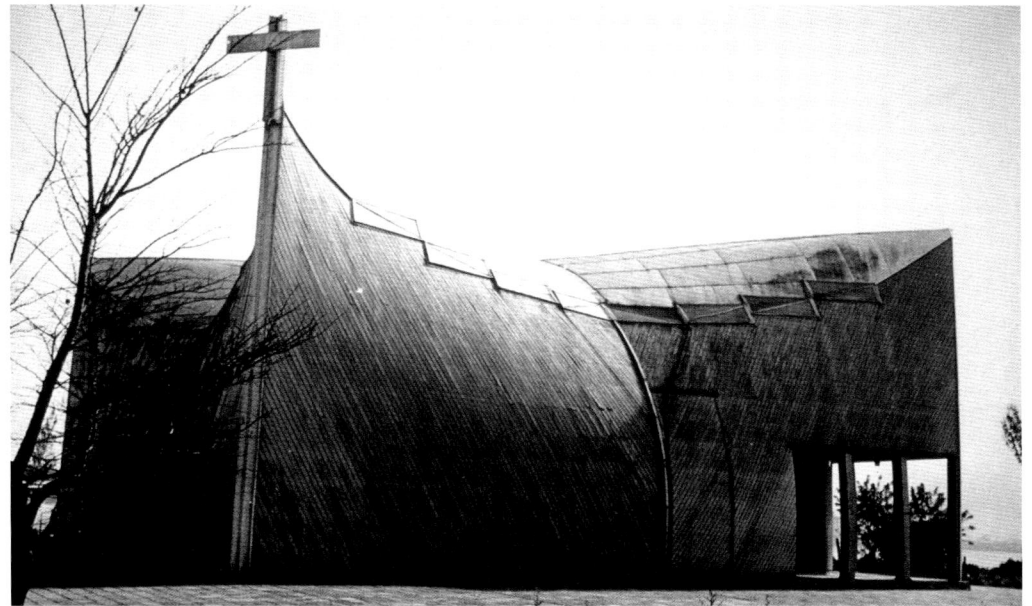

texes were connected at the highest points of the volume to generate the diagonal crossbeams of the roof, which coincided with the axes of the nave. The valleys, in contrast, divided the volume into four, creating arches which seemed to tie the volume to the ground. Between these and the square base of the floorplan there was a series of warped planes which gave the volume the continuity and attractiveness of the inverted hull of a ship, textured by the diagonal slats.

Given the continuity of the outer shell, the roof was only identified by a subtle change in material between the diagonal wooden slats and the covering of metallic sheet. This encounter was also used to good effect to place a series of rectangular windows arranged right over this kind of gently descending catenary in which the encounter occurred.

The possibility of extending the nave outwards was a reminder of what had already been proposed for the Los Pajaritos Chapel, except that in San Pedro the extension was created from behind the altar, through a series of panels raised to form a kind of canopy which acted as a threshold between interior and exterior. Thus, the altar was allowed to remain in a central position for the holding of ceremonies towards the exterior.

Of special interest was the wooden fencing which surrounded the pilgrimage enclosure. It was formed by a series of independent pieces of wood, freely interwoven to create a three-dimensional boundary. Unfortunately, the wooden structure of the church, built with enormous effort because of the scarcity of materials and labour, was seriously damaged by the abundant rain in the area, and had to be taken down in 1985. It was replaced by a larger church built with conventional materials.

Open City

Ritoque, Quintero
Cooperativa Amereida
1970 . . .

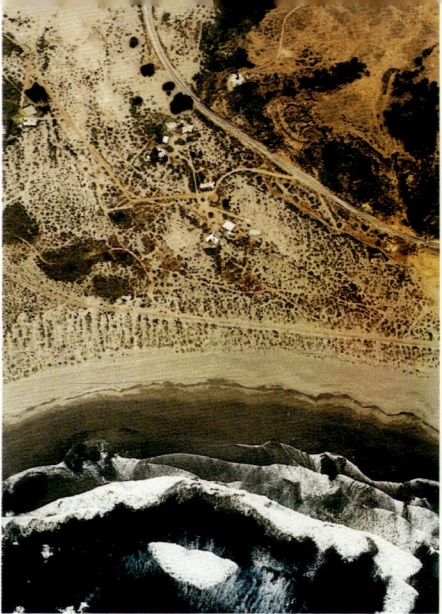
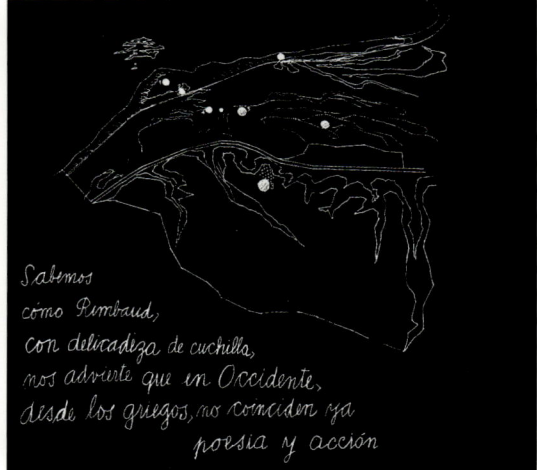

Along with the program of travesías, it is without doubt at the Open City where, by circumventing the framework of action of normal professional practice, the architects of Valparaíso have literally constructed a way of "doing" architecture in experimental conditions. Both undertakings, subject to strict budgetary contingencies and restrictions, are fully autonomous in nature, with the architects also taking on the role of managers or clients. It is for this reason that both projects enjoy an unusual degree of propositional freedom. The Open City is the site of the greatest concentration of works managed by the group and inspired by its spirit.

About 30 kilometres to the north of Valparaíso, the Open City is the last in a sequence of spa resorts which form a linear conurbation. The site unfolds along 3,030 metres of deserted beach. The prevailing climate is dry, with brief periods of seasonal rain. There are continual strong winds, predominantly from the southeast. Waves beat incessantly against the open sandy beach, whose only geographical feature is a small rocky island. Driven by the desire to create a space whose central purpose was to combine life, work and study, the professors of the schools of Architecture and Design, architects, designers, poets and artists, founded the *Cooperativa de Servicios Profesionales Amereida* (Amereida Professional Services Co-operative), the organization with overall responsibility for the project. In order to ensure the longevity of the experience, the site and works operate as a nonprofit making foundation whose assets are non-transferable. The statutes enshrine the principle of collective ownership—and exclude the possibility of individual private ownership—of the land and buildings. The ensemble is governed by the regulations which apply to a *Parque Costero Cultural y de Recreación* (Coastal Cultural and Recreation Park), thereby ensuring sufficient operational freedom once certain construction parameters have been met: for example, that the built surface does not exceed 9% of the land. The constructions are spread generously over the site and large open areas predominate.

A track divides the extensive 275 hectares of the site into two sectors: one of dunes and low-lying lands, towards the coast, and another inland sector of uneven mesetas and sloping planes of up to

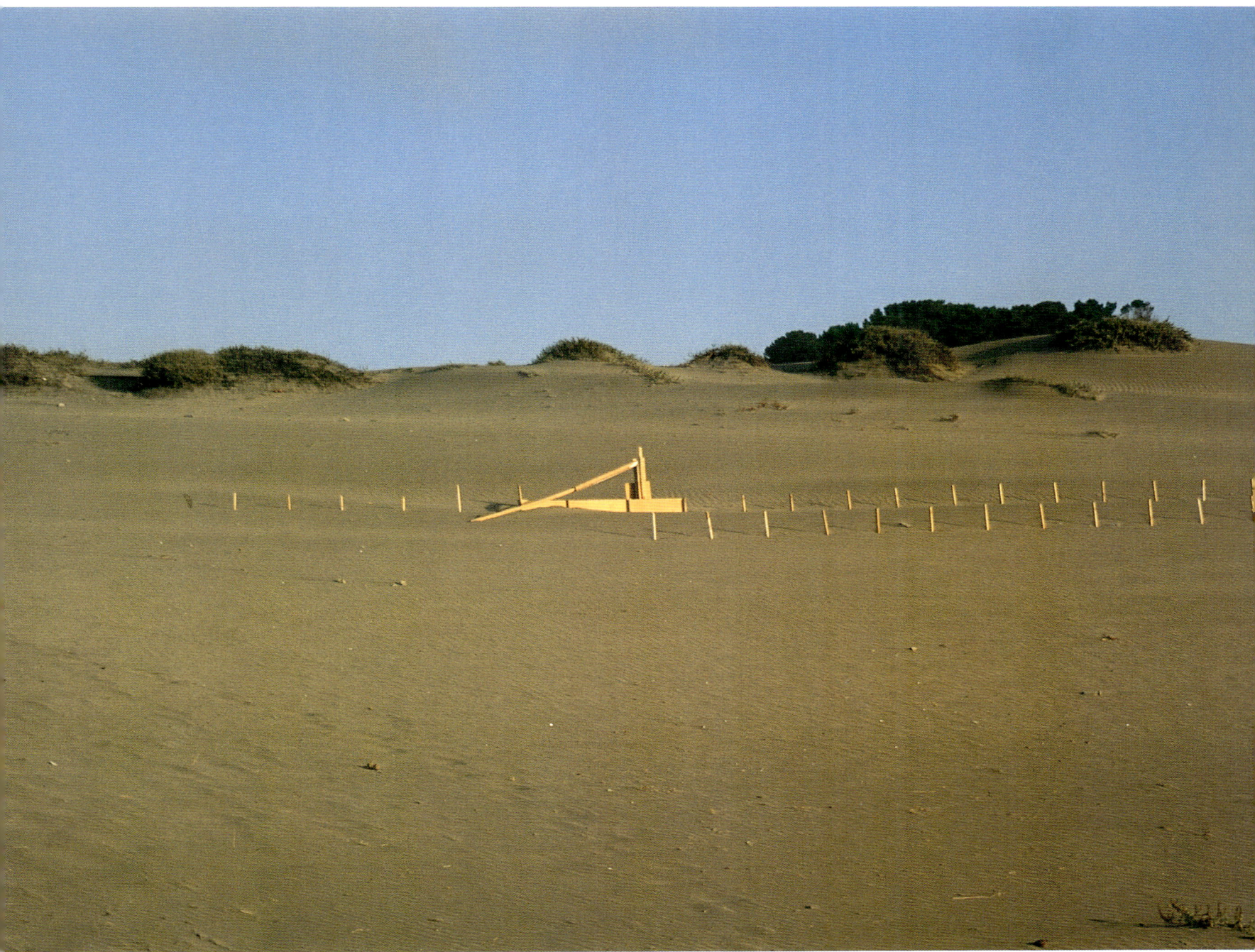

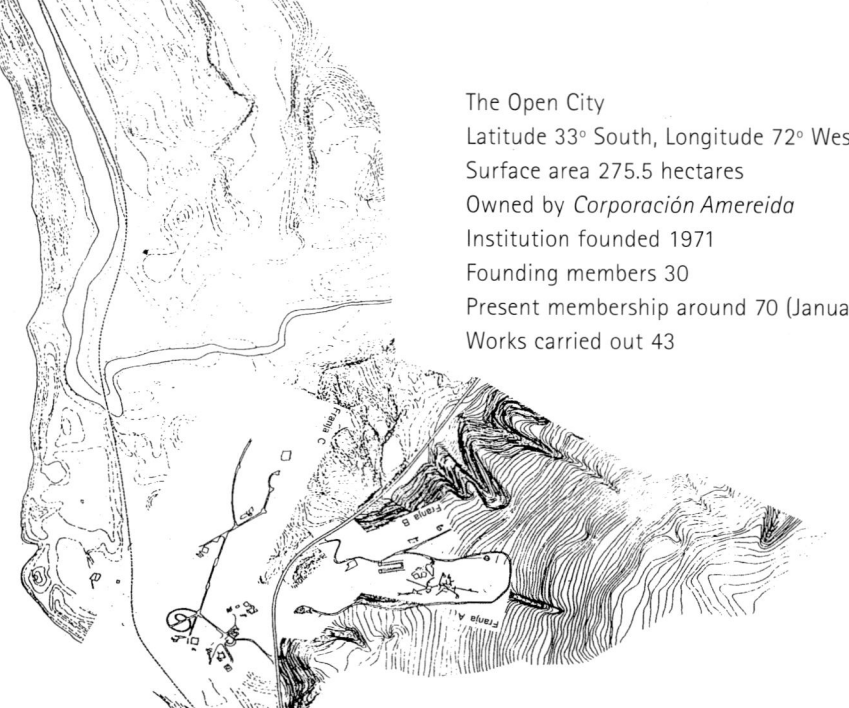

The Open City
Latitude 33° South, Longitude 72° West
Surface area 275.5 hectares
Owned by *Corporación Amereida*
Institution founded 1971
Founding members 30
Present membership around 70 (January 2002)
Works carried out 43

Detailed plan on page 142

120 metres in height. The topographical and material context provided by the site was of particular interest to the group, who inspected it both for its materials and its spatial conditions and for its capacity to act as a kind of metaphorical support for meanings. It is alluded to in many different ways, both in the works, because their locations are sensitive to the inflexions or subtle changes in the ground, and in the reasoning which has constantly accompanied the group's way of doing.

Within this context the presence of considerable areas of dunes stands out. The material of which they are made, the sand, is inert and unstable; their condition is, in a certain way, abstract and ambiguous: the dunes of sand are constantly losing their form and being reshaped; tracks disappear on ground which shifts, constituting a kind of halfway state between dry land and water. In a metaphorical sense, the group associated this constant re-shaping with the recovery of a state of innocence in the face of things, to the capacity to surprise permanently, exemplified in the wish to "*volver a no saber*", "to return to not knowing".

Postulated as a framework which was reluctant to encourage extremes between work and recreation, the Open City is rather indifferent to the extensive and attractive beaches which unfold along its long coastal flank. As a result, the usual hierarchies of location which one finds in a spa resort, and which are almost exclusively determined by accessibility to the seafront, are not present here. Nor are the buildings of the Open City located on the basis of the view they offer of the sea. Their façades do not provide evidence of any attempt at that visual dominance of the sea which is a normal characteristic of spa towns; quite the opposite. In fact, its windows, generally sealed, are blocked by walls which obstruct the view of the horizon. Strongly imbued with an extraordinary spirit, the Open City favours

1. Entrance Lodge and high ground
2. Entrance Lodge towards the Access Plaza

the more subtle effects of the sea: breeze, sounds, temperature, humidity, which give a greater value to the periodic reunion with the spectacle of the coast over and above that of its constant presence. The fact that the complex has been designated a "city" appeals to a certain spirit of public life which the group considers essential for a city: a sphere in which the free nature of the poetic experience and the capacity to surprise take priority over any other consideration or urban practice. This explains the proliferation of agoras, small squares and public meeting spaces and, furthermore, the total exclusion of a host of urban functions. These spaces are also valued as places where the cohesion of the group is put to the test by the need for collective decisions, as collective ownership entails the discussion of issues and the taking of decisions in collective meetings, assemblies in agora.

Work is overseen by a supervisor or director or a member who is leading the project, but is generally open to the participation of architects and designers in the development of the founding principles and the design concept. In many cases, buildings are erected collectively or in stages, through systems of *rondas* (literally "rounds" but here meaning "work in a circle"). The final configuration of a construction may be completely different from how it started out, and the notion of completeness is unknown. The method of conception and execution is such that small constructions may involve numerous co-designers, often including students whose project involves a small fragment of the overall design. This was the case, for example, with the Cubicle Lodges (*Hospederías la Cubicula*, begun in 1995) or the Double Lodge (*Hospederia Doble*, begun in 1974). The existence of collective authorship and execution by stages makes it difficult to attribute work to individual authors and to date the work. Beyond any similarity in form, this in itself distinguishes these works from those others whose

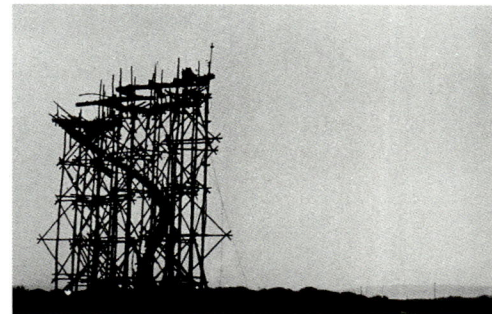
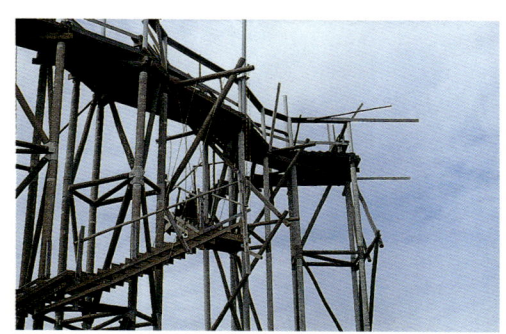

Plaza and Water Towers
(*above*: first version of 1974-1980)
Following page:
Gallery Lodge
and walled garden

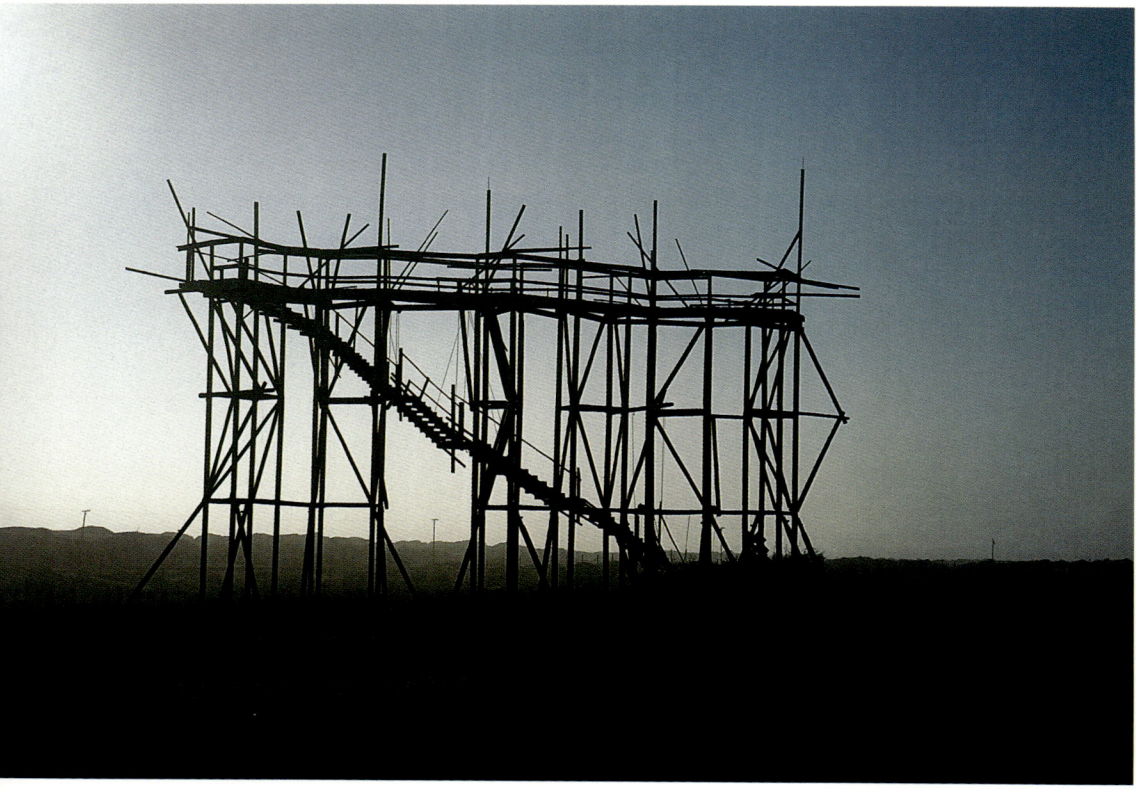

forms suggest aggregative processes, a distinction which reveals a radical attitude when compared with certain contemporary architectures obsessed with the identity of the author, the finite nature of the work and the conclusiveness of the process involved. Paradoxically, this later version of the ancestral principle of construction "in a circle" takes on a highly innovative slant in the Open City.

The ensemble includes lodges, a cemetery and open-air chapel, agoras and meeting places, workshops, as well as landscaping works, paths and roads, land consolidation work and support infrastructures. In the first years of minimal installations a constant presence was maintained on the premises through a shift system. Lacking water and electricity, initial occupation was along the lines of a camp though it benefited from the initial working installations, the igloo and a wood-impregnating shed. The possibility of doing without electricity was debated for a while, with the aim of preserving the virginity of the night.

Initially, rough and unfinished materials and simple building techniques were resorted to. Construction methods at the Open City have varied according to circumstances, leading to a wide range of materials and techniques, including at times the realization of works by outside subcontractors. Furthermore, the passing of time has revealed the short life cycles of some of the projects, whether because of their precarious construction, as they were only designed to be used for a limited amount of time, or as a result of vandalism.

Owing to the low number of permanent residents, the Open City is an unencumbered and relatively empty place: in general, the works dispense with gardens, and the activity of the

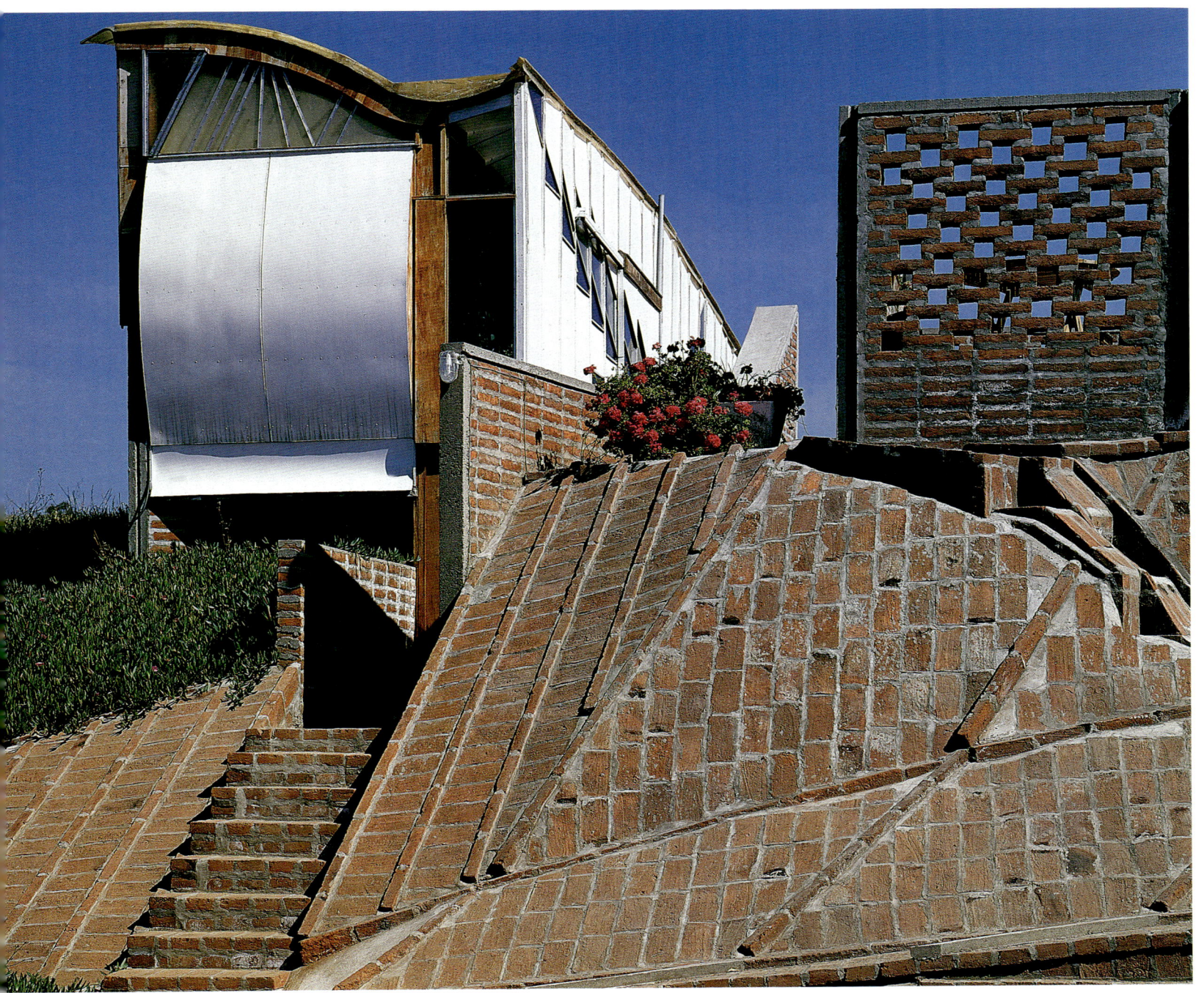

lodges is mainly turned inwards. Activities of a more public nature take place, staggered throughout the year, either for the academic community or for a wider public. On these occasions the reason for providing meeting places, the complex of esplanades, the small squares and the sites for hosting collective activities becomes clear. The high profile of these occasions is generally also guaranteed by the display of inventions associated with the act of playing, the receptions and banquets, inventions in which the designers participate actively, thus enriching the ritual and giving a note of individuality to the events. In a spirit similar to that of the baroque party, the works may be decorated on these occasions, while the food is laid out on supports specially designed in paper, metal or wood.

Although the Open City was originally established in what was the countryside, the effect of a budding neighbourhood of residential developments began to be felt at the turn of the century. This irreversible process is bound to affect significantly any decisions which have to be taken in the future, because for the first time the grounds of the Open City are becoming hemmed in by suburban growth. With the virginity of the horizontal vision lost, the debate about the site will be forced to consider the contingencies of a neighbourhood whose lineaments and ambitions arise from conflicting ideas and values. On the other hand, the arrival of new inhabitants could fire the Open City with new meanings regarding the public place.

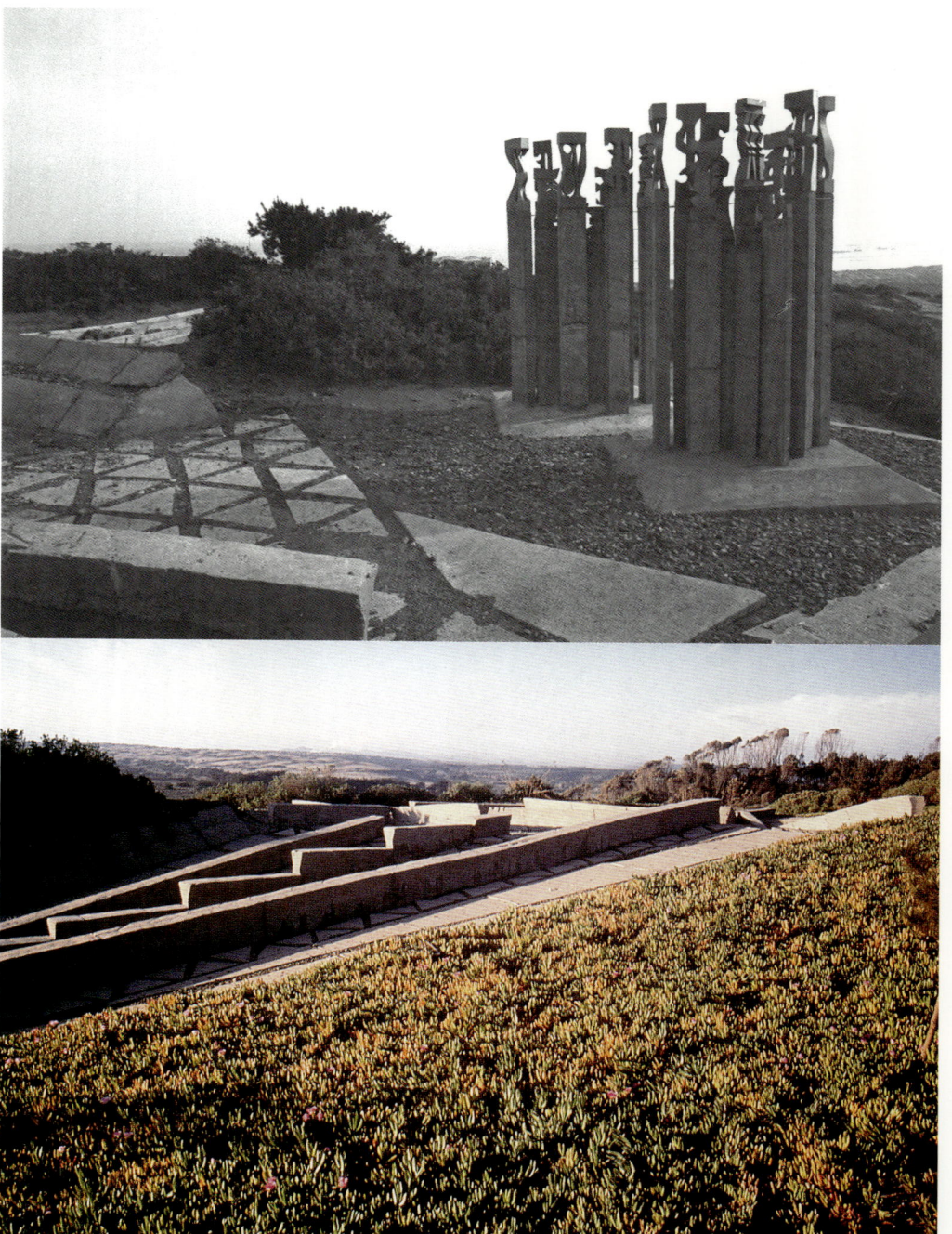

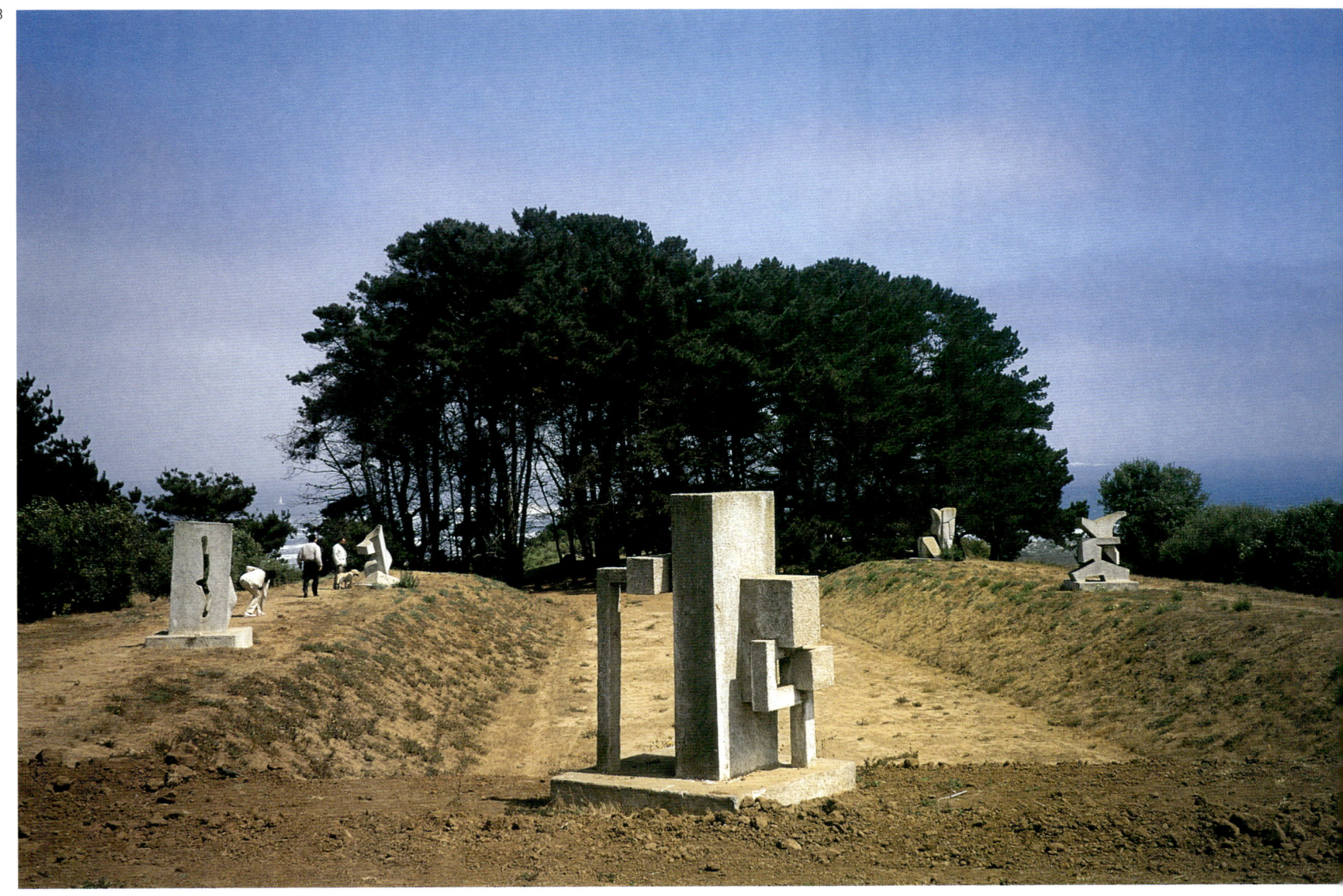

1 Bo Cenotaph Garden, group of sculptures by Claudio Girola
2 Bo Cenotaph Garden, paths and walkways
3 Guests' Agora: behind the trees, the Bo Cenotaph Garden, sculptures by Claudio Girola

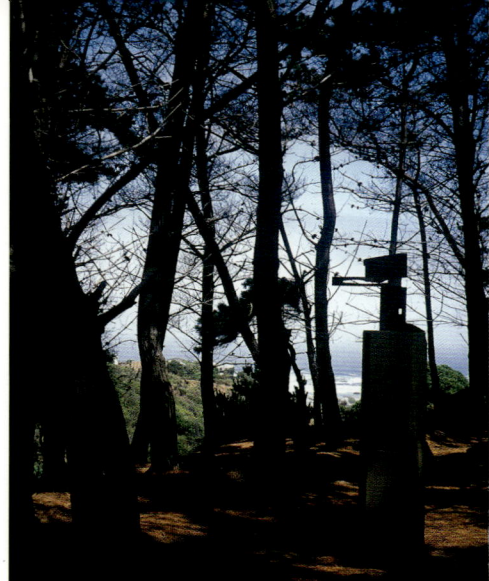

1. Pine grove in the Guests' Agora, sculpture by Claudio Girola
2. Act in the Henry Tronquoy Agora
3. Act with Claudio Girola in the foreground
4. The Track, with the Water Towers in the background

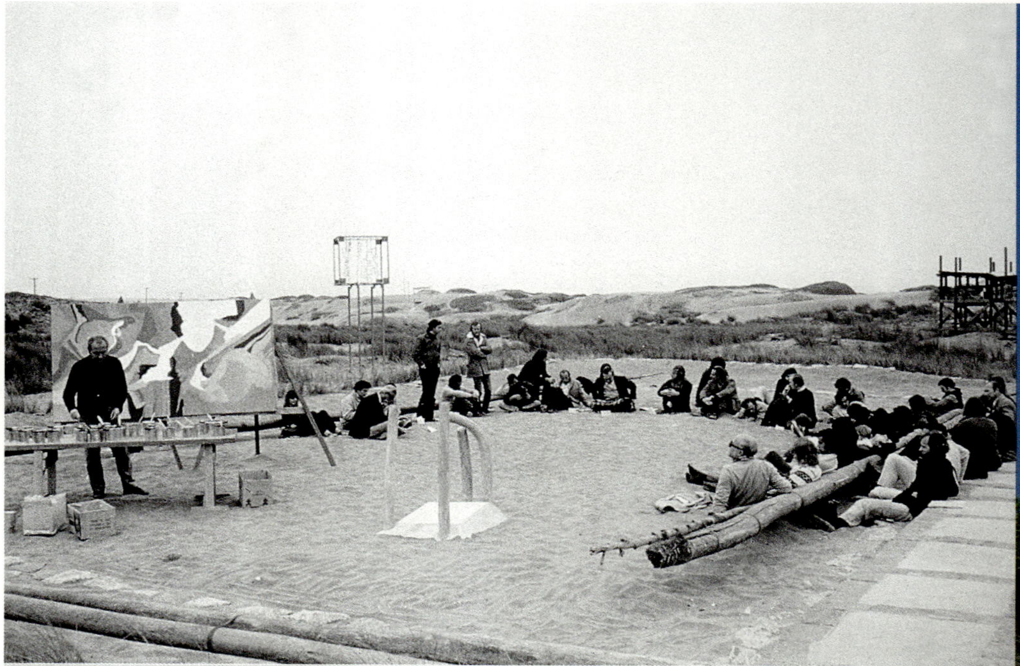

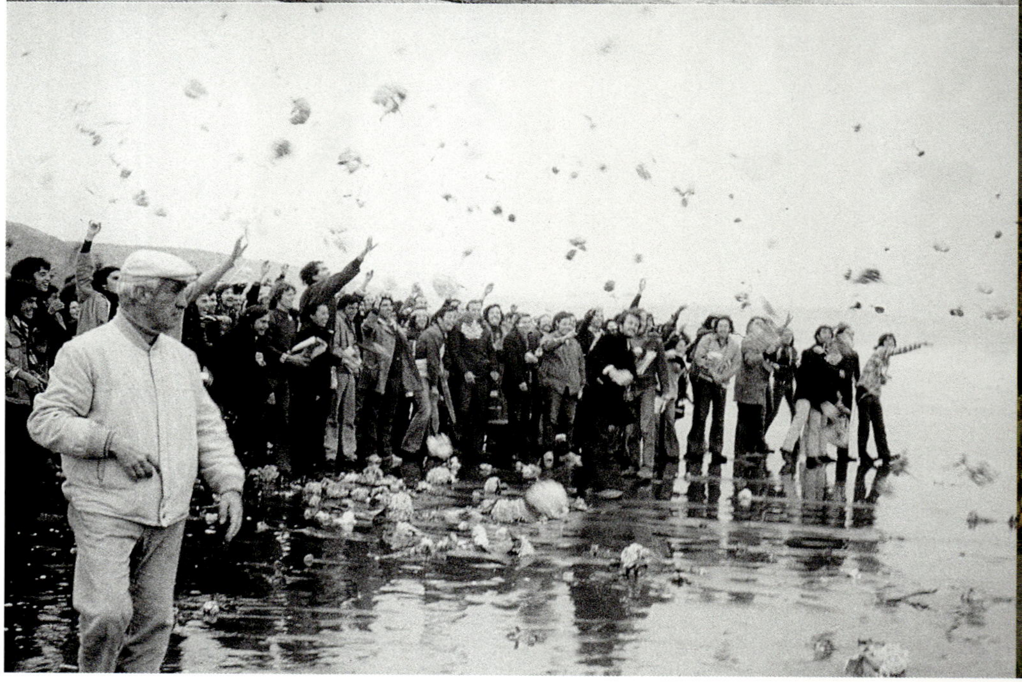

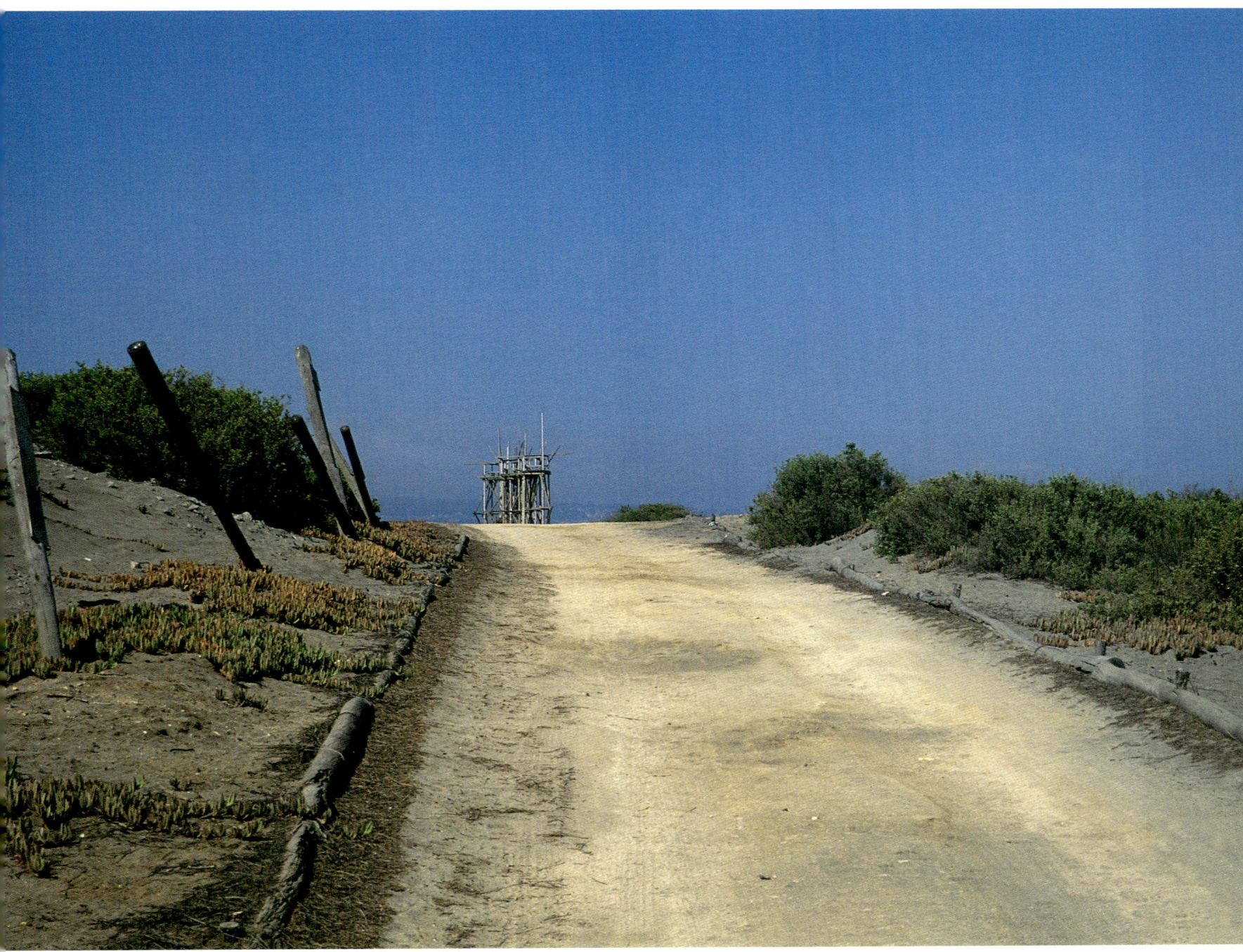

Music Room

Open City, Ritoque, Quintero
Alberto Cruz, Juan Purcell
1972

Faithful to the spirit of the ensemble, this inaugural work rejected the conventions of the spa town (such as the pre-eminence of the visual impact of the landscape), and instead turned in upon itself to create a place of meeting around music. A result of the desire to give priority to the creation of communal spaces over everyday sites, the Music Room was constructed before the buildings intended to provide accommodation. The Room deals with the relationship between music and space through the manipulation of light. And it is located in an area where the sound of the waves is still perceptible.

From the outside it appears as a single white rectangular box, of firm arrises, fitted with three access doors in its vertexes. It stands out clearly amid the landscape, and is one of the few pieces of the Open City which is perceived with the same clarity from a distance and from up close. It is constructed totally in wood, with diagonal crosshatching, in counterpoint to its orthogonal shape, a feature that recurs in the works and also the drawings of the authors. If the general forms are simple, a number of the arrises which hold the rectangular heads of the wooden planks in place have been left untrimmed, thereby creating articulations with a broken profile.

Once over the thresholds—all of which are of equal importance—we reach a warm one-roomed interior, of subtle shades of unpainted and uncoated wood. There is a single source of light, entrusted to a glass prism, a natural lighting device, which acts as both skylight and courtyard. Occupying the centre of the room it thus establishes itself as the main element. Conceived as a column of light, it spreads a diffused brightness through the room. Equipped with guillotine windows, it regulates the light, ventilation, acoustics and also the interior relationships, all

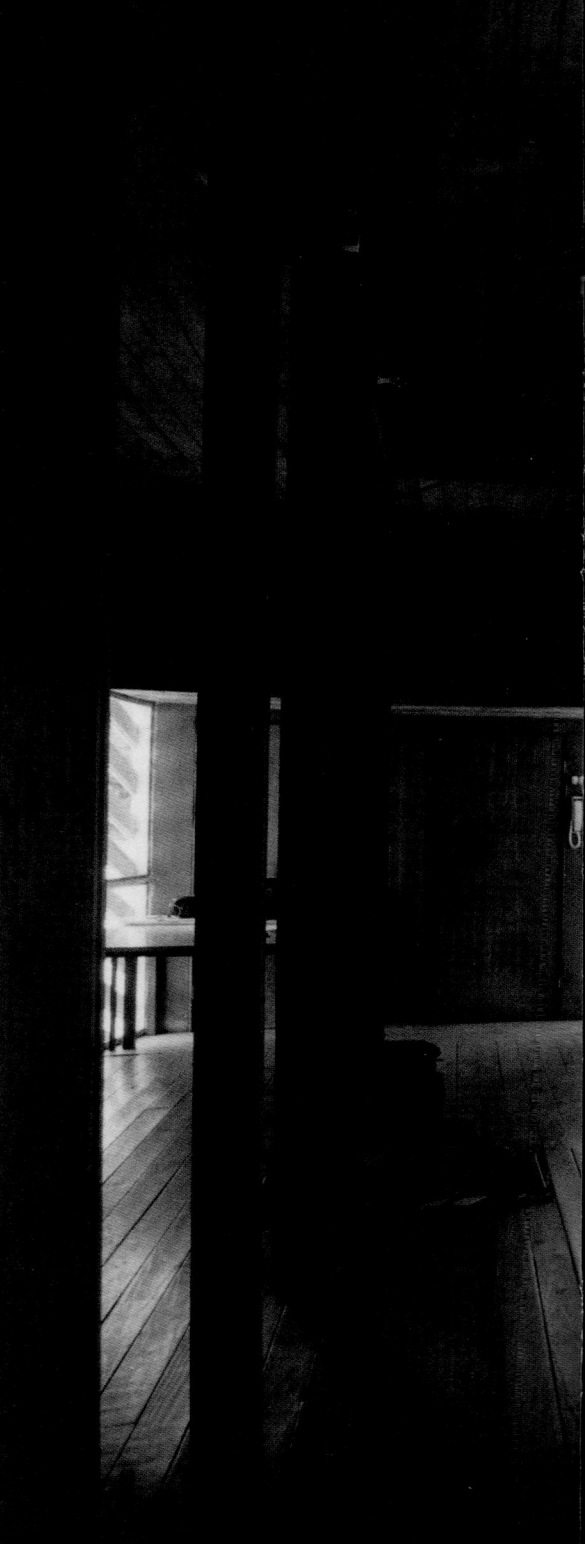

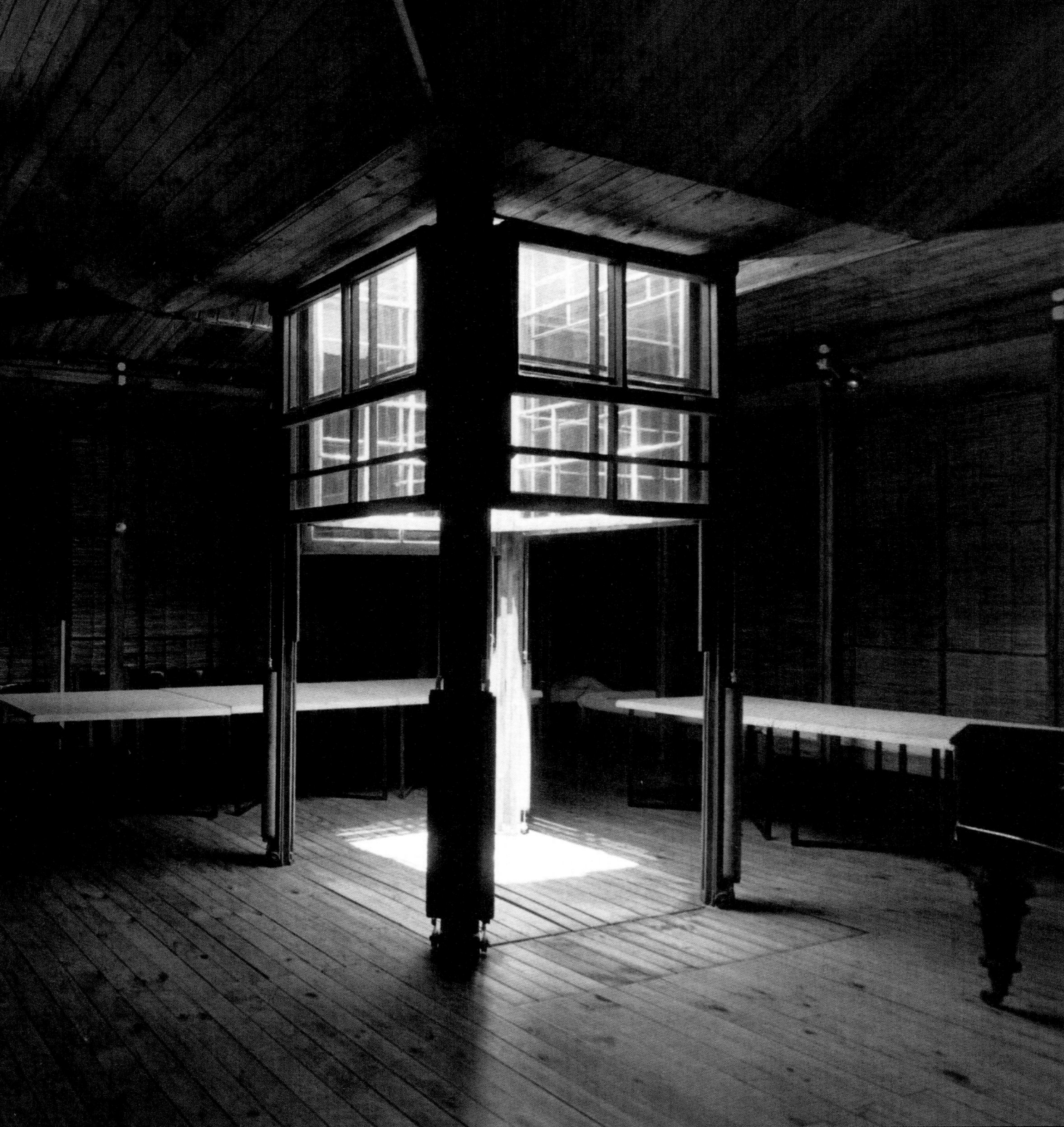

1

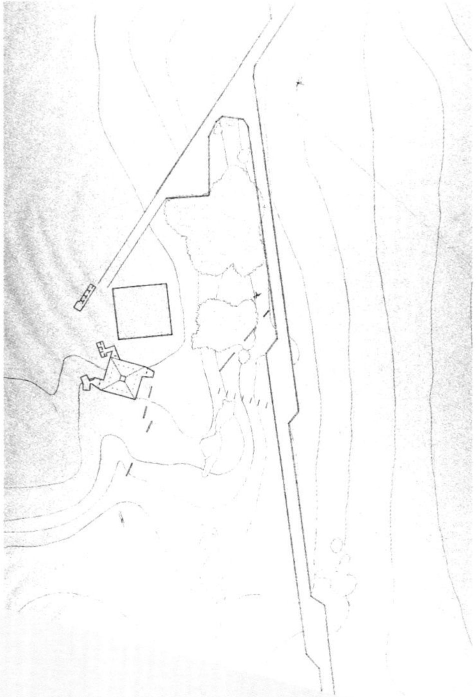

2

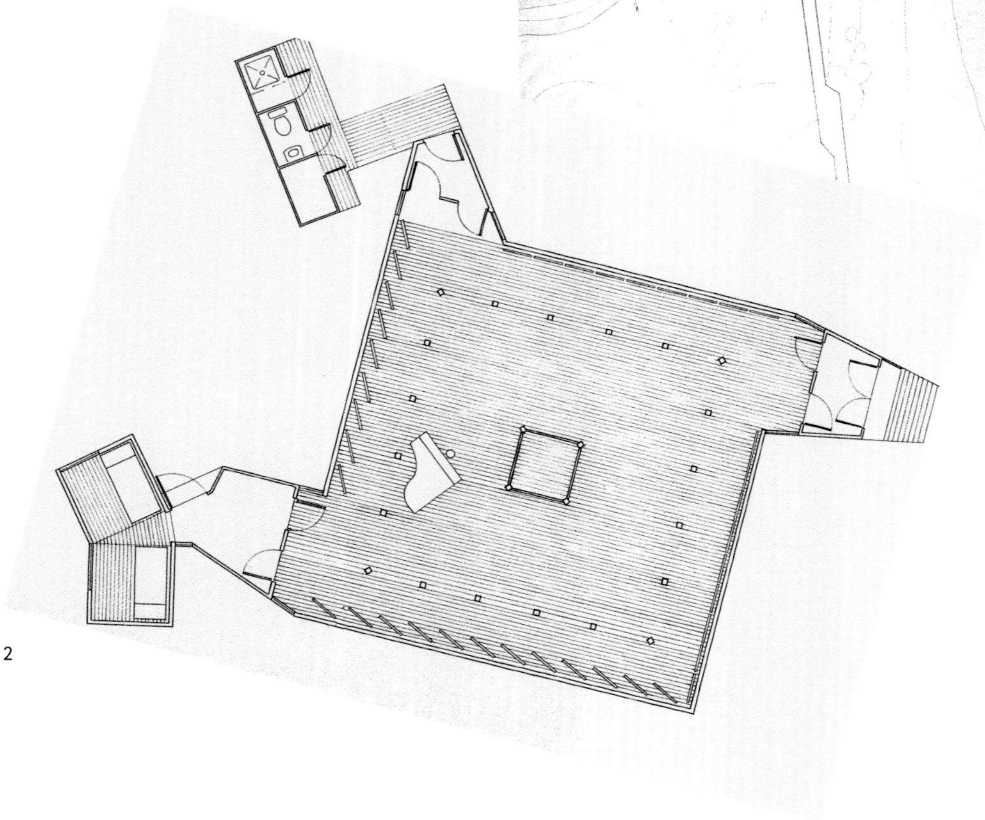

of which are heavily dependent on its presence. The location of the prism of light means that at every recital a choice must be made regarding the relationship between music and audience. Apart from this element of acoustic regulation, all of the outer panels can be moved. Constructed with wooden frames whose front and back are fitted with complementary acoustic attributes of reflection or absorption, they are suspended from rails in such a way that they can be moved and turned by hand to calibrate the acoustics of the room. The covering of locally obtained interwoven reed fibres reveals a readiness to work with any material and to entrust the material itself with the concept of the design, above and beyond its materiality, and with obtaining a result in tune with its environment.

The inward-looking nature of the Music Room, its radical introversion and the emphasis on the subtle effect of the light bring back memories of previous experiments by the group, for example, the Los Pajaritos Chapel in 1953, the church of Santa Clara Cubo, 1961-1969, and the study *Iluminación de Superficies Interiores con Luz Natural* (*Illumination of Interior Surfaces with Natural Light*—Miguel Eyquem, 1960).

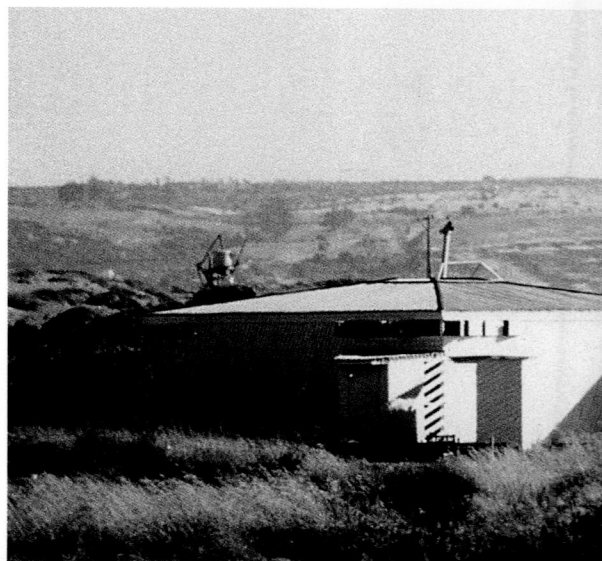

3

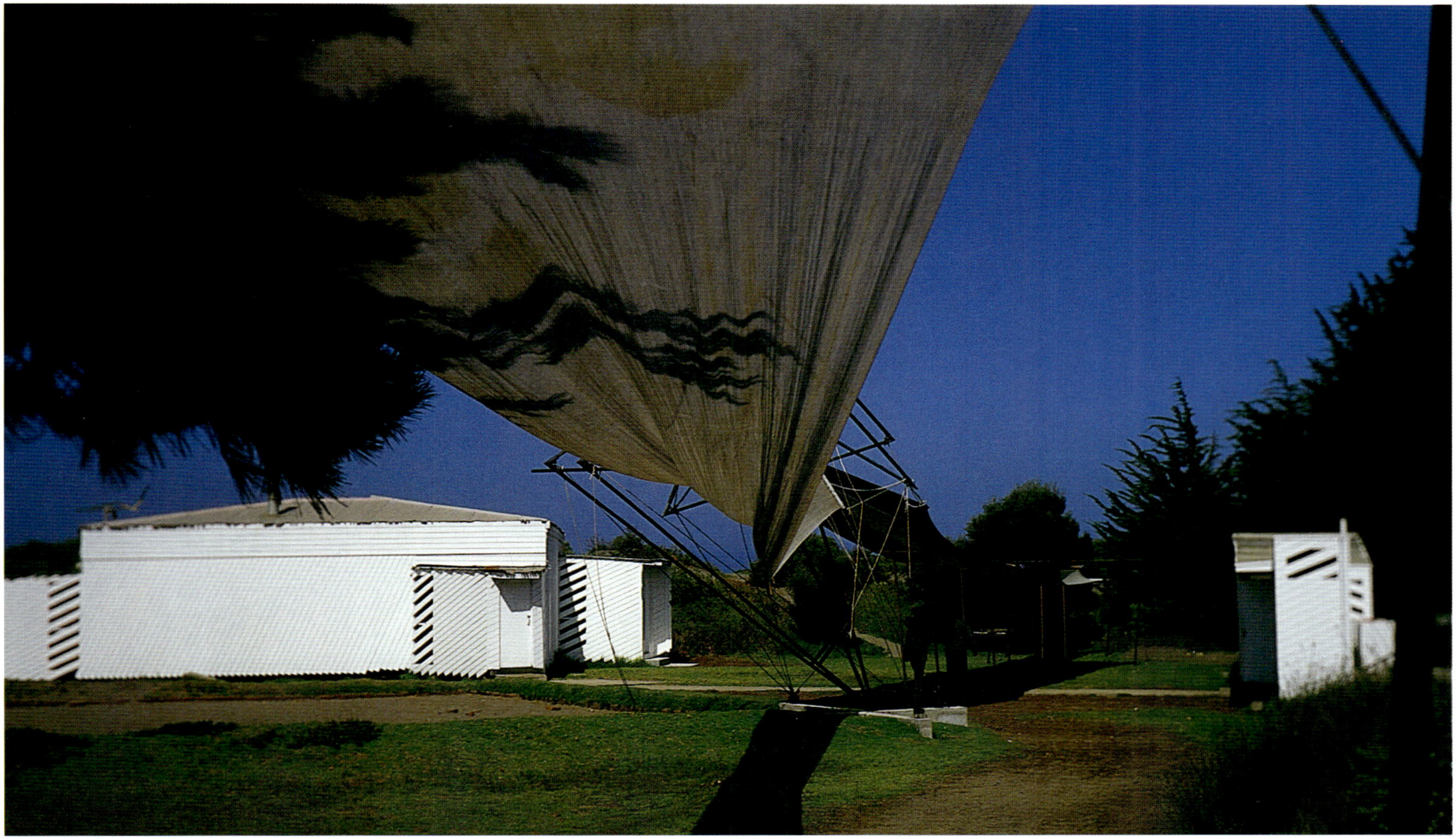

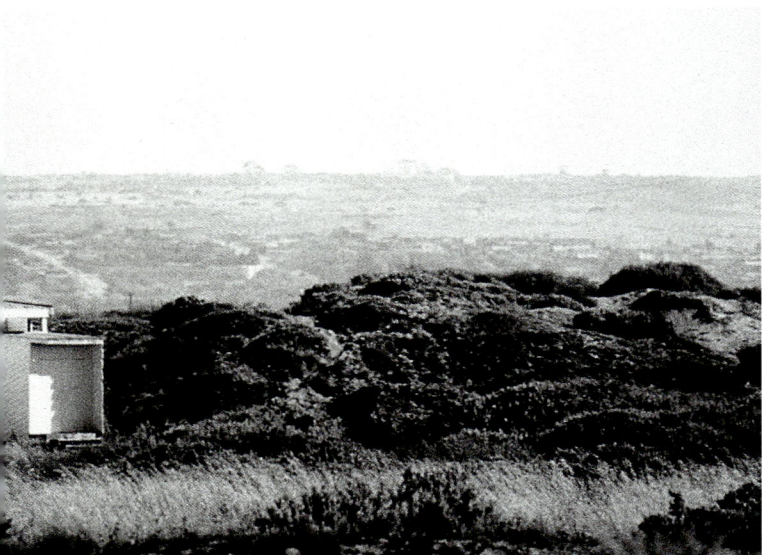

1 General site plan
2 Floor plan, with extensions which no longer exists
3 Music Room and access porches
4 Music Room with service pavilion on the right
   and temporary canvas for use on special occasions

Movable reed panels

Following page:
Detail of column of light and *impluvium*
and the column of light seen from inside the Hall

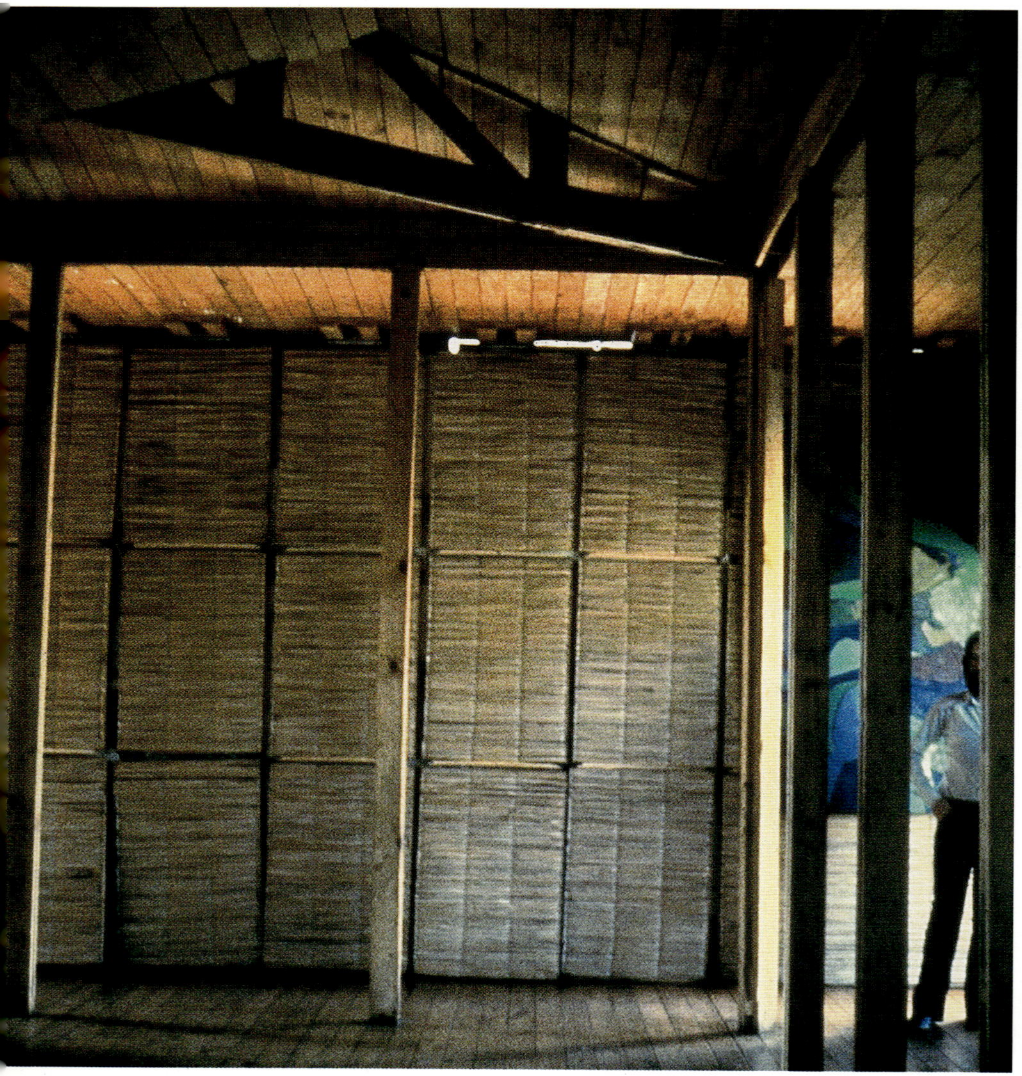

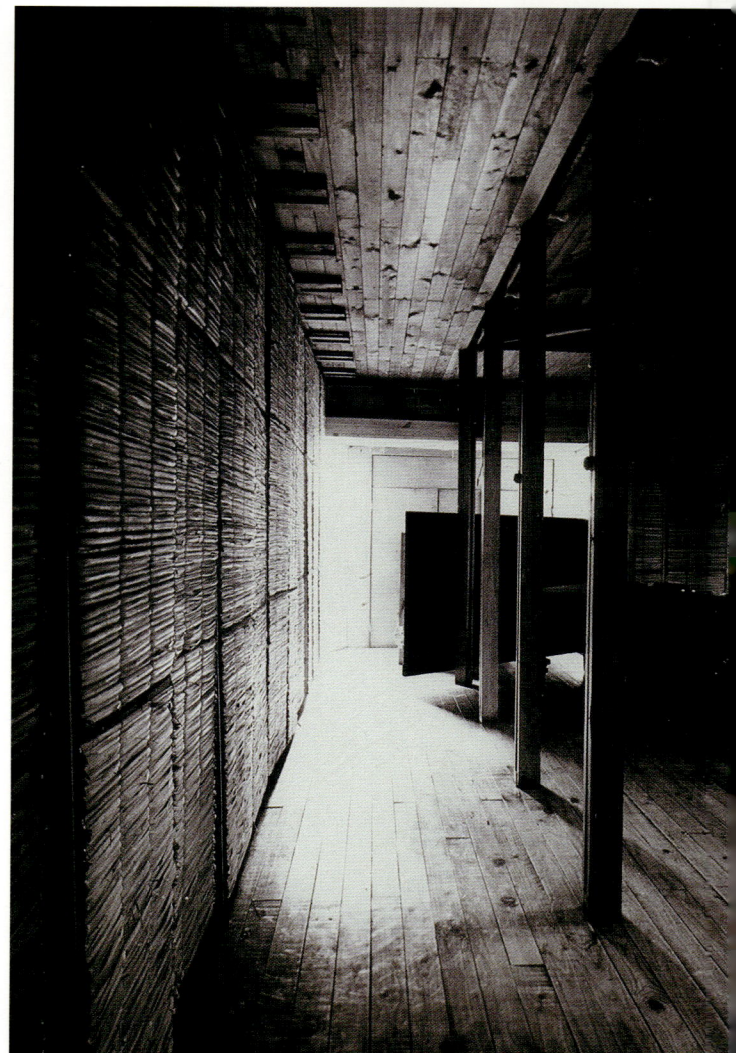

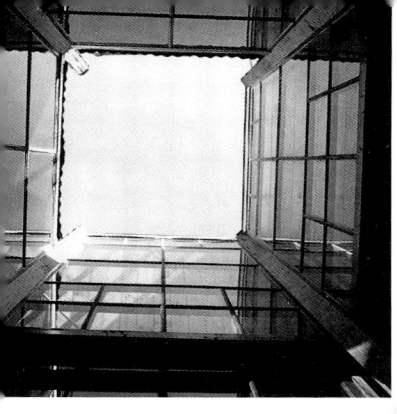

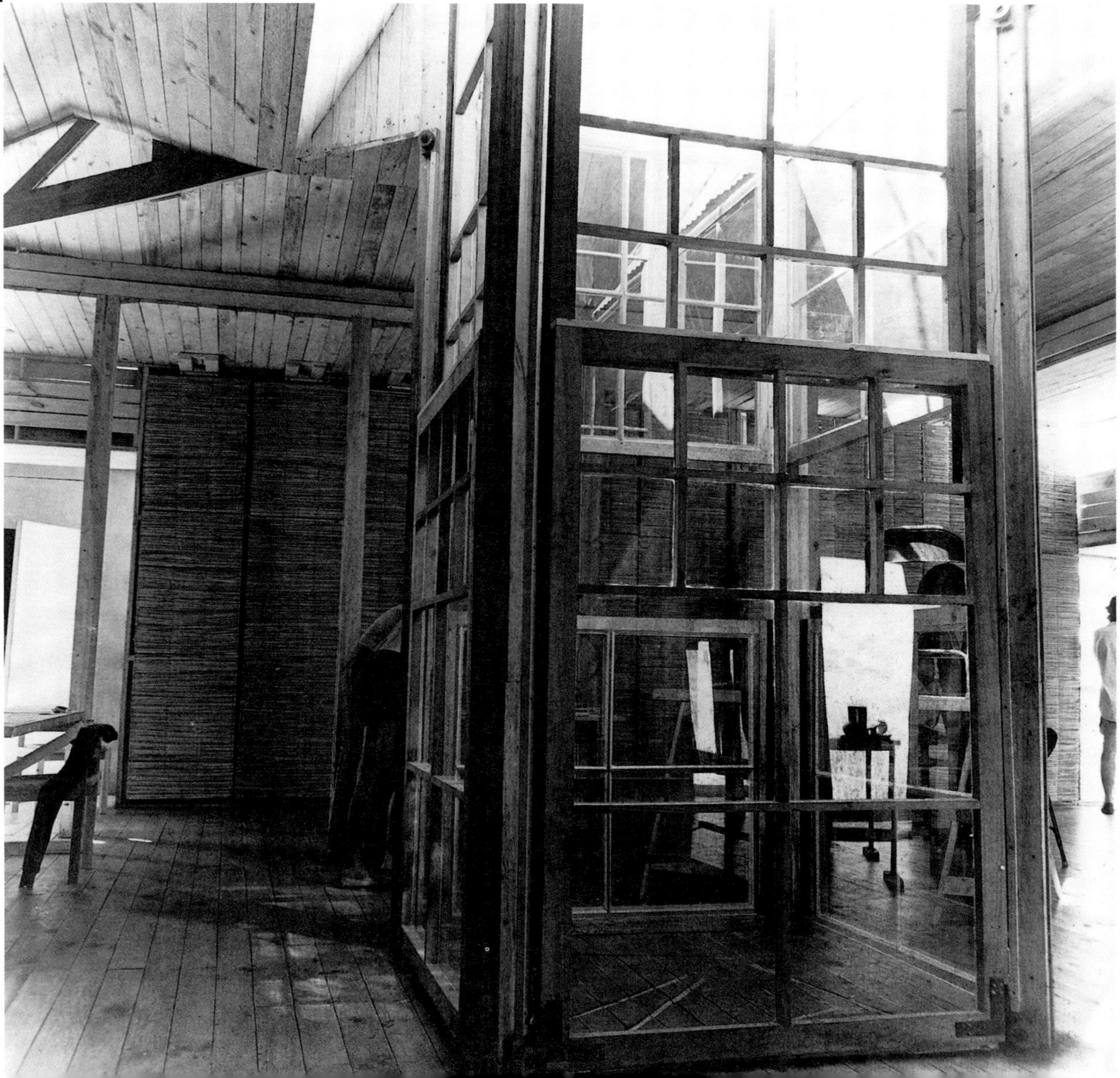

Palace of Dawn and Dusk
(Palacio del Alba y del Ocaso)

Open City, Ritoque, Quintero
1982

One of the most enigmatic pieces of the Open City, lacking any program and almost always empty, this structure of 986 sq. metres provides an insight into the procedures which inspired the construction of the ensemble. As with other buildings in the Open City, the project was initially intended as an open-ended work, to be built in stages without any definite idea of the final configuration. At one point, however, an agora decided that the work was finished, and its development was frozen at that moment.

The name of the work is an allusion to the pivotal nature of the appearance or disappearance of the light, a condition which sharpens or dissolves visible forms. The profile of the construction is highlighted by the homogeneous and vivid arrises standing out against the sky. The symmetry of the floor plan reveals the equivalence of the double orientation of the structure: land-sea, east-west; and yet there is nothing in its concrete structure to proclaim the symmetry of its floorplan.

The ensemble was originally intended to house two lodges and public baths. The grooves running across the courtyards remain as evidence of this intention of a program associated with water.

Built predominantly of red brick, the project is heavily conditioned by its monolithic quality, and by the structural criteria of self-bearing pieces. The modules dispense with steel structural reinforcement, obtaining their horizontal stability by means of a slight curvature of the floorplan. The arrangement combines this slightly arced layout of the lengths of wall with the logic of compensated weights in order to counteract seismic disturbances, which affect rigid structures particularly seriously. The walls are 2.22 metres high, with wide foundations of bricks buried in sand.

Subtle gaps like fissures separate the self-standing stretches of wall, creating relationships between enclosures and a flexibility in the articulations proposed by the general layout.

The ensemble appears as a system of interconnected courtyards in which interiority and first planes predominate. In spite of the uniform height of the walls, each courtyard reveals itself to be a distinct space, with the most remarkable being the one which acts as an organized walkway using ramps freely arranged. As one climbs the ramps the horizon of the sea reappears over the top of the walls. The grooves running across the courtyards were originally intended as water channels.

Heavily conditioned by structural criteria in its materials, dimensions and modular logic, the project is expressive of the limits of the material. After completion of the Palace, it was agreed for works to be built around it which would fully demonstrate the freedom of the architect. Thus, it was decided to create an informal meeting place in one of its vertexes, consisting of an arrangement of fixed furniture which would allow for different forms of seating. It was proposed as a condition that this seating should have capacity for a plenary session of the community of the Open City, that it should be built in two overlapping but independent order, and that it should be arranged in such a way that everybody would be looking naturally at each other.

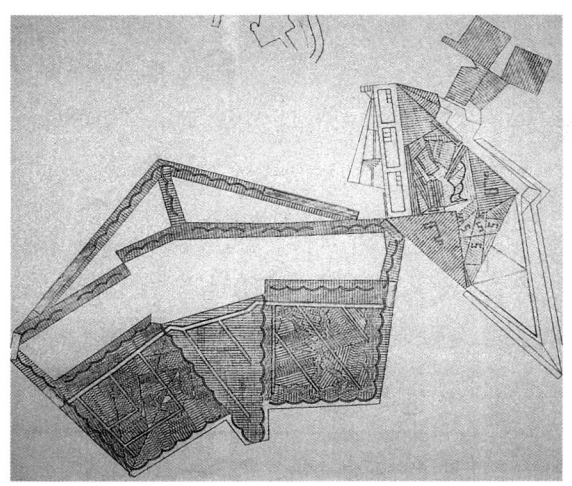

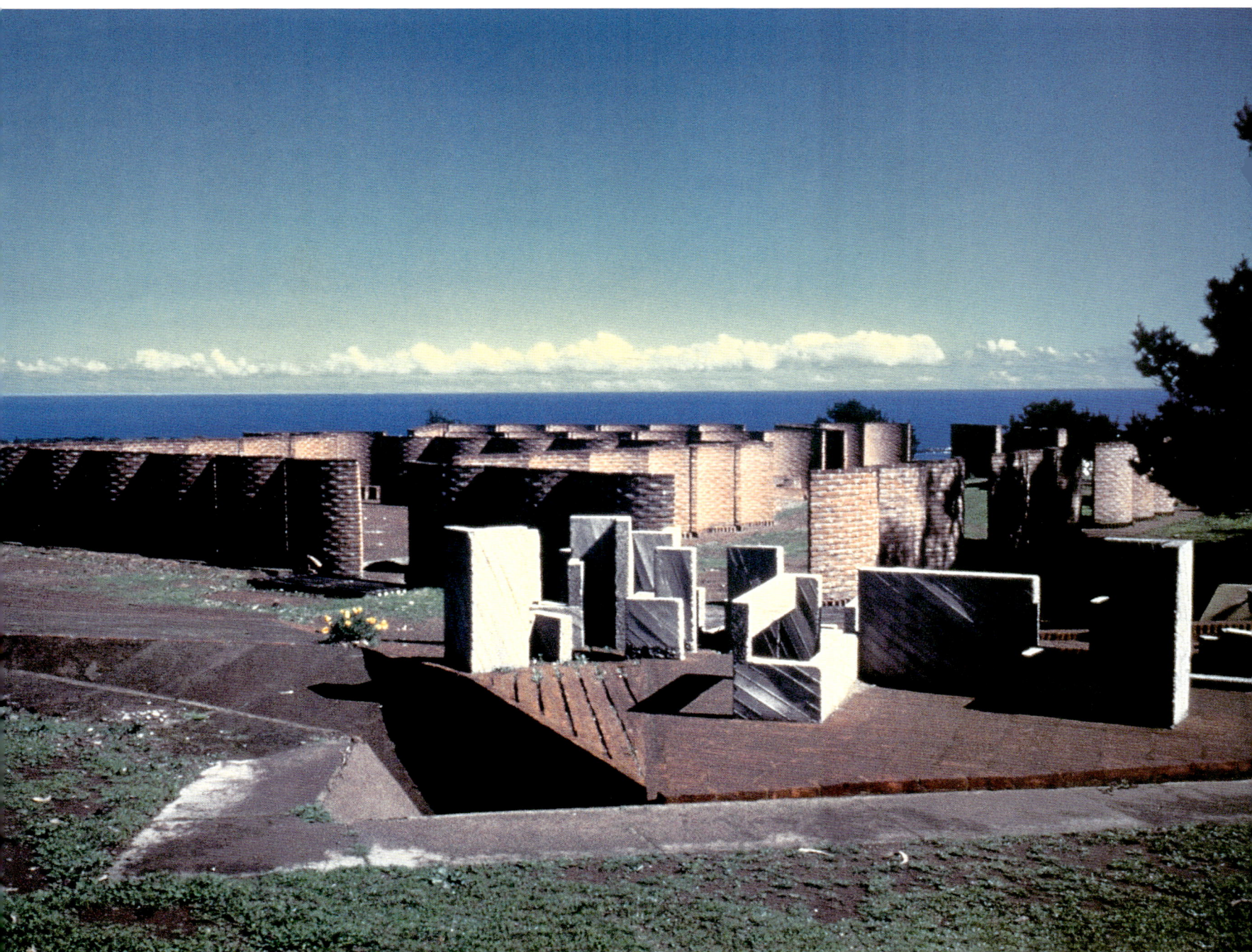

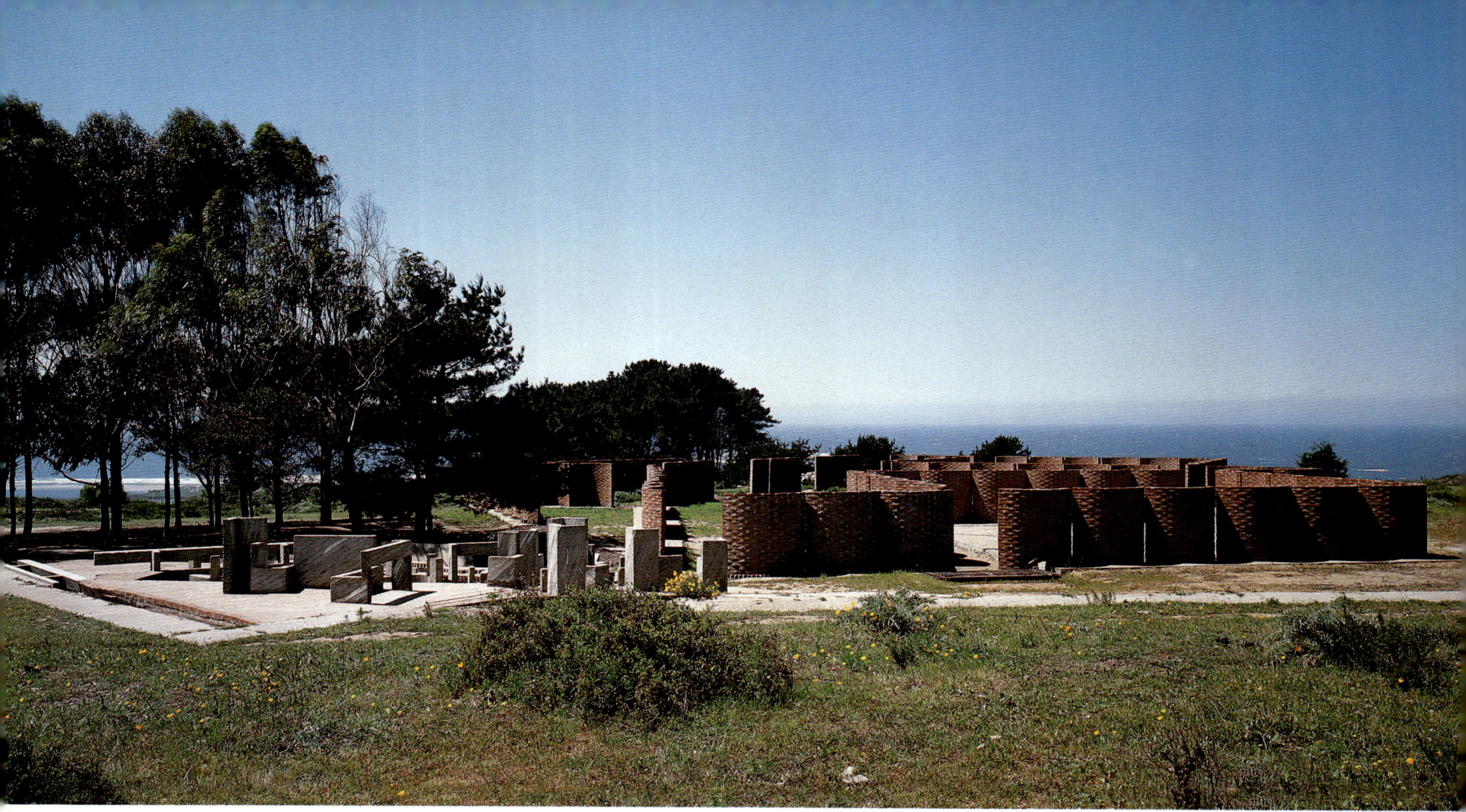

1

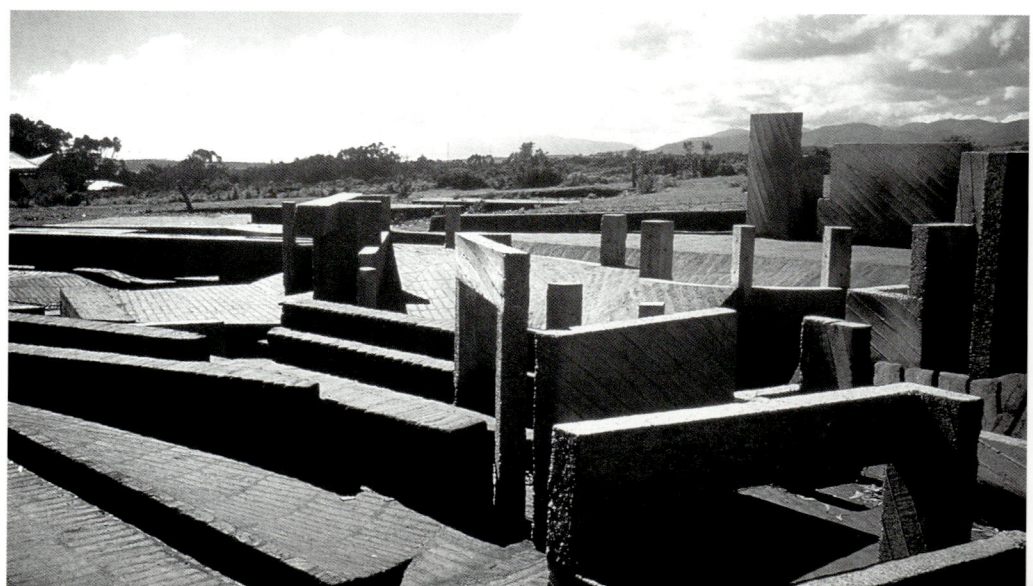
2

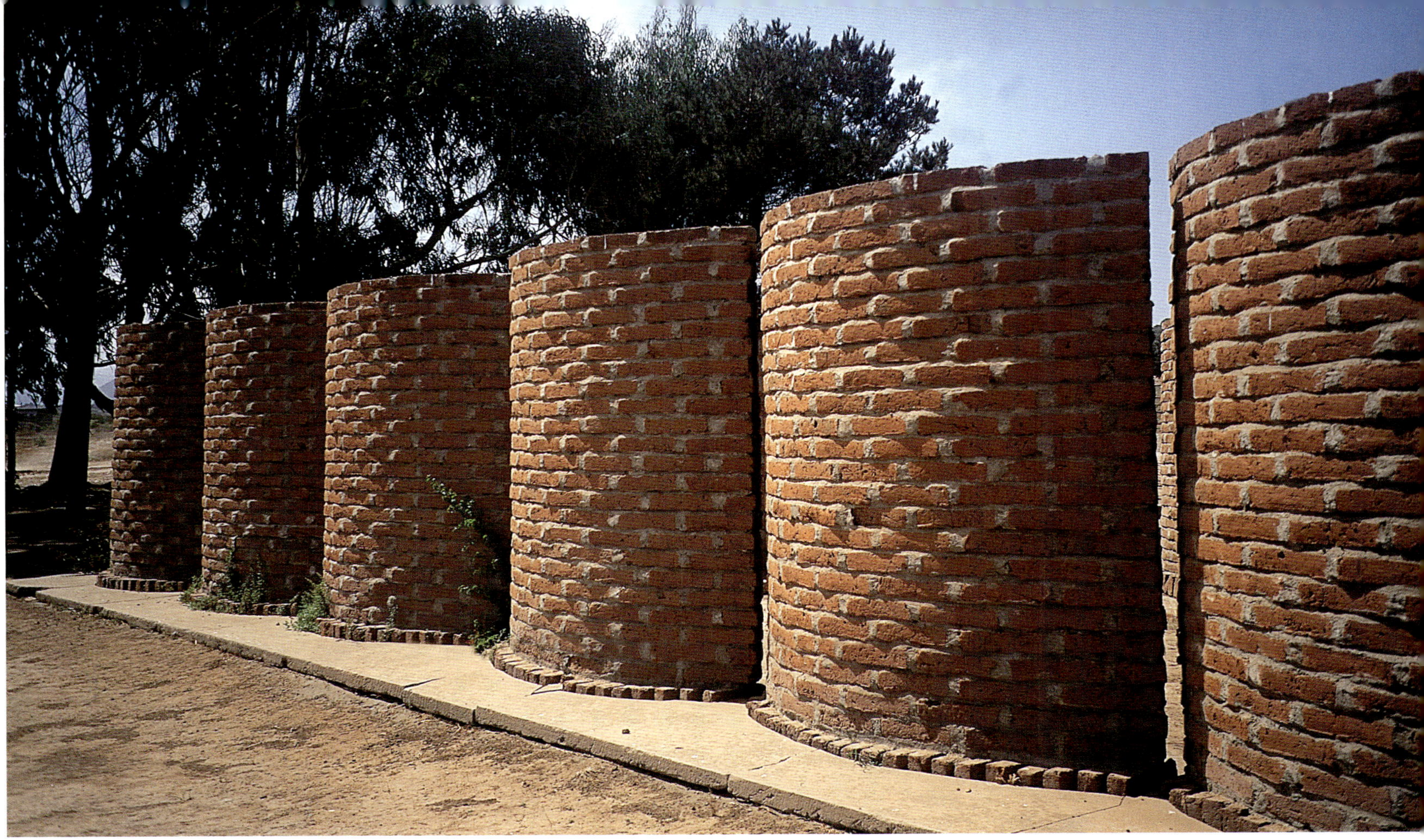

3

1 General view of the Palace of Dawn and Dusk
2 Concrete parapets
3 and 4 Self-bearing walls

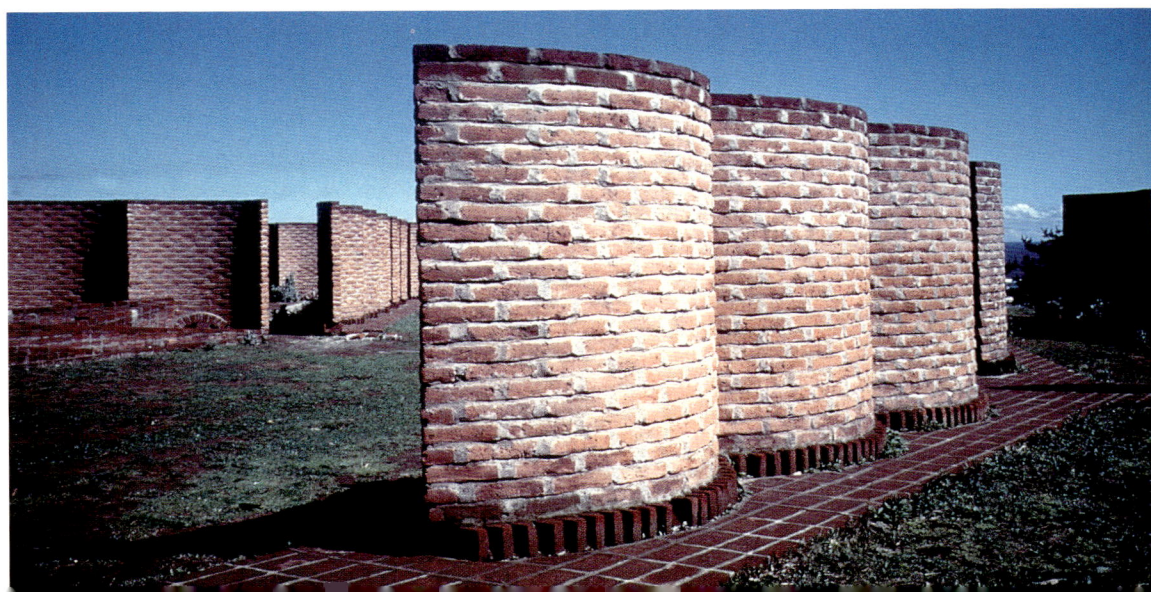

4

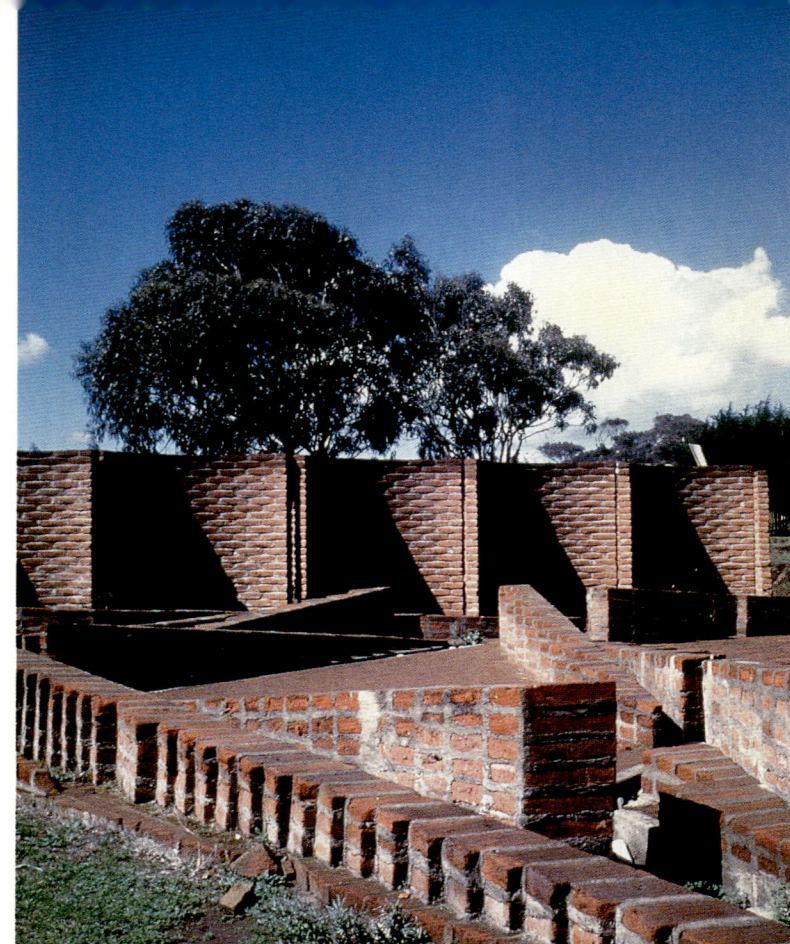

1 Inner courtyard
2 and 3 Walkways
4 Courtyard and water channels

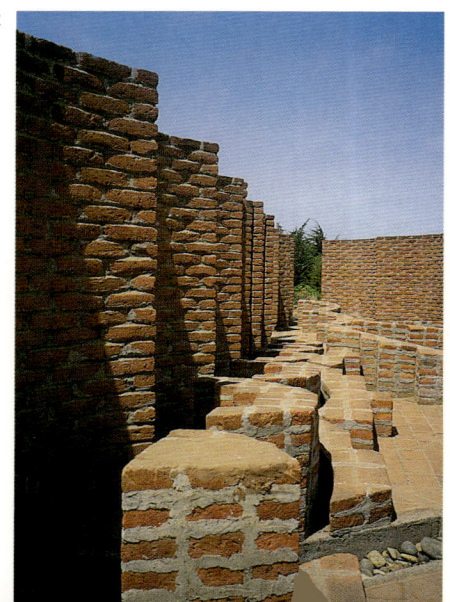

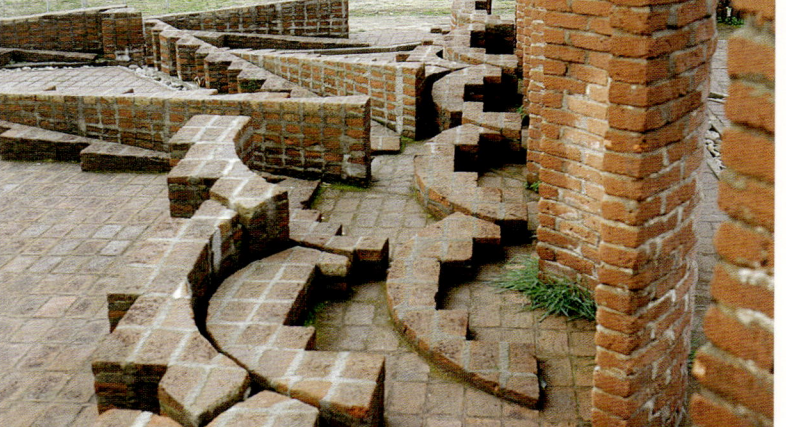

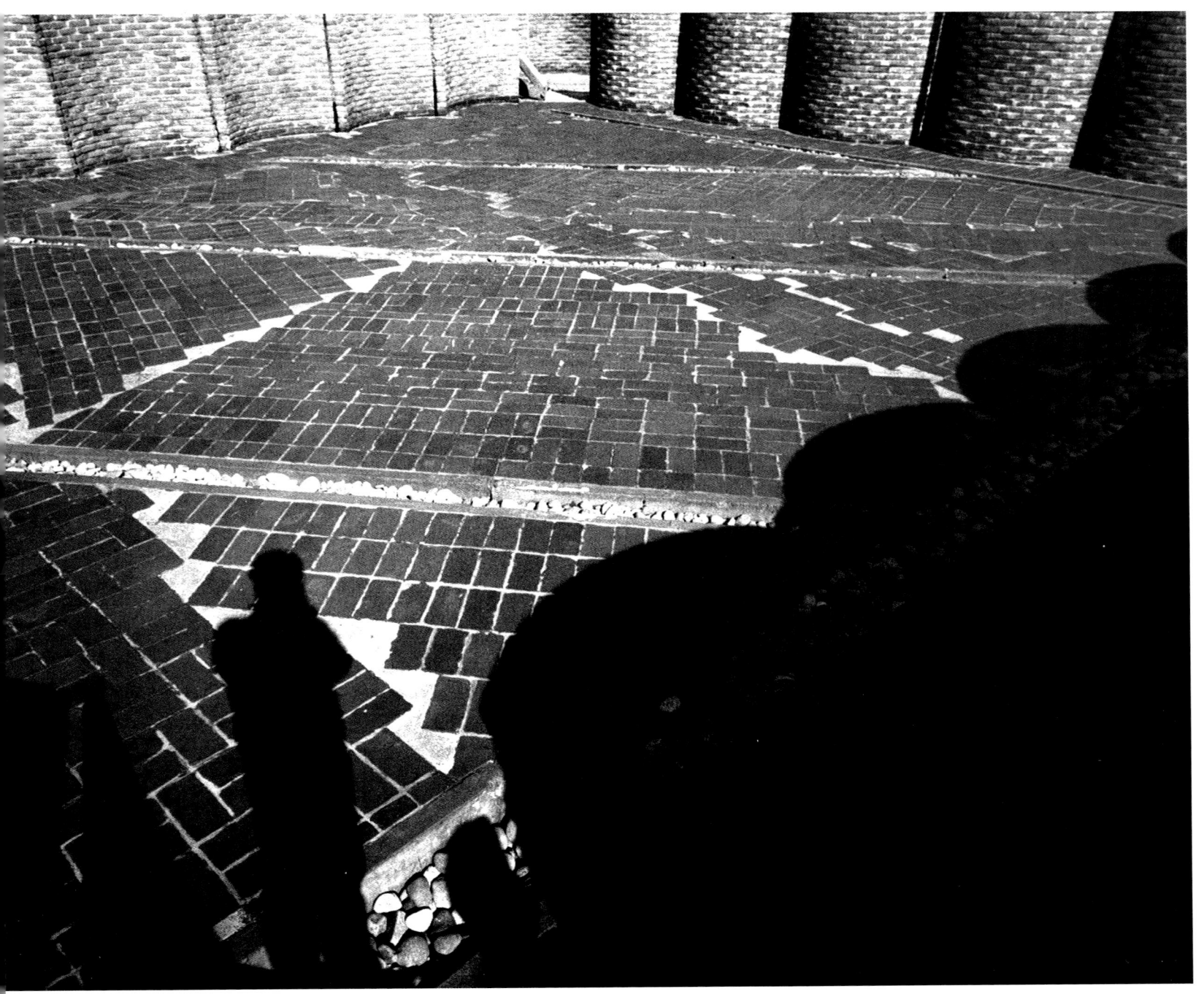

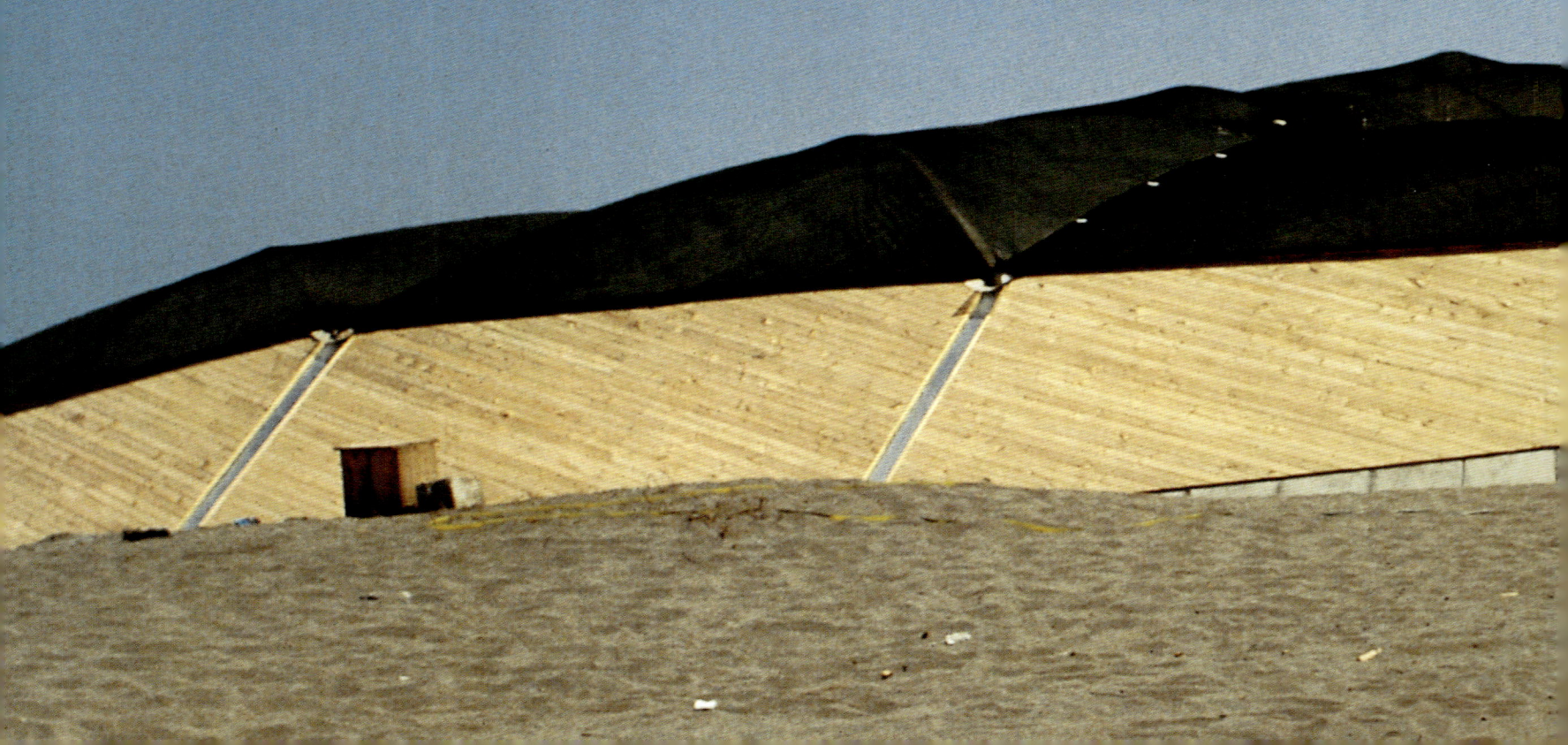

House of Names
(Casa de los Nombres)

Open City, Ritoque, Quintero
Boris Ivelic, Fabio Cruz, Salvador Zahr,
Ricardo Lang
1992
Demolished

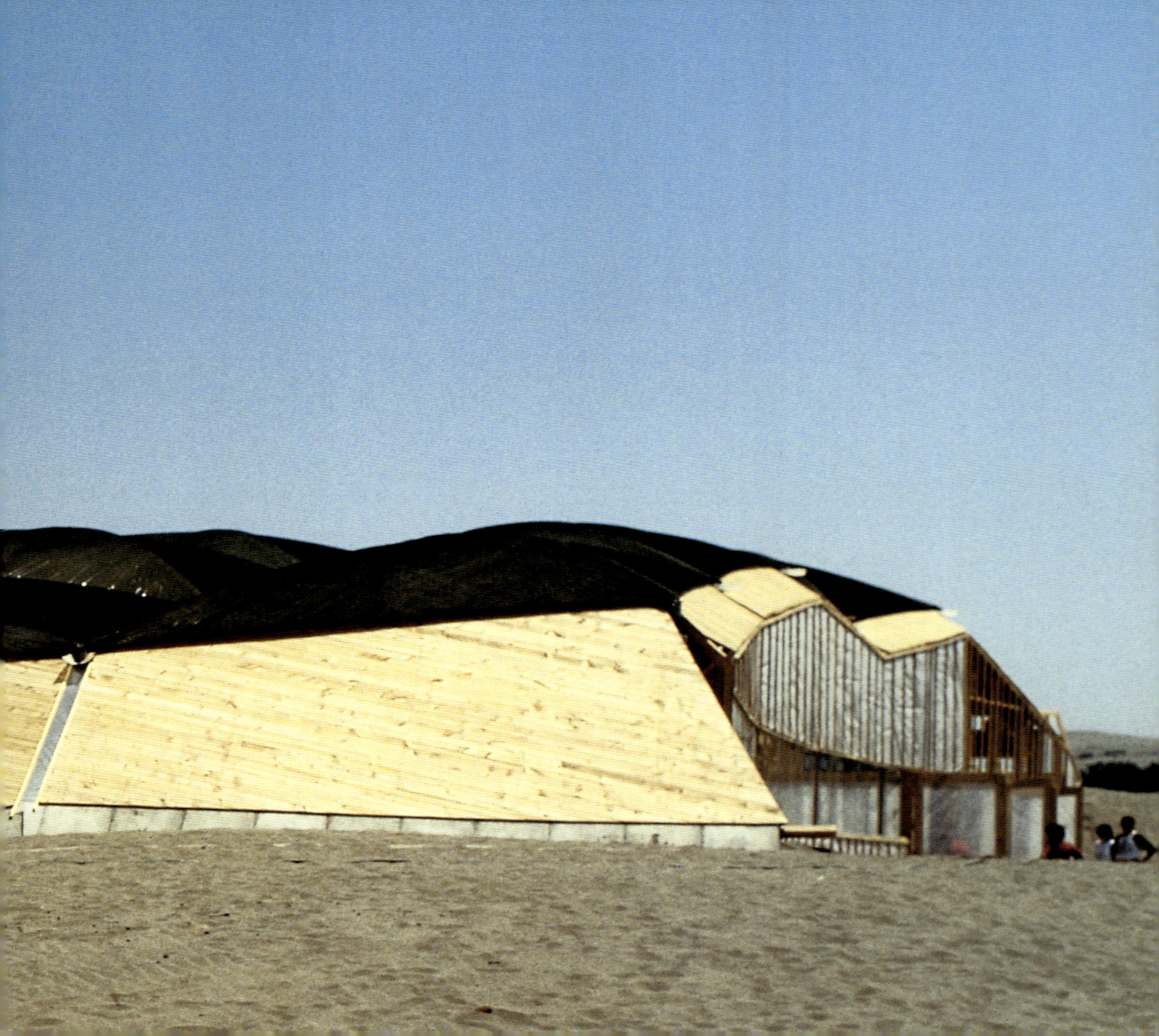

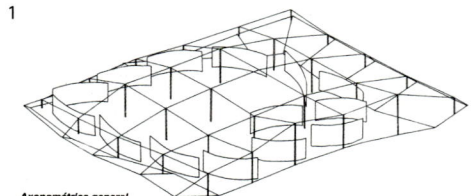

Axonométrica general

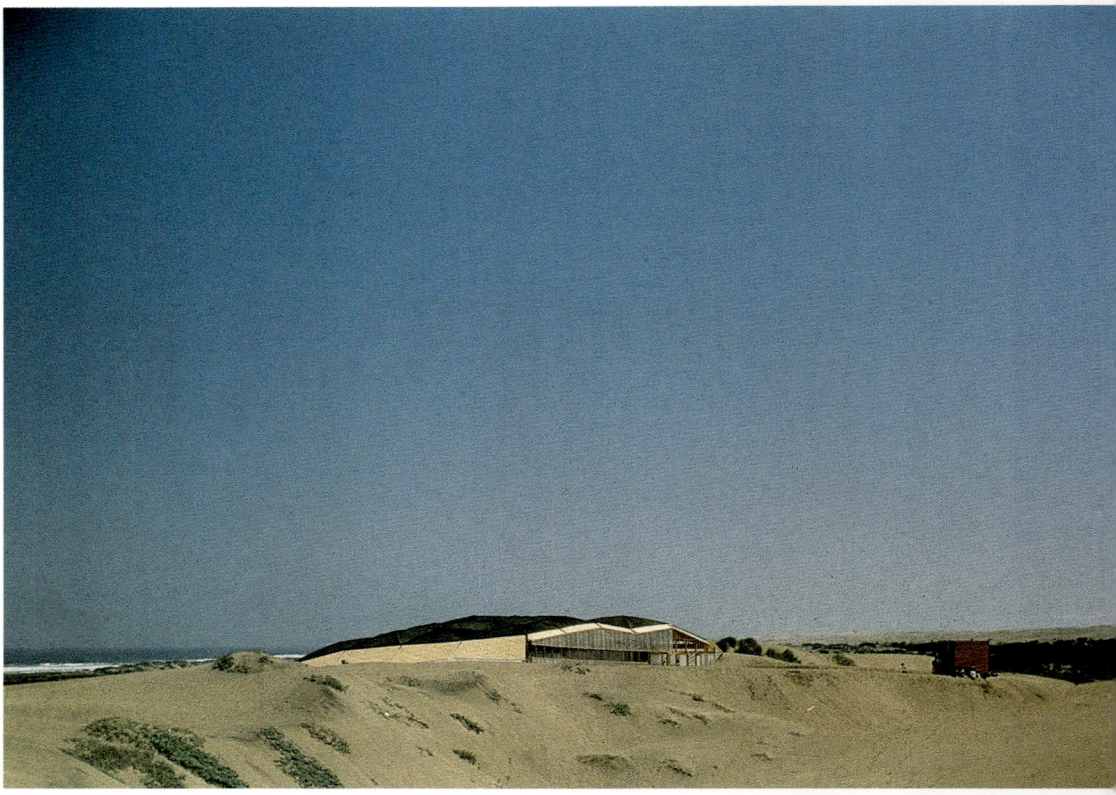

The hidden meaning of the work (reflected in its name) was indicated in a poetic act or *phalène*, as was its location on a stretch of moving sands on the border between the dunes and the esplanade of marsh. It was built to celebrate the 40th anniversary of the founding of the Institute of Architecture, as an exhibition pavilion and agora or assembly area for around 400 people. In this way, the commemorative exhibition held each decade could be hosted in the Open City, and would include material from the *travesías* of America.

Teachers and "circle" workshops participated jointly in the preparation of the project. This led to a strategy of definition by parts, with each part limited to an operation and a specific problem.

The sand played a major role in the project, both as the dominant topographical feature and because, together with the wind, it presented a challenge to the stability of any construction, whether because its implacable and tough luminosity required a clearly defined attitude to design or because the way in which it acted as an obstacle to the passage of people constituted an improbable basis for a work of architecture. In the face of the apparent contradiction of dealing with the dune as an architectural occurrence and an obstacle at one and the same time, it was decided to resort to the geometric shapes drawn by the wind, i.e. those undulations in the natural topography recognizable as the "natural surf of the sands".

The work was installed above a slight depression in the ground. Once the possible roof was planned, an upper layer was defined, consisting of a system of roofs formed by square caps: this criterion enabled the building to be designed and constructed from the top downwards. A transportable plastic canvas grid was used for the layout. Work began with the arrangement of the 29 prefabricated concrete pillars—representing the 29 people who participated in the founding act—by sinking them one by one to the pre-established level and tightening them in place according to a gridwork of meeting

1 Diagram of the installation of the panels
2 Access side
3 Continuity of the profile of the dunes

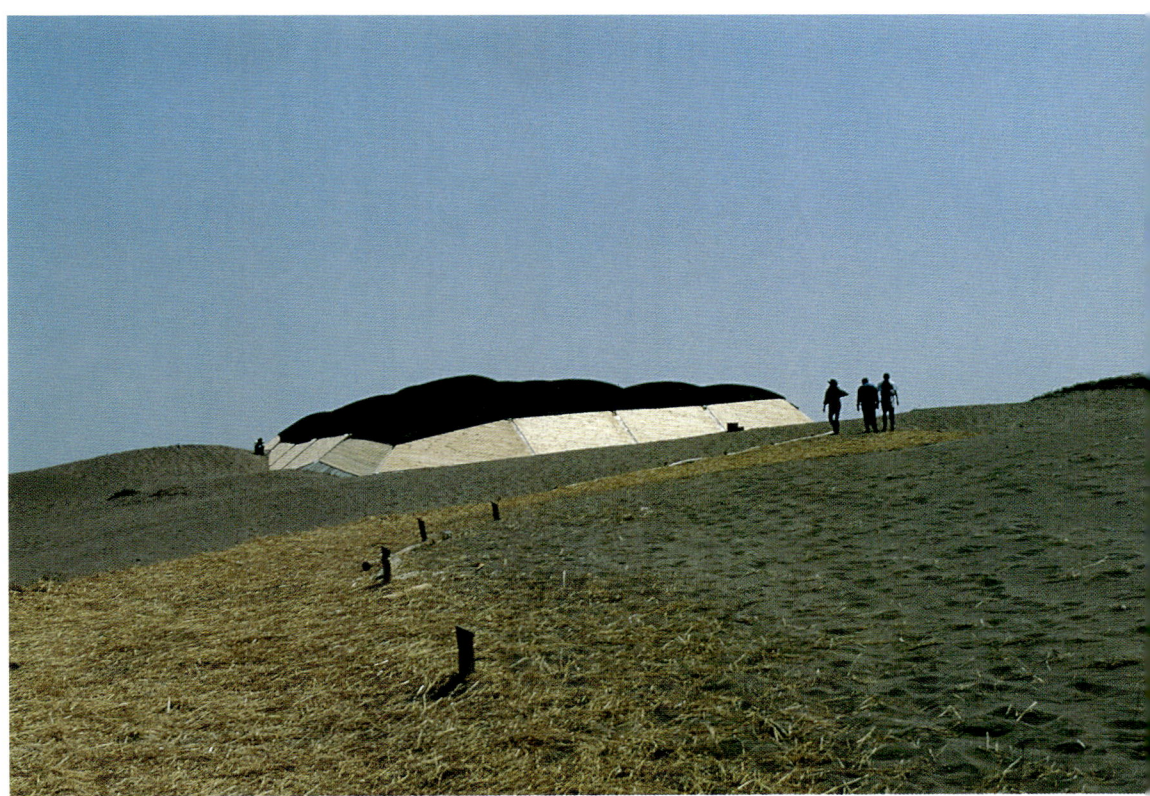

nodes whose angles varied between 90° and 63°. Mounted atop the pillars, the 20 stiff caps covered the surface whose floors retained their natural levels, except on the outer ring, where prefabricated concrete tiles were installed to consolidate the crown of the border in an aerodynamic shape which was empirically established.

The caps were made of black mesh and a polyethylene membrane. Joined by rainwater ditches in translucent plastic, they created a roof of black light and luminous nerves. Between the roof and the opaque outer ring a slatted skirt was built which ran round three sides of the floorplan. The fourth side, the access side, was erected with its back to the sea, by using vertical wooden panels with translucent membranes. Once shelter from the wind was ensured, the sand was excavated until the final levels were obtained. As a result, from the outside the work appeared opaque and compact— except under the artificial light and the low-set lighting—and is in continuity with the ridges of sand. The interior emptiness appeared, in contrast, as a display of linear figures, columns, structural nerves, grids and lines of light beneath the roof, which is black, translucent and dense like a storm cloud.

Today barely a few pillars remain, traces and evidence of that quality of appearance and disappearance characteristic of the landscape of dunes linked by the group to the idea of shedding, of a "return to not knowing". Thus, the work remains only as a memory or happening. Planned in relation to the effects and behaviour of the wind, the House of Names took the research begun in 1956 for the Naval Academy design, and would in turn see itself continued in even greater depth in the Wanderer's Lodge.

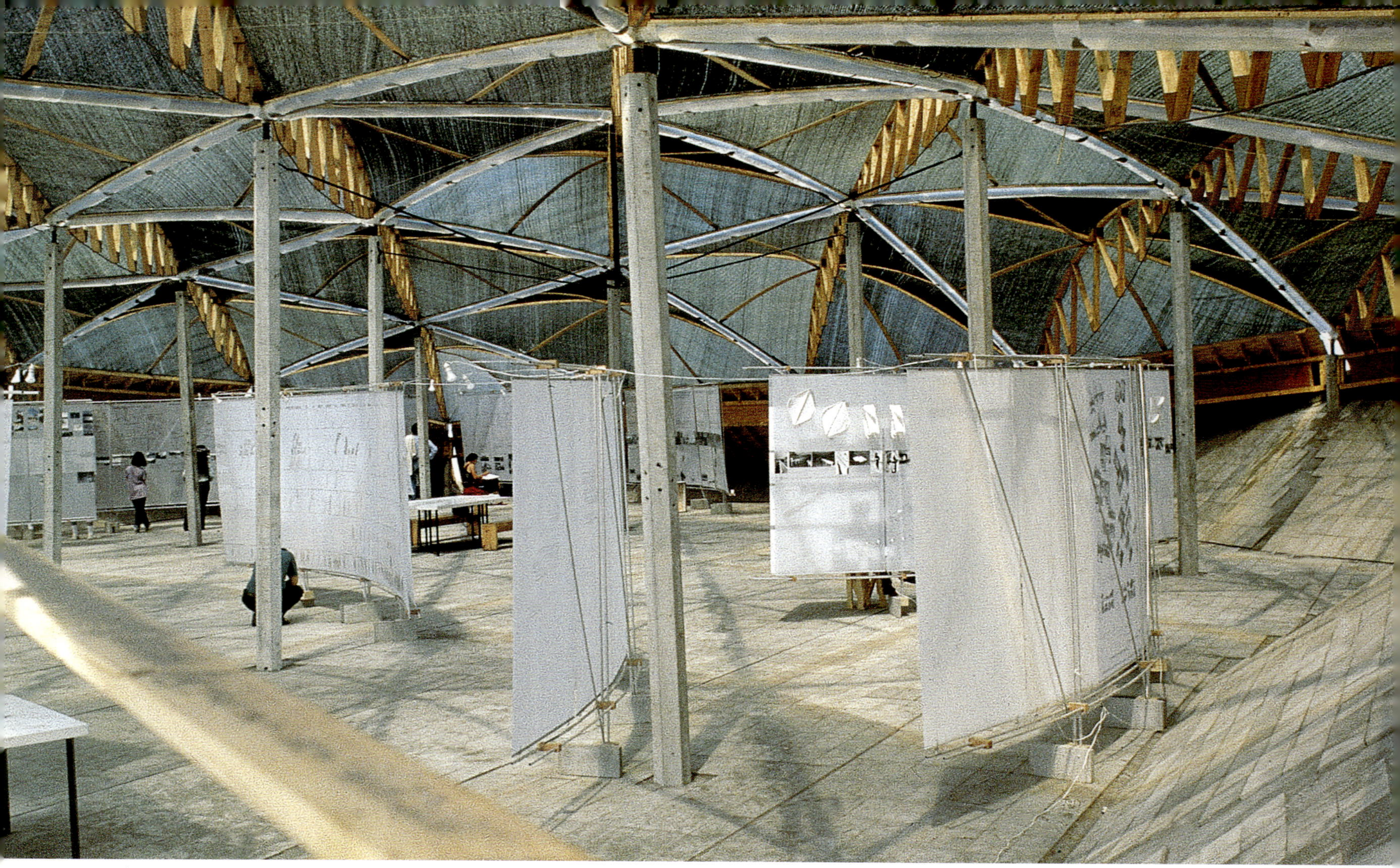

1

1 Assembly of the exhibition commemorating the 40th anniversary of the Institute
2 Cross section: continuity of the profile of the dunes, 7-metre-high concrete pillars
3 "Black light" and lines of light above rainwater ditches
4 Access side and detail of the structural system of the slat assembly

2

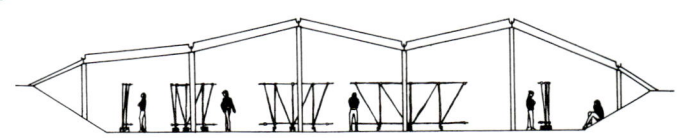

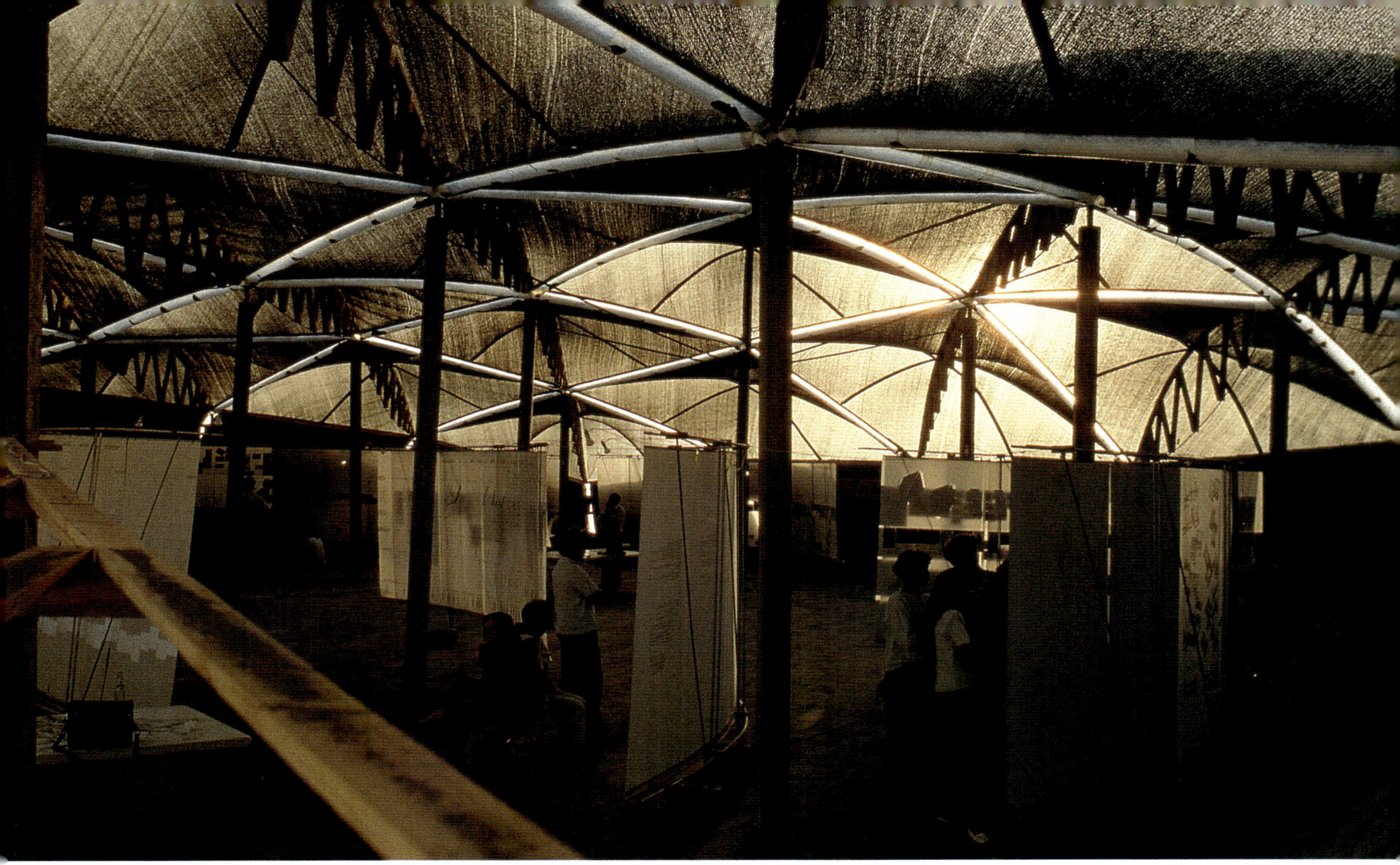

3

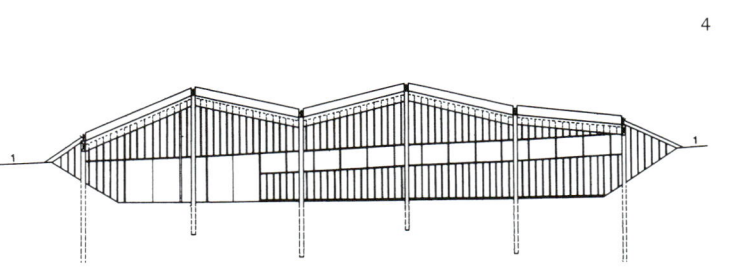

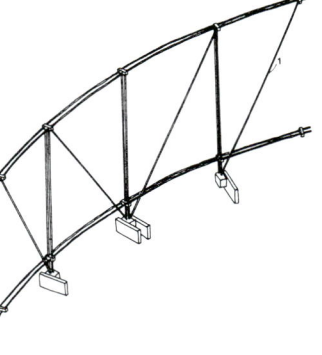

4

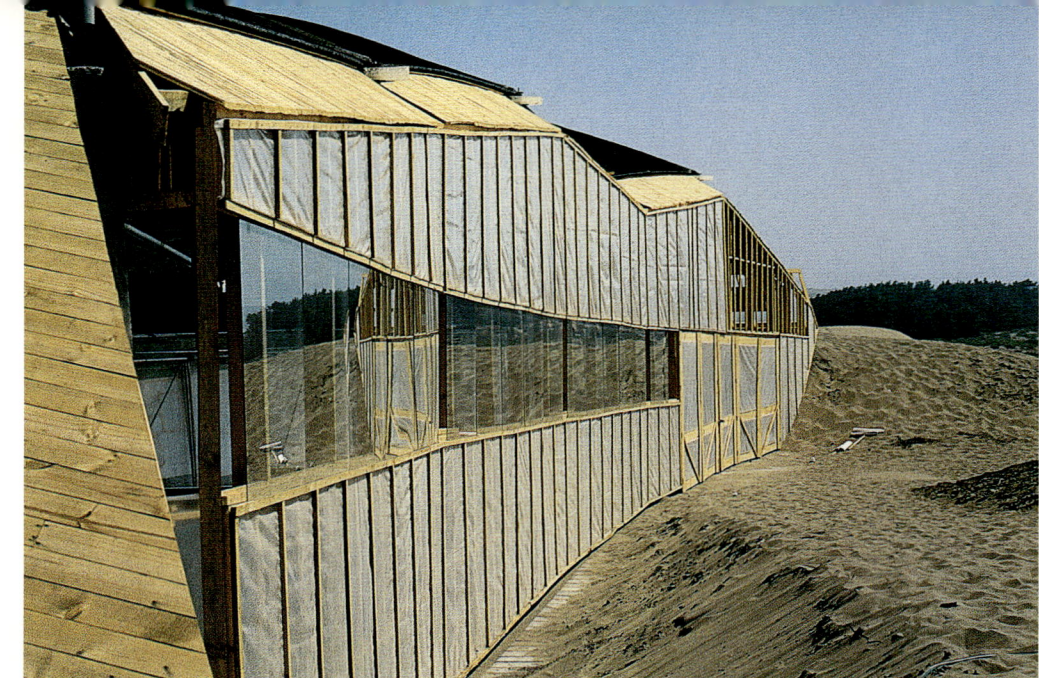

Right:
Partial view of the access façade

Below:
Partial view of the access façade, wooden slats and plastic membranes

Following page:
Roof of black Raschell mesh, 50% grid, and plinth with skirts of slatted wood of different heights

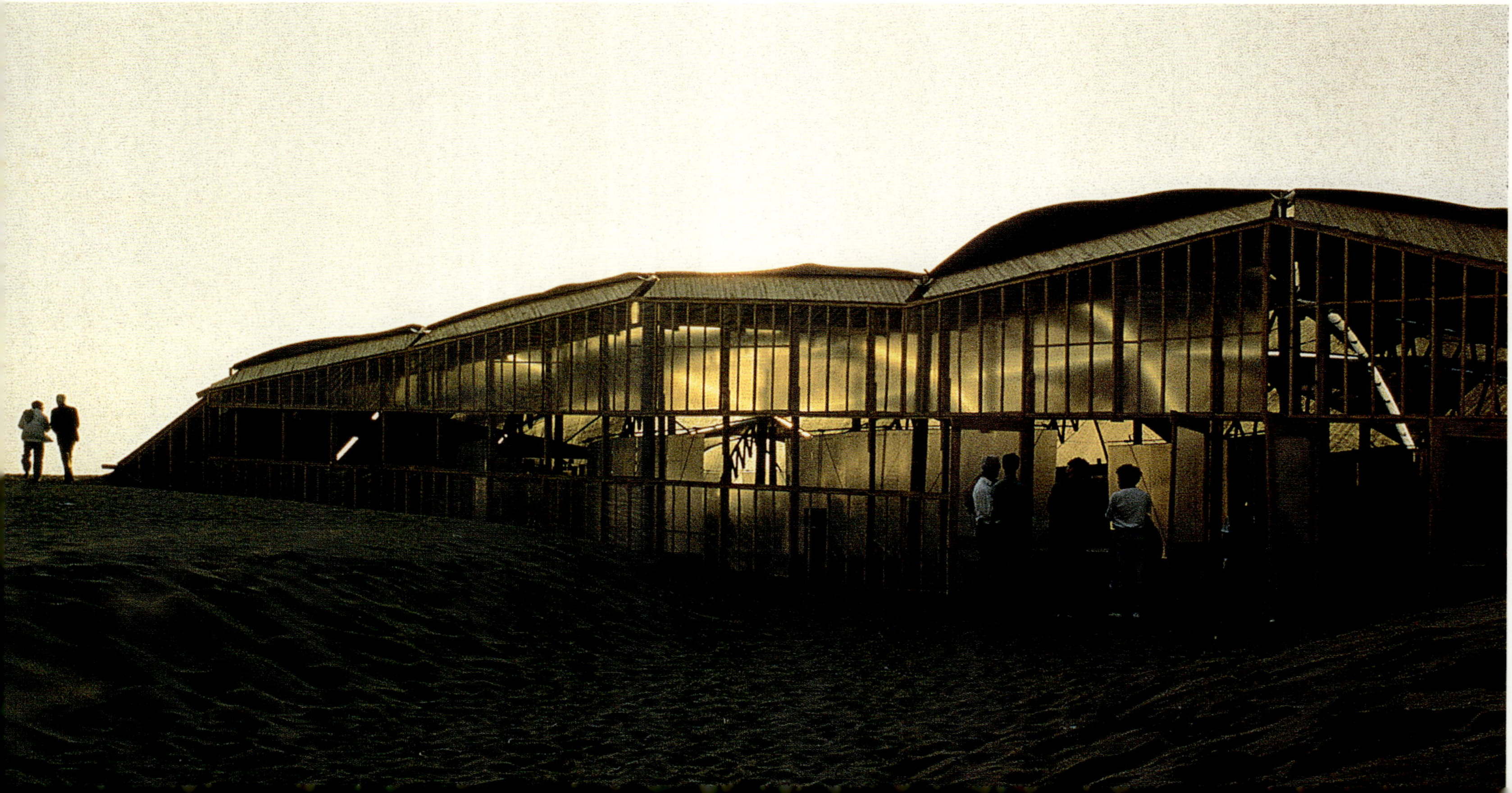

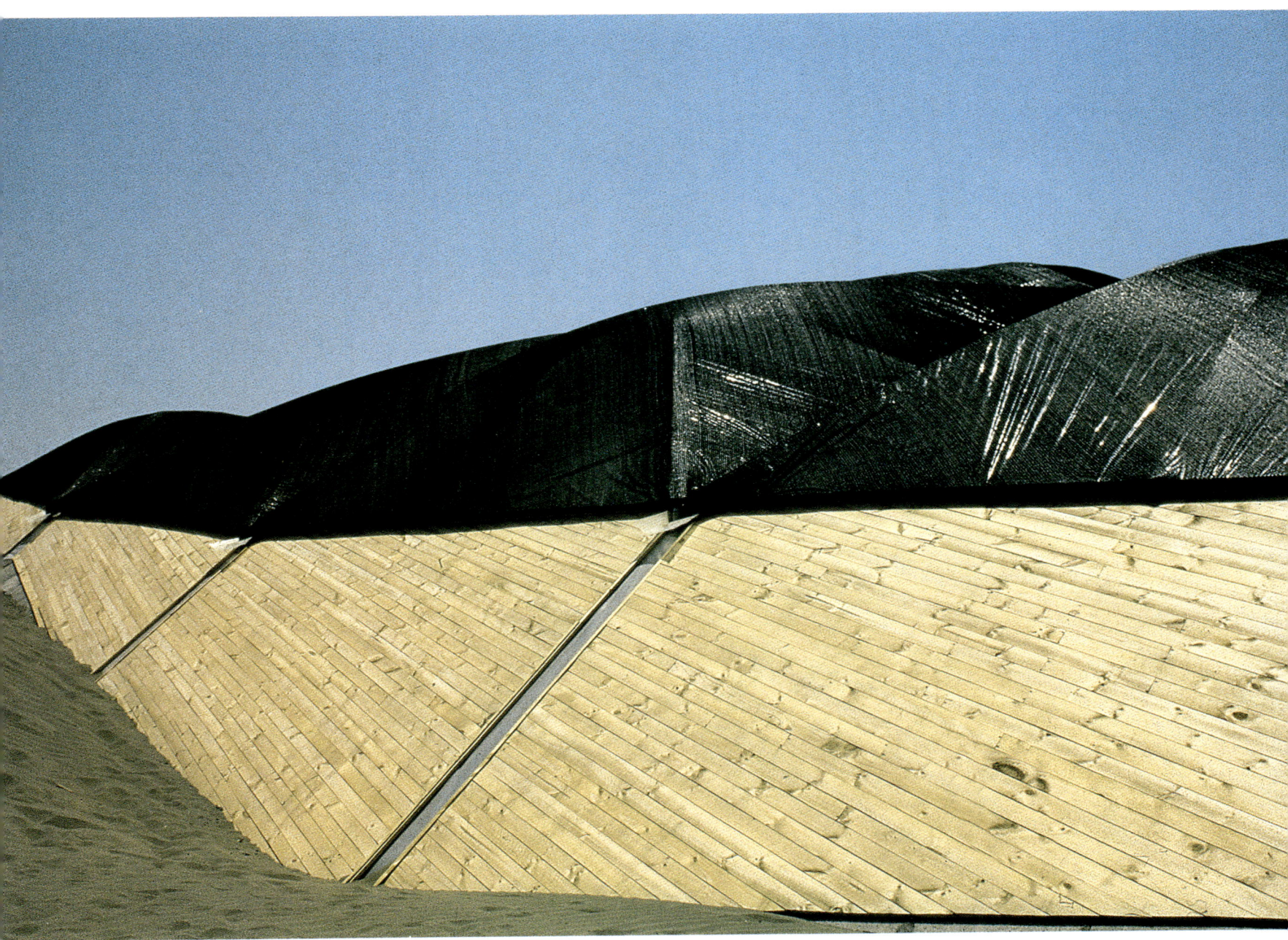

Wanderer's Lodge (Hospedería del Errante)

Open City, Ritoque, Quintero
Miguel Eyquem
First version, 1981
Demolished
Manuel Casanueva *et al.*
Second version, 1995

The first work, begun in 1981, was carried out with metallic and masonry parts donated to the Open City. Only the basic structure was ever built. This was left exposed to the destructive effects of time until the research project enabled it to be approached anew, as a search for a grading of the power of the elements.

The second stage of this work, involving the remodelling and reformulation of the first, formally embodied the identity of the project as research by registering it with the National Council of Scientific Research program, thereby submitting it to the rigours of the project review methods which are typical of such a procedure.

Research and work were carried out in successive workshops by disciplines integrated under the supervision of the architecture workshop in accordance with the principle of the relationship between theory and practice instituted in the study plan.

This design basically acknowledged two fields of research related to the natural energies of the elements: one dealing with luminosity, the other with the wind. To this end two concepts and the resulting mechanisms are involved which will define the characteristics of the outer shell: fuselages and lattices, in response to wind and light energy, respectively. The fuselages were conceived as technical elements capable of withstanding the flow effects of the wind and rain, and the lattices as a mechanism for controlling the light. Thus protected, the interior was seen as a space of residence, study and contemplation.

At the same time the virtual effect of the impact of a cube on the exterior cover was researched in such a way that the shape originated both in reaction to natural forces or effects and as a consequence of a plastic will associated with a geometric operation.

The corrosive effect of the coastal wind has been a constant subject of research throughout the history of the group, assuming greatest force in the Naval Academy Design of 1956 in Valparaíso and the House of Names, in the Open City in Ritoque, in 1992. When designing and building the Wanderer's Lodge flow laboratories were used as was an experimental tunnel built ex profeso.

Apart from the evident desire to calibrate the architectural form according to natural effects, the design sought to rethink certain assumptions made by modern architecture which gives rise to indiscriminate standards. The recourse to lattices, deep eaves and lengths of windows was an attempt to find an intermediate value of light between the shade typical of traditional masonry constructions and the excessive light of glass architecture. Set on the high grounds, not far from the Palace of Dawn and Dusk, the Wanderer's Lodge appears as a relatively hermetic body of folded white planes.

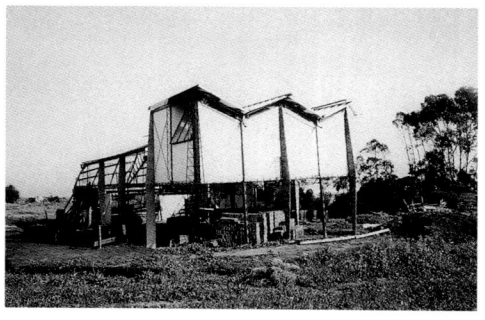

Left:
First version of the Wanderer's Lodge
Right:
Partial view of the second version with the nozzle exit, studio corner and "cubic impressions"

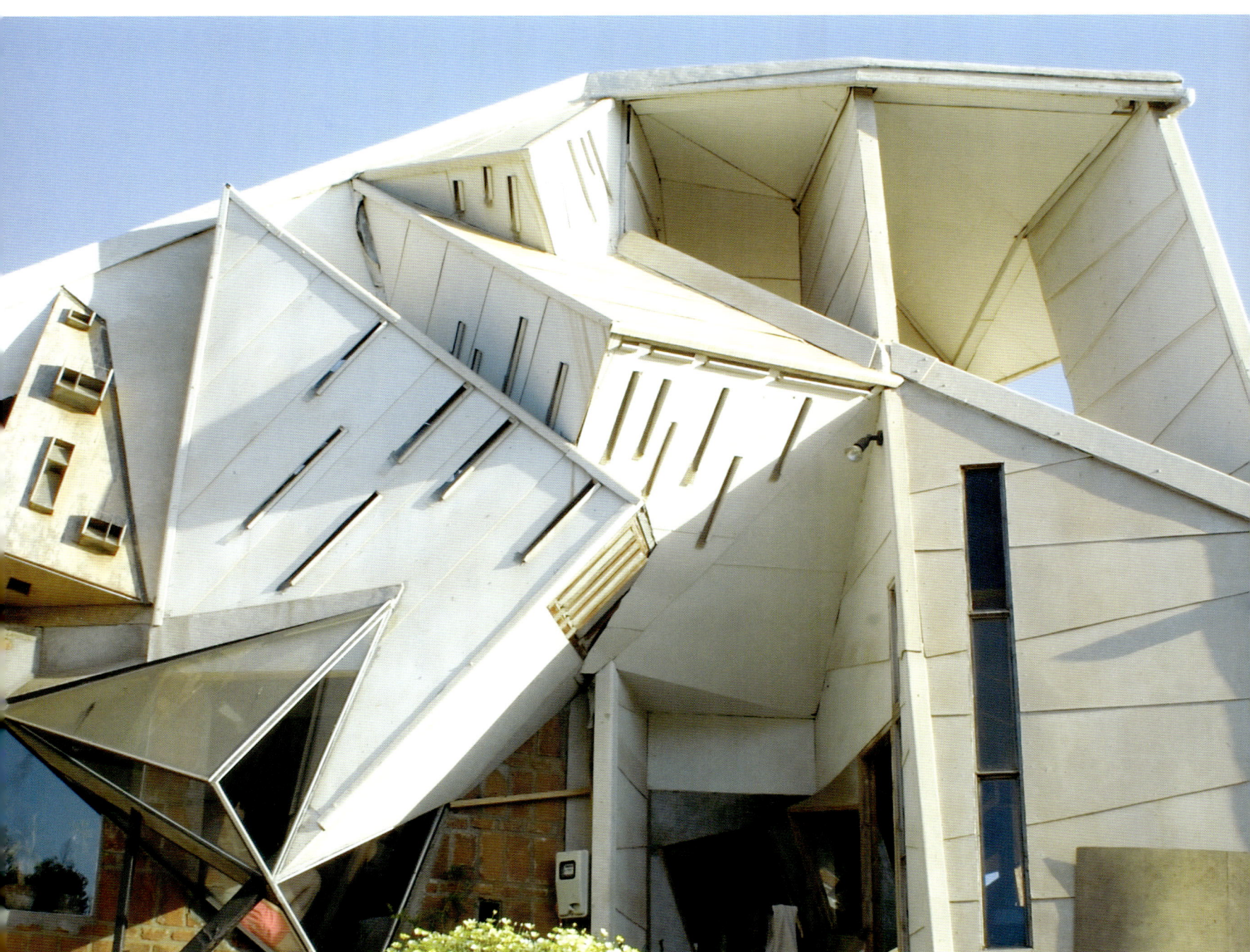

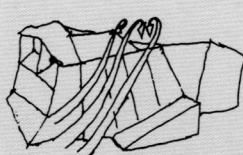

2a. *Sur-weste: 1/a)* El plano deflector produce un movimiento ascendente del viento que termina en zonas de turbulencia en el techo

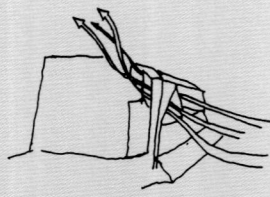

2a. *Sur-Weste: 1/b)* "Penacho", efecto estela proyectado hacia arriba, producto de la forma de la Tobera

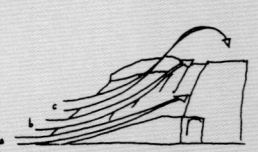

2b. *Primera Sesión Sur-Weste: 1/a)* Plano deflector: El aire en su capa inferior (a), choca con la rampa y se eleva, se forma una capa límite. La capa intermedia de aire (b), sube por el deflector y la capa superior (c), es deflectada y produce una zona Eddy en el techo

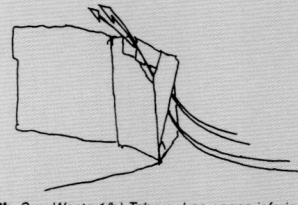

2b. *Sur-Weste: 1/b)* Tobera: Las capas inferior e intermedia del flujo se introducen en las aberturas de la Tobera, siendo expulsadas a gran velocidad y con dirección ascendente, formando un "Penacho" resultante del efecto Estela y efecto Venturi

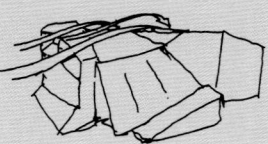

2a. *Weste: 2/a)* La concavidad que tiene el techo (dos pendientes que terminan en una canaleta), producen zonas de baja presión que conducen al aire, el cual baja en forma turbulenta

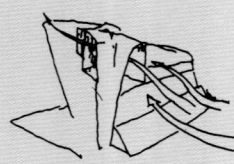

2a. *Weste: 2/b)* Efecto minimizado al colocar un pequeño plano deflector en la base del plano

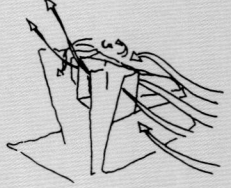

2b. *Sur-Weste: 1/c)* La capa superior se deflecta rodeando este "Penacho" y creando una turbulencia en el techo. Zona Eddy

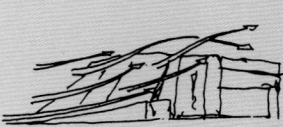

2b. *Segunda Sesión Sur-Weste: 2/a)* Plano deflector: Ocurre algo similar a la sesión anterior, pero esta vez, como se le agrega el resto del techo y la estructura de la puerta, se observa la continuidad producida por la estructura de techumbre en general, es decir, no se producen turbulencias mayores sobre el techo

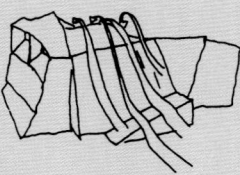

2a. *Sur: 3/a)* el plano deflector conduce al aire con facilidad, elevando y produciendo turbulencias en la zona del techo

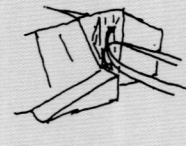

2a. *Sur: 3/b)* La estructura de Puerta, por su verticalidad, presenta un frente de choque a barlovento

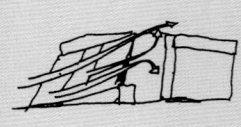

2b. *Sur-Weste 2/b)* En la estructura de la puerta, se observa un choque del aire contra un plano vertical, lo que indica que se produce una zona Eddy en el acceso

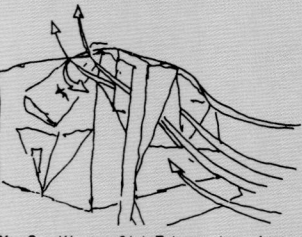

2b. *Sur-Weste: 2/c)* Tobera: los efectos aerodinámicos producidos por la Tobera son similares a la sesión anterior, por lo que se puede concluir que la Tobera no influyen de forma alguna la estructura del techo ni el rincón de estudio

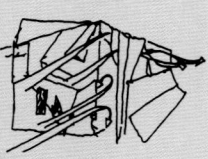

2a. *Norte: 4/a)* la Tobera funciona en sentido contrario conduciendo el aire por los expulsores hacia el weste; sin embargo se enfrenta el aire a la abertura del patio interior norte de la tobera y se crean zonas de baja presión en este lugar

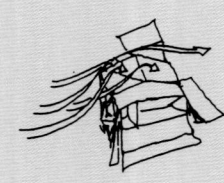

2a. *Norte: 4/b)* Se producen turbulencias en los techos de la Hospedería, sin embargo en los paños paraboidales el flujo se mantiene laminar

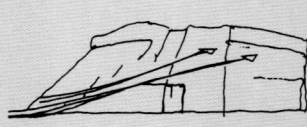

2b. *Weste: 2/d)* Plano deflector: Se produce una canalización del aire por el muro deflector y la rampa de acceso al segundo piso

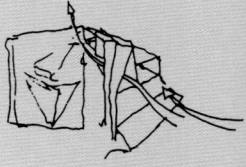

2b. *Tobera: 2/e)* el efecto de vórtice acostado al pie de la Tobera desaparece gracias al pequeño plano colocado en la base del frente de la Tobera

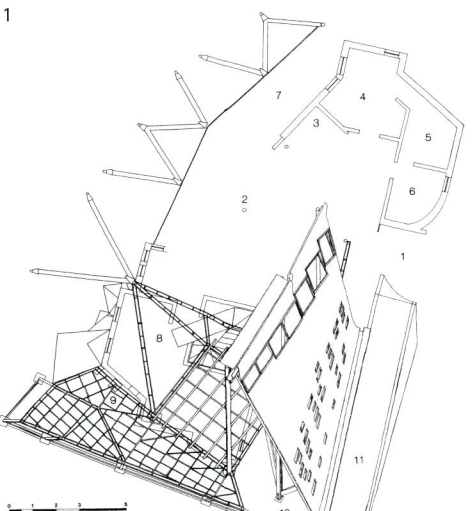

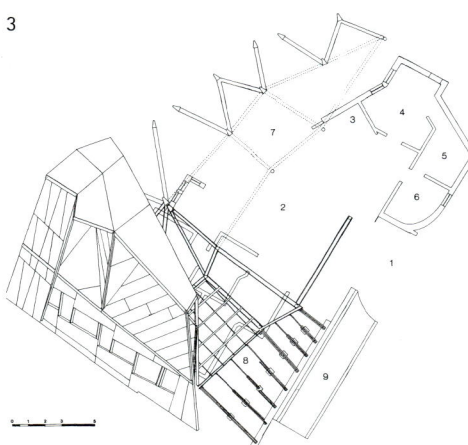

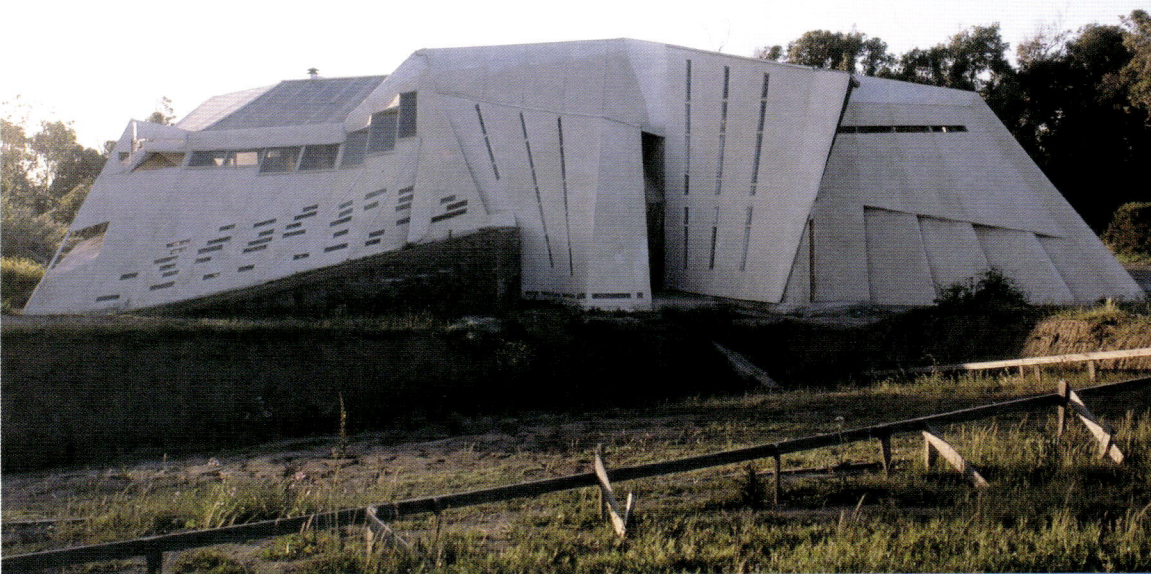

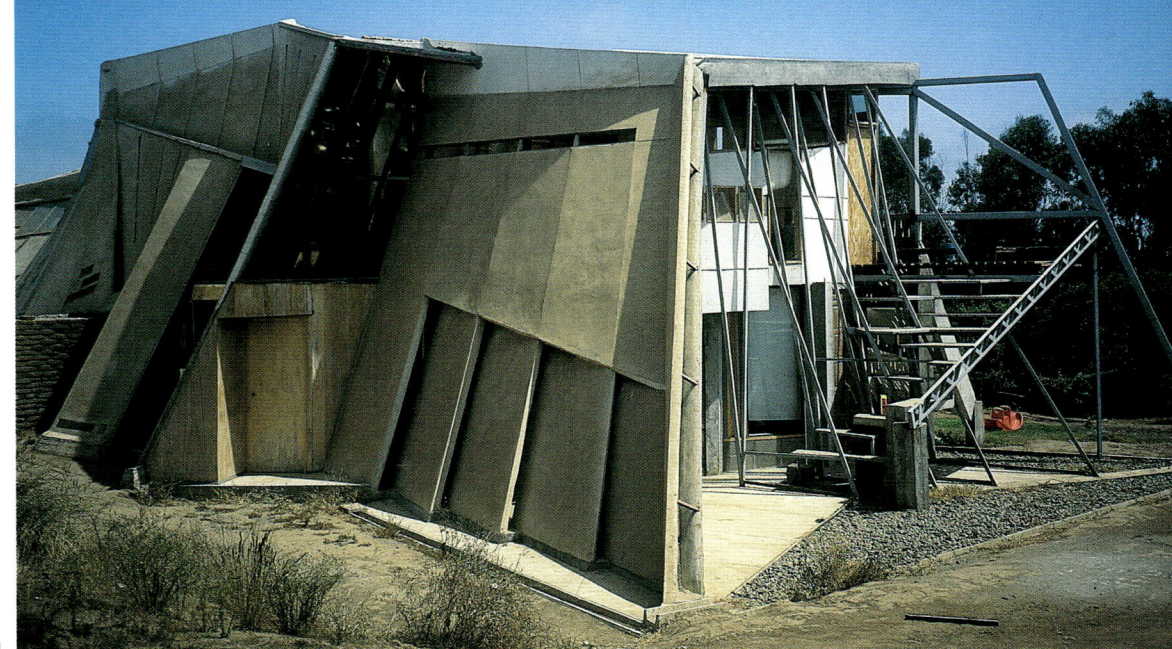

Left:
Schematic drawings of the wind flows affecting each of the sides

1 Axonometric projection and general plan of the aerodynamic deflector
2 View of access façade
3 Axonometric projection and general plan of nozzle
4 View from the southeast

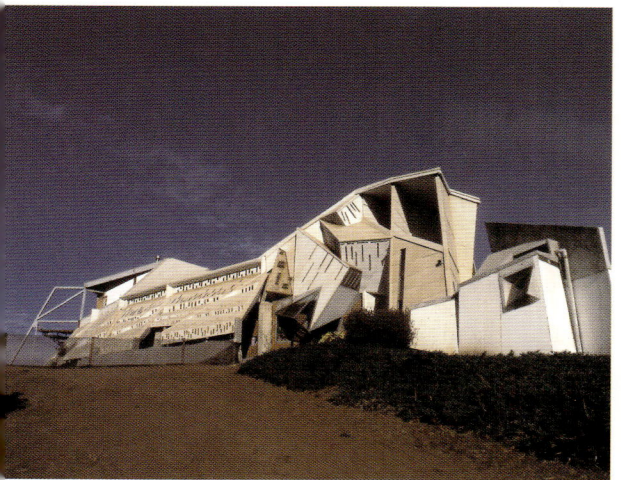

1

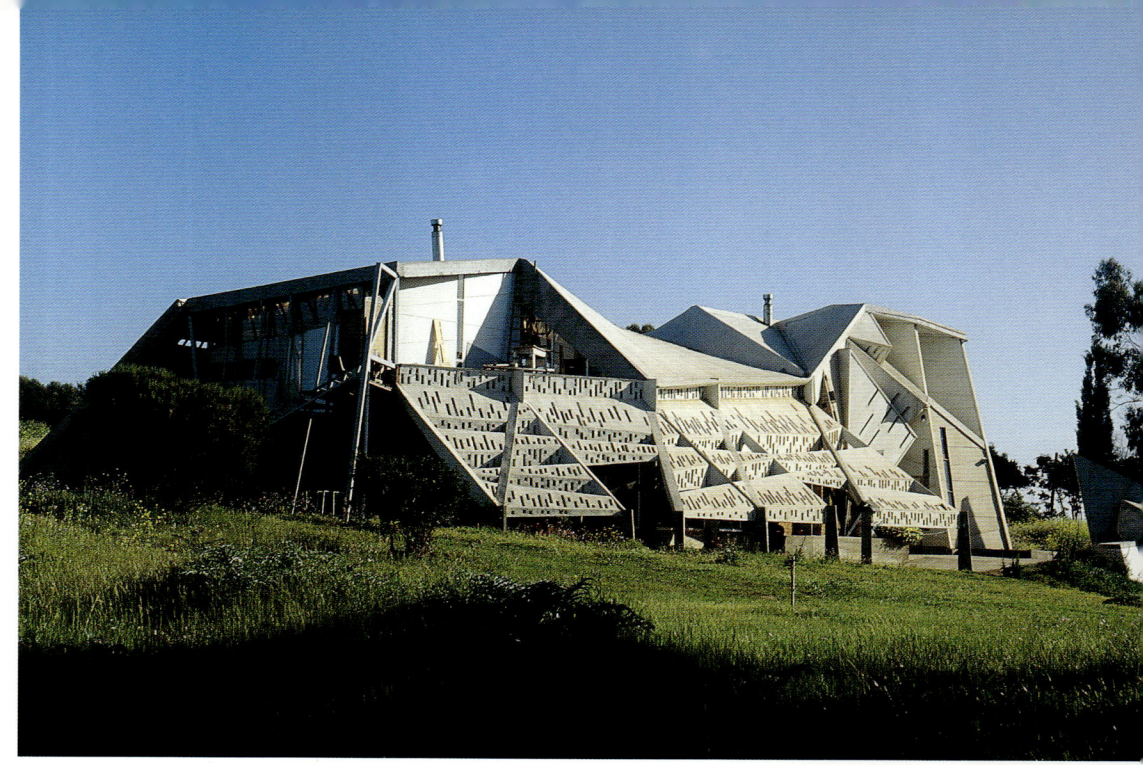

2

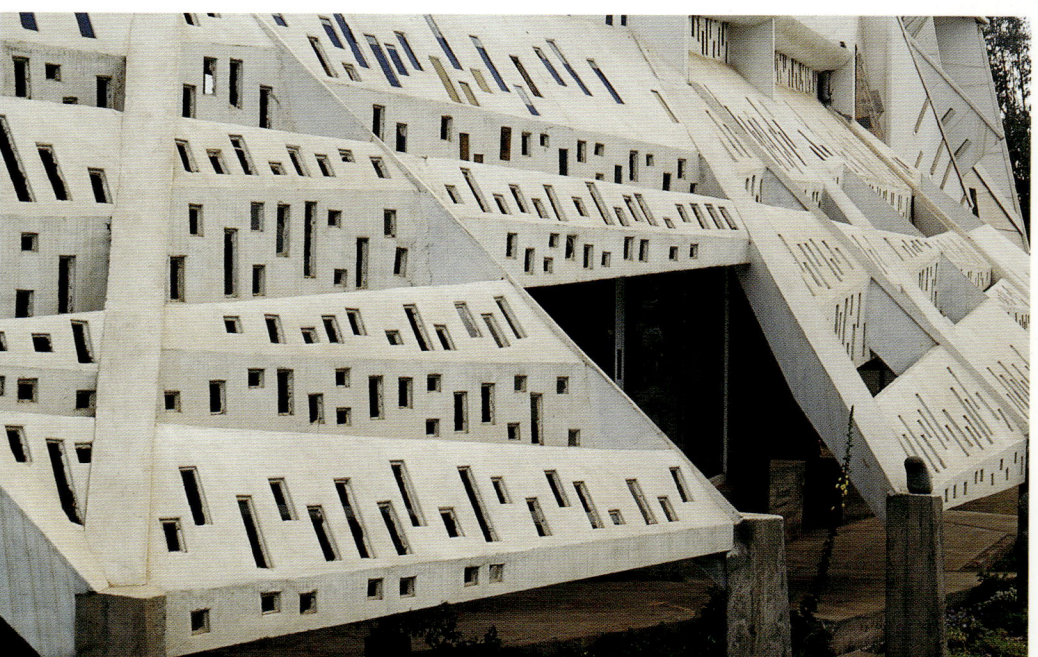

3

1 Northern side stained glass window; deflector exit on right
2 Northwest façade
3 Partial view of the exterior vitral and the passage underneath it
4, 5 and 6 Details of the vitral

Next two pages, from top to bottom:
Axonometric projections and general plan of stained glass window; axonometric projection and general plan of stairwell and studio corner; and sketch of studio corner
Right: View from the northwest

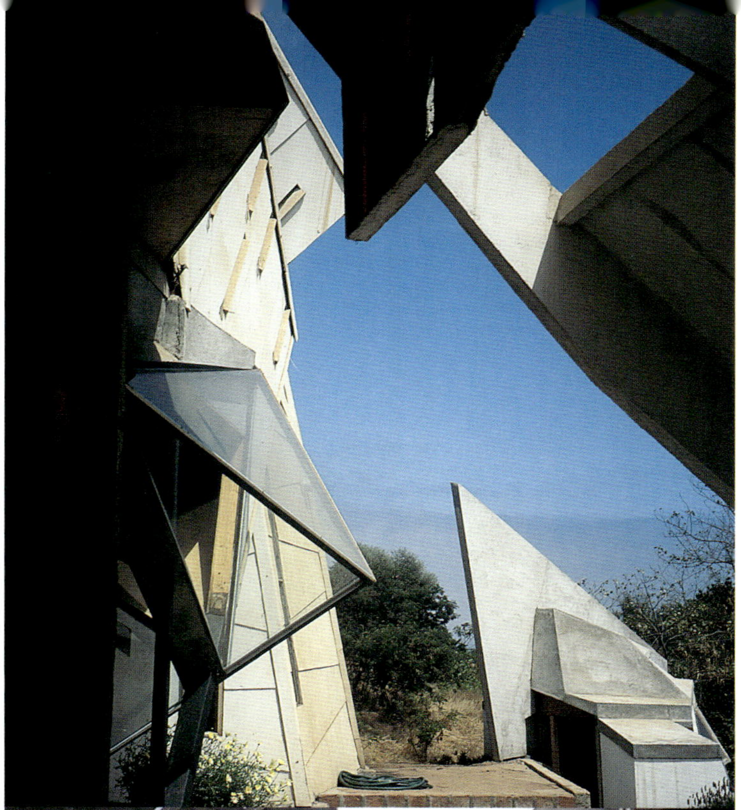

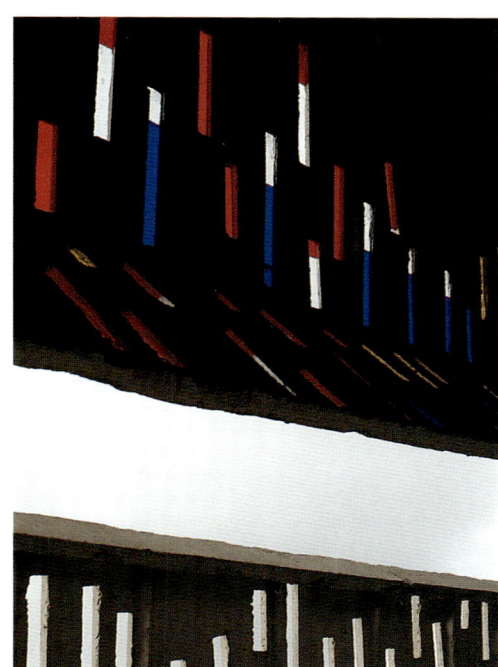

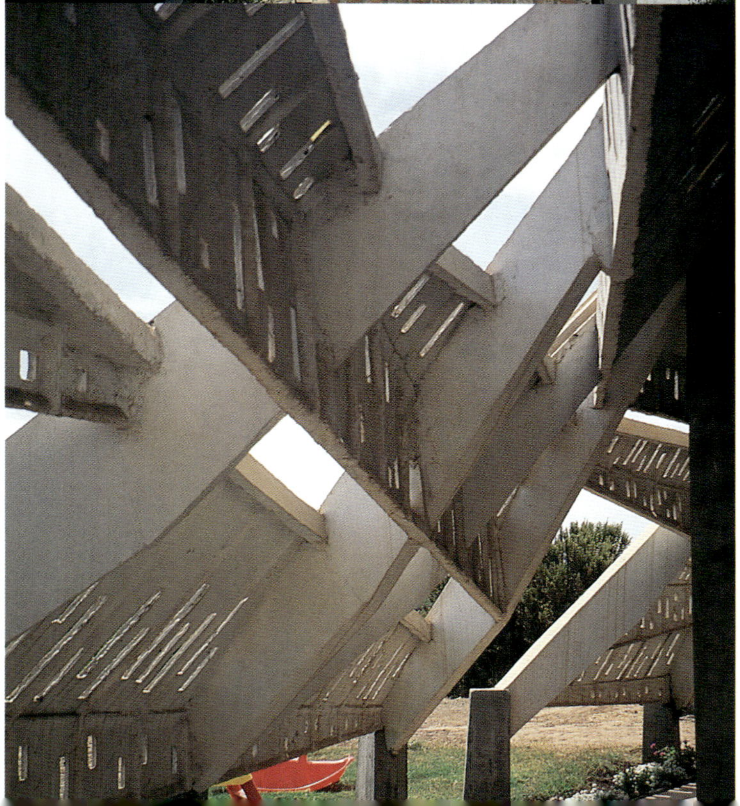

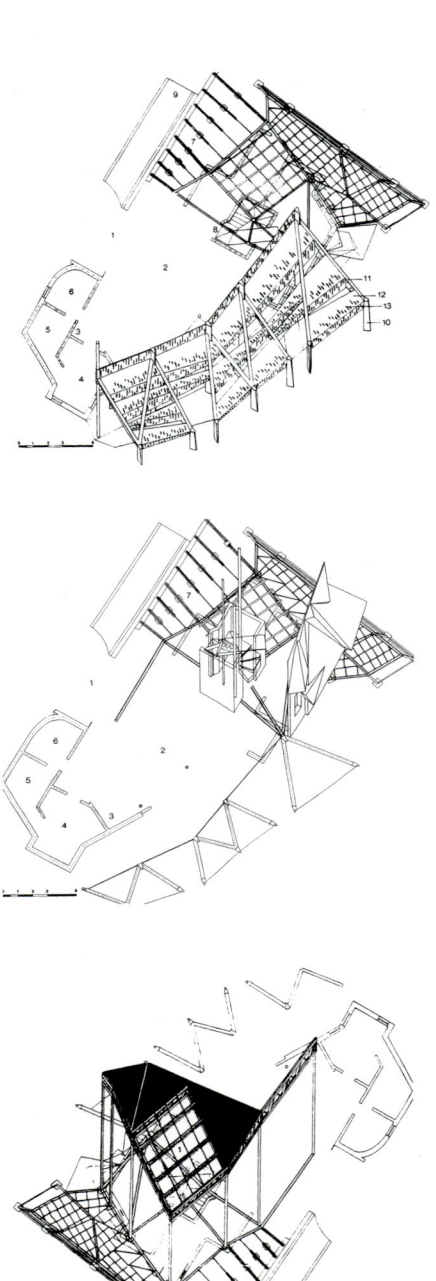

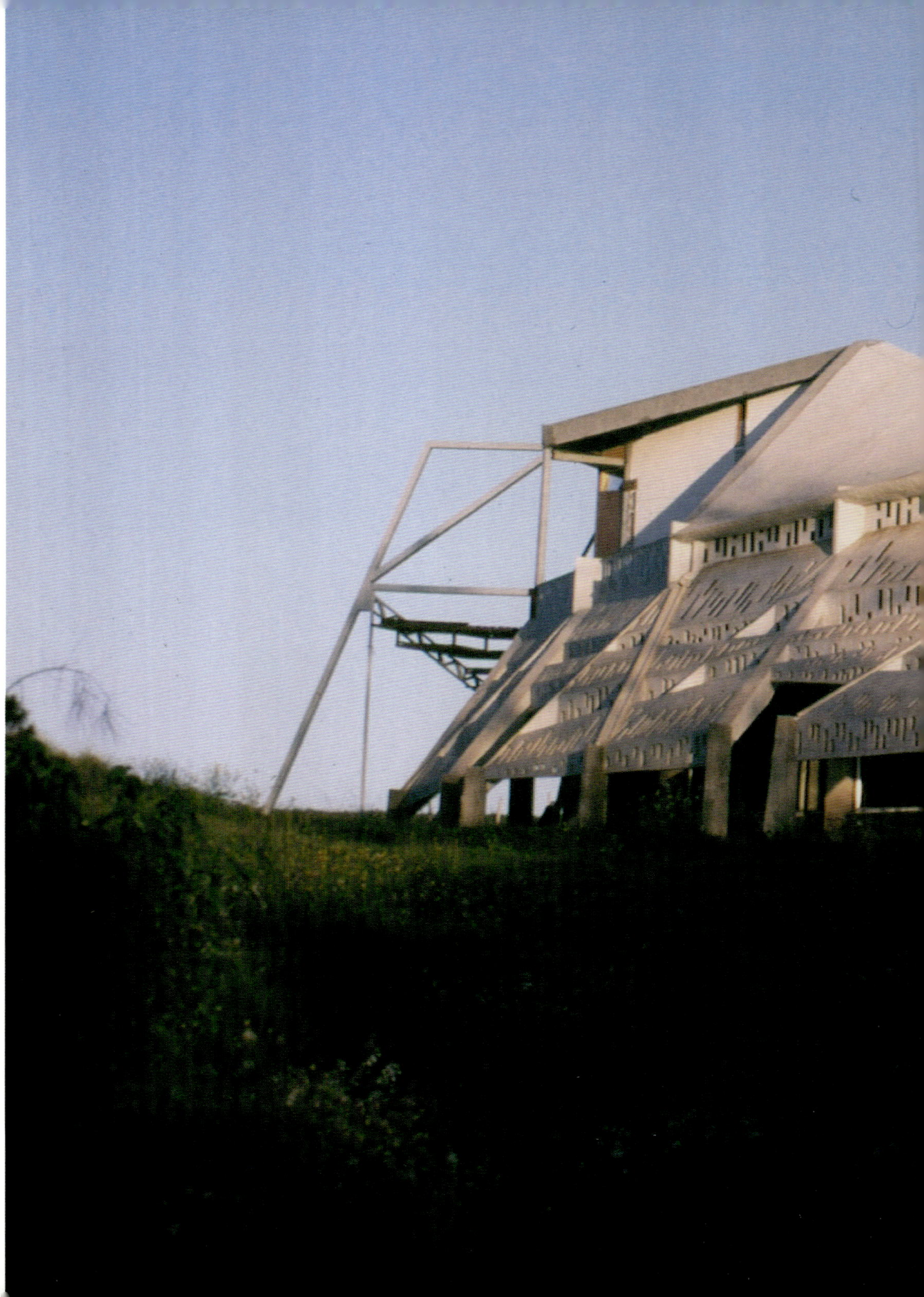

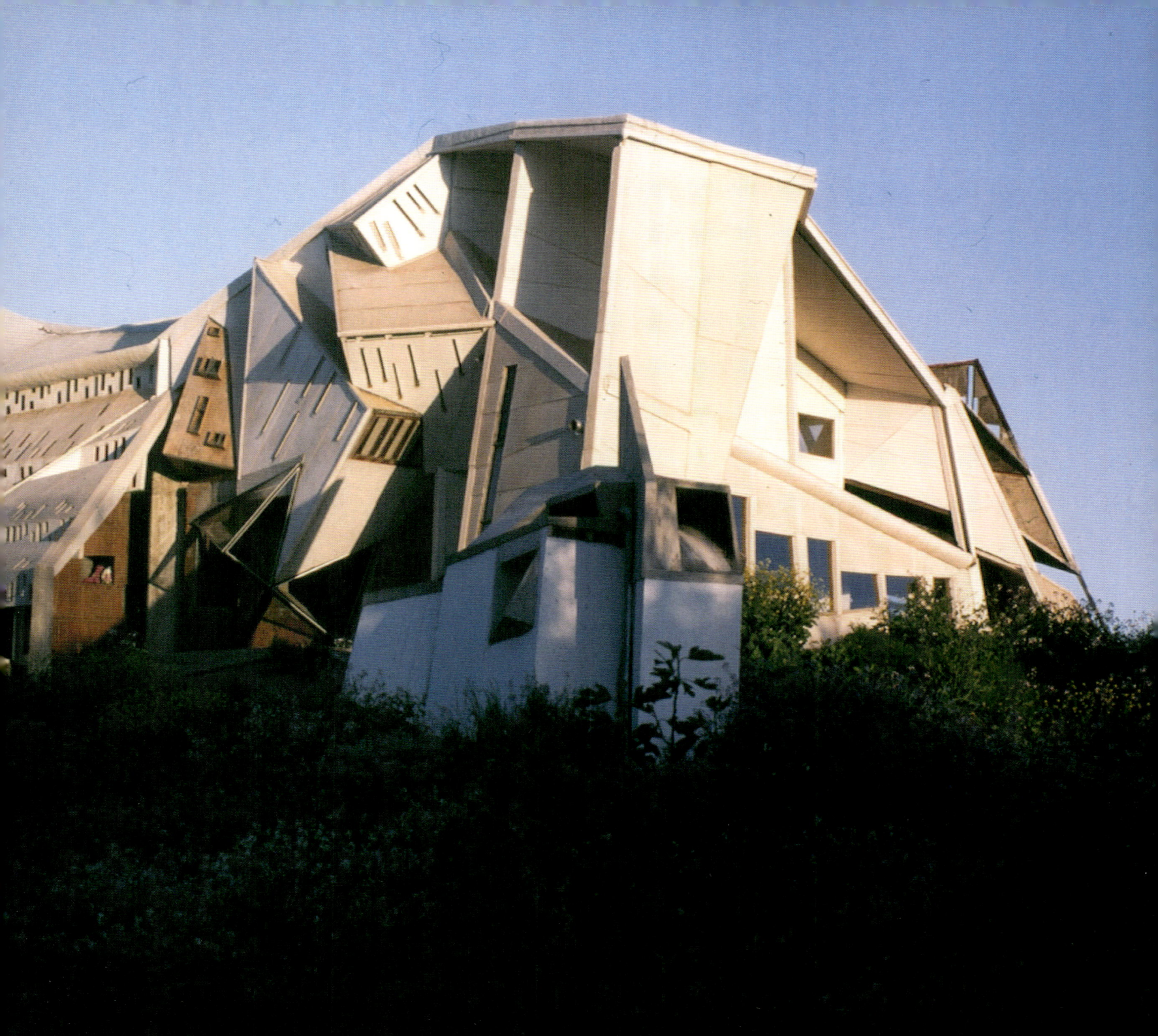

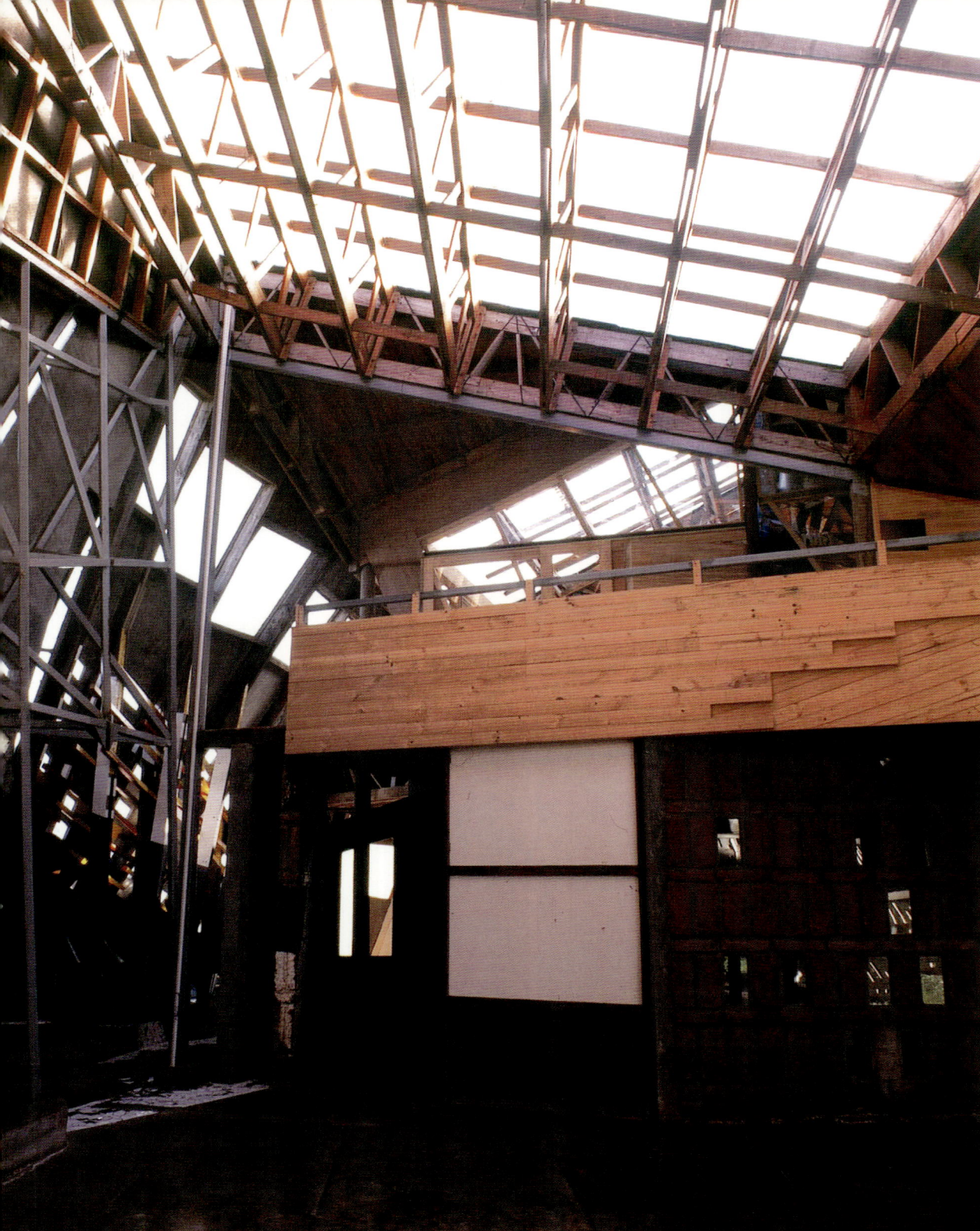

1 Inner atrium, studio and attic
2 View from the first floor: stained glass window, metallic structure covered with ferrocement 5-cm-wide perforations

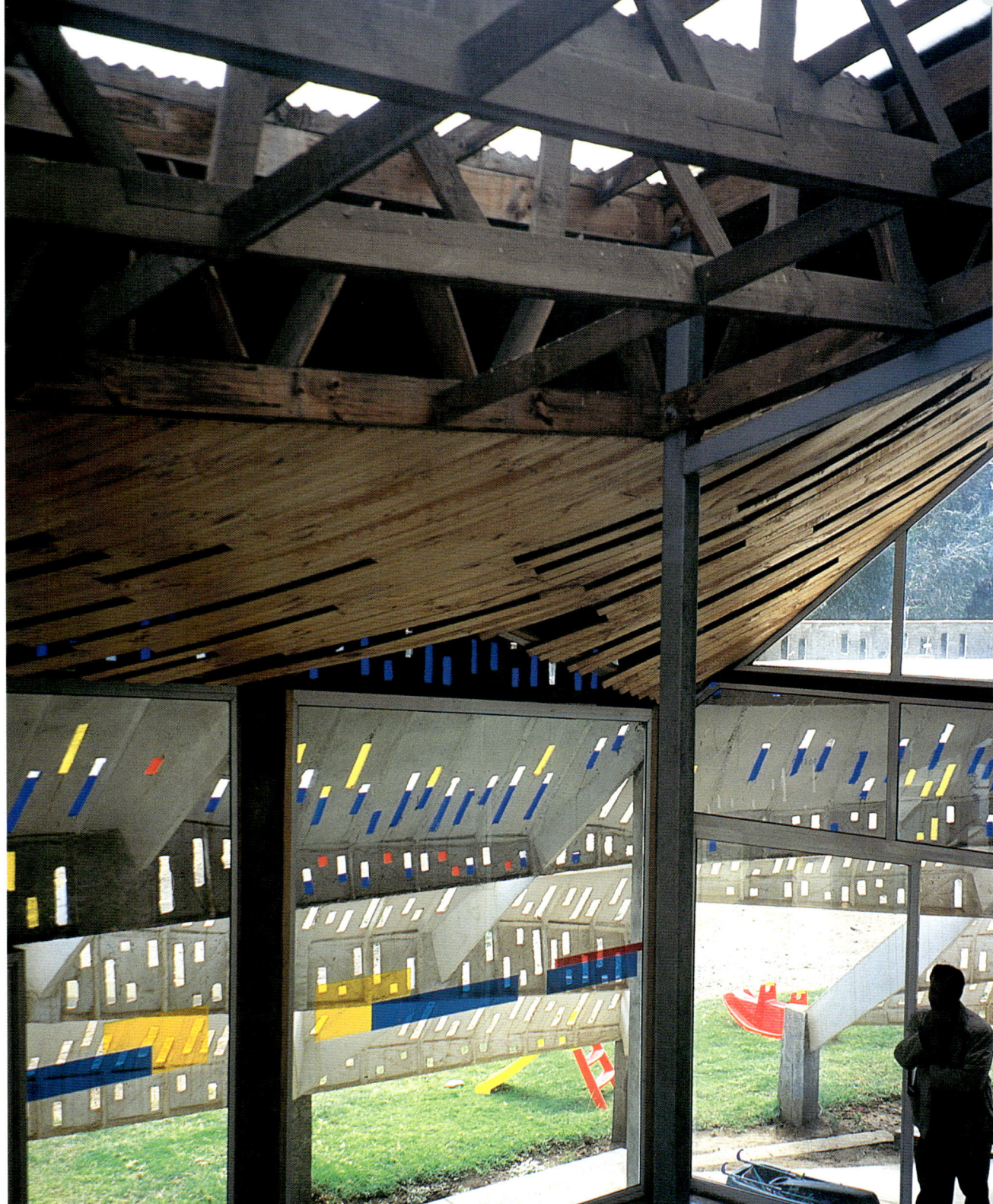

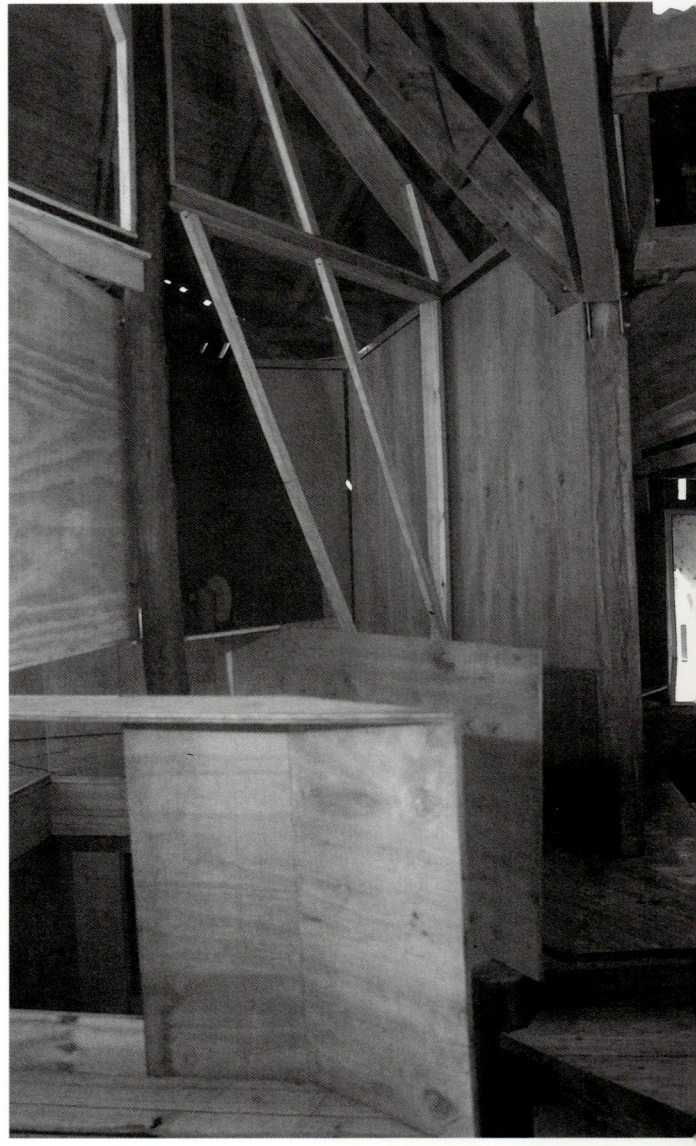

1 Interior of the southeast cover, deflector and nozzle
2 Second floor landing
3 Detail of the interior of the studio corner
4 Interior view of the access door

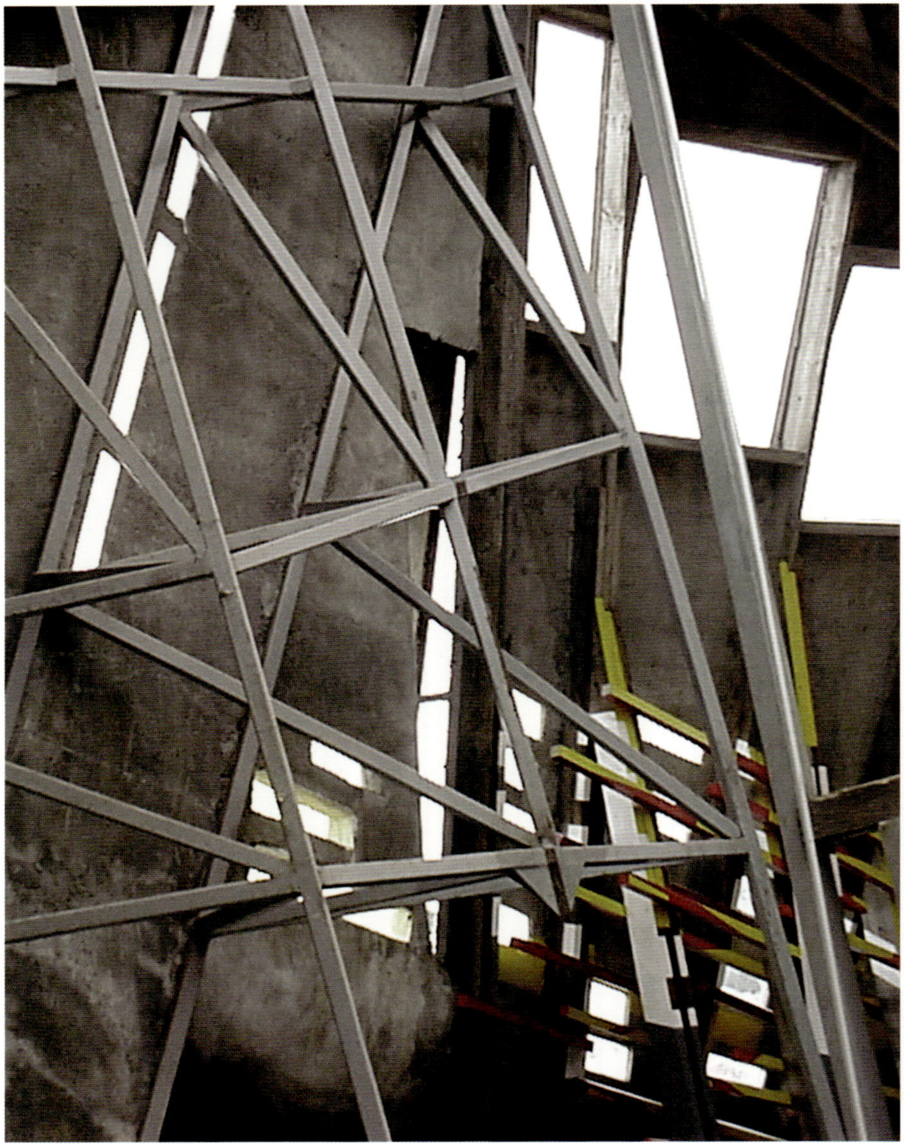

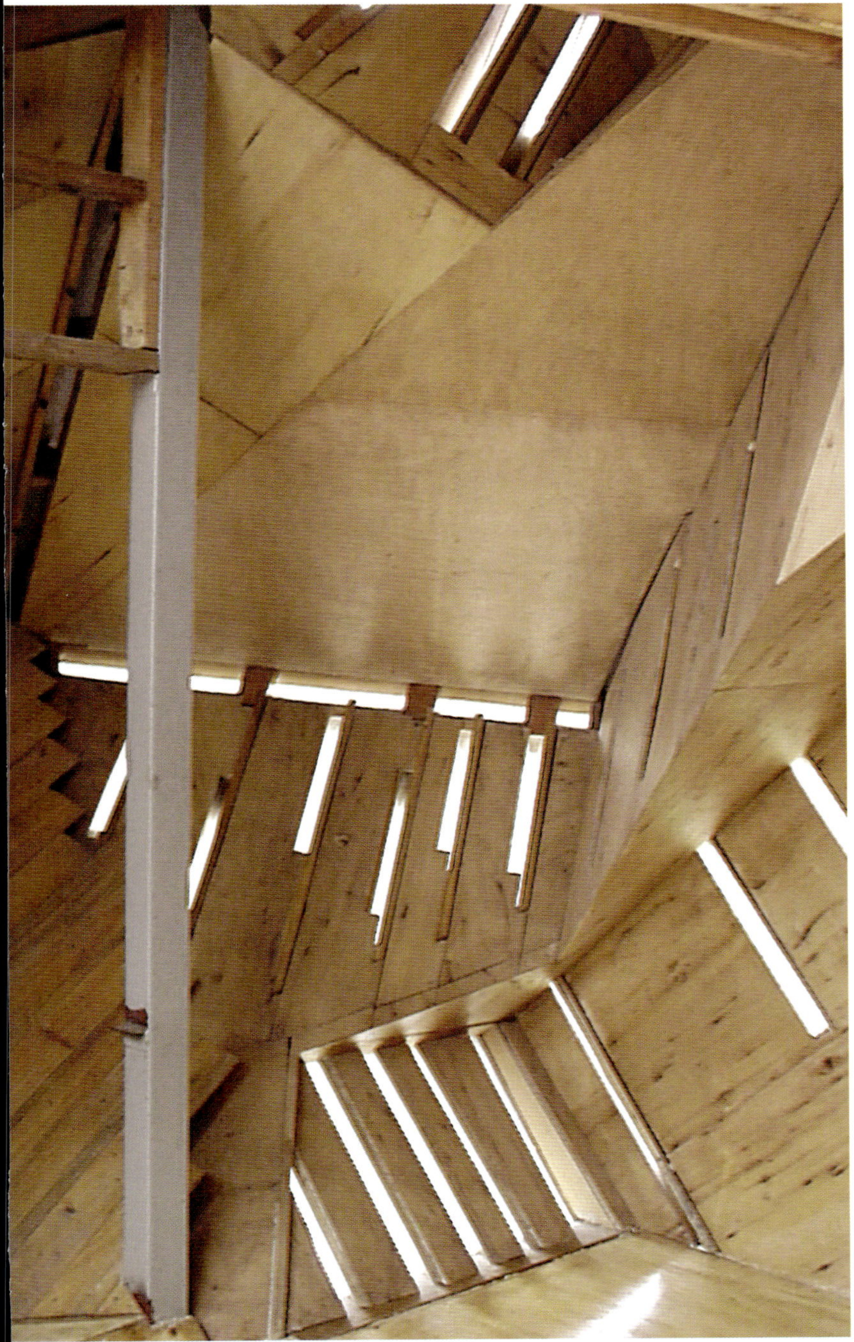

3

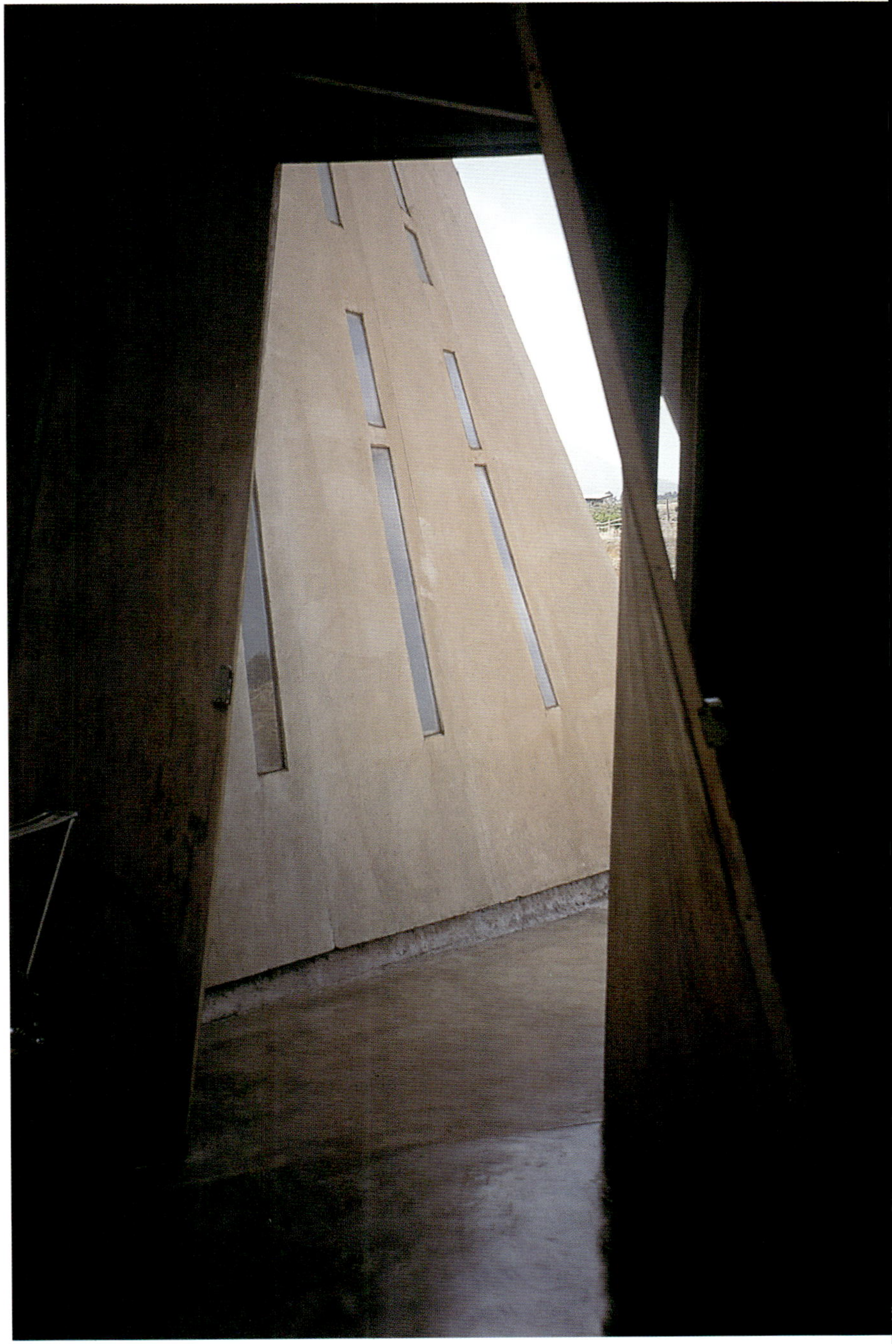

4

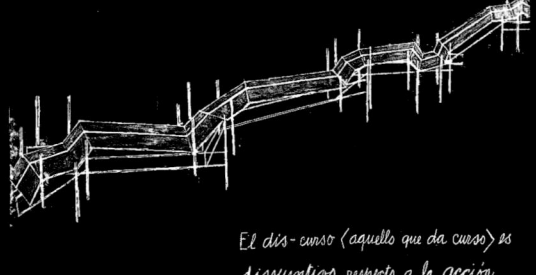

El dis-curso (aquello que da curso) es disyuntivo respecto a la acción

The poet Henri Tronquoy was temporarily associated with the Valparaíso group, from which he was prematurely separated by his demise in a plane crash over the Caribbean on the way back to France from Valparaíso. This pioneering work was built in his memory.

Located above the sands, the Agora comprises a springy upper walkway, which threads its way towards the Caribbean and a rhomboidal esplanade, whose floor is divided into an area of combed sand and a section of hard flooring, the undulating surface of which induces balance control of the body and the distance taken up between people in conversation with each other.

The Agora contains two sculptures by Claudio Girola, one of which rises like a stake to give a sense of vertical magnitude. As with other early works, this one had a small, lightly built elementary cubicle—named Vestal—attached. This was because of its role as permanent guardian of a collective asset.

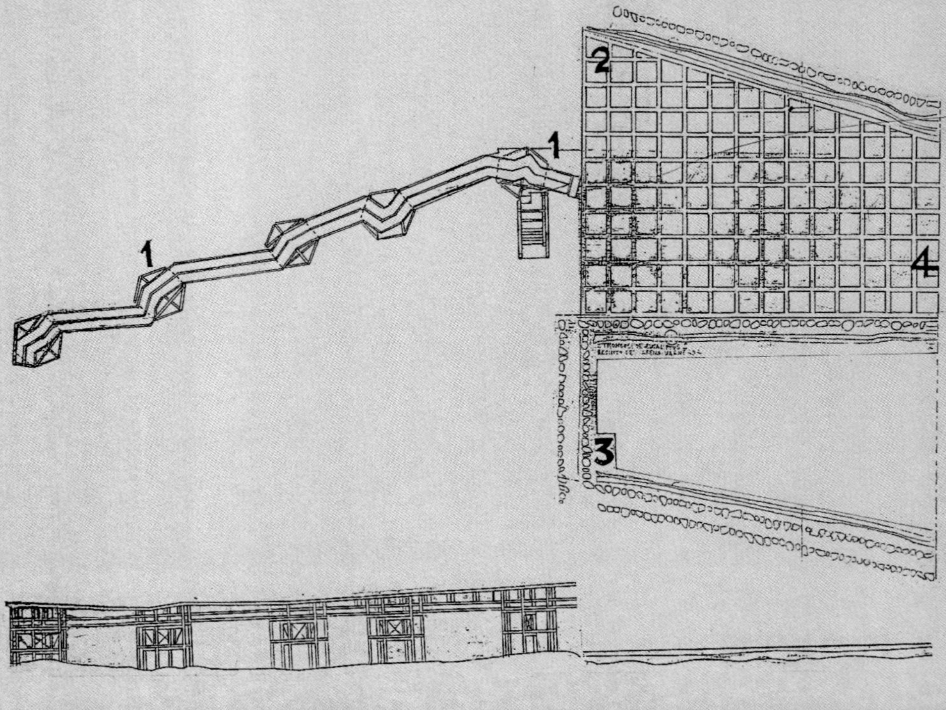

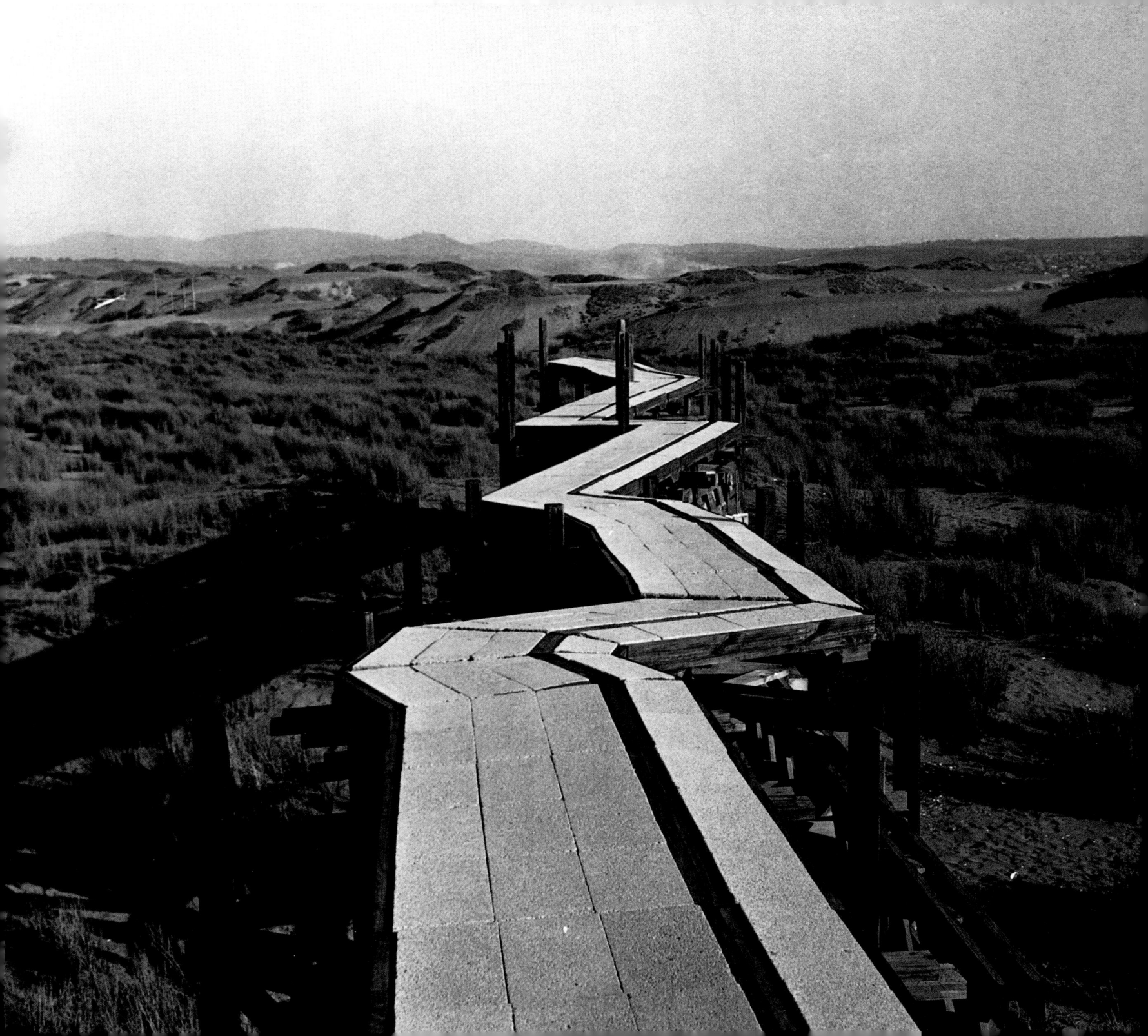

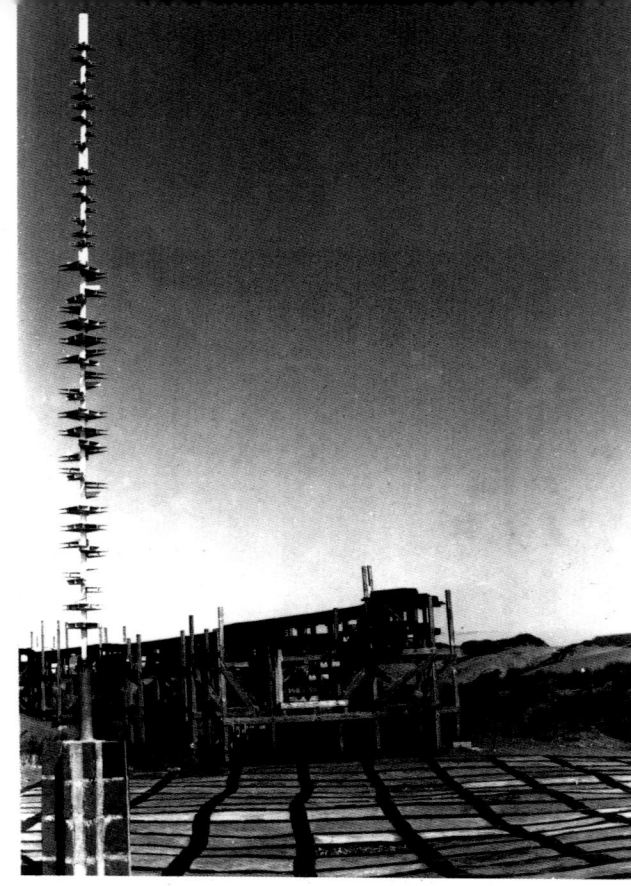

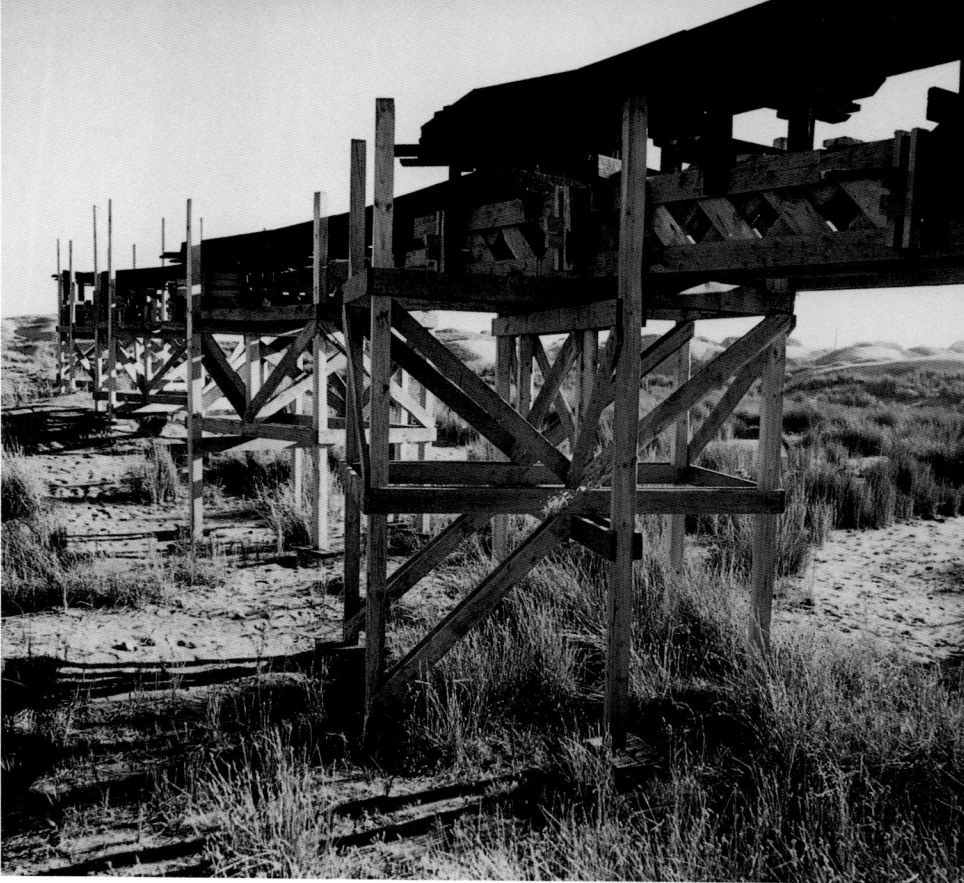

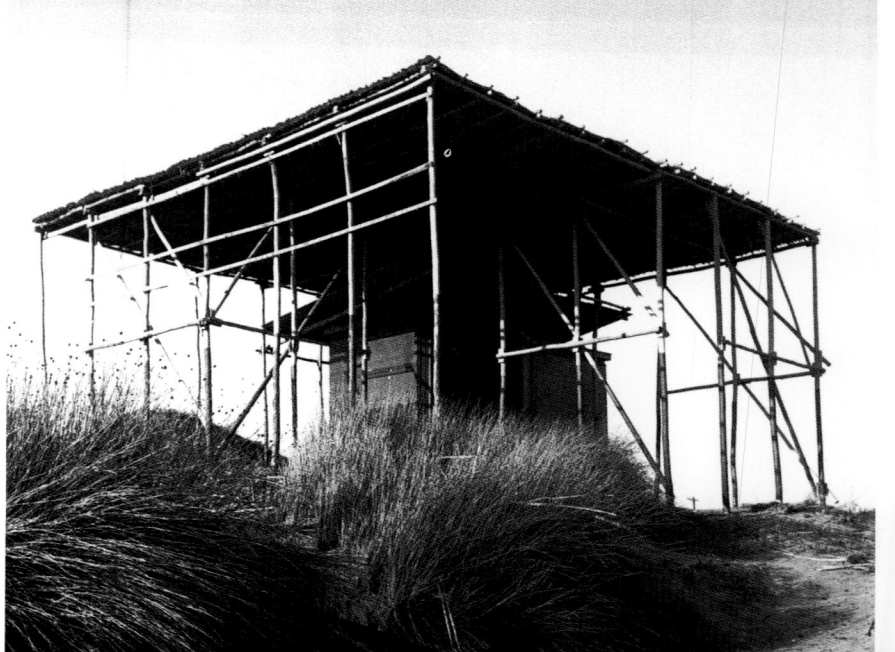

1 Sculpture by Claudio Girola, undulating floor and walkway
2, previous and following pages: Raised walkway
3 Vestal: the small cubicle is a place of study

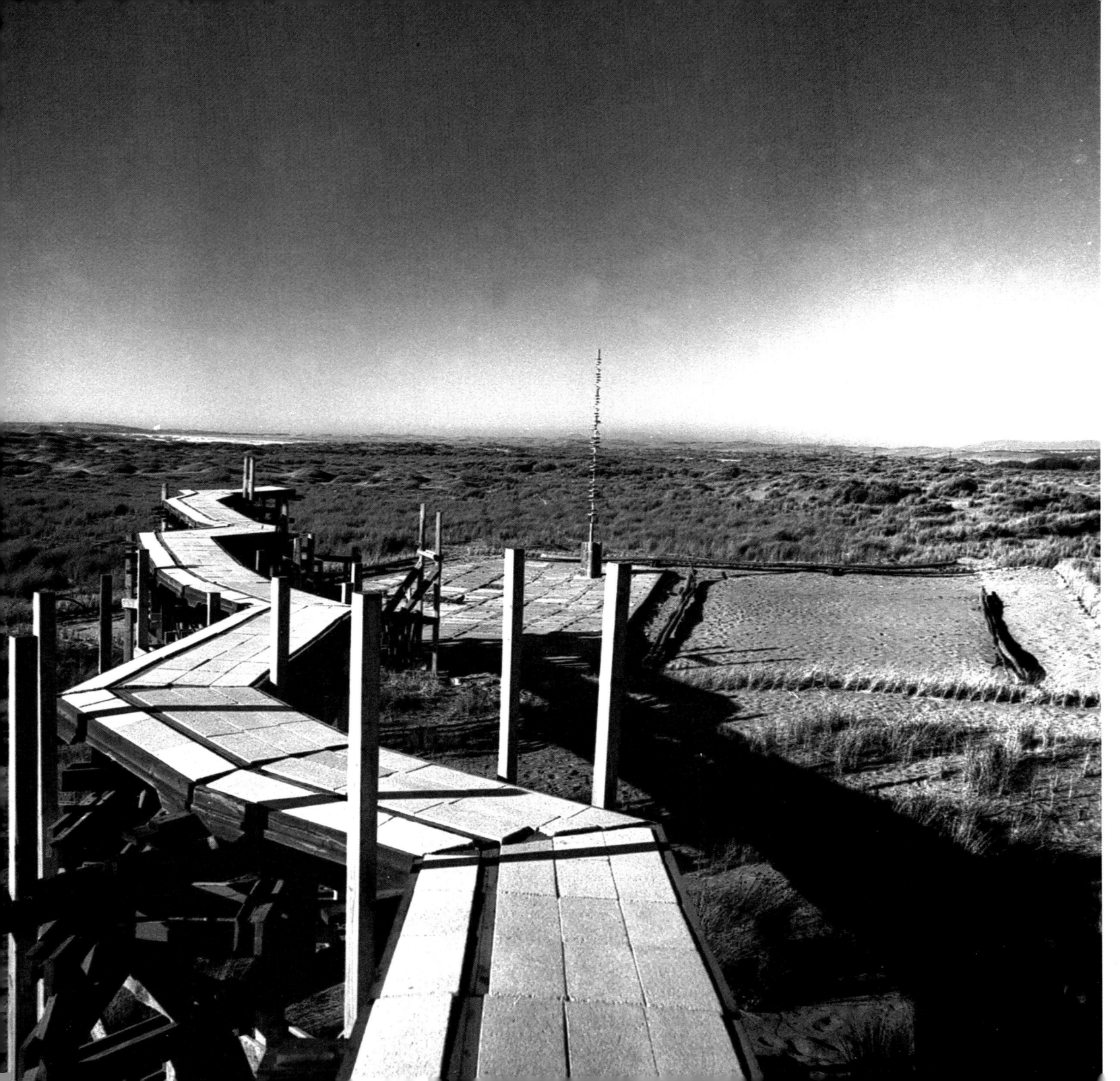

Double or Banquet Lodge (Hospedería Doble or del Banquete)

Open City, Ritoque, Quintero
Alberto Cruz, Juan Mastrantonio, Open City Group
1974

The notion of *trabajo en ronda* or "work in a circle" becomes clear in this project, the product of multiple related initiatives. Taking the two end *nuclei* as a starting point, the addition of a third element, called *El Confín*, gave the ensemble a sense of unity. Its external expression is almost chaotic and barely intelligible, as opposed to the Music Room and other designs, whose perception is always clear. The design was developed from the inside out through a series of successive operations of conception and construction of the perimeter, whereby the enlargement is evidence of a transition from the regular interior order to the heterogeneous and irregular exterior order. By consolidating its internal, more secret forms, and leaving the outer edge in a state of uncertainty, the procedure inverted more typical design methods, which establish the general appearance as the starting point of a design. Over time, both the façade and the roof of the ensemble have been recovered with new layers. The centrifugal logic of the design can also be appreciated in the details, as in the way the floors of the room are surrounded by a perimeter border of sand that separates them from the enclosing walls. Although the concept of *hospedería* or lodge gives more weight to the notion of hospitality by assigning greater status to the rooms and tables, this lodge has always seemed more of a home—or several interconnected homes—more suited to the life of a family. Generally endowed with a Mediterranean air, these common spaces are lit from different sources, which include overhead lighting, a light not accompanied by views. In the distribution schemes, which favour alternative routes and the alveola quality of passages, the almost chronic lack of halls or corridors as a means of connecting the different spaces is highly noticeable. As is generally the case in the works which comprise the Open City, natural colours predominate: where there is paint, it appears as a fragment in its mural condition, perhaps reflecting a private search for light or space.

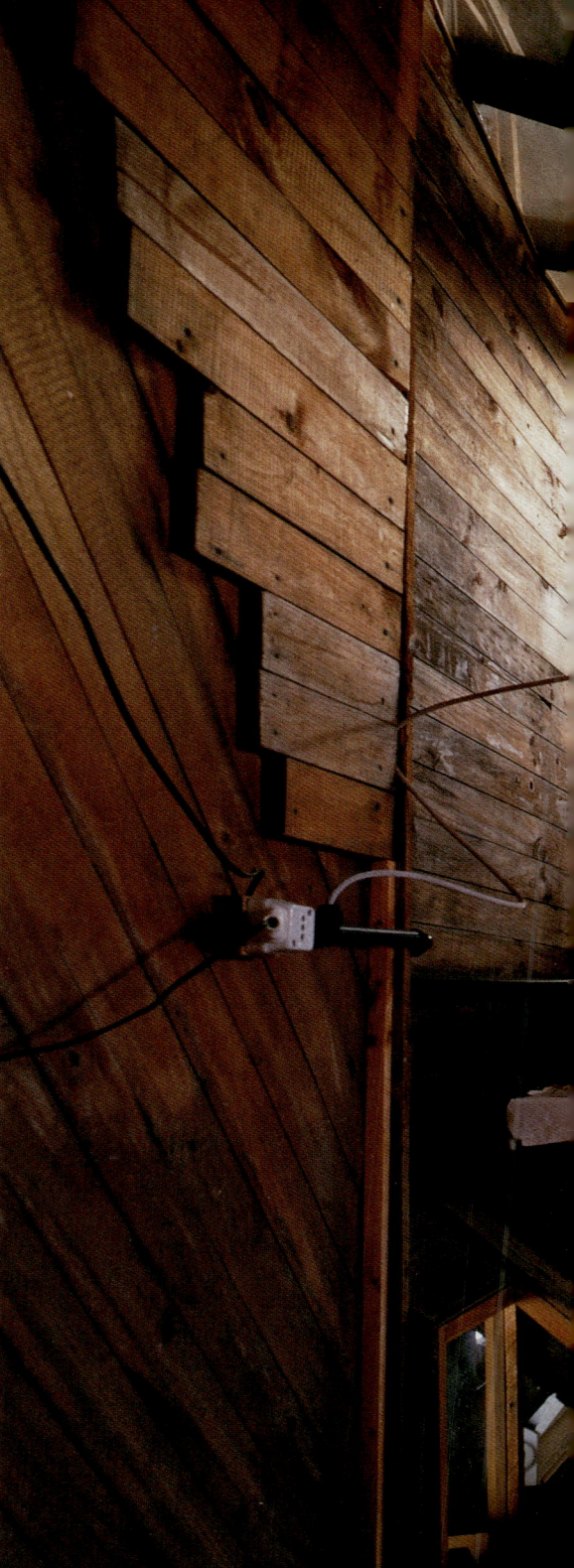

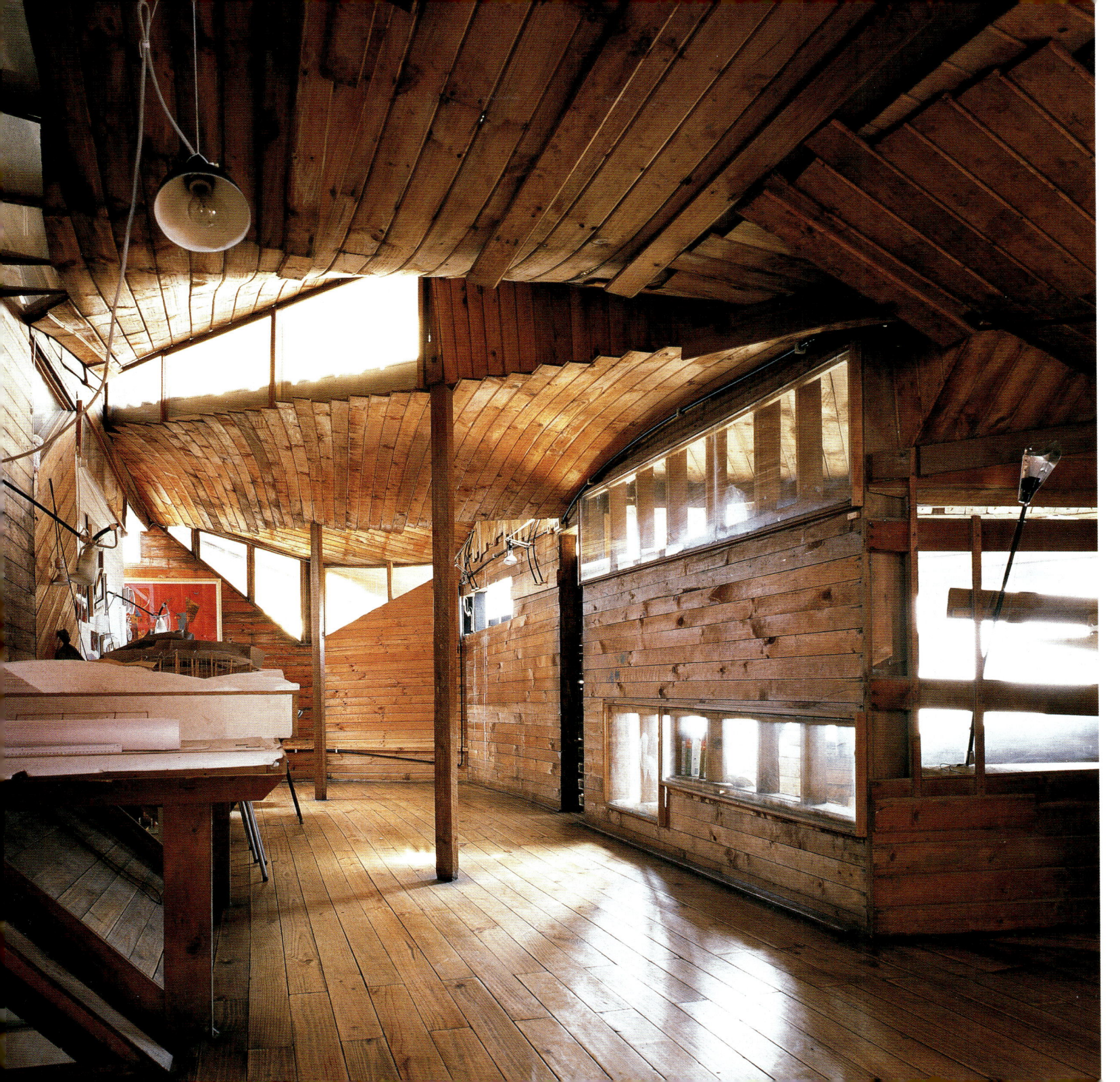

1

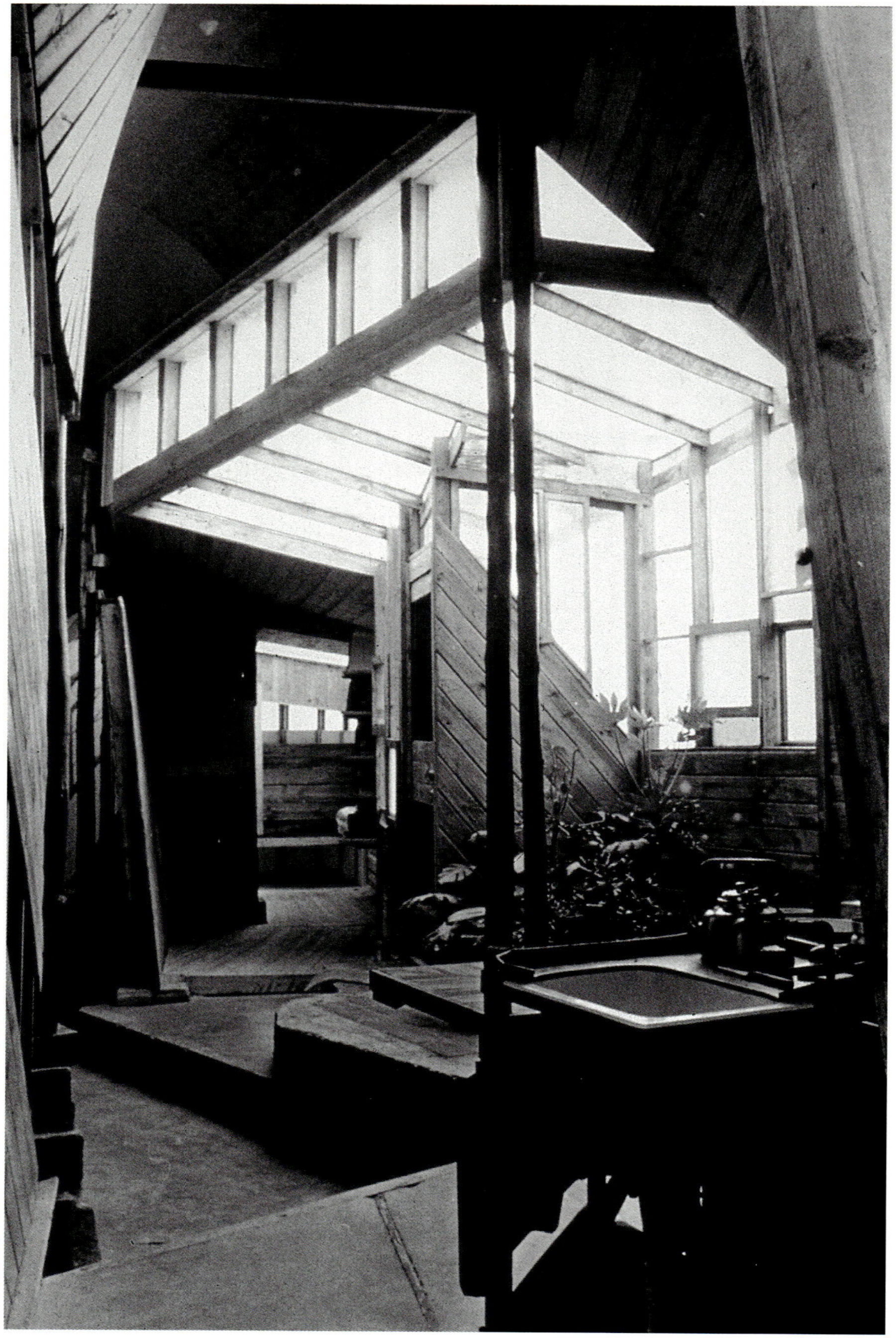

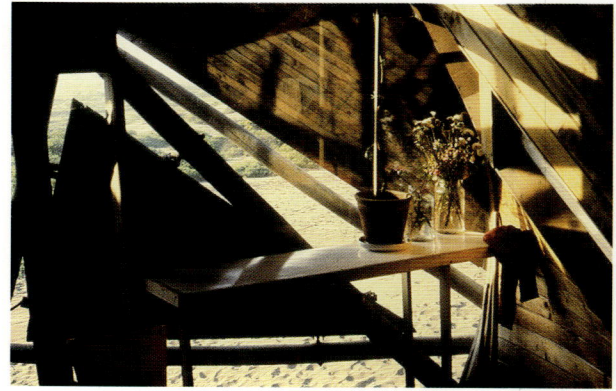
2

104

1 Interior view from the kitchen
2 Detail of the interior paintwork of the walls
3 Exterior view and access to *El Confín*
4 General plan: the *nuclei* of the two end lodges are square-shaped; the constructions grow in an irregular fashion towards the outer edge

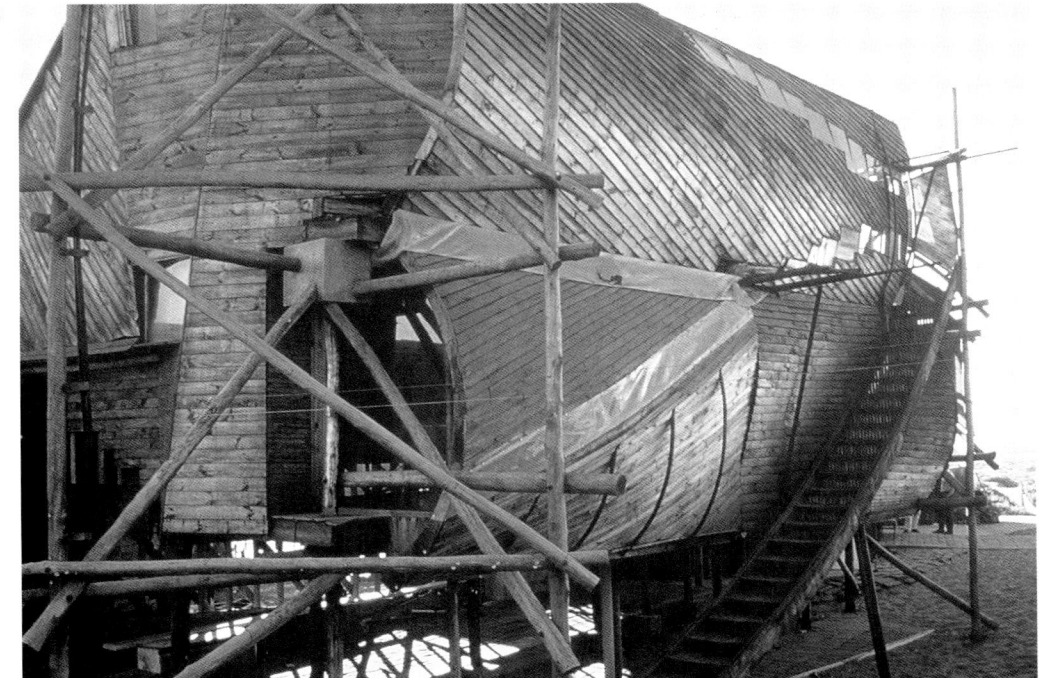

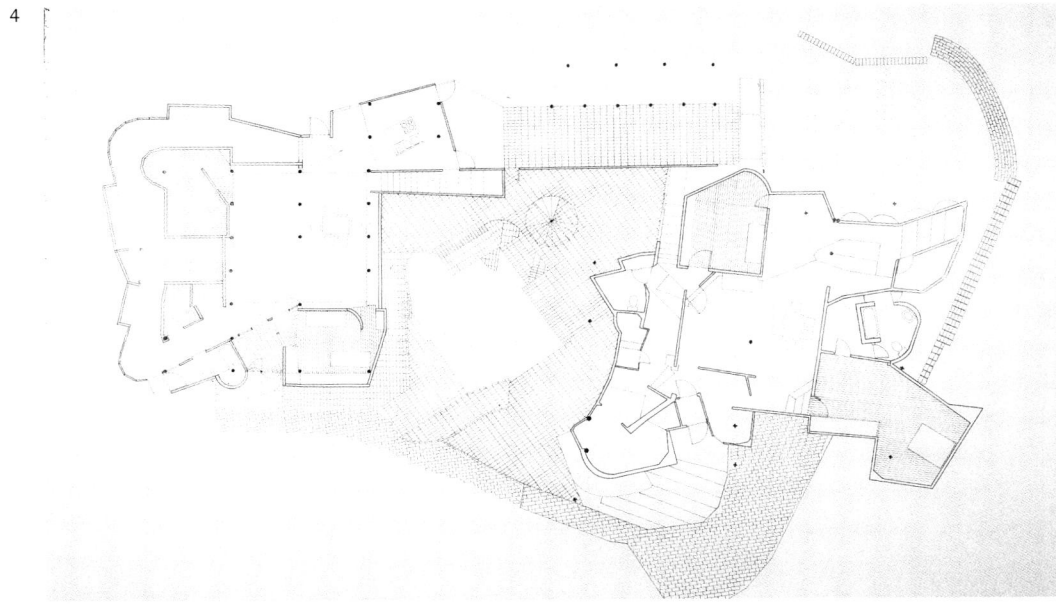

1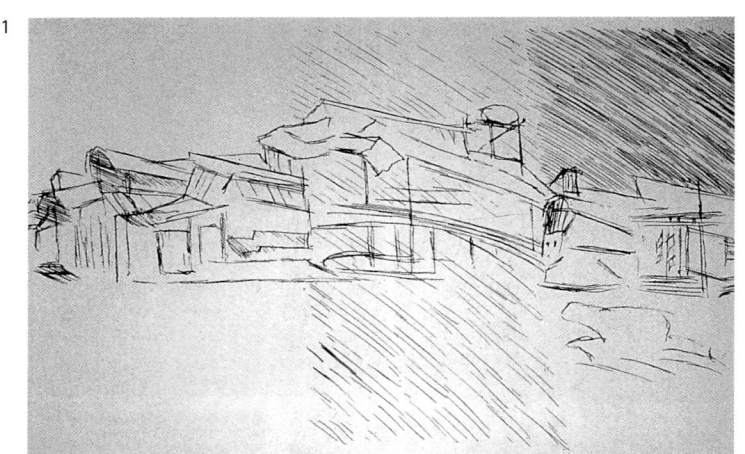

2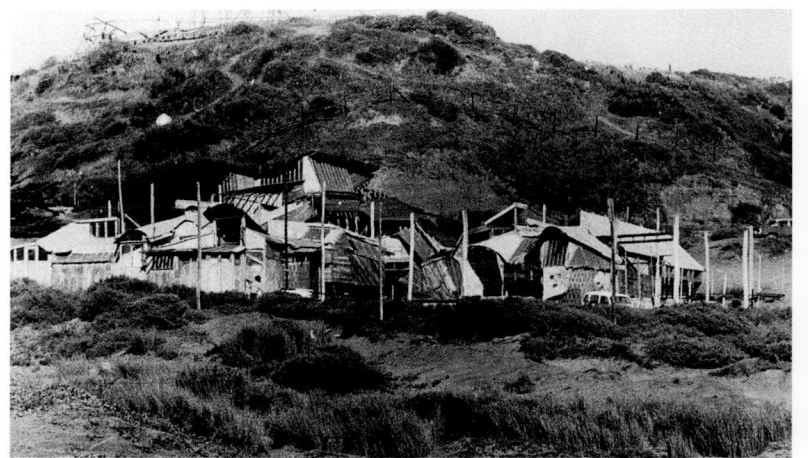

3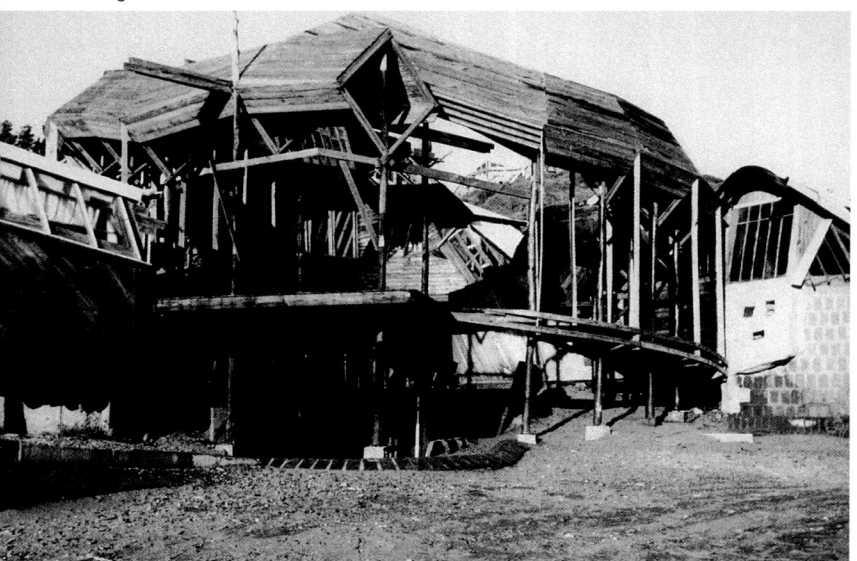

4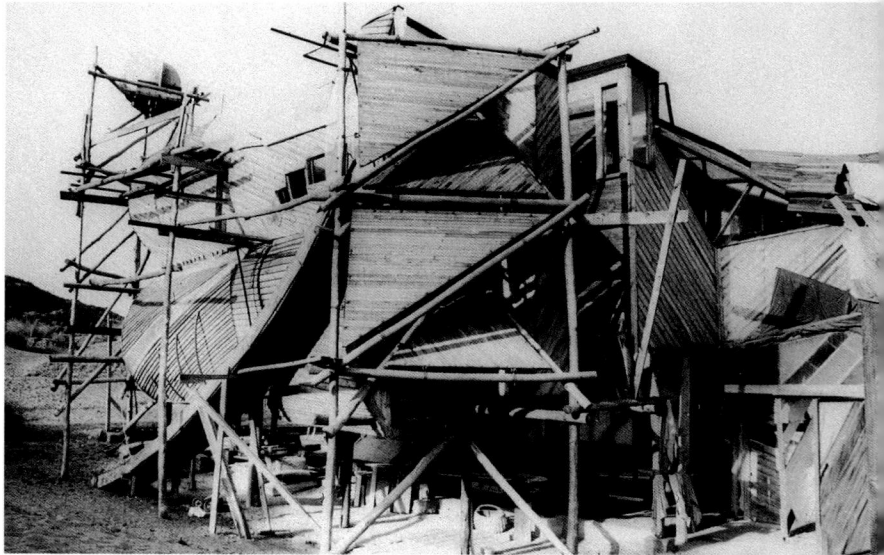

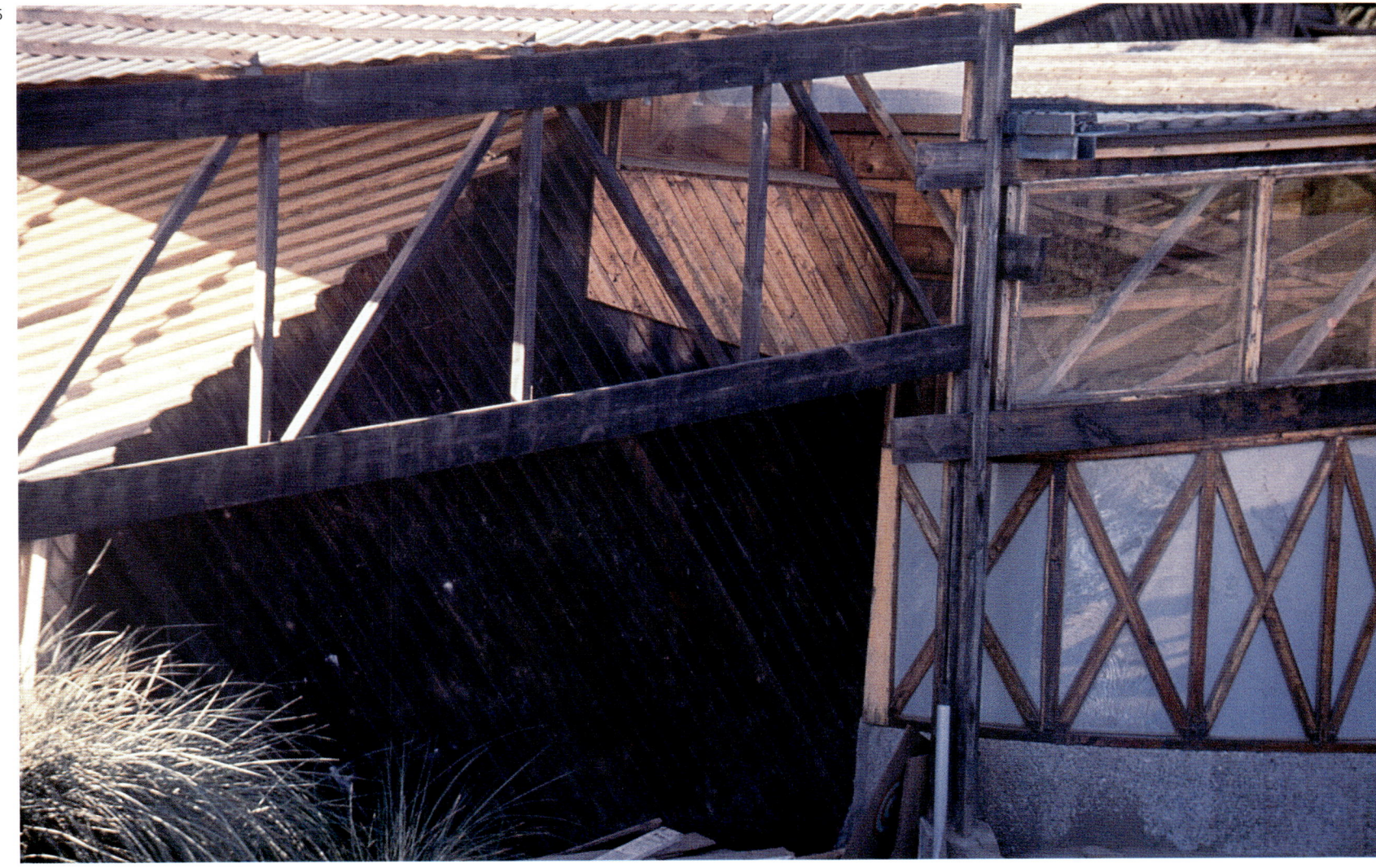

1 Sketch by Alberto Cruz
2 General view prior to the construction of the double roof
3 View from the access *patio*
4 First version of *El Confín*
5 Detail of the double roof

Temple, Cemetery and Gully

Open City, Ritoque, Quintero
Juan Ignacio Baixas, Jorge Sánchez, Juan Purcell
1976 ...

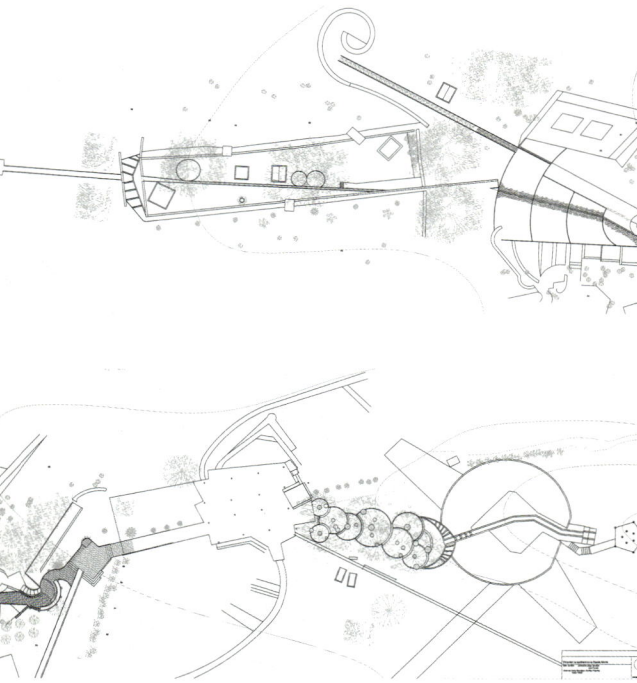

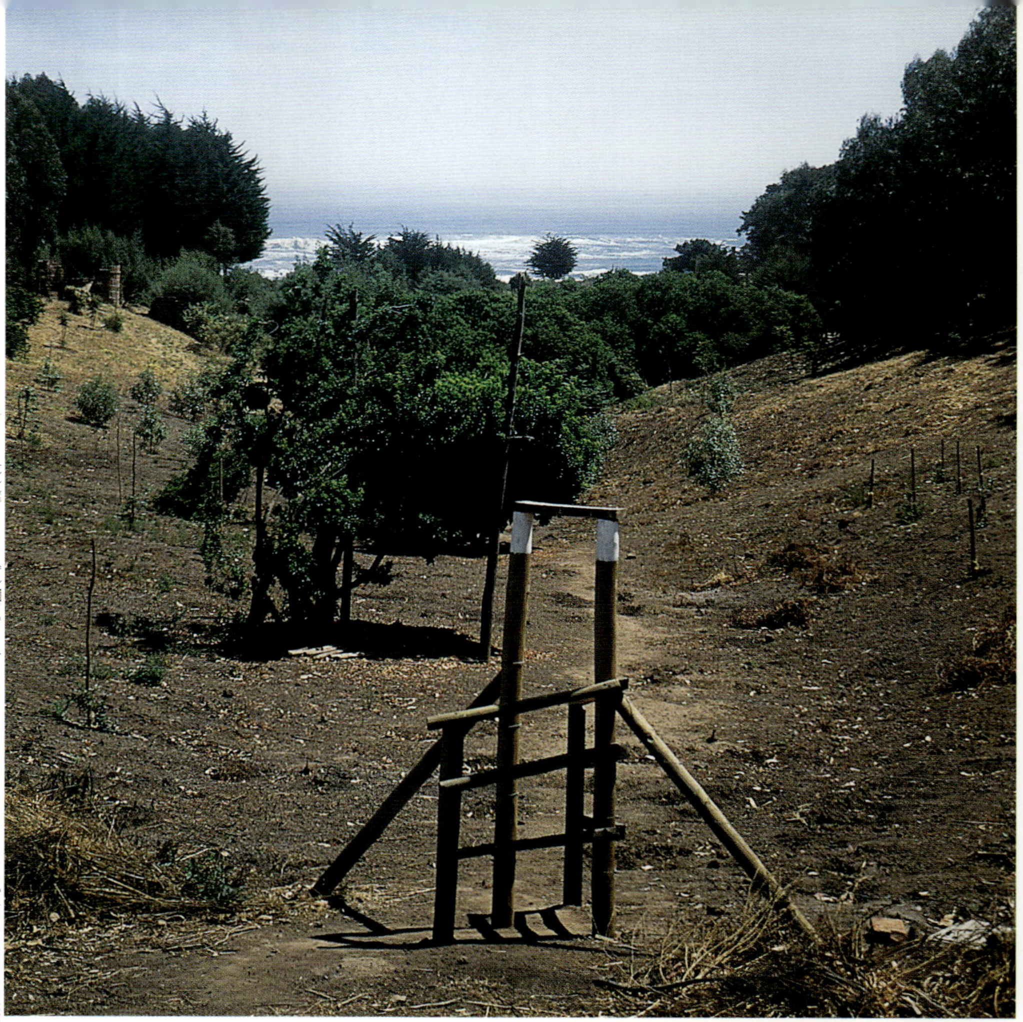

A *phalène* or poetry-reading act was held before building work commenced on the site. Four fires were consecutively lit at the end of four paths. The reading began while the first fire was burning. By the end of that reading the following fire was already burning. Lines were paced out between each of the fires to create a trapezoid that marked the layout of the work.

In the cemetery, located on the floor of a gully, the values of the landscape predominate: ground, vegetation and views. The foliage consists mainly of a tight mass of indigenous perennial trees and bushes, growing more densely towards the lower end of the gully, where other exotic species, such as palms and cypresses, were planted. In this way the cemetery has acquired the characteristics of a park—an interior space in the middle of the extensive untamed ground of the Open City.

The layout of the design took into consideration the dead and their links with the Open City. Three groups were defined, each with its own area in the cemetery: an area for the guests, one for the founders and one for their relatives. The works extend along a system of long axes, each one following a different direc-

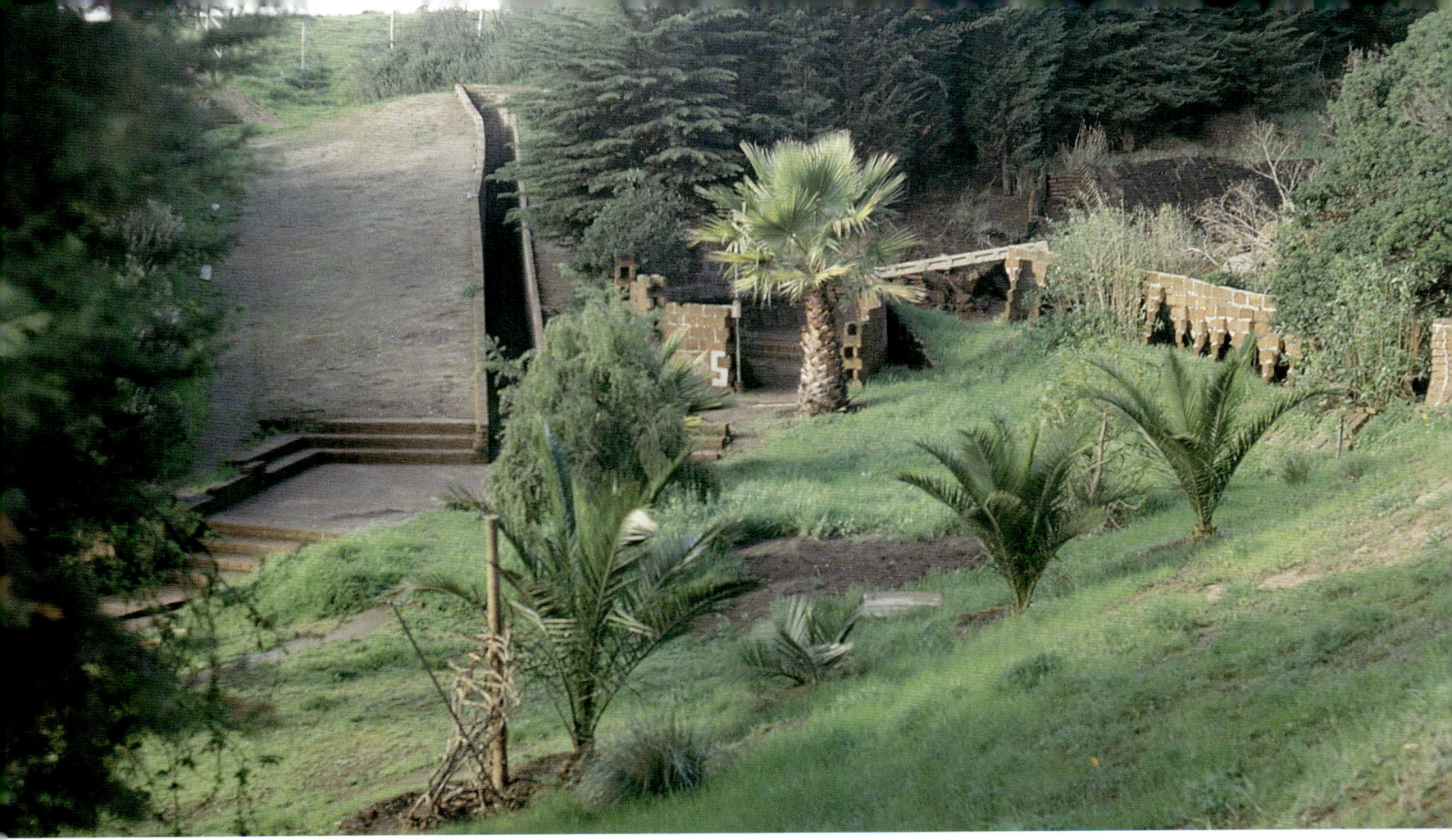

tion. All of the axes have headpieces, formed by individual works. Each pair is made up of complementary pieces; thus, each construction forms part of another. The headpieces are arranged in spiral patterns, to establish a transition between the concentrated and the extensive. The crossover nodes offer a choice of routes along the bottom of the gully or over the hills towards the higher ground. The *nuclei* of tombs are spread along the paths, arranged in accordance with the three groups described above.

The central *nucleus* of the ensemble is defined by the chapel, the meeting point of all the axes, whose shape has recently been altered to accommodate a new altar and a roof of translucent membranes that unfold like a series of sails over the brickwork floor: naturally, this site fulfils the role of the ceremonial area of the cemetery.

Owing to its location, the cemetery can only be perceived from nearby and from above. The sails of the chapel stand out above the foliage. Its interiority is such that the horizon of the sea cannot be seen from the bottom of the gully.

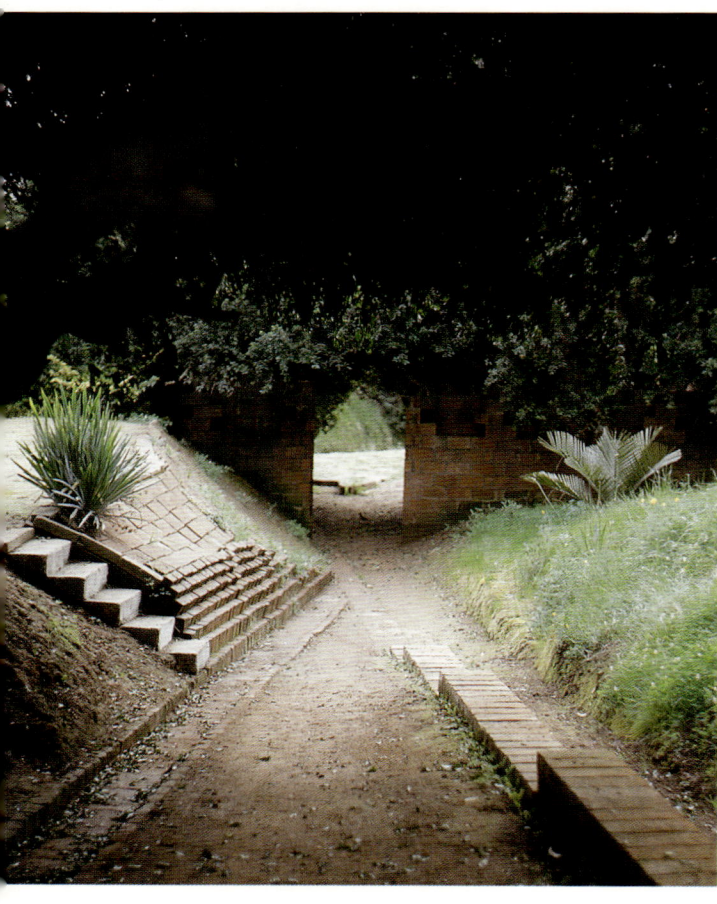

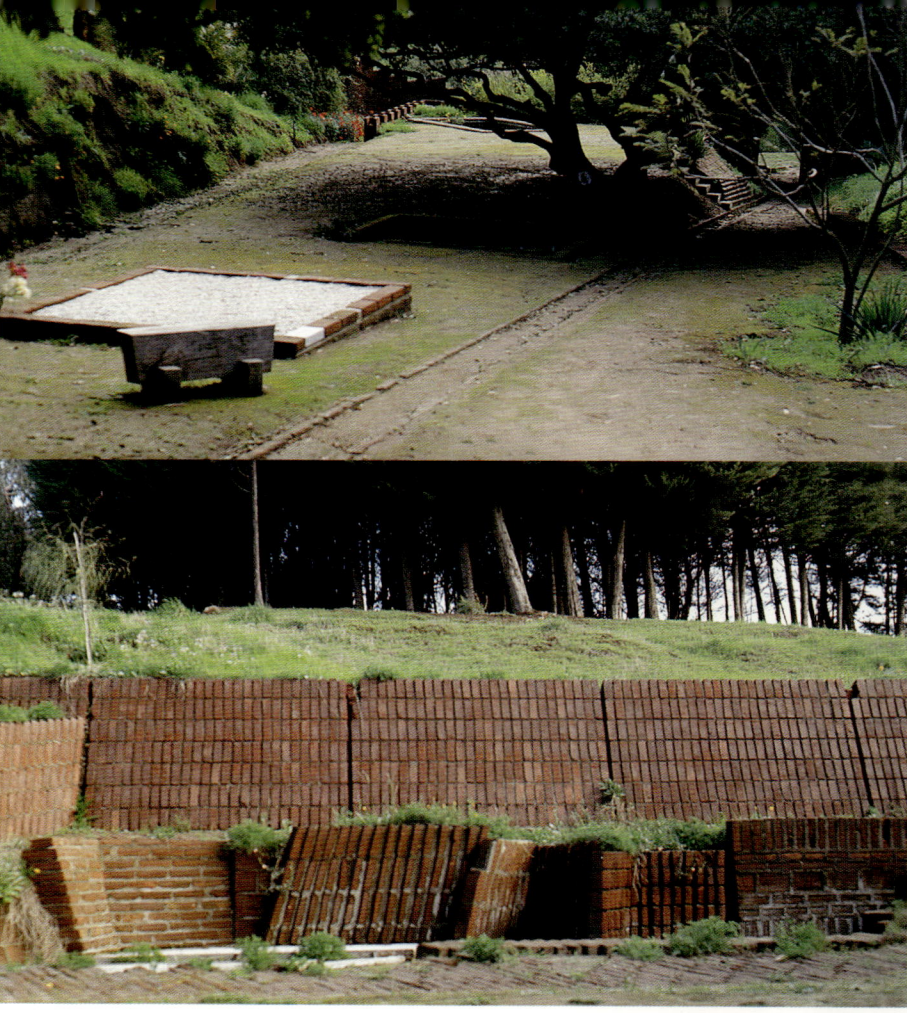

1, 2 and 3 Long axis: banks and tombs constructed in red brick
4, 5 and 6 *The Well*, sculpture by Claudio Girola

The sculpture titled El Pozo (The Well) was made by Claudio Girola as part of a poetic act. During the event, the sculptor drew an outline on the side of the hill and drilled into it, thereby making the first excavation on site without the aid of any plans. At first, the work consisted simply of a hole carved in the side of the hill. But once the conditions of the terrain were considered, containing walls were constructed to ensure that the work would survive. As a result, in this bas-relief sculpture, the definition of the arris outlining the rupture of the surface has been highlighted.

The transition towards the interior follows a horizontal path that turns before reaching a chamber of quadrangular contours where, in the absence of any other horizon, the presence of the sky is strongly felt. The elbow or bend in the path was conceived as a site of sufficient intensity to counteract the relationship between passageway—preamble and chamber—destination. Subtle differentiations characterize the walls, whether in their geometries and forms, or in their

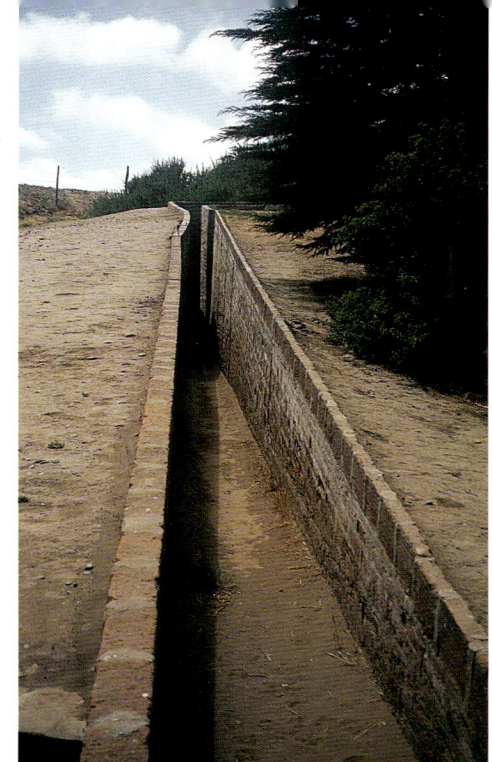

4

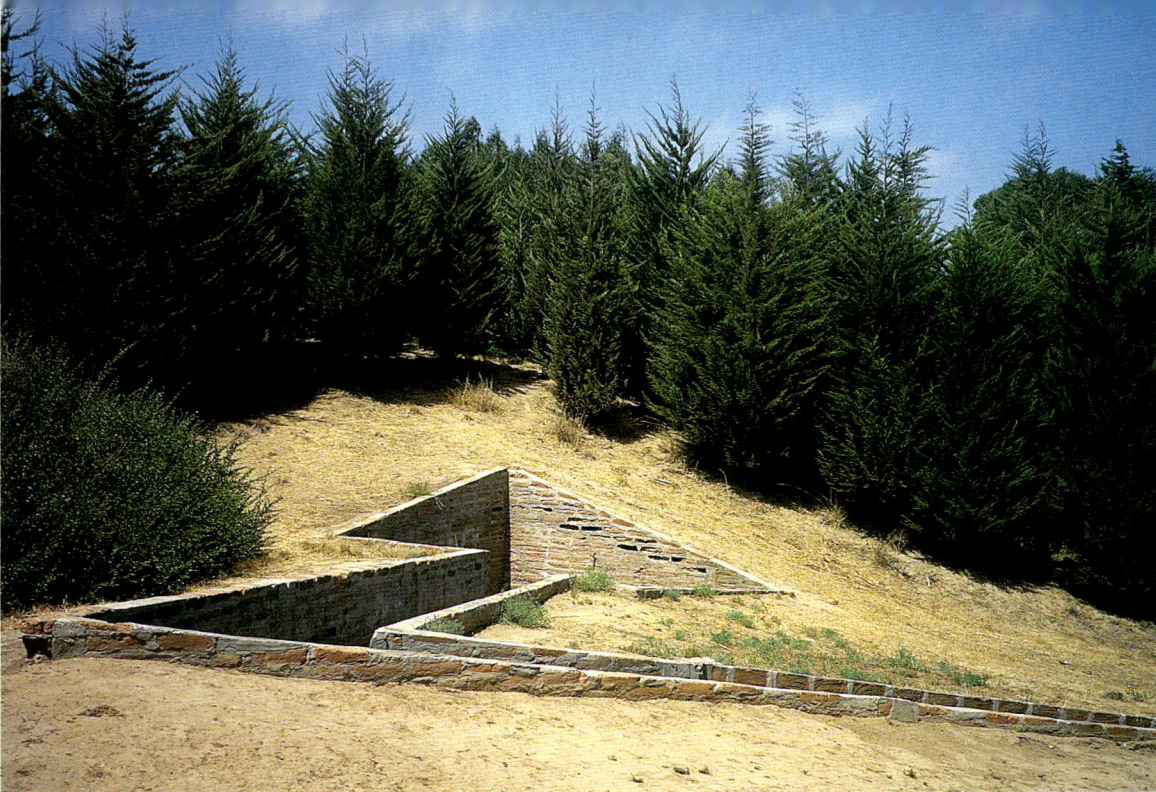

5

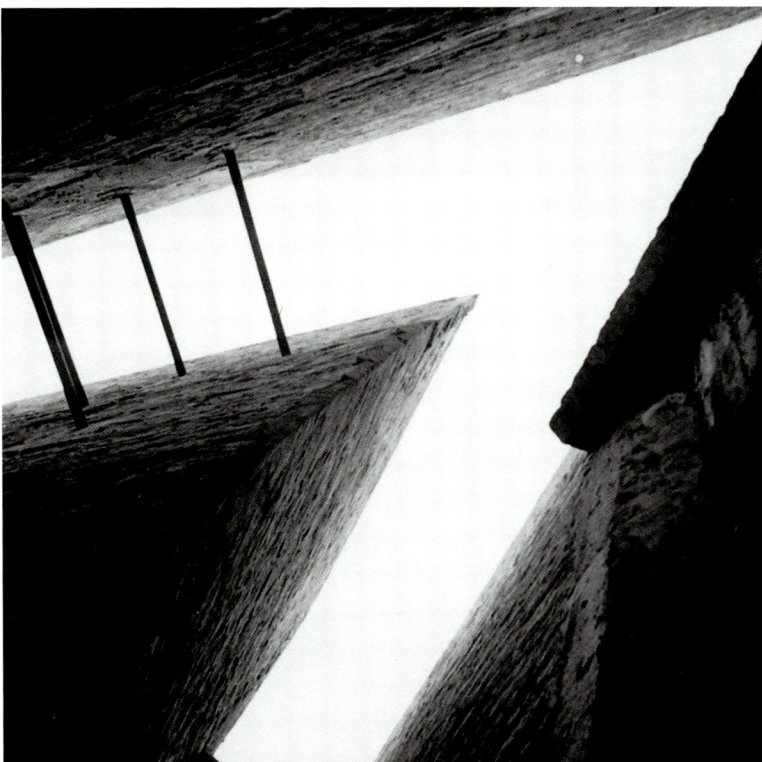

6

material textures. As with other sculptures in the Open City, The Well calls into question the traditional notion of the sculptural plinth, albeit with a greater degree of radicality.

In similar fashion to the Palace of Dawn and Dusk, brick is the dominant material here, both for the floor and the containing walls, furnishings, tombs and individual objects. But in the cemetery the earth, too, acquires a special value, particularly in the areas where the roots of the trees have been uncovered by excavations, revealing them as an inverted structure of interwoven branches forging a path through the earth.

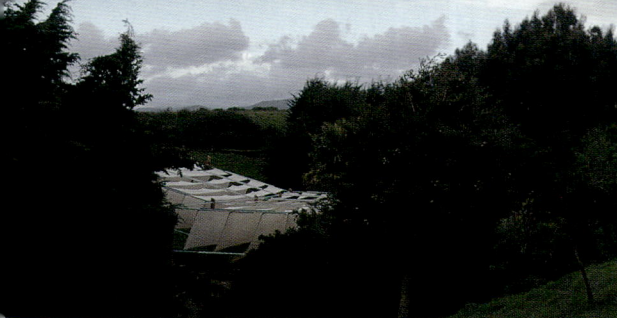

General view and details of the open-air chapel: red brick floor, roof of white mesh over a metal and wooden structure

Facing page, clockwise:
Promenade at the bottom of the gully, towards the chapel, in the form of an atrium or antechamber to the church
Amphitheatre
Stairway to the gully and detail of the handrail, by first year students at the School

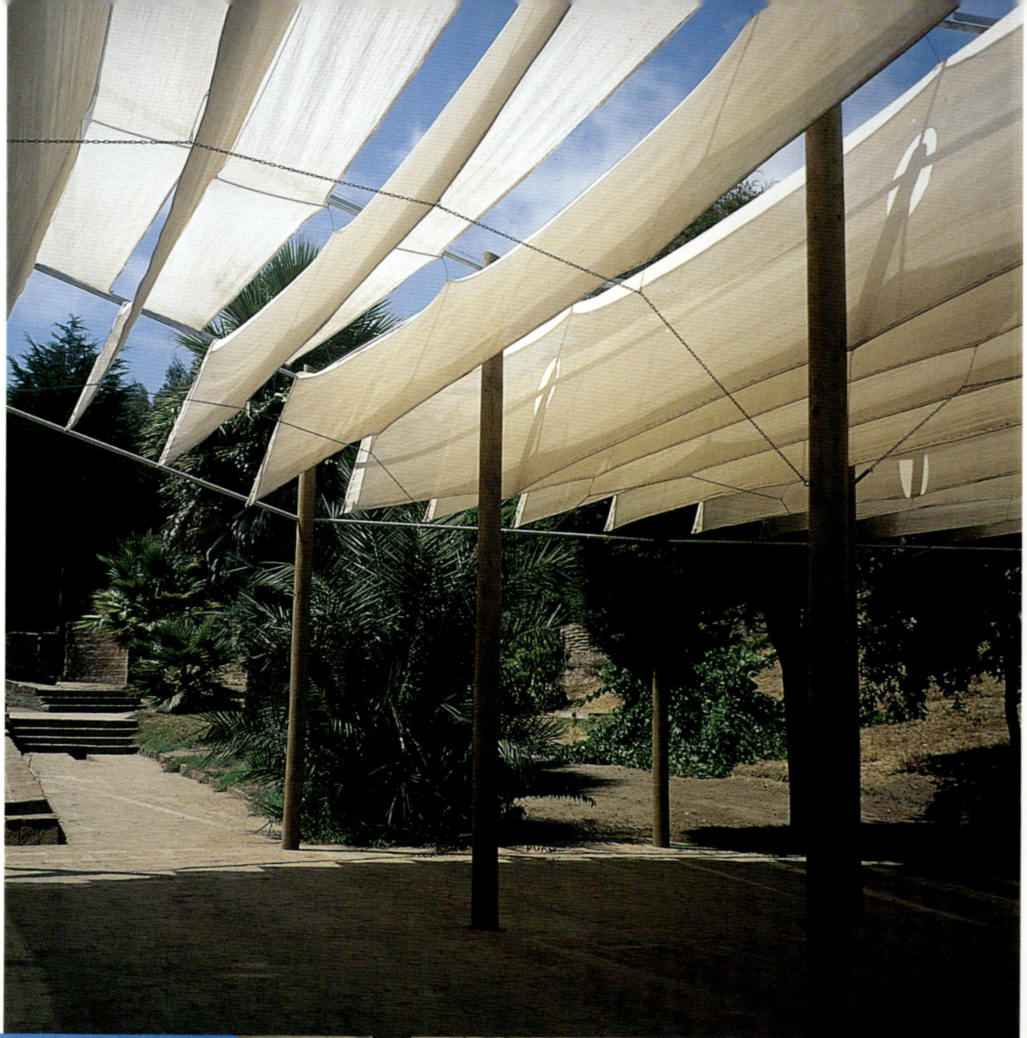

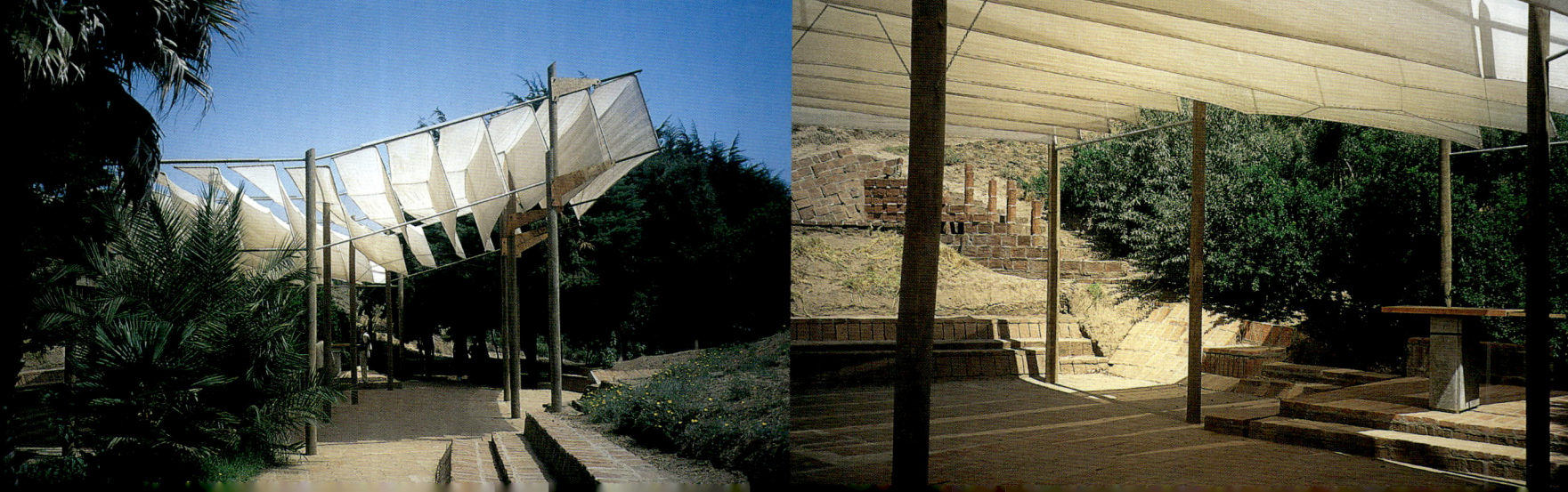

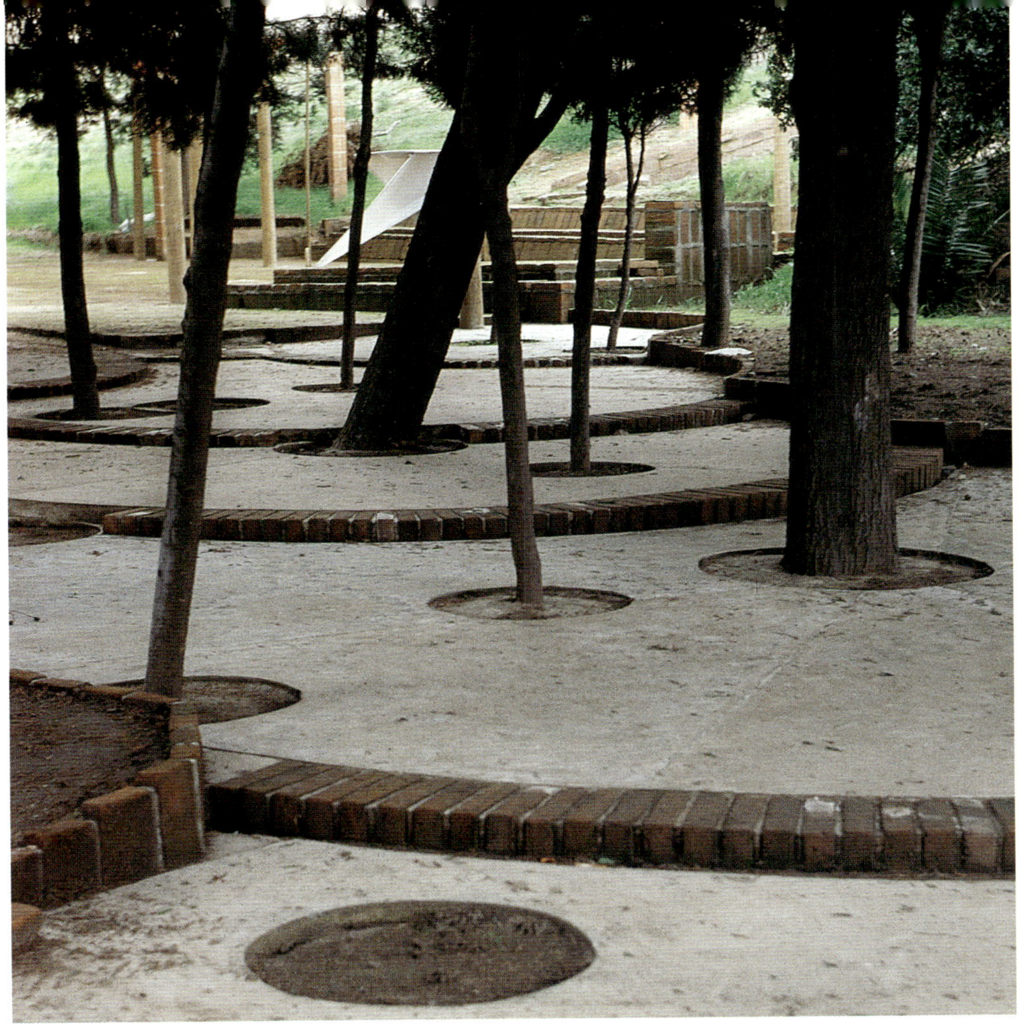

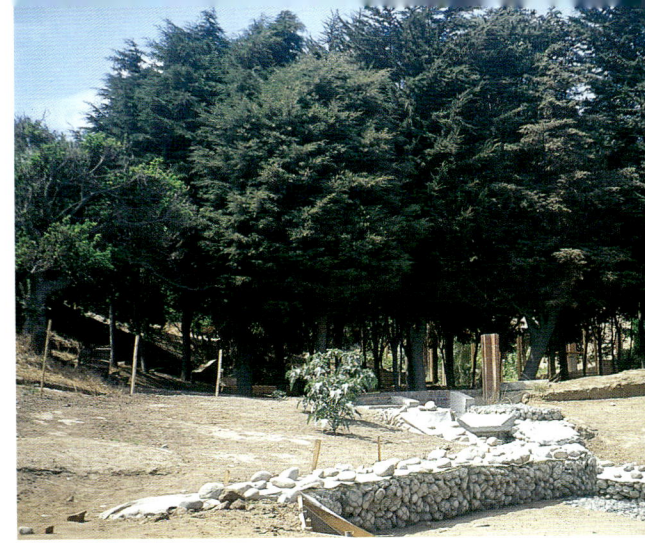
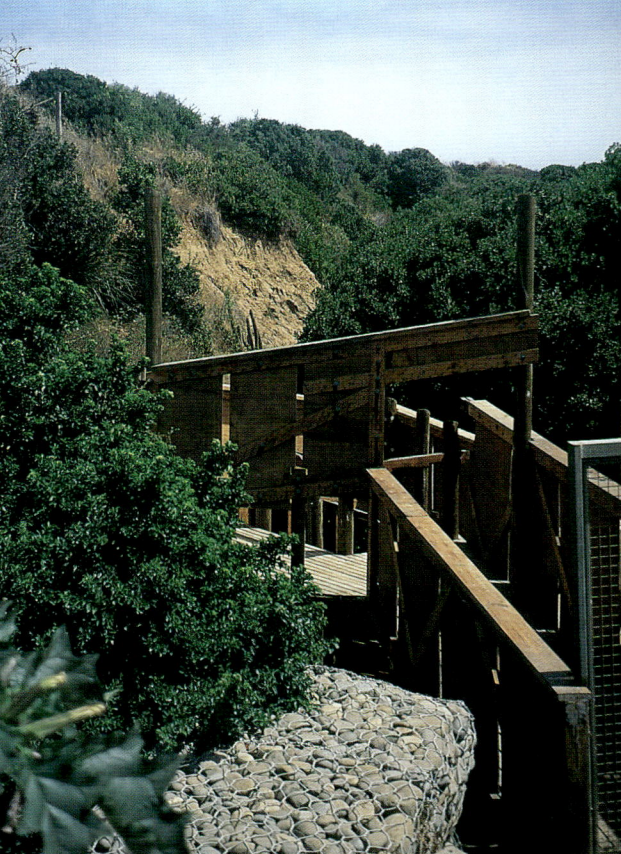
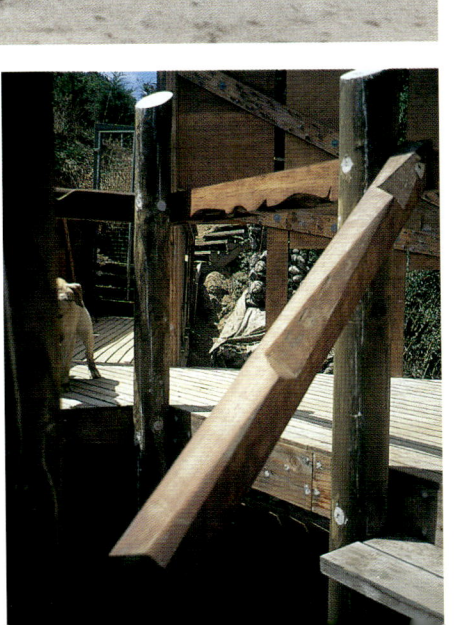

Prototype Workshop

Open City, Ritoque, Quintero
Boris Ivelic, Fabio Cruz, Juan Ignacio Baixas,
Open City Group
1990

The workshop was built by Object Design students during a period of *travesía* in two work shifts, each one lasting three weeks and formed by a group of 16 students who first prefabricated the construction elements and later assembled them on site. The excavation work and the masonry were carried out by skilled workers. The half-buried interior has two main walls—an open wall made of glass and a closed wall leaning against the ground—and can be accessed from both sides. The worktables were planned by designers, as were the lighting mechanisms. The upper plane, occupied by structural systems, generates a dense, foliage-like grid, while the lower visual horizon is open and clear. There are two workshops in the immediate neighbourhood, forming an ensemble of manual workshops sharing common exterior spaces. Once again, a reformulation of the idea of the sculptural pedestal appears in this work, this time formed by the sloping plane of the roof terrace, the surface of which was initially left free and later provided the setting for the group of sculptures by José Balcells.

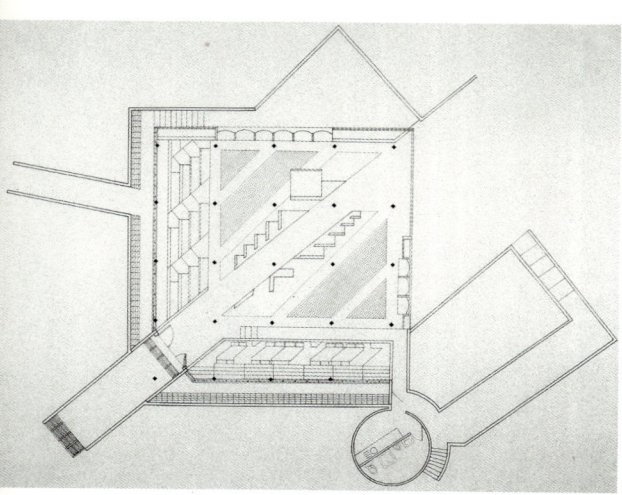

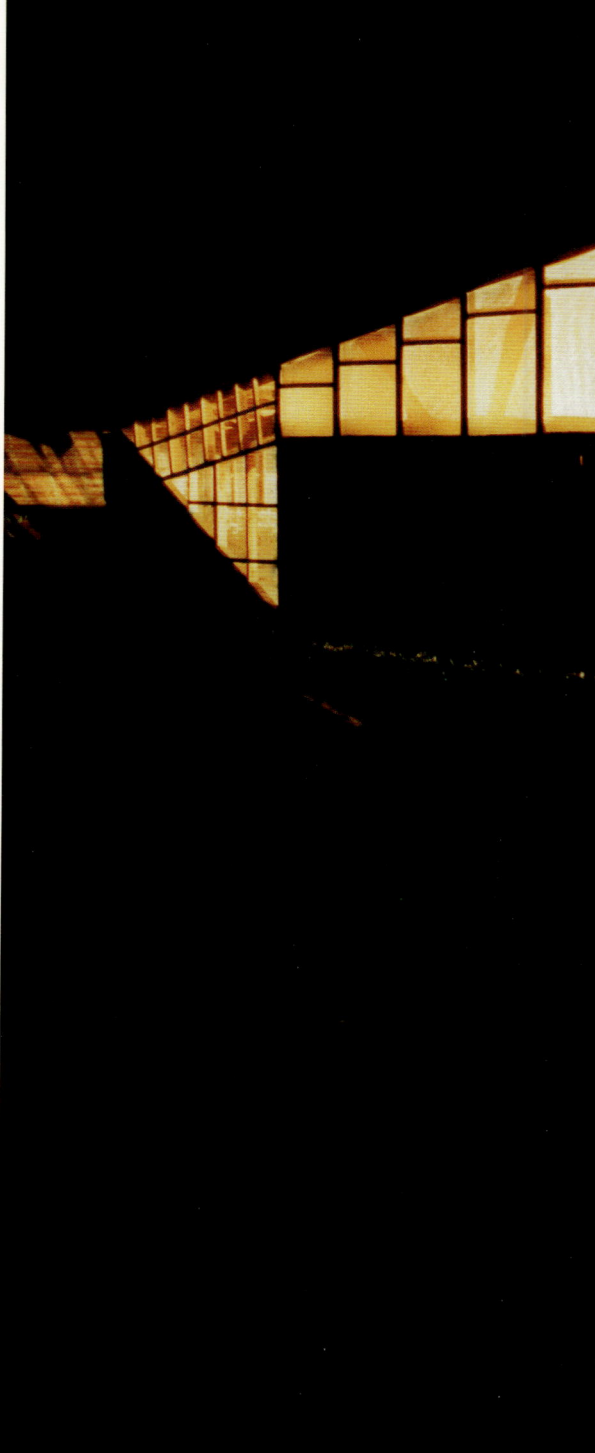

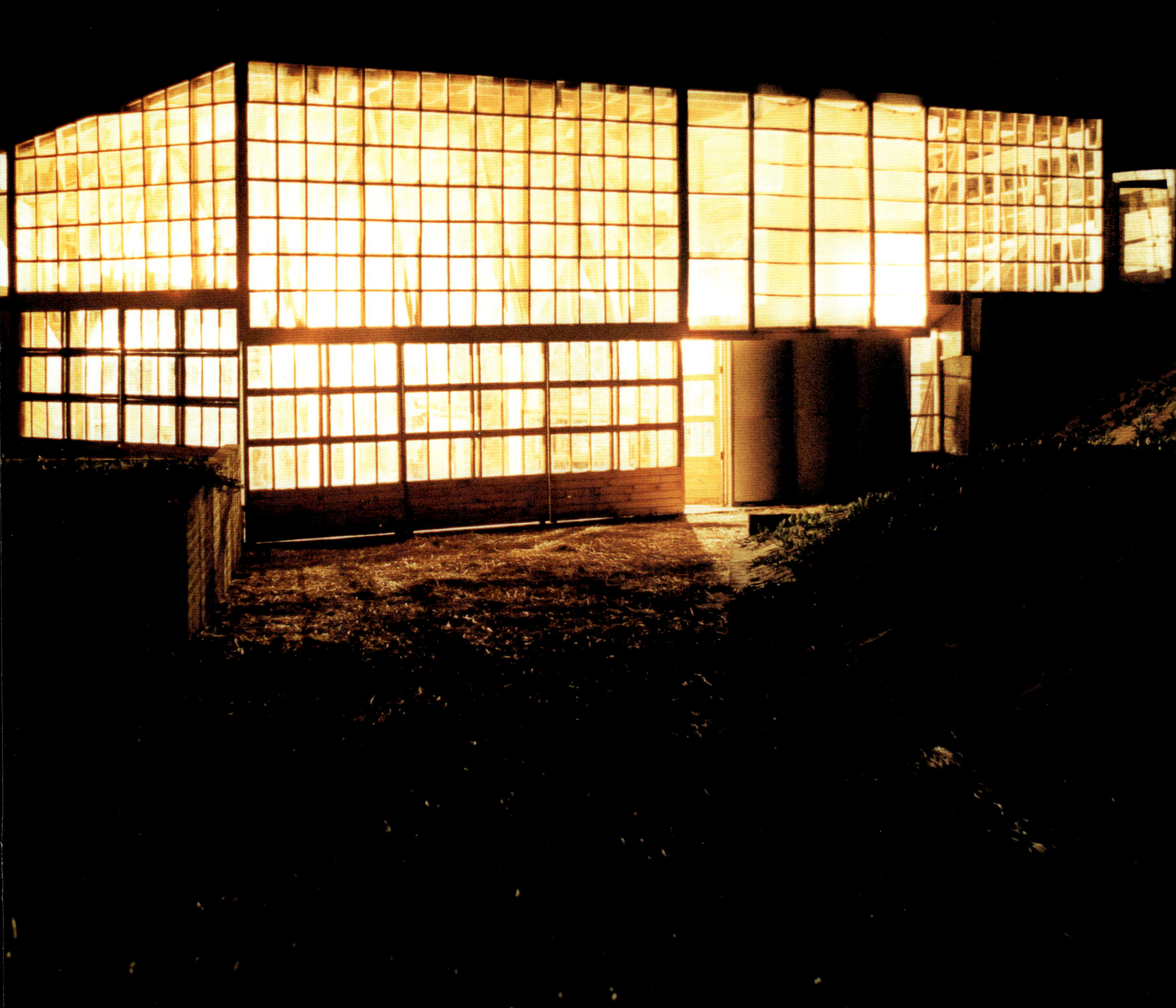

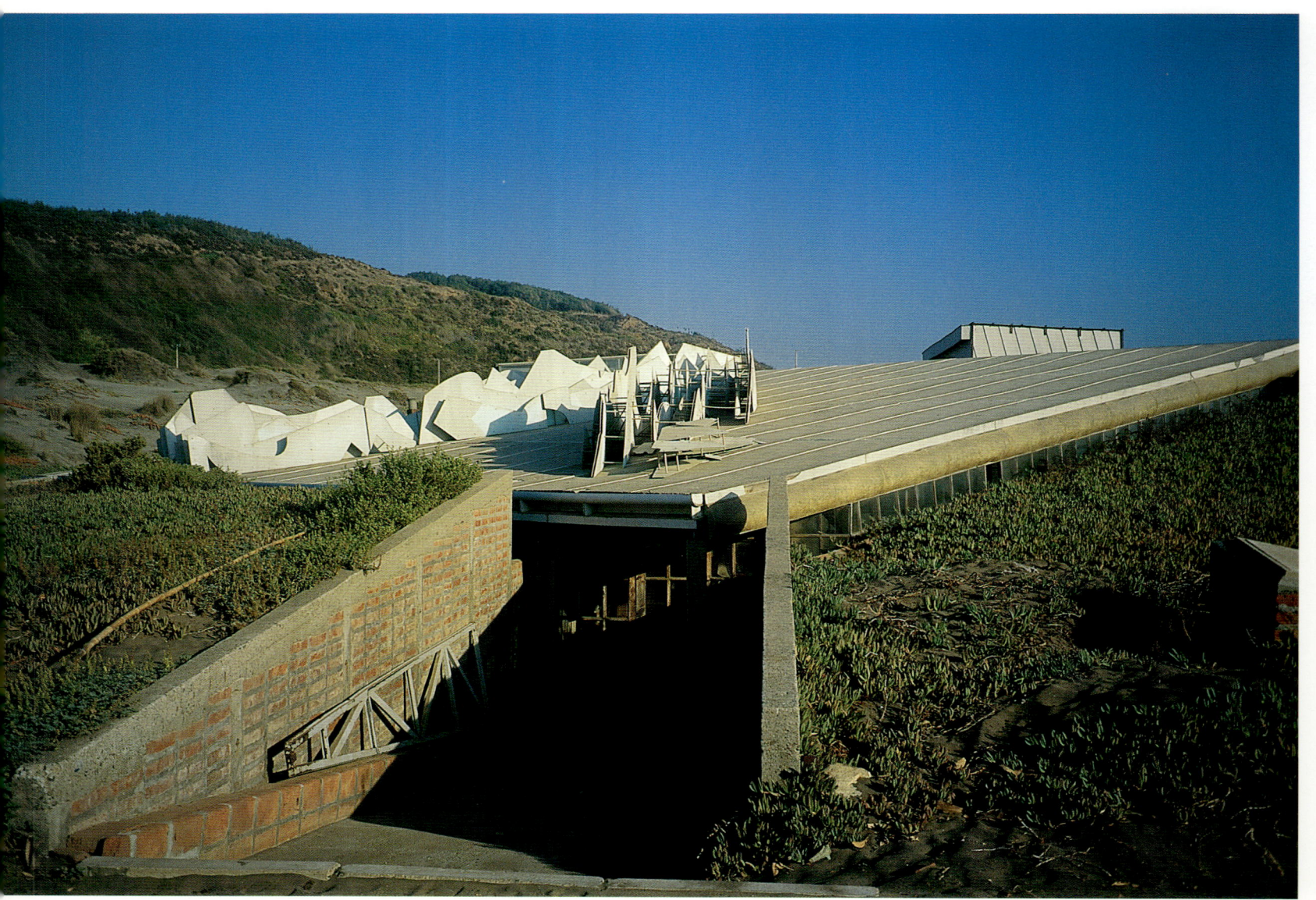

Access vertex

Right:
Access trench and roof with sculpture by José Balcells, and *above*, access to the workshop in its initial state

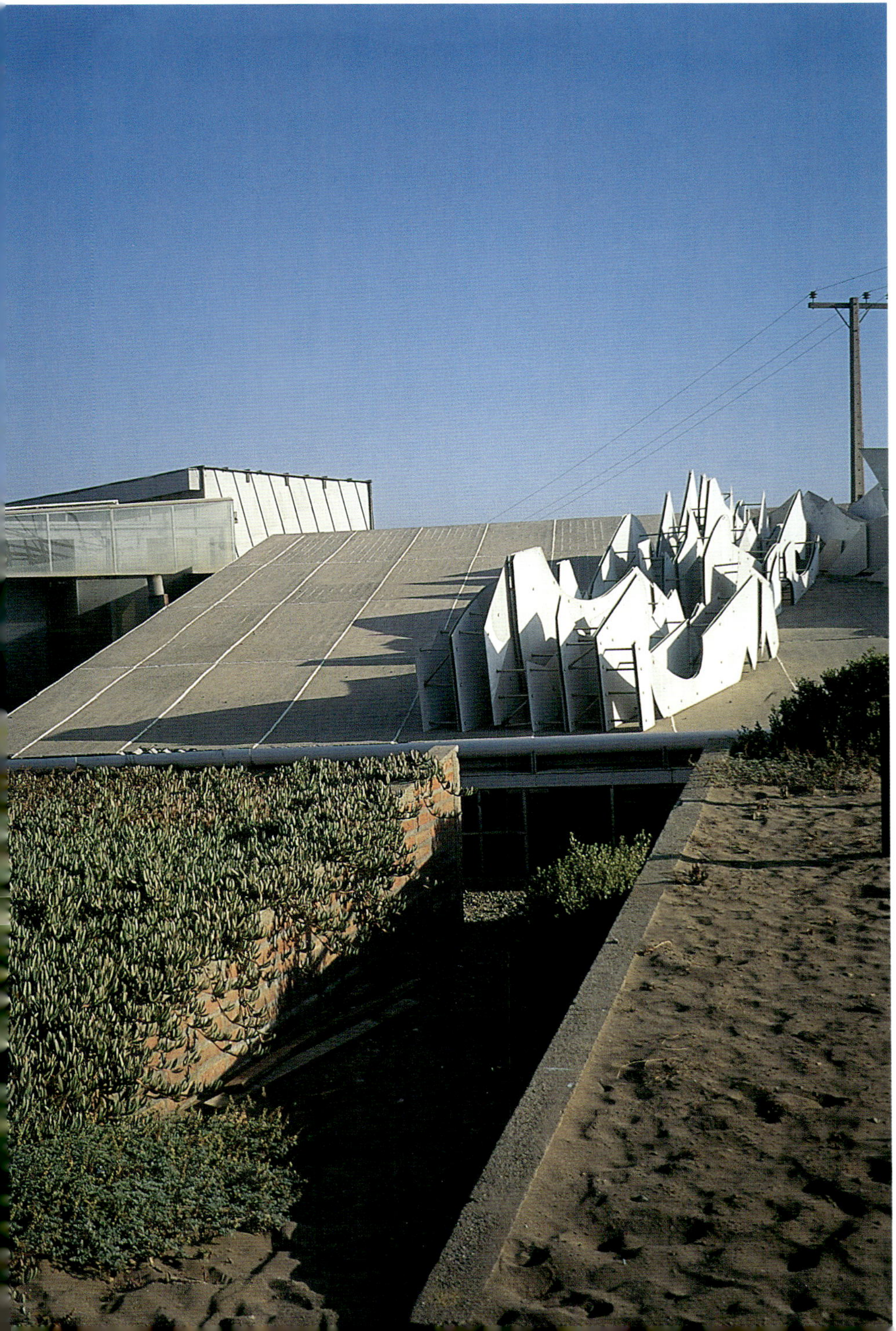

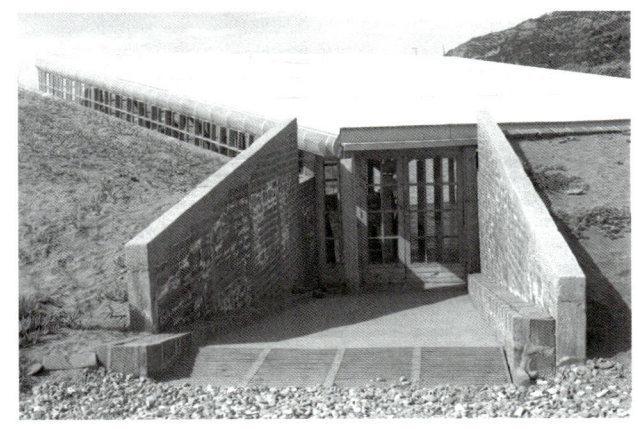

1

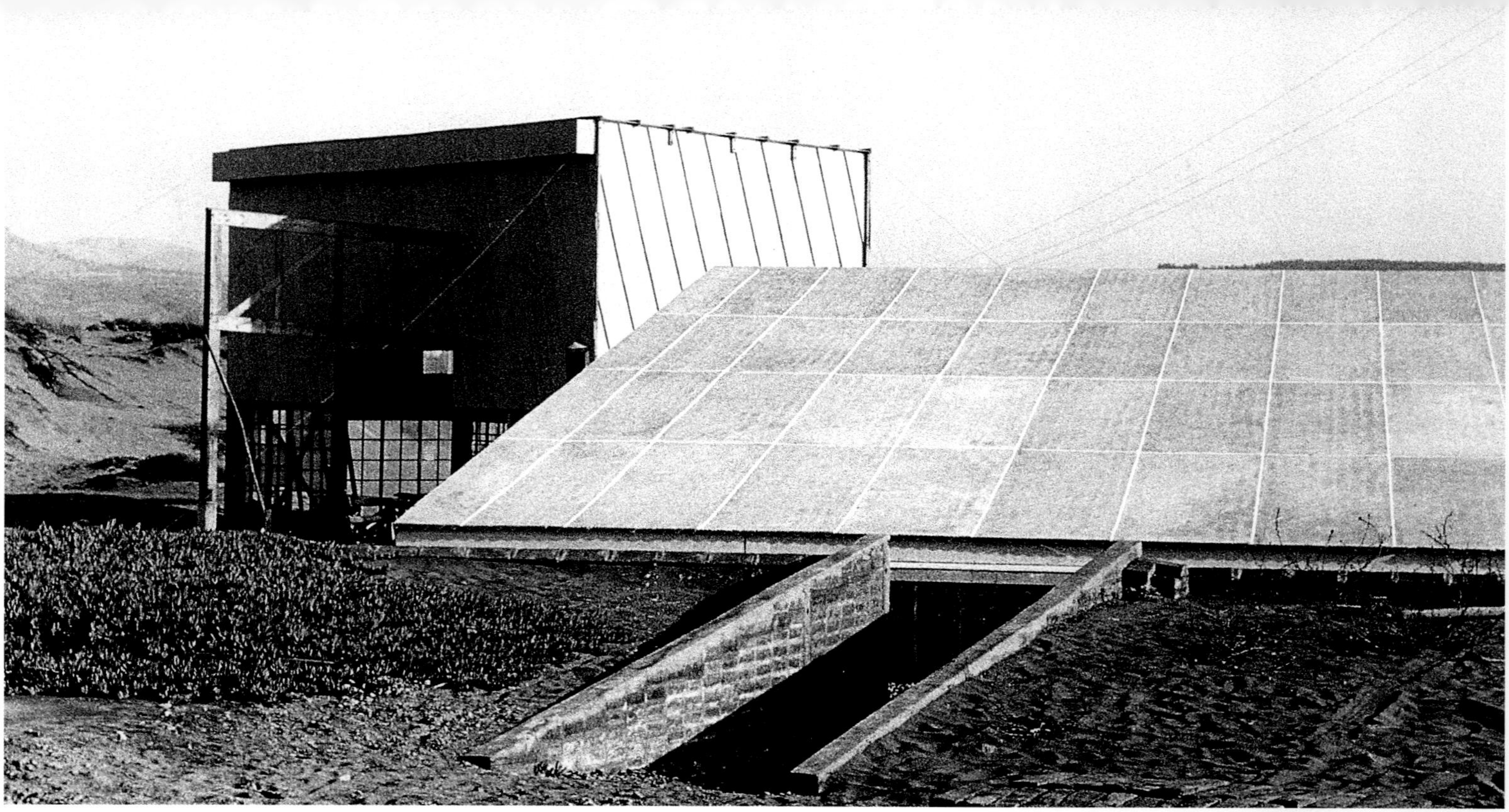

2

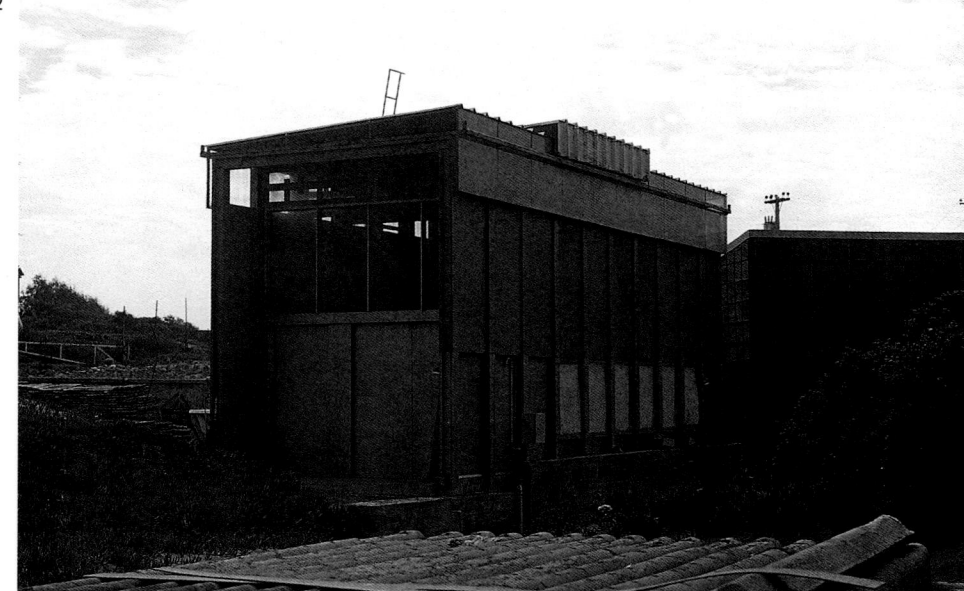

1 Workshop
2 Sculptor's Workshop
3 Interior of the Prototype Workshop
4 Interior plinth of the Prototype Workshop in its initial state
5 South window of the Prototype Workshop

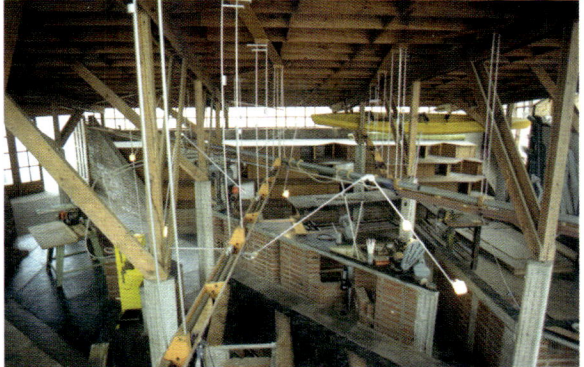
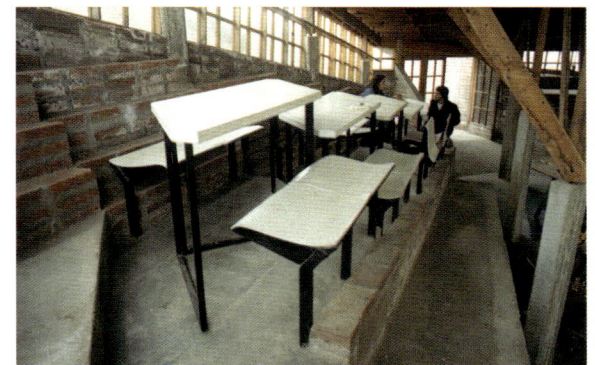

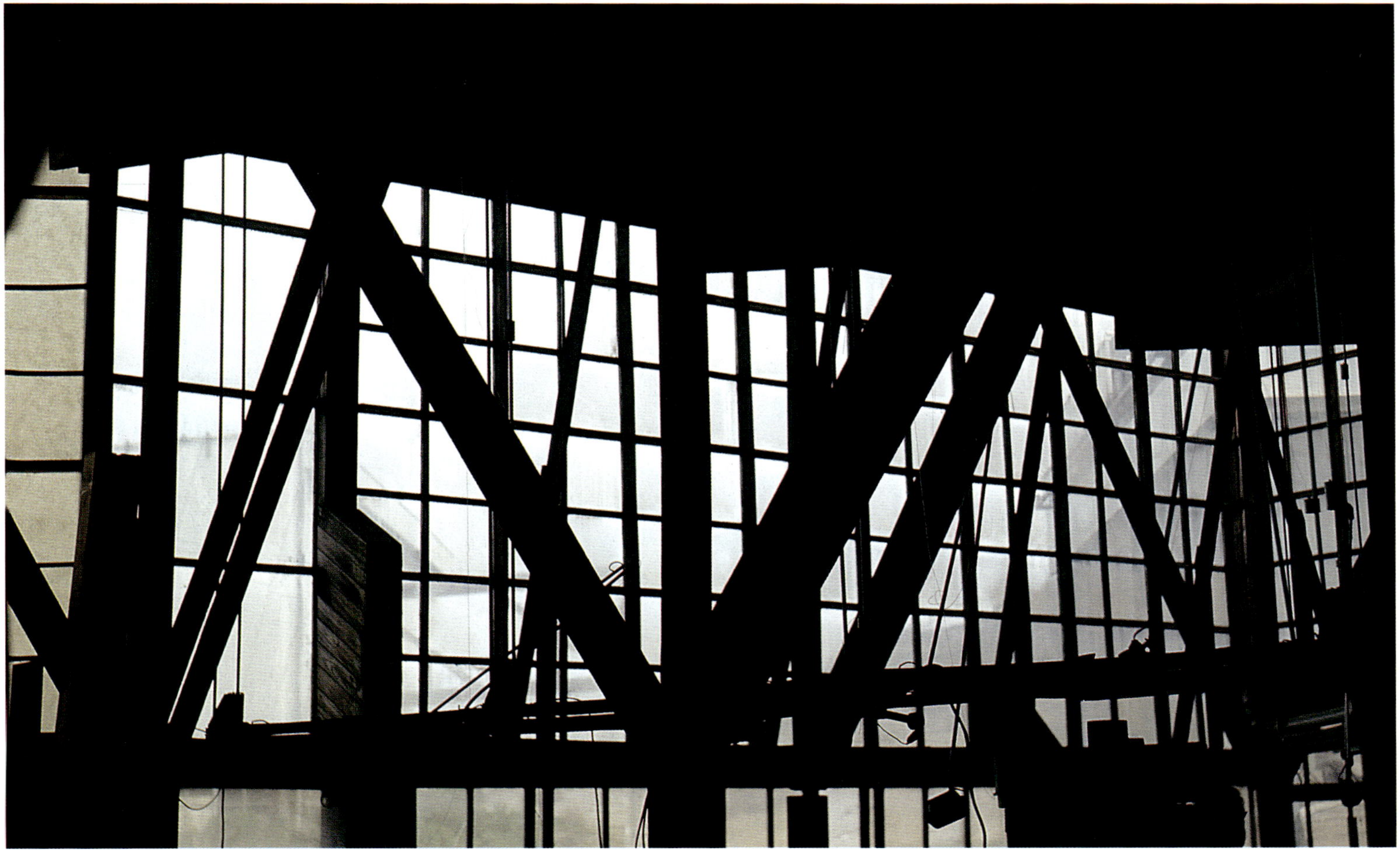

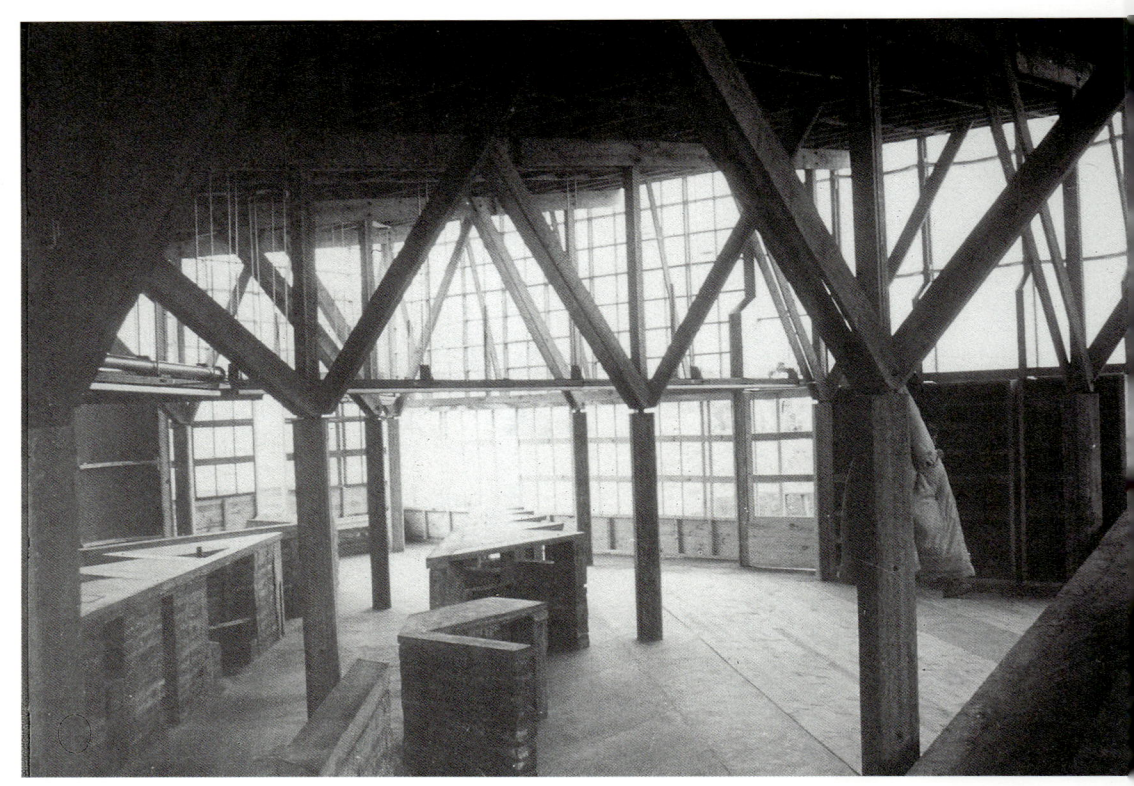
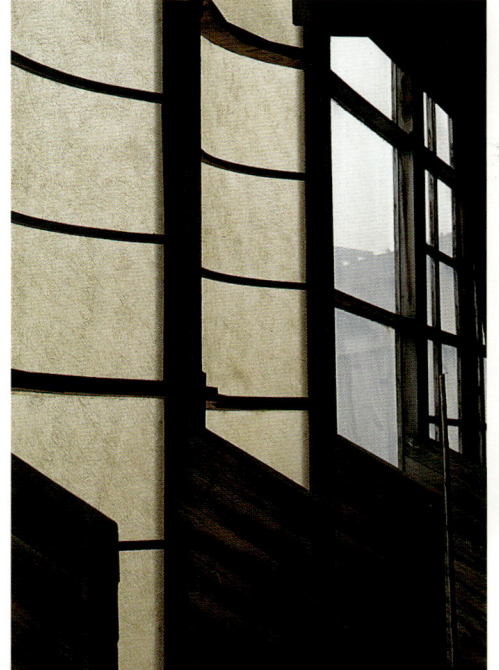
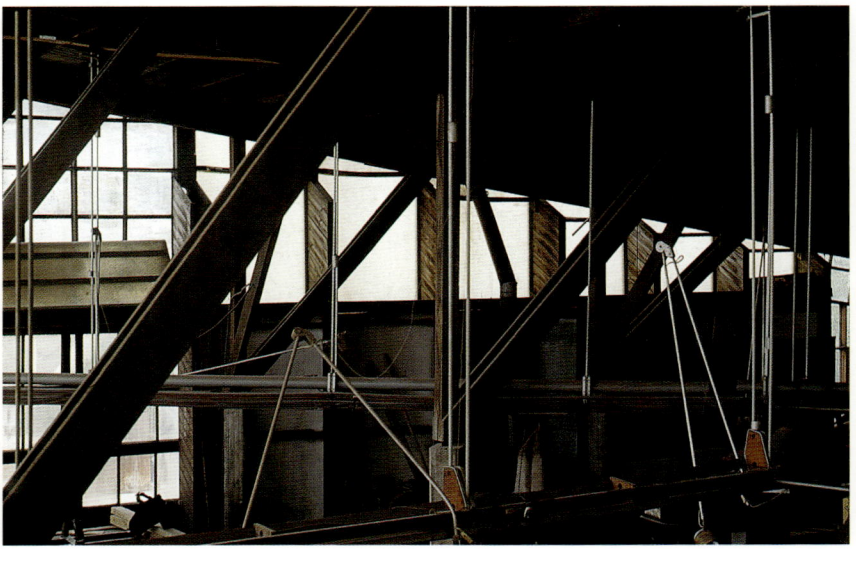

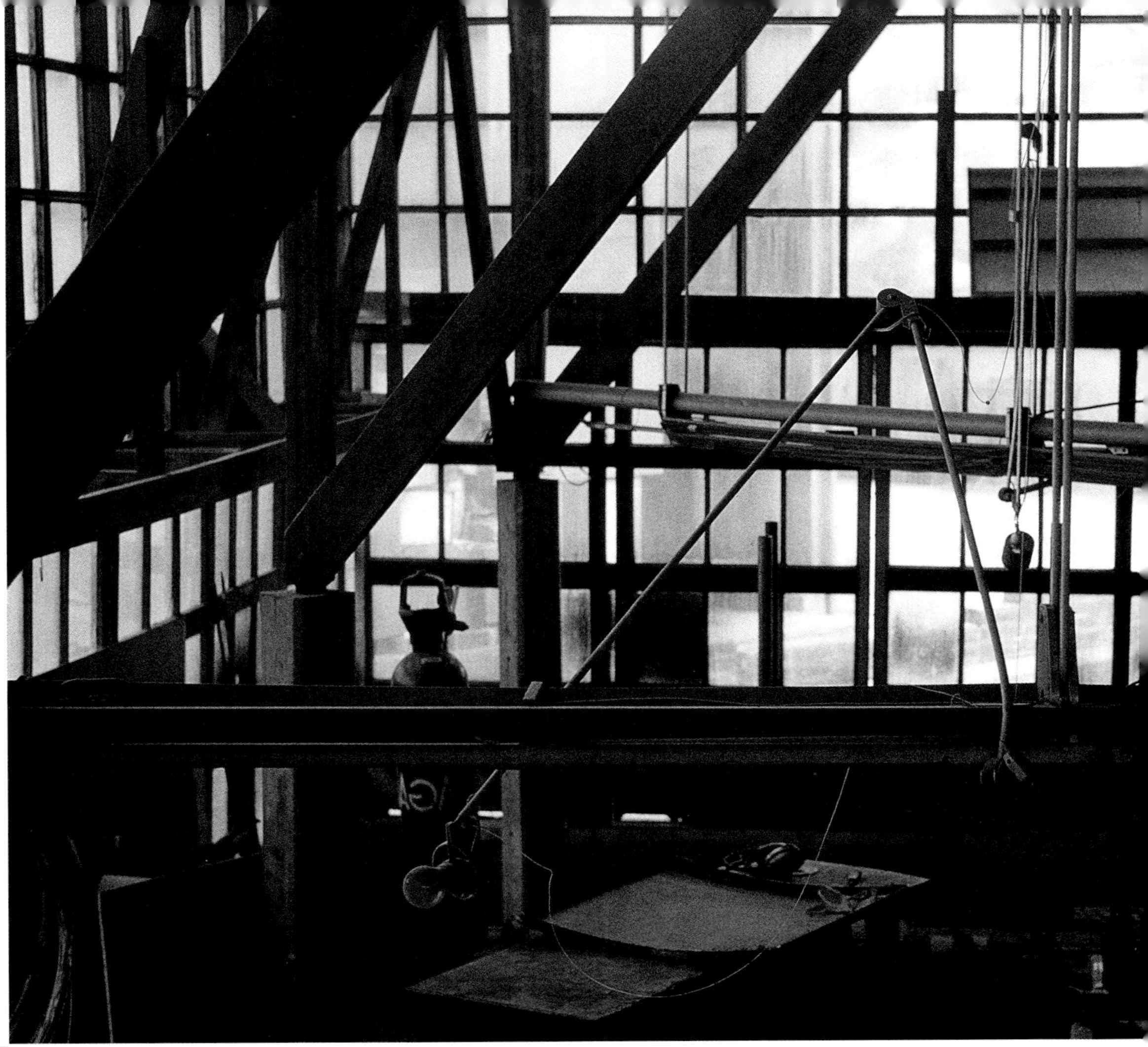

Prototype Workshop:
Previous page:
Glass and fibreglass skin
This page:
Details of knots and electrical installations

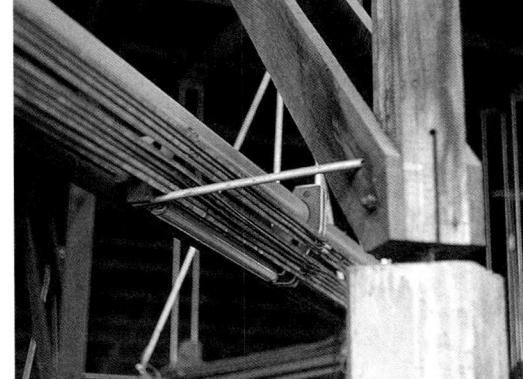

Works in Travesías

As there were nearly a hundred of these experiences, it is only natural that a large degree of diversity should manifest itself within the genre. As regards the motivations behind these *travesías*, some were undertaken at the request of a director of municipal works, while others came about as a direct result of an *Amereida* imperative. All of them, however, constituted a field of specific teaching experience of an educational nature, a field which stimulated the sense of opportunity of each undertaking, the capacity for improvisation, organization and the group sense. Little by little, the network of journeys undertaken covered the spaces of the American continent, with a greater density of *travesías* around certain poles which, for various reasons, became stable reference points. The Huinay Fjord, in the archipelago region of southern Chile, an area in which the Valparaíso group is seeking to collaborate decisively in the uncertain process of colonization, is the most important of these. It was in connection with this project that the *Amereida* vessel was constructed, a floating classroom which heralds the opening of a new and second front of works, potentially comparable in importance to the Open City, albeit far to the south.

In general, the journeys have been undertaken jointly by architects and designers, although more recent trends suggest a separation by specialities. When the *travesía* is undertaken on a joint basis, each group deals with those tasks involved in the journey which are more closely related to its area of specialization, both regarding the voyage and the work at the point of destination.

As far as the works themselves are concerned, there are several types: some act as signs, while others serve as inhabitable places. Sometimes, the ensemble of installations and events prepared by the group constitutes a kind of celebration of the site, in episodes that can involve the direct and active participation of local artists, designers or architects. There are profoundly urban *travesías*, to villages and cities, and there are wild *travesías*, to spaces of great solitude, such as mountain peaks or islands. When there are many people at the site, there may be acts and banquets when utensils devised by designers and architects are used.

In many cases, sculptures have been carried on the *travesías* to be located at the works, while in other cases, sculptures have been completed on site. In this way, these works of art survive as more or less permanent traces of, or testimony to, a fleeting presence.

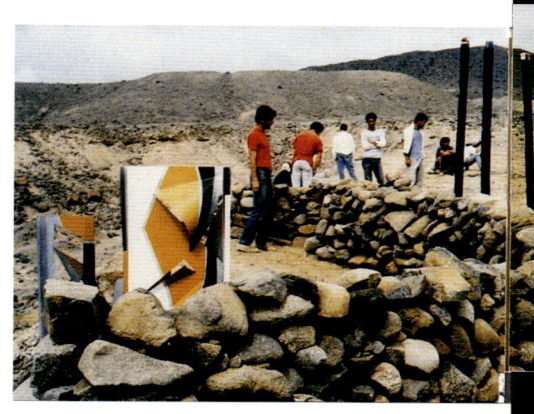
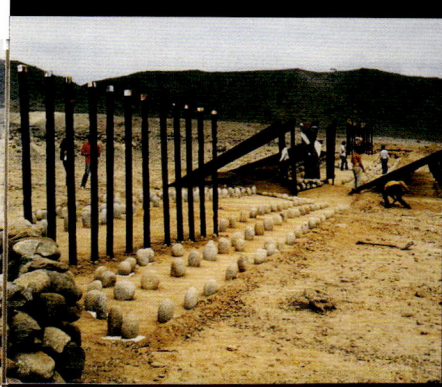
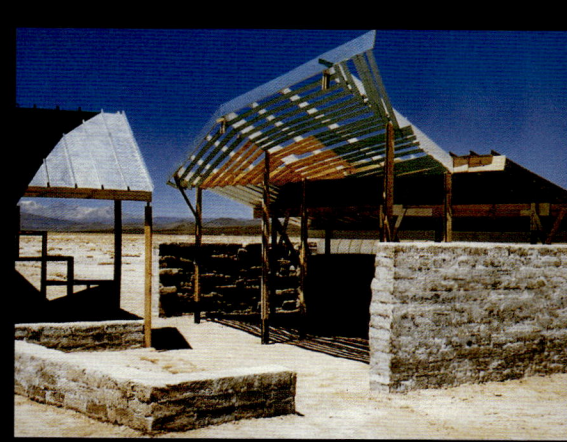

Below, from left to right on this double page:
Travesía to Morro Copiapó, Caldera.
Travesía to Salar de Coipasa
Mejillones *Travesía*
Huinay *Travesía*, sculpture by José Balcells
Juncal *Travesía*, sculpture by Claudio Girola
Right:
From *Amereida*

    y más que sur

           ¿no es ella nuestro norte

    y su extremo

        cumbre

           aparecida

                a quienes

por primera vez la remontaron?

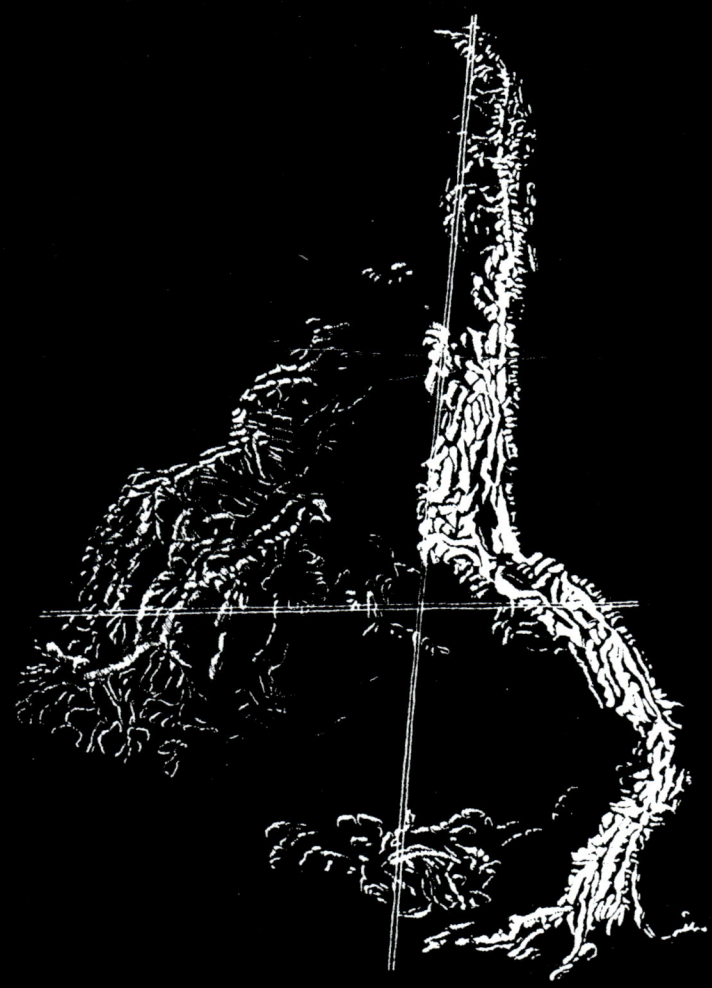

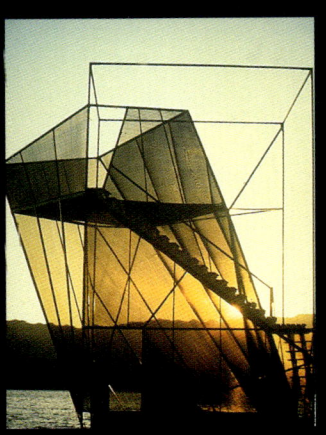

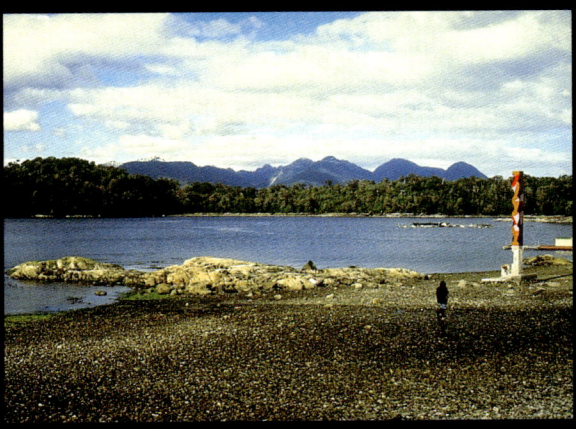

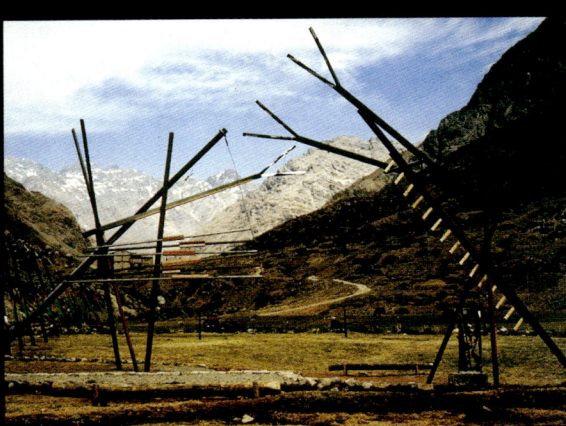

Travesía to Lake Titicaca
Amantani Island, Bolivia, 1985
Professors Manuel Casanueva, Ricardo Lang and 2nd Year Architecture and Object Design Workshops
Collaboration in previous studies, physicist Carlos Werner

Following a sequential plan, this *travesía* was undertaken after the crossing to the Juan Fernández Islands in the Pacific Ocean. Its first framework of reference was established by a map of the continent crossed by co-ordinates. The vectors Cape Horn—Easter Island and Easter Island—Belem form two sides of an equilateral triangle whose third side, tangent to the Chilean coastline, crosses Valparaíso and continues inland to the north where it coincides with Lake Titicaca. The mere existence of this image is an eloquent manifestation of the simultaneousness of visions and horizons of the *travesías*.

The journey to Lake Titicaca, which is situated in the "roof of America", at a height of 3,800 m above sea level, was undertaken in search of specific conditions of visibility for the construction of a *mirador* or observation point. The crystal-clear air at the lake provides optimum visual conditions, while accentuating the contrasts between the shores, which are illuminated by a burning light, and the opposite shores which are submerged in dense shadow. In this atmosphere, "colours vibrate between illumination and eclipse", while from the western side of the continent clouds of an intense whiteness rise over the lake, coming from the enormous vastness of the Amazon, America's "inland sea" (see page 16). The reflection of the clouds creates a "perpetual condominium of seas": such is the description of the scene and motivation for the work.

The technical characteristics of the work, essentially a pontoon—a floating classroom and observation point—were formerly studied in Valparaíso. In order to establish the correct conditions of floatability, technical-spatial studies were carried out previously with the use of stereometric models made of wire and transparent

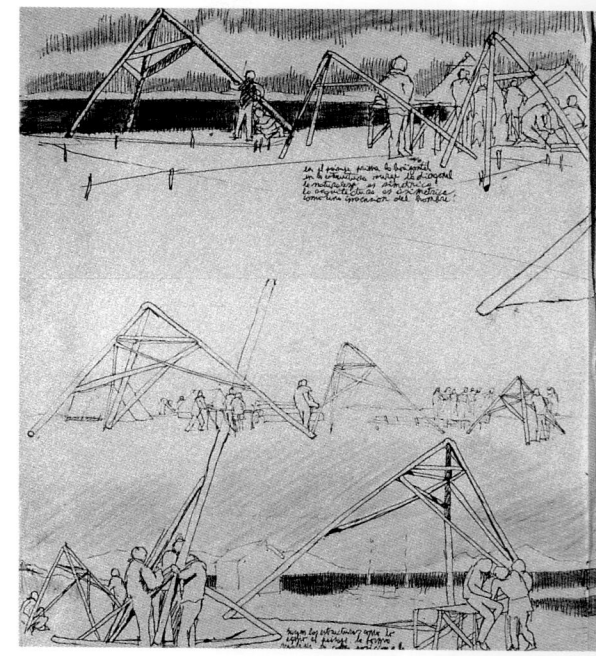

1

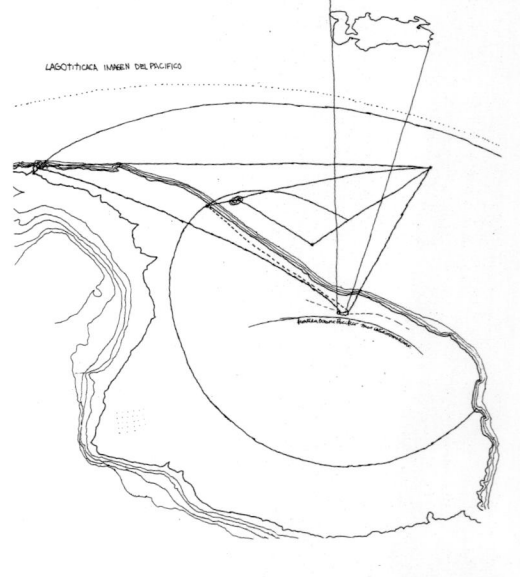

2

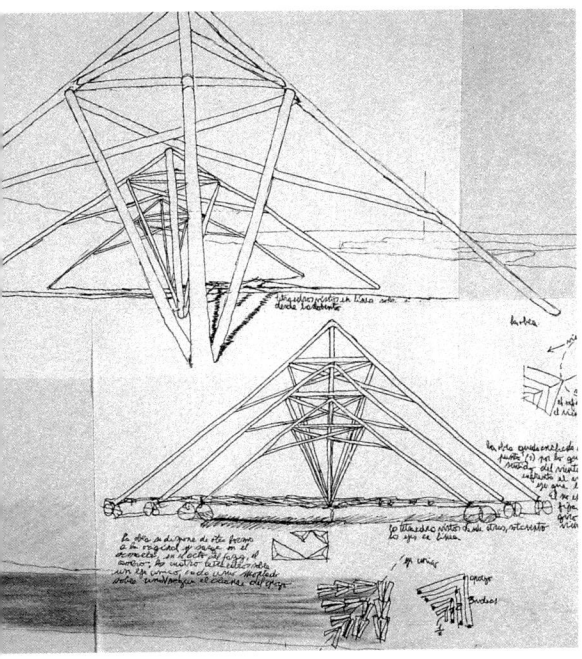

plastic sheets. The construction was built on site by teams of architects and designers, using reeds from the lake—the material traditionally used for vessels—combined with cylindrical sleeves sealed with polyethylene. Joined together in pairs, the cylindrical modules create four ensembles in angles of growing size. The floors and the respective polyhedric lattices were supported on top of this structure, extended over a floorplan the general dimensions of which are comparable to those of the Pazzi chapel (15th century, Florence). The total weight of the pontoon is 1.5 metric tonnes. This floating structure, which rotates in the water around its anchoring point, has a precise and definite location, but entirely lacks a fixed orientation.

The work was donated to the authorities of the island, descendants of the original native inhabitants.

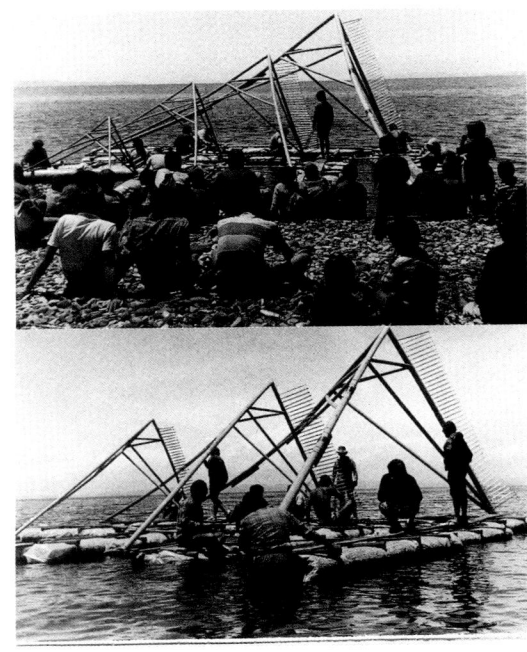

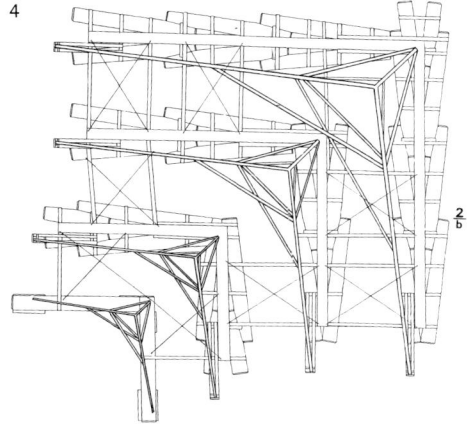

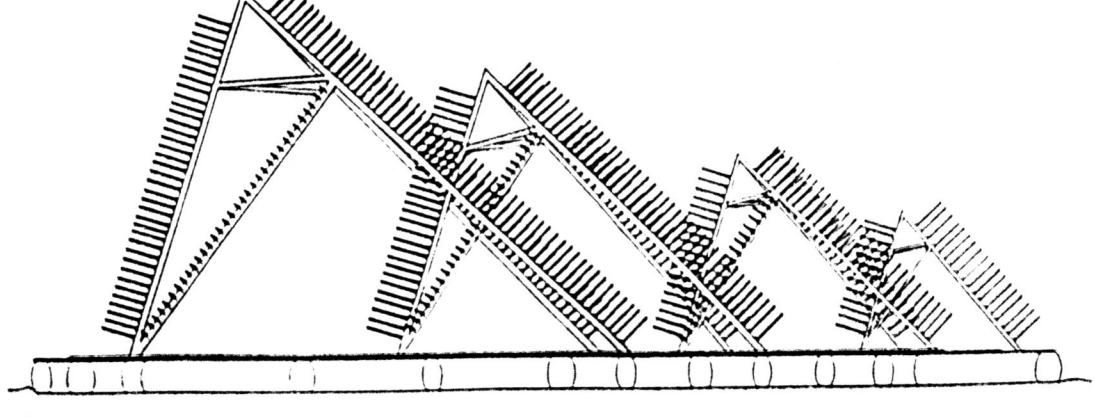

1 Sketch by Alfonso Noguera
2 Geographical co-ordinates
3 The work on Lake Titicaca
4 Plan of the pontoon and lattices
5 Elevation of the pontoon and lattices

Travesía to Caldera
Cerro Montevideo, Chile, 1986-1987
Professors Manuel Casanueva, Ricardo Lang
and 2nd Year Architecture
and Object Design Workshops

The lonely peak of Cerro Montevideo, 10km from the village of Caldera, was designated as the site for an aerial plaza or observation point from which the village could see itself and acknowledge the similarities of its two empty territories: the Pacific Ocean and the Atacama desert. The design entailed the construction, on top of the 310-m-high hill, of an artificial peak consisting of eleven walkways rhythmically arranged as stands following the typical tread and riser layout of a staircase. Each unit of this "staircase", consisting of a walking surface, a section of the profile and a fragment of the peak, was assigned to a student. The ensemble established distinct circulation paces according to the rhythms imposed by each unit. Below these, as a result of the leaning plane which supported them, a shady area was created where the effect of the stands was similar to a protective lattice. The conception and development of the work was influenced not only by mathematical studies, but also by research into European baroque architecture. In its firm commitment to bodily postures and gestures, the work presented similarities with the routes established in the Bo Garden and the Palace of Dawn and Dusk, in the Open City.

As with other *travesía* works, this one reflected a series of concerns that expressed themselves in research, texts and concrete works, linking theory and experimentation in an educational context. The designers showed a particular interest in the study of the furnishing, designing the celebration table, whose top of metallic mesh was reminiscent of bodily gestures. Two stays at the site were necessary in order to build the work, which the local inhabitants acknowledged and used as a place for strolling.

The work was destroyed during army manoeuvres.

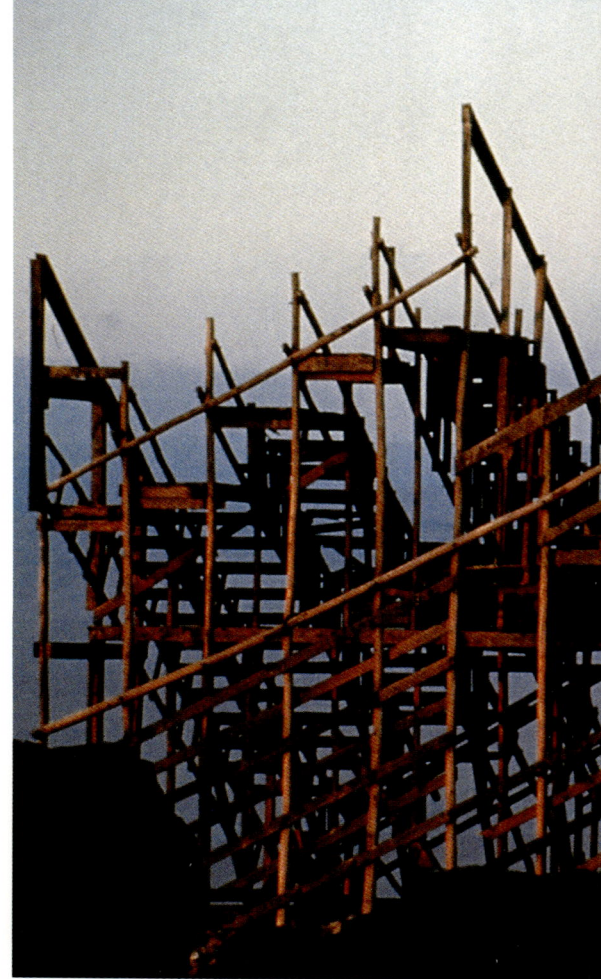

1 Protective lattice and stands
2 Systems of stands: elevation and plan
3, 4 and 5 The work in place on Cerro Montevideo

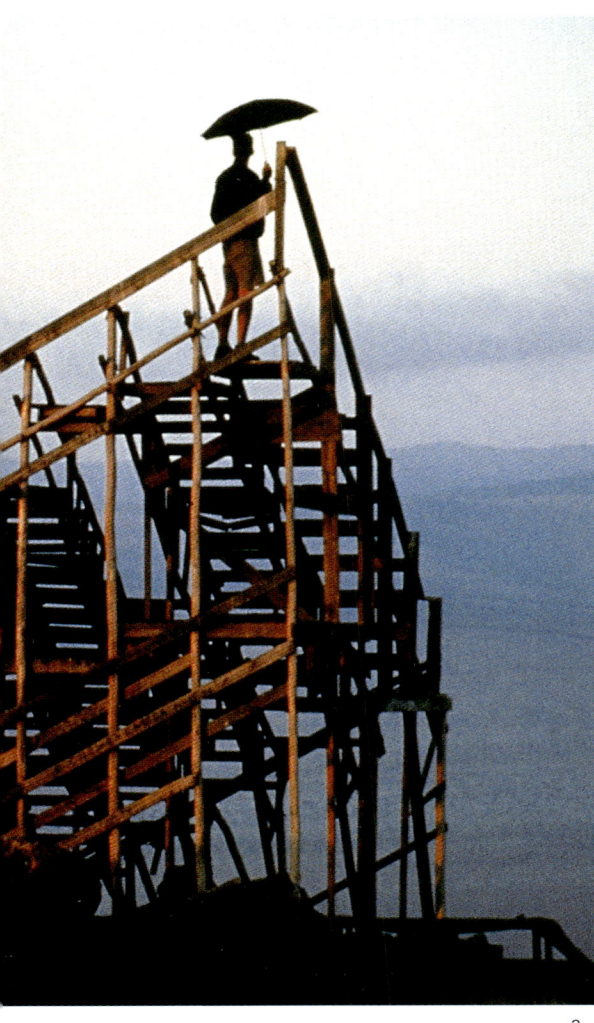
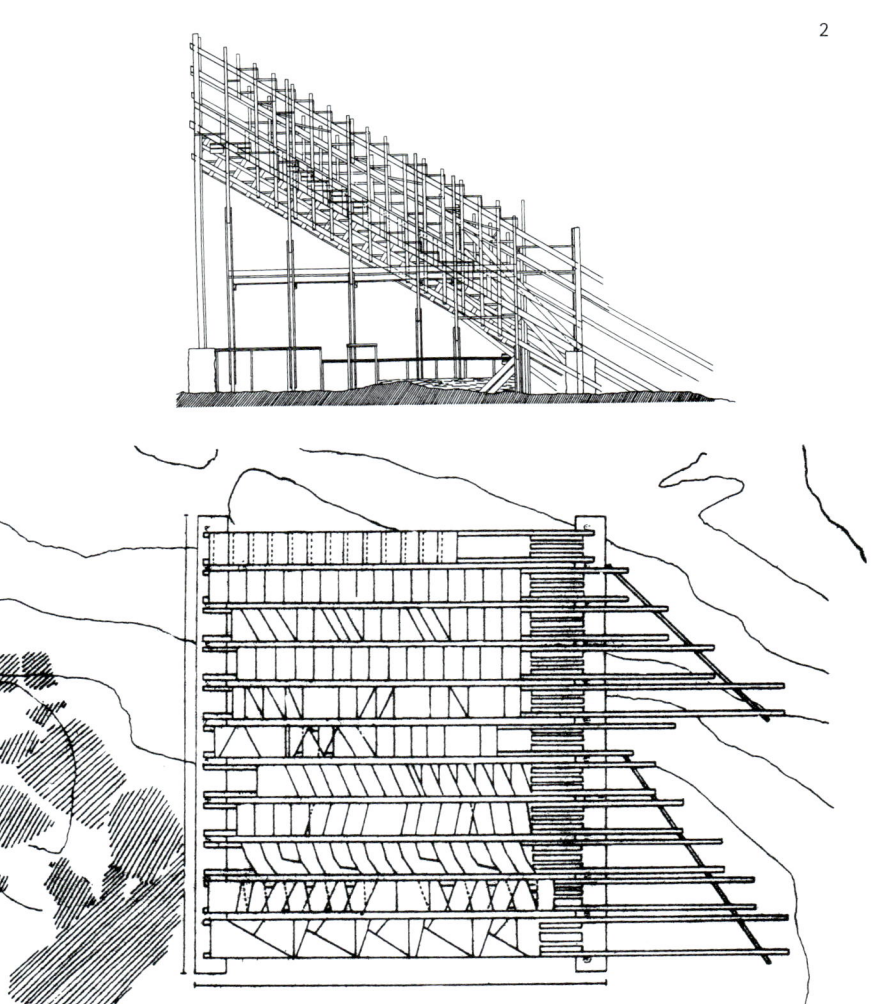
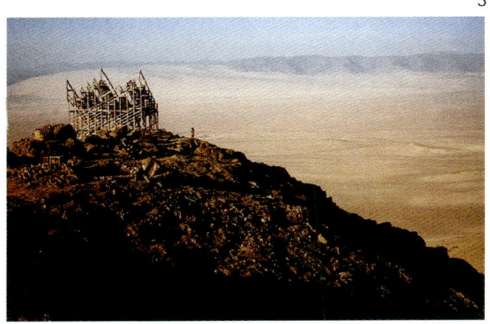
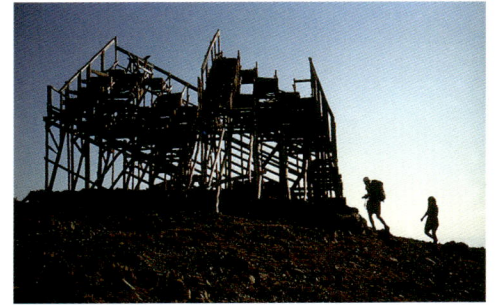
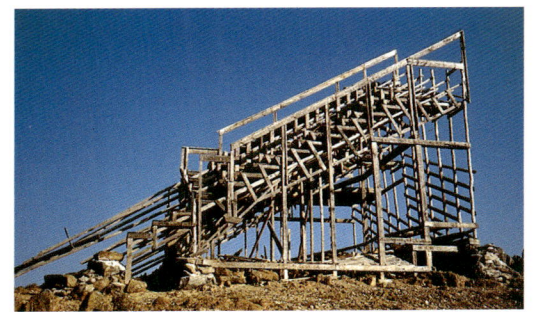

127

Travesía to the Plains of Curimahuida,
or Stone *Travesía*
Chile
Professors Juan Ignacio Baixas, Fabio Cruz,
Boris Ivelic, Bruno Barla with
3rd Year Architecture Workshops and
3rd Year and Final Year Object Design
Workshops

Situated towards the interior of the Andes mountain chain, the plains of Curimahuida coincide approximately with the western edge of the wilderness which the poem *Amereida* describes as an "Inland Sea". After previous reconnaissance missions into the Andean massif, this site was chosen as the place where the Andes Mountain chain was closest to the Pacific Ocean.

The plain is 3,300 m above sea level. Just as the southern *travesías* assert the possibility of inhabiting inhospitable climates, so did the Curimahuida *travesía* propose to recover the ancestral capacity of the pre-Columbine cultures to live at great heights.

Although the work was initially conceived as both a lodge and a sign—a place of shelter for the potential traveller, whether he be a miner, a shepherd, engineer or mountaineer—it gradually embraced the idea of a nave as its architectural key. A precarious refuge on the site was considered as the possible location and original nucleus of the project, but was later rejected as a result of its primitive structure. The idea of a nave led to the creation of an atrium, defined by a longitudinal wall. On an empirical basis, it was decided that the wall should be sixty metres in length to reflect adequately the dimensions of the site, and that it should be constructed in segmented stretches. Slightly pivoted with regard to the axis, these stretches serve to deflect the prevailing winds. Three rooms, one of them covered, were placed at the highest end and given different properties: thus, the largest—4.97 m in length—defines the smallest space which would allow the group to meet while leaving an empty space in the centre; the smallest—2.13 m in length—establishes a space that is more tactile than visual. The covered room consists of two planes placed at different levels.

The work required approximately 116 metric tonnes of stones quarried on site, as well as pieces hauled with great difficulty from the road 30 km away. Foreseeing these conditions, the designers devised a portable folding machine to handle the metal sheets, giving them rigidity. The collapsible windows are all the same size. The nucleus of the camp was formed by the Froward Classroom, a 120 m² polyethylene marquee big enough to hold the entire workshop.

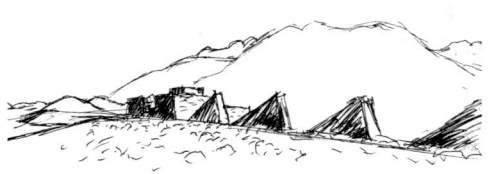

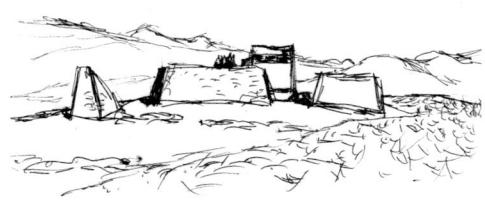

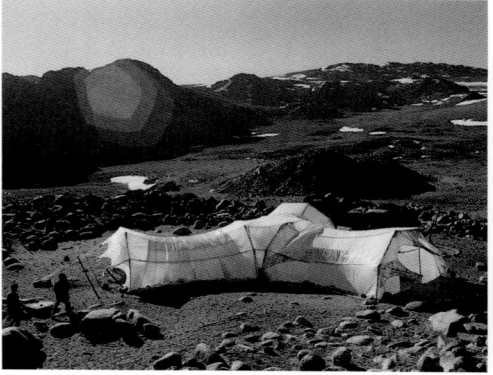

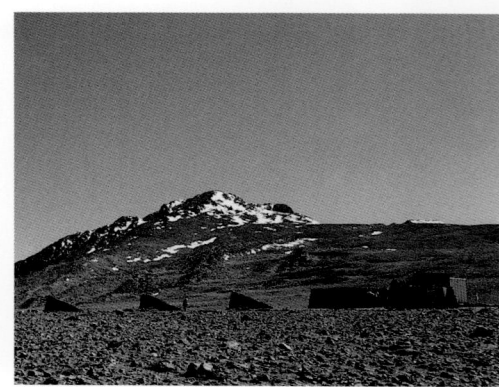

Facing page:
Sketch by Fabio Cruz, marquee-classroom and side view

This page:
Right, elements from the site and elements transported to the site: stone wall, cubicles and metal window
Below: interior of the marquee-classroom

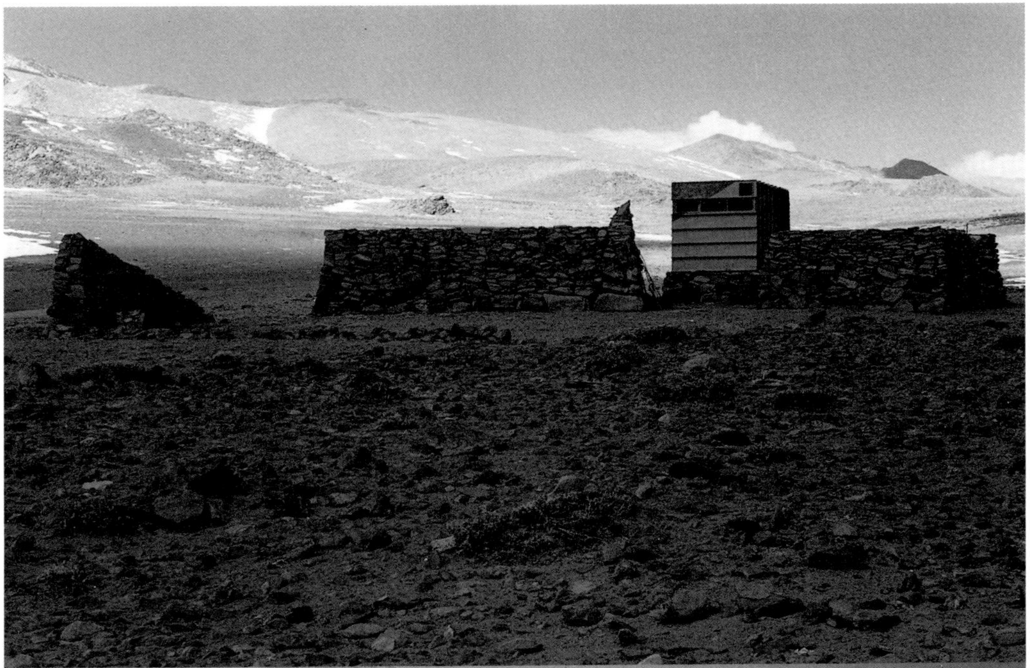

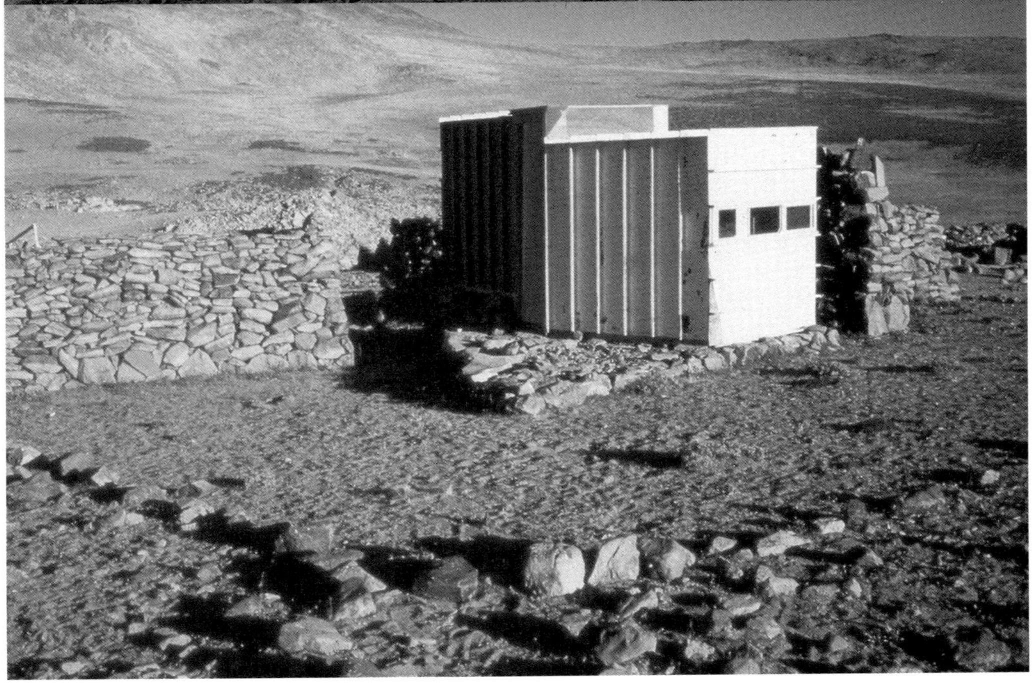

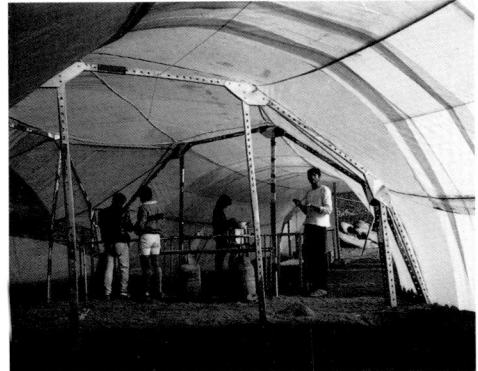

Travesías to Comau Huinay Fjord, Chile, and the *Amereida* Vessel
Professors Juan Ignacio Baixas, Boris Ivelic, Fabio Cruz, Ricardo Lang, Bruno Barla and 3rd Year Architecture and 3rd Year Object Design Workshops

Amereida Vessel for the Southern Region
Boris Ivelic
Co-researchers Juan I Baixas, Arturo Chicano, Marcos García Alvarado, Sergio Ostornol Varela, Naval Electrical Engineer, UCV Workshops

The *Travesías*

In 1969, the group began conducting investigations around the territory of the fjords. The results of this field research have been published under the title *Maritorios de los Archipiélagos de la Patagonia Occidental* (Marine Territories of Western Patagonia), a document that looks at the means of land, air and sea transport that could be used to connect the different towns, and analyzes the conditions needed to increase the networks and frequencies of communication. In other texts it is argued that, contrary to the expectations rooted in the national culture, which perceive this territory to be essentially inhospitable, the latitudes of these fjords are comparable to those of some of the more densely populated regions of the Northern Hemisphere.

The different *travesías* to Huinay have gradually come to form part of a plan which might eventually create a second pole of works in addition to those of the Open City. Regarded as a frontier to be colonized, the fjord region in southern Chile is beginning a slow process of opening up and integrating with the rest of the country. Nevertheless, its dislocated geography makes any kind of permanent settlement extremely difficult.

On the basis of specific experiences, the group has concluded that, paradoxically, it is the sea and not the land which constitutes the true "floor" of the labyrinth of archipelagos that make up Chile's southern region. The *Amereida* vessel arose as a response to this approach and, specifically, given the lack of access routes, as a response to the need to establish a centre of operations in a region that shows signs of being a territory with long-term possibilities. In this way the search for solutions to the logistical difficulties of the area is being undertaken. As with the Wanderer's Lodge, the project is being carried out as part of the National Program of Scientific Research.

The Vessel

The vessel satisfies the need for workshops and temporary residence. For this reason, it is equipped with manipulable devices which adapt the interior to its different functions: floats are deployed from the hull to extend the deck for use as a workshop platform, sometimes covered with a climatic membrane, thereby transforming the vessel into a trimaran. The berths, attached to the hull, fold away during the day to become seats. The tables, used both as dining tables and as drawing boards, are kept under the deck of the vessel.

In spite of its strong individual identity, the project combines several of the parts and fragments designs devised in the framework of the university workshop experience and inspired by the same spirit that guided the experiences of the Open City in its expression as a pedagogical project, its nature as a collective project developed by multiple managers, and its experimental character, which places it on the level of a prototype in the research chain. It is a project that strongly recalls the designers. As is only to be expected, the technical factor is more demanding in this case, given the very essence of the task.

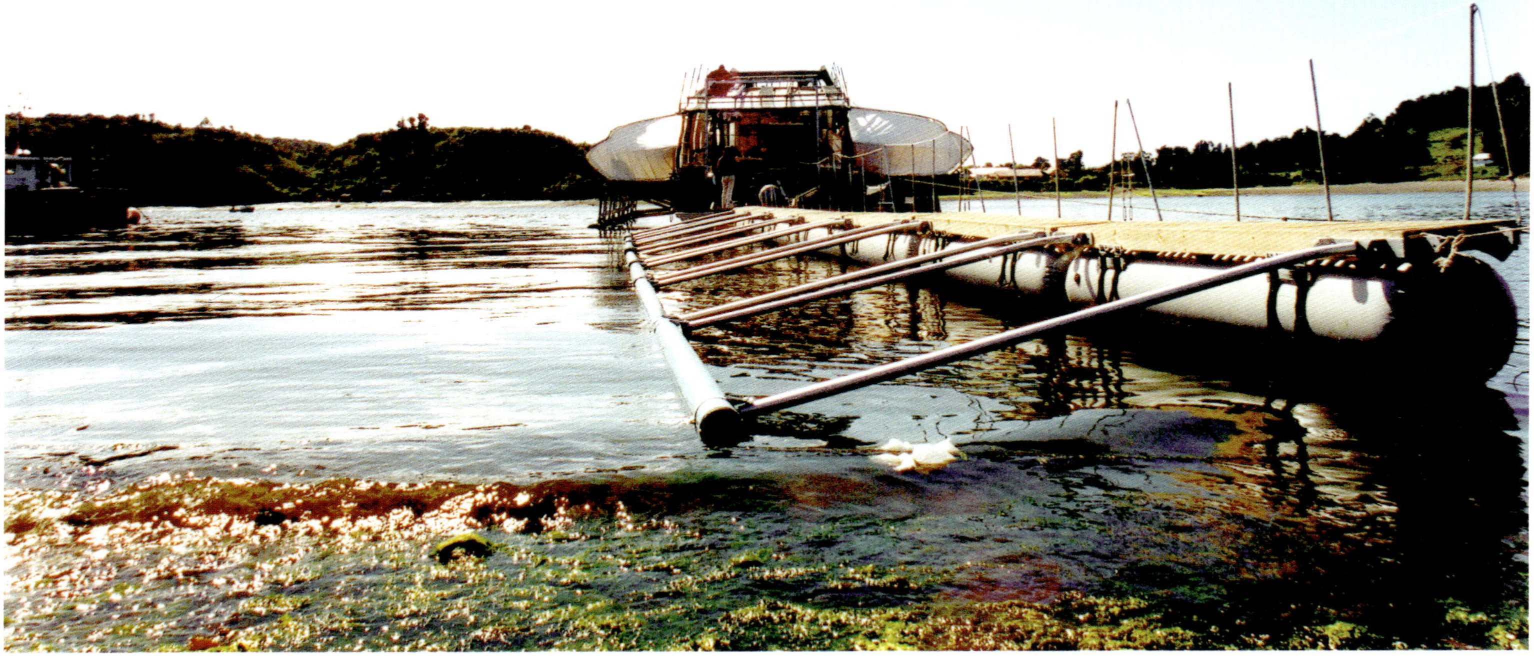

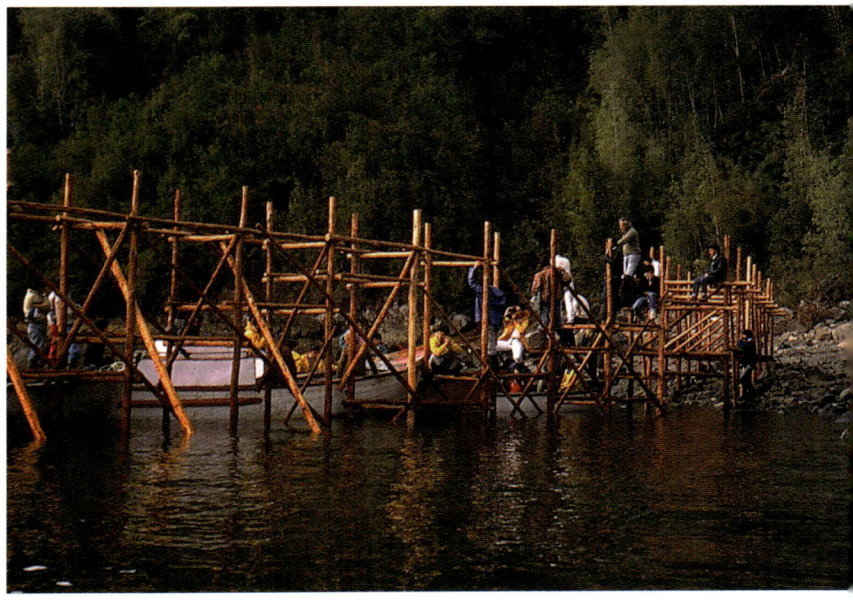

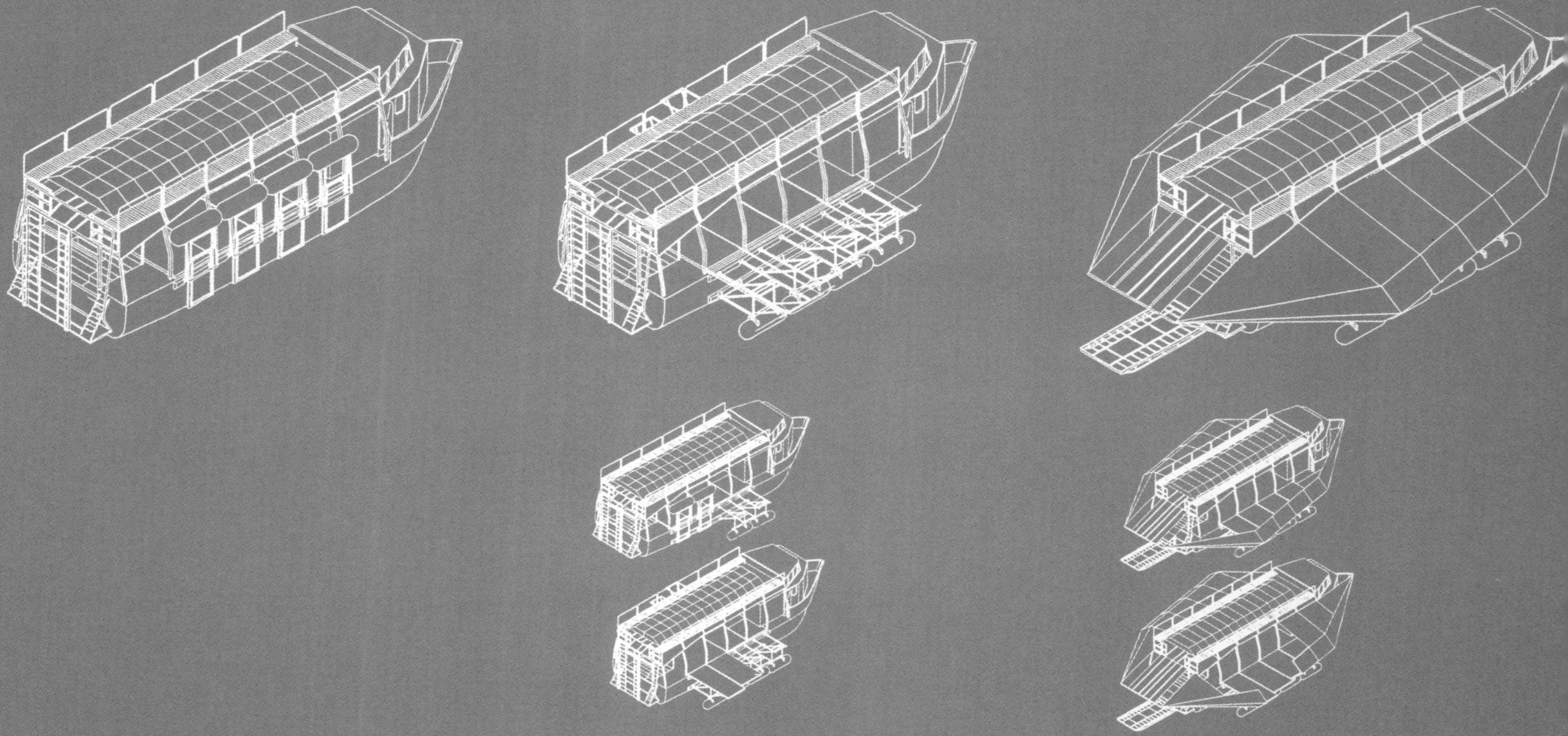

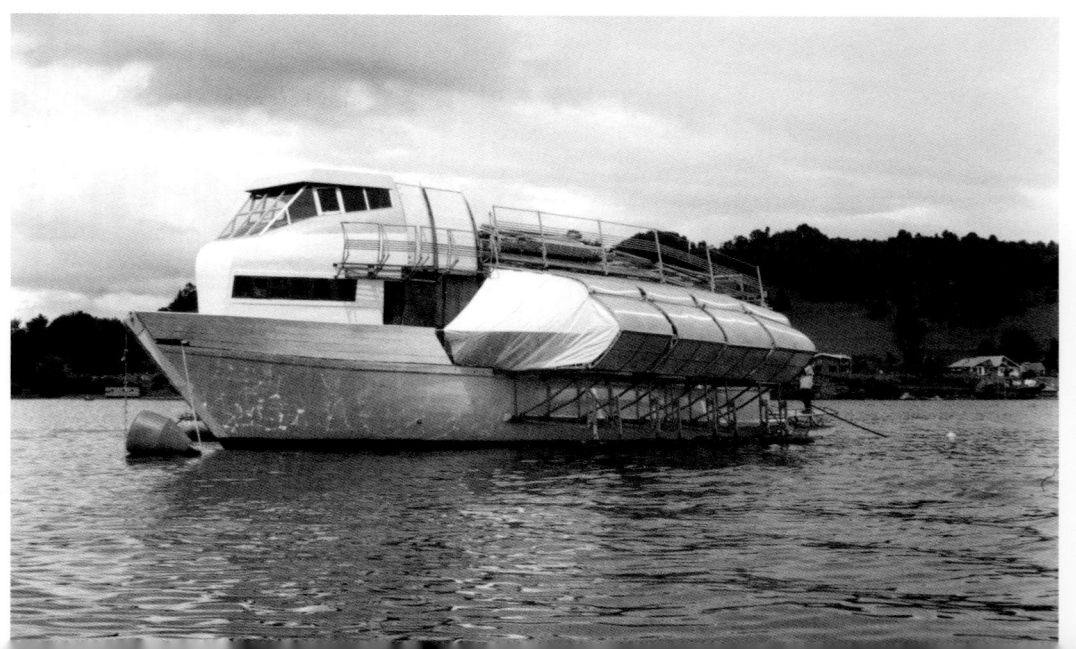

132

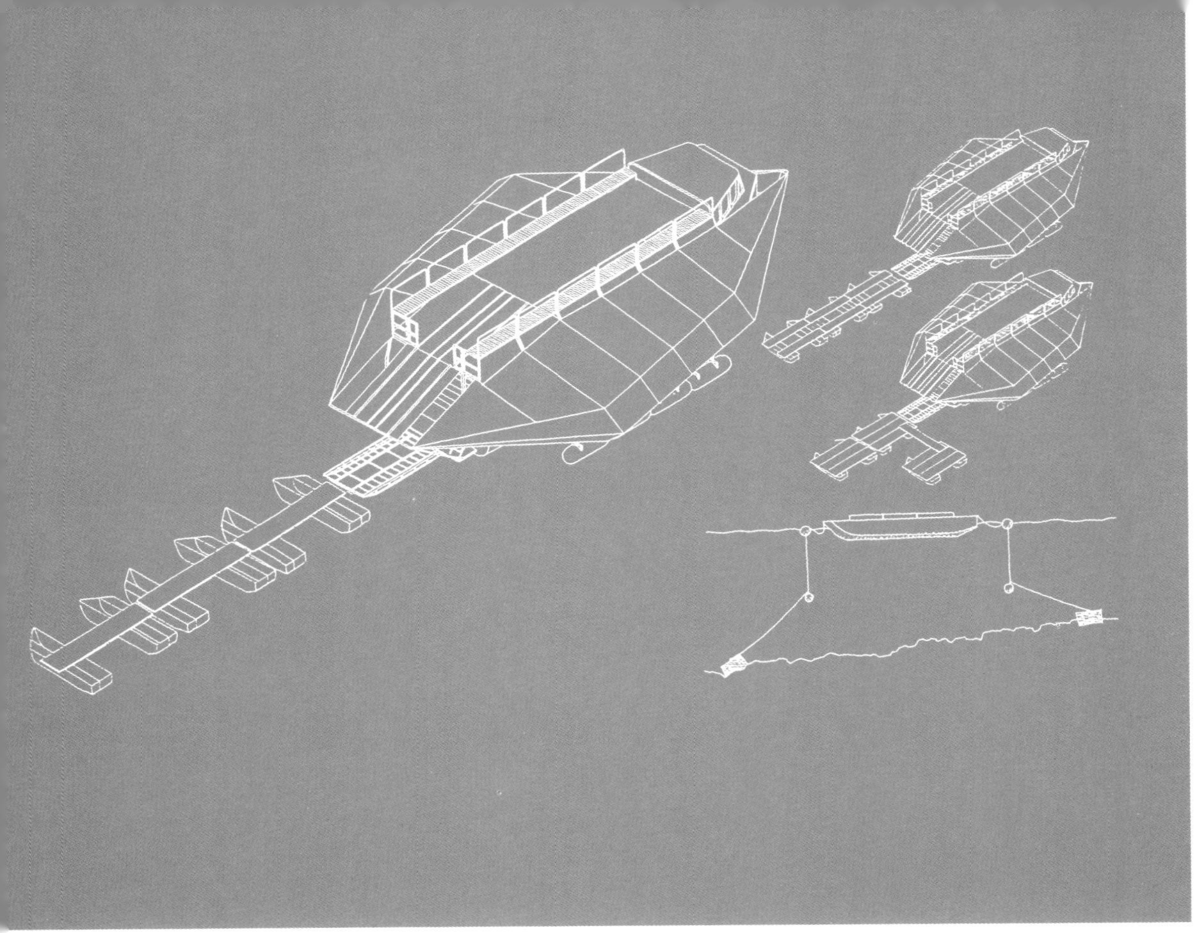

Axonometric projection of the *Amereida* vessel and the different ways it can be extended
Below, from left to right:
General view of the *Amereida* vessel at anchor, detail of the interior of the deck set up as a dining room, and its lateral structures extended to provide space for workshops

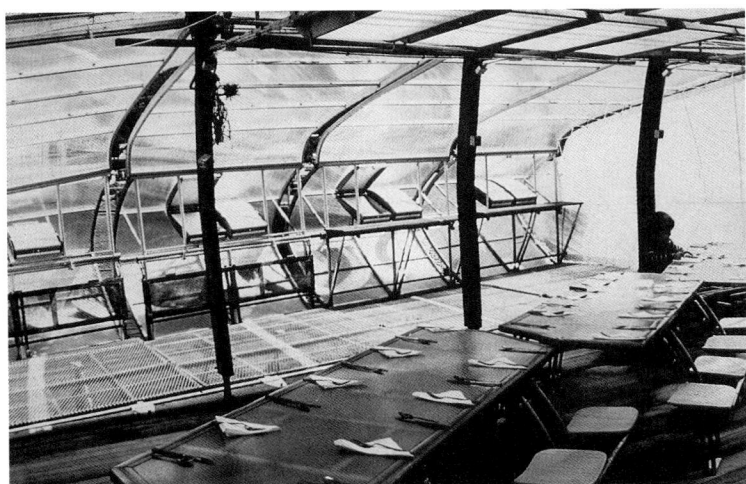
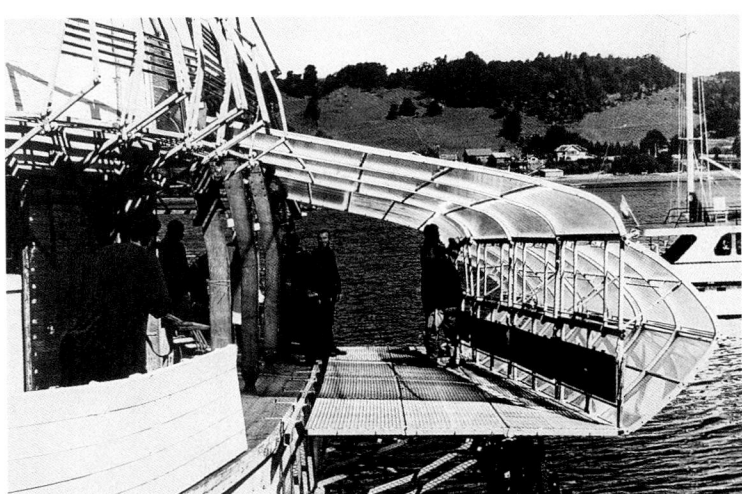

Works and Designs

1   **Houses for the Armed Forces**
    Puente Alto
    1950, Alberto Cruz, Arturo Baeza, José Vial

2   **Ford Agency**
    Curicó
    1950, Alberto Cruz, Jaime Bellalta

3   **Fabio Cruz Property Division into Plots**
    Santiago
    1950, Francisco Méndez et al

4   **Plot Division and Construction on Calle Diego de Almagro – Design**
    Santiago
    1950, Francisco Méndez et al

5   **"Lago Buenos Aires" – Graduation Project**
    Aisén
    1950, Arturo Baeza

6   **"Unidad Agraria Chile Chico" – Graduation Project**
    Aisén
    1950, José Vial

7   **Fabio Cruz House Extension**
    Santiago
    1950, Fabio Cruz Prieto

8   **Los Pajaritos Chapel – Design**
    Maipú, Santiago
    1952, Miguel Eyquem

9   **Los Pajaritos Chapel – Design**
    Maipú, Santiago
    1952-1953, Alberto Cruz
    See pages 24-27

10 **Museum – Design**
    Valparaíso
    1953, Francisco Méndez

11 **Navy Yacht Club – Design**
    Valparaíso
    1953, Institute of Architecture

12 **Achupallas Urban Development Project**
    Viña del Mar
    1954, Alberto Cruz, Institute of Architecture
    See pages 20-23

13 **Cerro Castillo Urban Development Project**
    Viña del Mar
    1954, Arturo Baeza

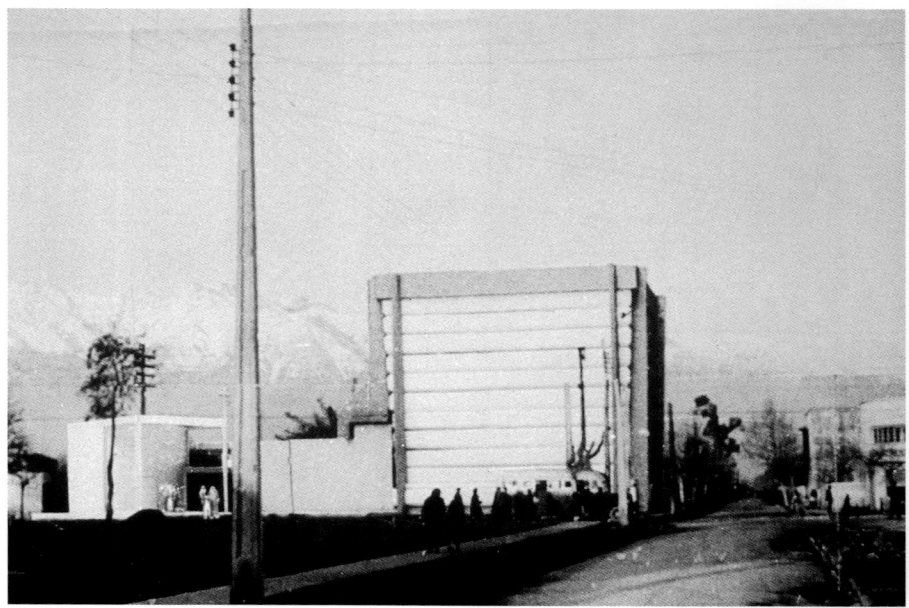

20

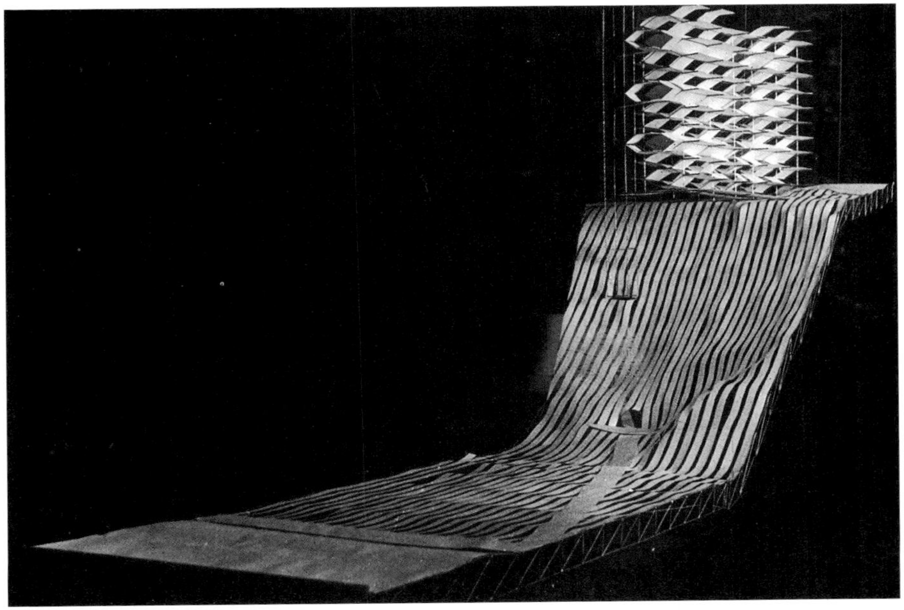

14 Undurraga House – Design
Reñaca
1954, Miguel Eyquem, Alberto Cruz, Jaime Bellalta

15 Airfield – Design
Rodelillo
1954, Miguel Eyquem

16 Subida Latorre – Design
Viña del Mar
1954, Institute of Architecture

17 Benedictine Monastery – Draft Design (competition)
Las Condes, Santiago
1954, Jaime Bellalta, E. Cromie, O. Sotomayor,
F. Mena and L. Rodriguez

18 Church of Santa Clara – Design (cubic version)
Santiago
1954, Institute of Architecture

19 Benedictine Monastery – Design
Las Condes, Santiago
1954-1955, Jaime Bellalta
See pages 36-41

20 Exagón Building – Design
Viña del Mar
1955, Arturo Baeza, José Vial, Fabio Cruz

21 Astaburuaga House
Santiago
1955, Jaime Bellalta

22 Vitacura Parish School
Las Condes, Santiago
1955, Jaime Bellalta

23 Commander Correa House – Design
Valparaíso
1956, José Vial

24 Cruz House – First Draft Design
Calle Jean Mermoz, Santiago
1956, Fabio Cruz and Institute of Architecture

25 Naval Academy – Design (competition)
Valparaíso
1956, Francisco Mendez, Institute of Architecture
See pages 28-31

26 Recreo Yacht Club – Design
Viña del Mar
1957, Miguel Eyquem

27 Saint Marie House – Draft Design
Cajon del Maipo
1958, Jaime Bellalta, Miguel Eyquem

28 Cruz House – Successive Designs and Building Plans
Calle Jean Mermoz, Santiago
1958-1961, Fabio Cruz, Institute of Architecture
See pages 42-47

29 Sagrados Corazones School – Design
Valparaíso
1959, Institute of Architecture

30 Paseo Gervasoni – Design
Valparaíso
1959, José Vial

31 Workshop Loft, House-School of Architecture
Calle Matta, Recreo, Viña del Mar
1959, Institute of Architecture

32 Design and Assembly of the UCV School of Architecture Exhibition held at the School of Architecture of the Catholic University of Chile, Santiago
1959, Institute of Architecture

33 Benedictine Monastery – Design
Santiago
1960, A. Cruz, A. Baeza, J. Vial, Institute of Architecture
See pages 36-41

34 Grassi House – Draft Design
Ischia, Italy
1960, Miguel Eyquem

35 Prieto House – Design
Santiago
1960, Fabio Cruz

36 Bevilocqua House – Design
Concón
1960, Arturo Baeza

37 Urban Development Study for the Parish of Valdivia
Valdivia
1961, Institute of Architecture

38 Urban Development Study for the Parish of Osorno
Osorno
1961, Institute of Architecture

39 Urban Development Study for the Parish of Temuco
Temuco
1961, Institute of Architecture

40 Urban Development Study for the Parish of Santiago
Santiago
1961, Institute of Architecture

41 Urban Development Study for the Parish of Coronel
Coronel
1961, Institute of Architecture

42 Church of Nuestra Señora de la Candelaria
San Pedro, Concepción
1960-1961, Arturo Baeza
Demolished
See pages 54-55

43 Coronel Church – Draft Design
Coronel, Concepción
1961, Institute of Architecture

44 Coronel Church
Coronel, Concepción
1961, Arturo Baeza

45 Parish Church – Draft Design
García Hurtado de Mendoza, Osorno
1961, Institute of Architecture

46 Gil de Castro School Church – Design
Valdivia
1961, Institute of Architecture

47 Corral Parish Church
Bahía de Corral seaside promenade, Valdivia
1961, José Vial
See pages 51-52

48 Paillaco Church
Paillaco
1961, Institute of Architecture

49 Osorno Cathedral – Design
Osorno
1961, Institute of Architecture

50 Church of Santa Clara (final horizontal version)
Santiago
1961-1969, Alberto Cruz, Juan Purcell

51 Misión de Rahue School of Agriculture – Design
Valdivia
1961, José Vial, Institute of Architecture

52 **Parish Church of Santa Cruz – Design**
Valparaíso
1961, Institute of Architecture

53 **Puerto Montt Mother Church**
Puerto Montt
1962-1964, José Vial, Institute of Architecture
See pages 50-51

54 **Arauco Parish Church**
Arauco
1962-1963, Arturo Baeza
Demolished

55 **Curanilahue Parish Church**
Curanilahue
1962-1963, Institute of Architecture

56 **Lebu Parish Church**
Lebu
1962-1963, Arturo Baeza, Institute of Architecture

57 **Florida Parish Church**
Concepción
1962-1963, Institute of Architecture

58 **Carampangne Chapel – Design**
Concepción
1962, Institute of Architecture

59 **Coronel School**
Coronel
1962, Institute of Architecture

60 **Paillaco Church Renovation**
Paillaco
1962, Institute of Architecture

61 **María Gaete School**
Quillota
1963, Institute of Architecture

62 **Arauco Church Enclosure**
Arauco
1963, Institute of Architecture

63 **Florida Parish Church Enclosure**
Florida
1963, Institute of Architecture

64 **Curanilahue Parish Church Enclosure**
Curanilahue
1963, Institute of Architecture

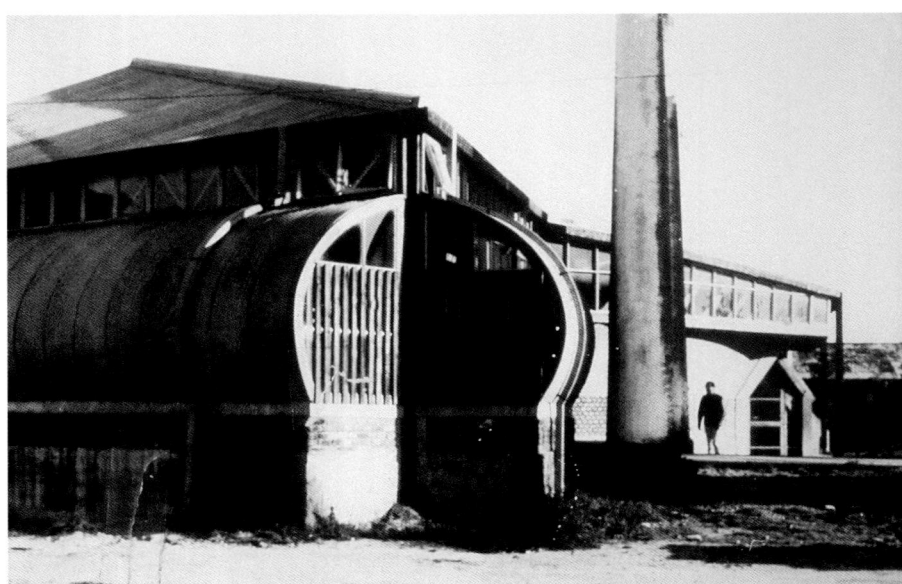

52

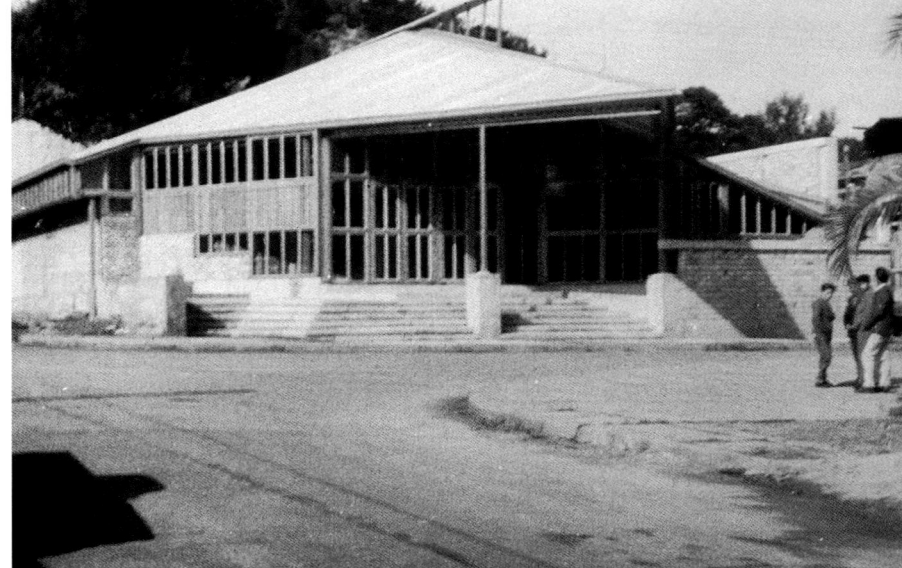

56

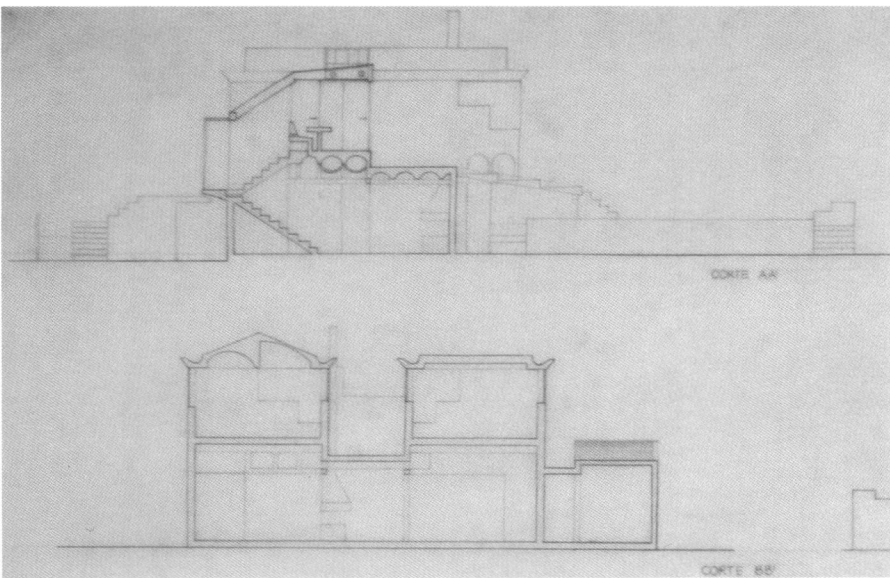

68

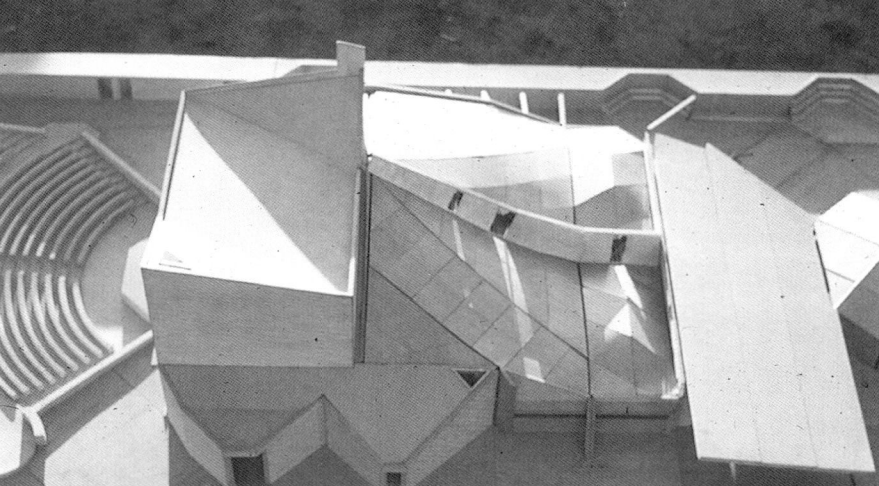

74

65 School of Agriculture – Design
Valparaíso
1963, Arturo Baeza, Institute of Architecture

66 Polpaico House – Draft Design
Polpaico
1963, José Vial

67 Cosmelli House – Draft Design
Lago General Carrera (formerly Buenos Aires)
Chile Chico, Aisén
1963, Arturo Baeza, Alberto Cruz, José Vial

68 Arias House
Santiago
1964, Fabio Cruz

69 Lebu Parish House
Lebu
1964, Institute of Architecture

70 Curanilahue Plaza
Curanilahue
1964, Institute of Architecture

71 Sagrados Corazones, School Church and Gymnasium
Viña del Mar
1964, Institute of Architecture

72 Avenida Apoquindo Section Plan Study
Las Condes, Santiago,
1965, Arturo Baeza

74 Church of Santa Teresita
Quillota
1966, Miguel Eyquem

75 Donoso House – Design "A"
Santiago
1966, Arturo Baeza

76 Donoso House – Design "B"
Santiago
1966, Arturo Baeza

77 Florentino Baeza House – Design
Santiago
1966, Arturo Baeza

78 Municipality of Las Condes Airfield – Design
Las Condes
1966, Miguel Eyquem

79 Santa Inés Gymnasium – Design
Viña del Mar
1966, Miguel Eyquem, Arturo Baeza

80 UCV Campus in Agua Santa – Design
Viña del Mar
1967, Institute of Architecture

81 Lo Beltrán House – Design
Santiago
1967, Arturo Baeza

82 Subida Bellavista Remodelling – Draft Design
(competition)
Valparaíso
1967, Institute of Architecture

83 UCV Bacteriological Institute – Design
Valparaíso
1967, Francisco Méndez, Institute of Architecture

84 Hammersley Building – Final Plans
Valparaíso
1968, Jorge Sánchez

85 Bar Alemán Building – Final Plans
Valparaíso
1968, Jorge Sánchez

86 Huth Building – Final Plans
Valparaíso
1968, Jorge Sánchez

87 Greater Valparaíso – Project (COREM)
Valparaíso
1968, Alberto Cruz, School of Architecture

88 Reñaca Buildings – Draft Design
Reñaca
1969, Juan Purcell

89 Avenida del Mar – Project
Coastline from Valparaíso to Viña del Mar
1969, Arturo Baeza, Alberto Cruz, Institute of Architecture
See pages 32-35

90 Río Bueno Cinema-Theater
Río Bueno
1969, Arturo Baeza

91 UCV School of Agriculture – Design
Quillota
1969, Alberto Cruz

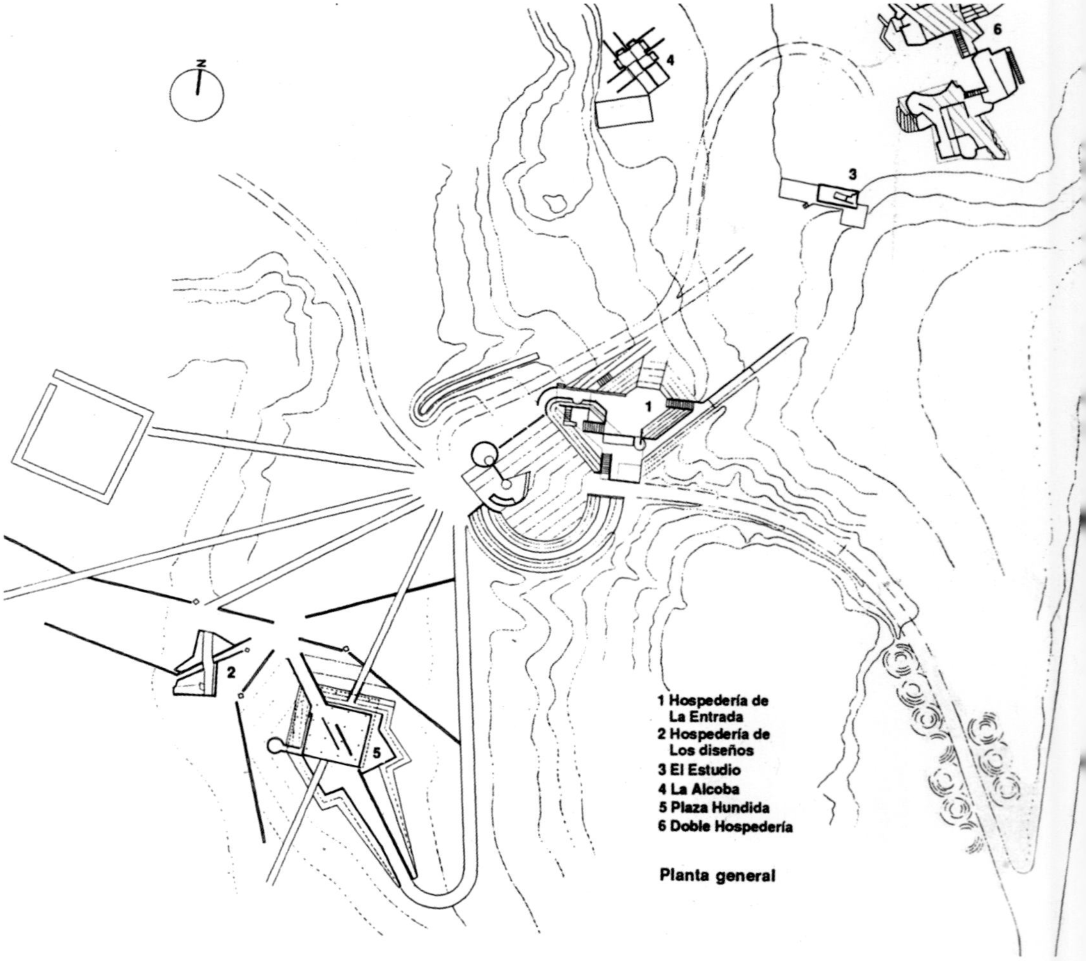

1 Hospedería de La Entrada
2 Hospedería de Los diseños
3 El Estudio
4 La Alcoba
5 Plaza Hundida
6 Doble Hospedería

Planta general

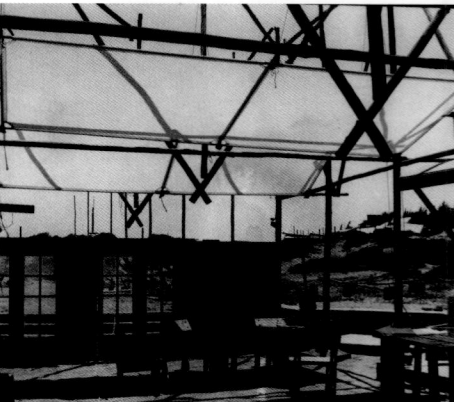

97

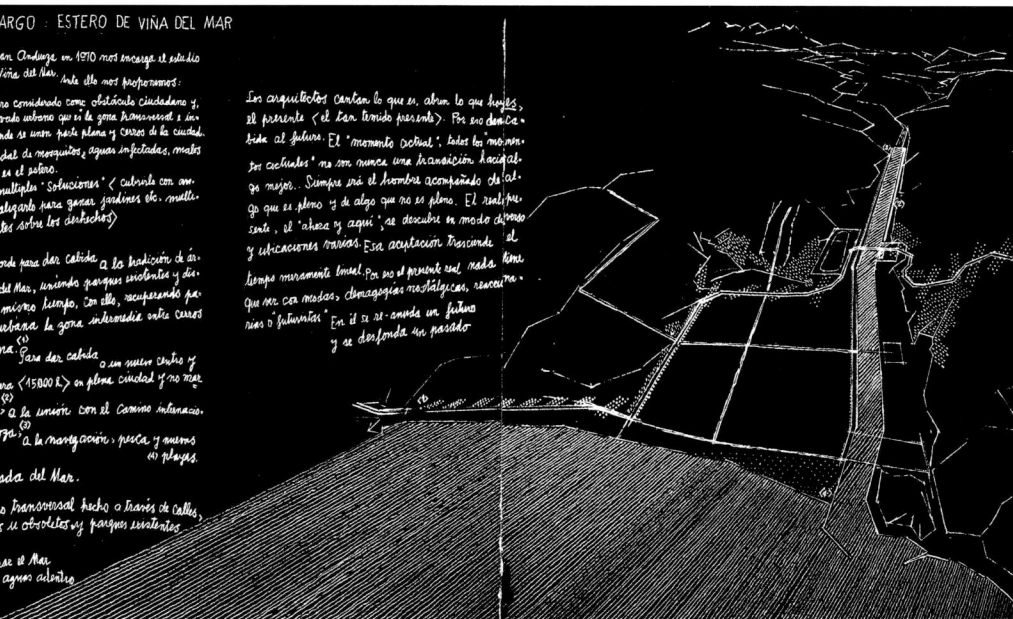

99

92 **Pudahel Airport – Design**
    Pudahuel
    1969, Jaime Sepúlveda

93 **Greve House**
    Concón
    1969, Arturo Baeza

94 **Open City Section Plan**
    Ritoque, Quintero
    1970, Amereida Corporation, Open City Group
    See pages 56-65

95 **Portal Alamos Building – Design** (competition)
    Viña del Mar
    1970, Open City Group

96 **San Luis Urban Development – Project**
    CORMU Project
    Las Condes, Santiago
    1970-1974, Miguel Eyquem
    National Town Planning Award

97 **Igloo**
    Open City, Ritoque, Quintero
    1971, Boris Ivelic

98 **Open City Bathrooms – Design**
    Open City, Ritoque, Quintero
    1971, Boris Ivelic

99 **Estero Viña del Mar Section Plan**
    Viña del Mar
    1971, José Vial, Arturo Baeza, School of Architecture

100 **El Almendral Section Plan, site of the Catholic University of Chile at Valparaíso**
    Valparaíso
    1971, Arturo Baeza.

101 **Tronquoy Agora**
    Open City, Ritoque, Quintero.
    1972, Open City Group

102 **Design and Assembly of the UCV School of Architecture 20th Anniversary Exhibition**
    Museum of Fine Arts, Santiago
    1972, School of Architecture

103 **Tronquoy Agora Vestal**
    Open City, Ritoque, Quintero
    1972, Alberto Cruz, Jorge Sánchez
    See pages 98-101

104 Music Room
Open City, Ritoque, Quintero
1972, Alberto Cruz, Juan Purcell, Open City Group
See pages 66-71

105 Olivetti House – Design
Santiago
1973, Alberto Cruz, Miguel Eyquem

106 UCV-BID Campus in Agua Santa – Design
Viña del Mar
1973-1976, Alberto Cruz, Boris Ivelic, School of Architecture

107 Ancient Palace
Open City, Ritoque, Quintero
1973-1982, Alberto Cruz, Open City Group
Demolished

108 Terraced Building for the San Luis Housing Unit – Design
CORMU Project
Santiago
1974, Arturo Baeza, Miguel Eyquem

109 Double Lodge: Hospedería de las Máquinas (Machine Lodge) and Hospedería del Banquete (Banquet Lodge)
Open City, Ritoque, Quintero
1974, Alberto Cruz, J. Mastrantonio, Open City Group
See pages 102-107

110 Water Towers (first version)
Open City, Quintero
1974, Isabel M. Reyes, Open City Group Demolished
See page 60

111 Six Houses in Concón – Draft Design
Concón
1975, Arturo Baeza.

112 Chilean Air Force Building Refurbishment
Iquique.
1975, Arturo Baeza.

113 Cemetery
Open City, Ritoque, Quintero
1976, Open City Group
See pages 108-113

114 El Pozo Sculpture
Open City, Ritoque, Quintero
1976, Claudio Girola
See pages 110-111

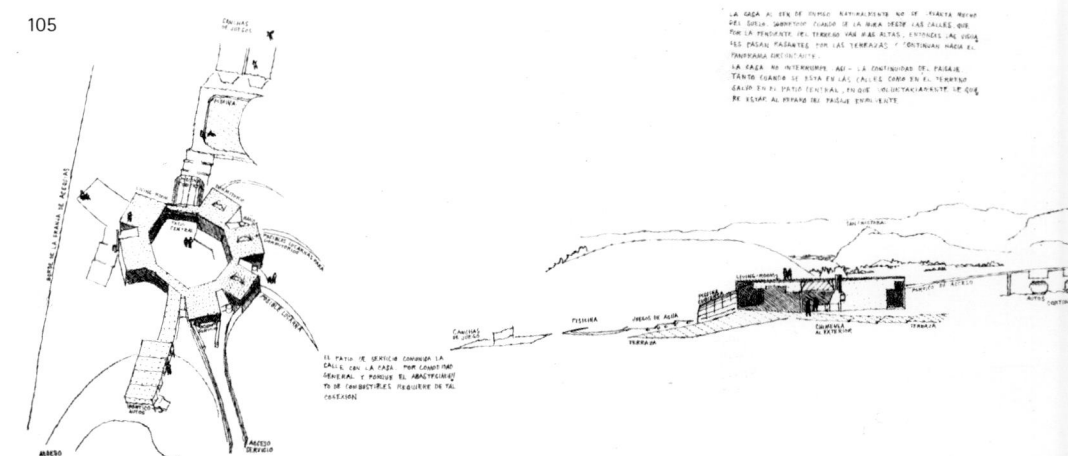

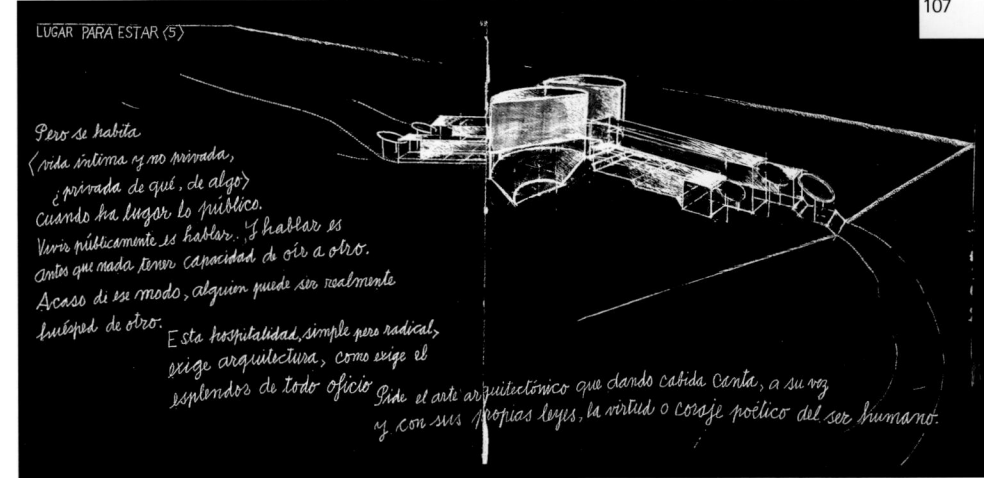

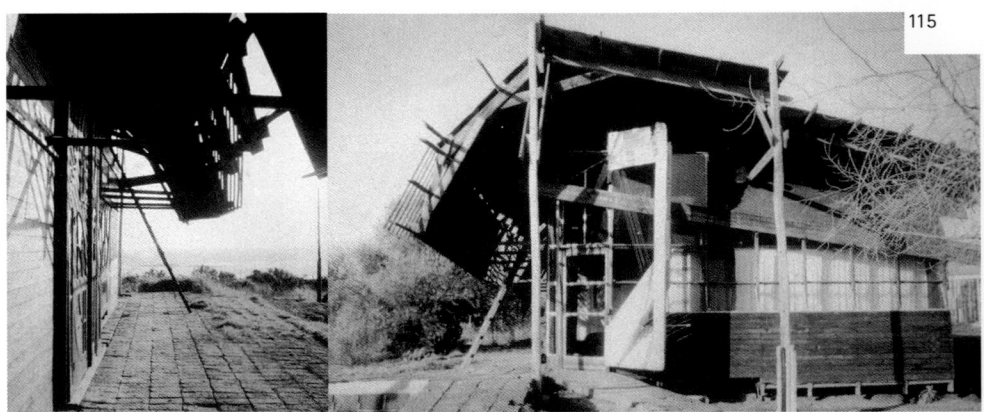

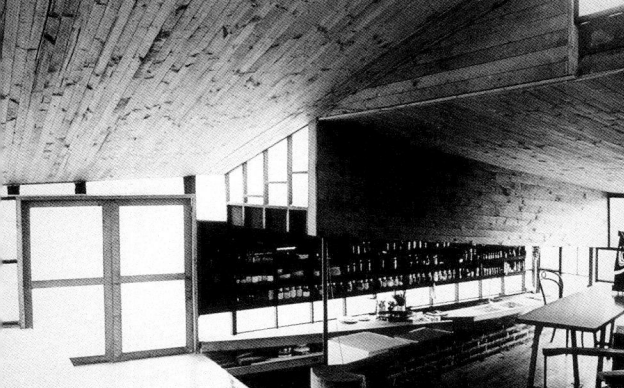

116

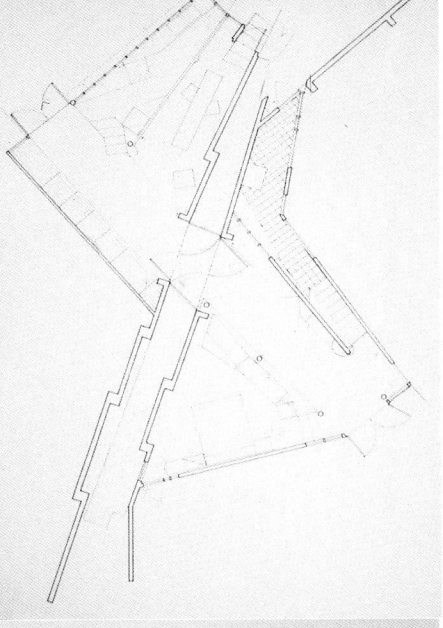

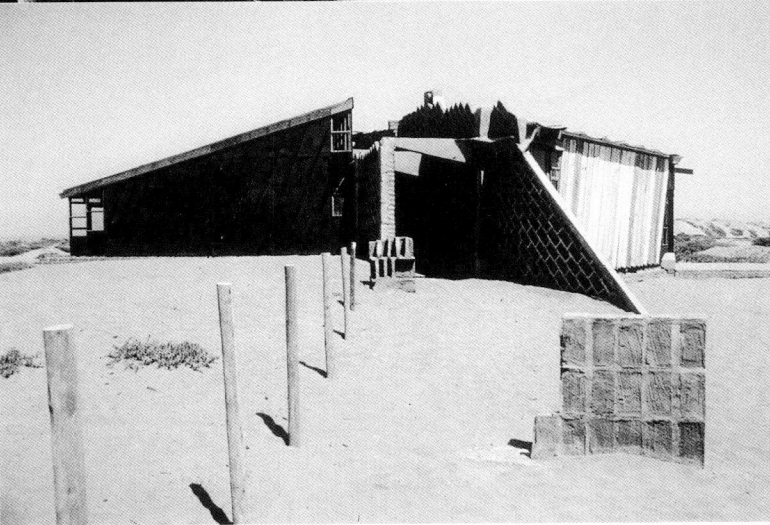

118

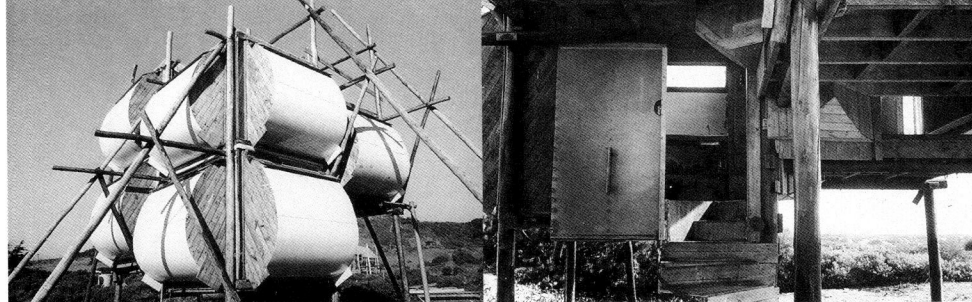

115 Hospedería Pie de Cruz (Pie de Cruz Lodge)
Open City, Ritoque, Quintero .
1977, Fabio Cruz, Open City Group

116 Hospedería de los Diseños (Design Lodge)
Open City, Ritoque, Quintero
1977, Open City Group

117 Greater Valparaíso Proposal
COREM
Valparaíso
1978, School of Architecture, Alberto Cruz

118 Hospedería de la Alcoba (Dormitory Lodge)
Open City, Ritoque, Quintero
1978, David Jolly, Open City Group

119 Agora de los Huéspedes (Guest Agora)
Open City, Ritoque, Quintero
1978, Juan Purcell, Open City Group
See pages 63-64

120 Peña House in Colina
Santiago
1979, Miguel Eyquem

121 Children's Home – Design
Valparaíso
1979, Alberto Cruz, Valparaíso Workshop

122 El Confín
Open City, Ritoque, Quintero.
1979, Open City Group

123 Quillota Urban Development – Project
Aconcagua
1980, José Vial, Arturo Baeza, Jorge Uribe,
Boris Ivelic

124 Hospedería de la Puntilla (Nail Lodge)
Open City, Ritoque, Quintero
1980, Open City Group

125 Hospedería del Errante I (Lodge of the Wanderer I)
Open City, Ritoque, Quintero.
1981, Miguel Eyquem, Open City Group.
Replaced by a new version: see work 191 and page 86

126 Hospedería de la Puerta o de la Entrada
(Entrance Lodge)
Open City, Ritoque, Quintero.
1982, Boris Ivelic
See page 59

127 Bo Cenotaph Garden
Open City, Ritoque, Quintero
1982, Alberto Cruz, Tomás Browne
See page 62

128 Palacio del Alba y del Ocaso (Palace of Dawn and Dusk)
Open City, Ritoque, Quintero
1982, Alberto Cruz, Jorge Sánchez, Open City Group
See pages 72-77

129 Palace of Dawn and Dusk Faubourg
Open City, Ritoque, Quintero
1983, Isabel M. Reyes, Tomás Browne, Patricio Cáraves,
David Jolly, Building Workshop

145 Hospedería del Estudio (Studio Lodge)
Open City, Ritoque, Quintero
1987, Fabio Cruz, David Jolly, Juan Purcell

164 Taller de los Diseños (Prototype Workshop)
Open City, Ritoque, Quintero
1990, Fabio Cruz, Juan Ignacio Baixas
See pages 114-121

168 Taller del Trabajo (Workshop)
Open City, Ritoque, Quintero
1991, Patricio Cáraves, David Jolly

169 Mesa Luna, (Moon Table) design for the Wanderer's Lodge
Open City, Ritoque, Quintero
1991, Manuel Casanueva, Miguel Eyquem

176 Casa de los Nombres (House of Names) **and Assembly of the UCV School of Architecture 40th Anniversary Exhibition**
Open City, Ritoque, Quintero
1992, Boris Ivelic, Fabio Cruz, Salvador Zahr, Ricardo Lang
Demolished
See pages 78-85

177 El Camino (The Road)
Open City, Ritoque, Quintero
1992, Jorge Sánchez, Juan Purcell
See page 65

181 Aula Viga (Beam Hall) **at the School of Architecture**
Recreo, Viña del Mar
1993, Juan Ignacio Baixas, Fabio Cruz

183 *Travesía* Amereida Vessel
Fondecyt Project
1994-2002, Boris Ivelic
See pages 130-133

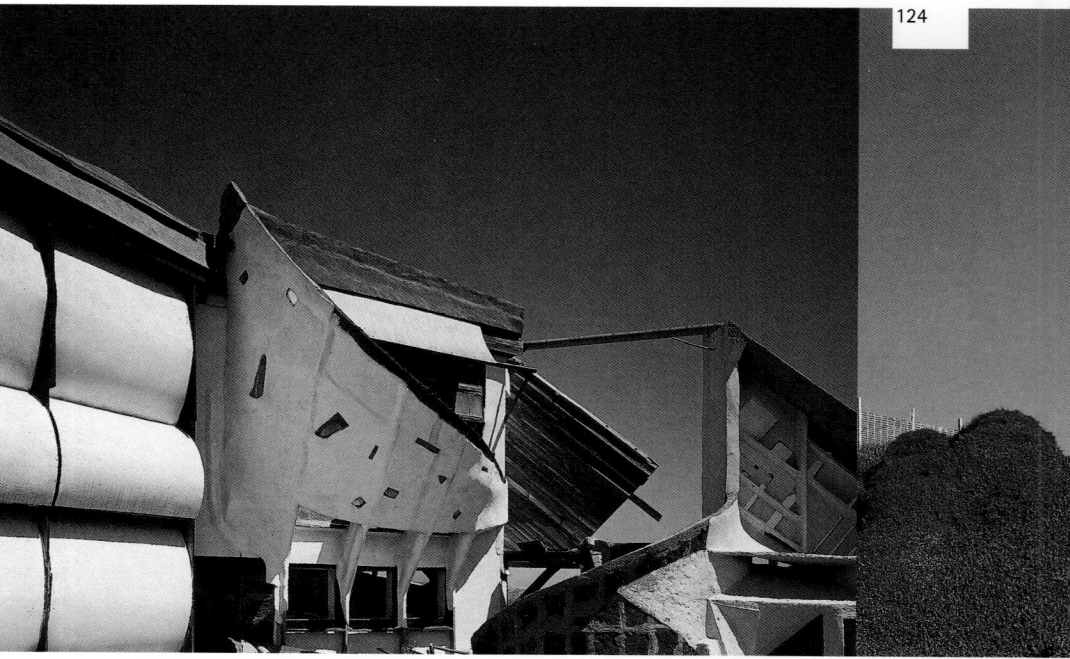

124

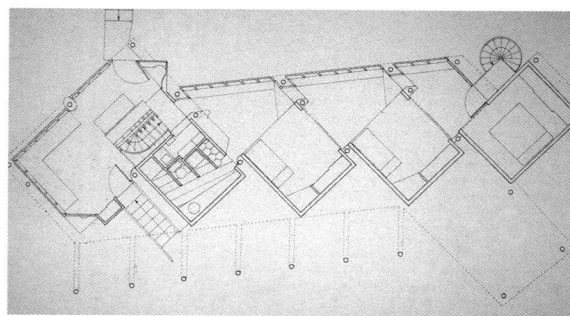

126

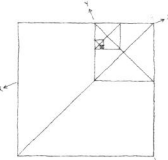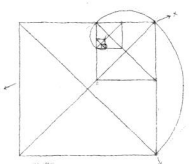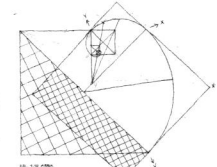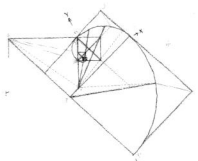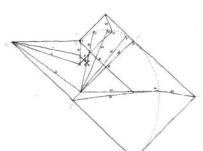

127

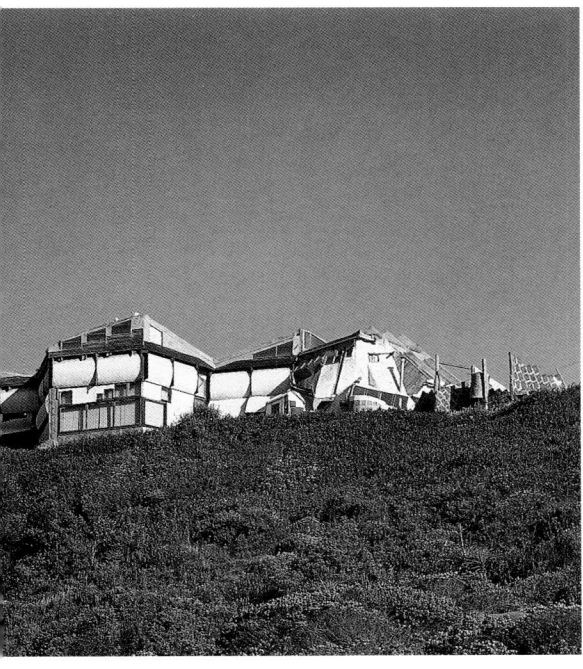

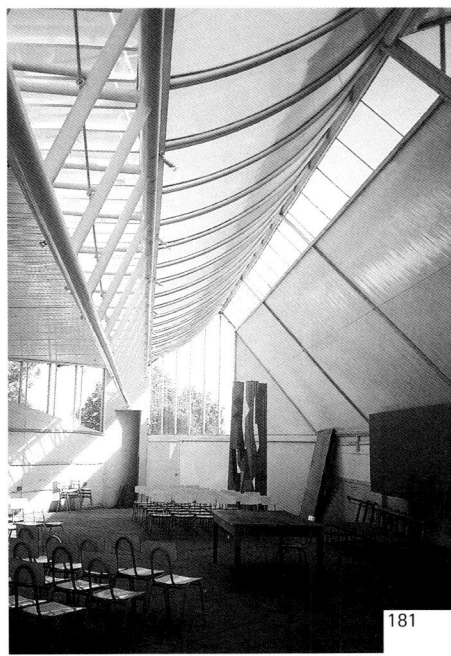

181

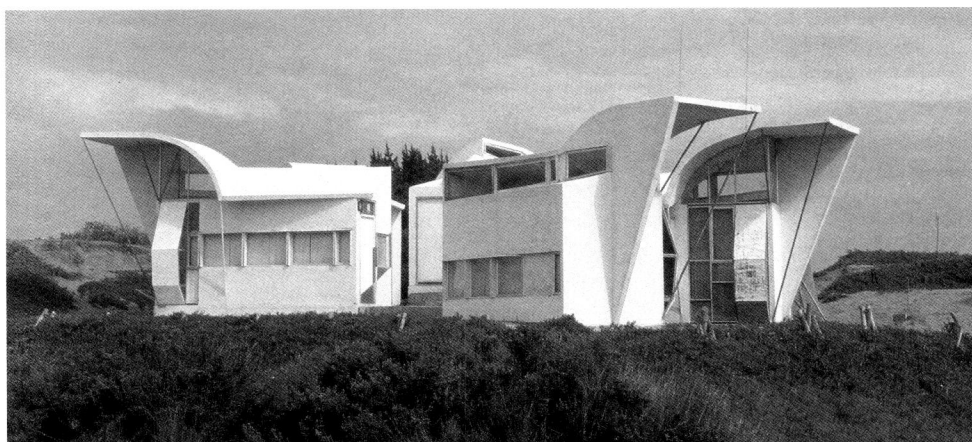

217

- **191 Nueva Hospedería del Errante** (New Lodge of the Wanderer) Fondecyt Project
  Open City, Ritoque, Quintero
  1995-2000, Manuel Casanueva
  See pages 86-97

- **200 Mesa del Entreacto** (Interval Table)
  Open City, Ritoque, Quintero
  1996, David Jolly, Patricio Cáraves, Open City Group

- **201 Galería de la Puntilla** (Nail Gallery)
  Open City, Ritoque, Quintero
  1996, Open City Group

- **215 Water Towers – Tensegrity Towers**
  Open City, Ritoque, Quintero
  1998, Miguel Eyquem
  See page 60

- **216 Sculptor Workshop**
  Open City, Ritoque, Quintero
  1998, Salvador Zahr, Fabio Cruz, Open City Group

- **217 Hospedería Rosa de los Vientos** (Compass Card Lodge)
  Open City, Ritoque, Quintero
  1998, David Luza, Building Workshop

- **218 Hospedería del Jardín** (Garden Lodge)
  Open City, Ritoque, Quintero
  1998, Iván Ivelic

- **226 Cemetery Chapel**
  Open City, Ritoque, Quintero
  1999, Patricio Cáraves, Jorge Sánchez, Juan Purcell,
  Open City Group
  See pages 108-113

- **234 Design and Assembly of the 30th Anniversary Exhibition of the Open City**
  Museum of Fine Arts, Santiago
  2000, School of Architecture

- **235 Avenida Brazil – Project**
  Valparaíso
  2000, School of Architecture

- **243 Cemetery Amphitheater**
  Open City, Ritoque, Quintero
  2001, Jorge Sánchez, Juan Purcell, Open City Group

- **244 Hospedería de los Signos** (Lodge of the Signs)
  Open City, Quintero
  2001-2002, Rodrigo Lorca, Open City Group

Travesías

73   ***Amereida Travesía*** across the continent, from Punta Arenas (Chile) to Santa Cruz de la Sierra (Bolivia). 1965, Alberto and Fabio Cruz (architects), Godofredo Iommi, Edison Simonds, Michel Deguy and Jonathan Boulting (poets), Henri Tronquoy, Claudio Girola (sculptors), François Fedier (philosopher), Jorge Pérez Román (painter)

130   **Froward Cape *Travesía***, Chile
1984, Fabio Cruz, Juan Ignacio Baixas, Boris Ivelic, Francisco Méndez, Bruno Barla, UCV Workshops

131   ***Travesía* to Róbinson Crusoe Island**
Archipelago of Juan Fernández, Chile
1984, Manuel Casanueva, Ricardo Lang, Salvador Zahr, Juan Mastrantonio, José Balcells, UCV Workshops

132   ***Travesía* to Marudá**, Brazil
1984, Juan Purcell, Jorge Sánchez, Justo Uribe, UCV Workshops

133   ***Travesía* to Paraná River**, Argentina
1984, Miguel Eyquem, Alberto Cruz, Claudio Girola, Victor Boscovic

134   ***Travesía* to Froward Cape**, Chile
1985, Juan Ignacio Baixas, Fabio Cruz, Boris Ivelic, Francisco Méndez, Bruno Barla, UCV Workshops

135   ***Travesía* to the River Plate**, Buenos Aires, Argentina
1985, Alberto Cruz, Miguel Eyquem, Claudio Girola, UCV Workshops

136   ***Travesía* to Easter Island**, Chile
1985, Salvador Zahr, Juan Mastrantonio, José Balcells, UCV Workshops

137   ***Travesía* to Amantani Island,** Titicaca Lake, Peru, 1985, Manuel Casanueva, Ricardo Lang, UCV Workshops

138   ***Travesía* to Bajos de Santa Rosa**, Patagonia Argentina
1985, Patricio Cáraves, David Jolly, Tomás Browne, Isabel M. Reyes.

139   ***Travesía* to San Pedro de Atacama**, Chile
1985, Juan Purcell, Jorge Sánchez, Justo Uribe

140   ***Travesía* to Pozo Colorado**, Chaco, Paraguay
1986, Juan Purcell, Jorge Sánchez, Justo Uribe

141   ***Travesía* to Llanos de Curimahuida**, Chile
1986, Juan Ignacio Baixas, Fabio Cruz, Boris Ivelic, Bruno Barla

142   ***Travesía* to Trehuaco**, Chile
1986, Miguel Eyquem, Alberto Cruz, Claudio Girola, Alejandro Garretón, Silvia Arriagada, Victor Boscovic

143   ***Travesía* to Morro Copiapó**, Caldera, Chile
1986, Salvador Zahr, Juan Mastrantonio, José Balcells

144   ***Travesía* to Malargüe-Usno**, Argentina
1986, Patricio Cáraves, David Jolly, Tomás Browne, Isabel M. Reyes

146   ***Travesía* to Churrecué, Chonos Archipelago**
Chile
1987, Salvador Zahr, Juan Mastrantonio, José Balcells

147   ***Travesía* to Florianópolis**, Brazil,
1987, Jorge Sánchez, Juan Purcell, Justo Uribe

148   **Athenea *Travesía***, Santiago, Chile
1987, Miguel Eyquem, Alberto Cruz, Claudio Girola

149   ***Travesía* to Salar de Coipasa**, Chile
1987, Juan Ignacio Baixas, Fabio Cruz, Boris Ivelic, Ricardo Lang, Bruno Barla

150   ***Travesía* to Cerro Montevideo**, Caldera, Chile
1987, Manuel Casanueva, Ricardo Lang

151   ***Travesía* to Pehuencó**, Bahía Blanca, Argentina
1987, Patricio Cáraves, David Jolly, Tomás Browne, Isabel M. Reyes

152   ***Travesía* to La Serena**, Chile
1988, Alberto Cruz, Claudio Girola, Isabel M. Reyes, Miguel Eyquem, Patricio Caravés, David Jolly, Tomás Browne Víctor Boskovic, Alejandro Garretón, Silvia Arriagada, Ricardo Lang

153   ***Travesía* to the Pampas, Cordillera Chulo**, Perú and Argentina
1988, Juan Purcell, Jorge Sánchez, Justo Uribe

154   ***Travesía* to Quebrada Verde**, Valparaíso, Chile
1988, Manuel Casanueva

155   ***Travesía* to Huinay**, Chile
1988, Juan Ignacio Baixas, Fabio Cruz, Boris Ivelic, Ricardo Lang, Bruno Barla

156   ***Travesía* to Pisagua**, Chile
1988, Salvador Zahr, Juan Mastrantonio, José Balcells.

157   ***Travesía* to Aconcagua Valley**, Chile
1988, Fabio Cruz, Bruno Barla

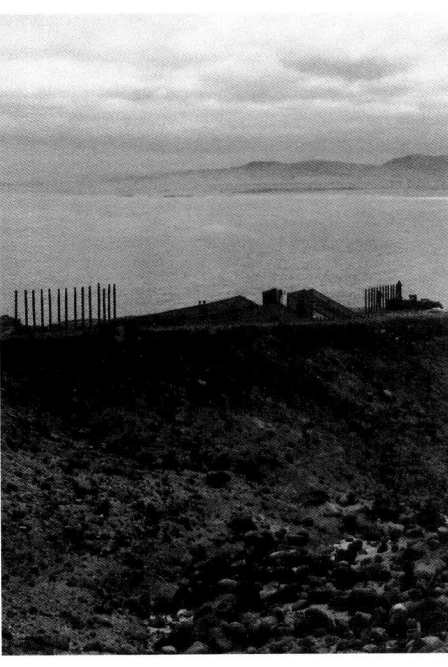

158 *Travesía* to **Colliguay**, Chile
1989, Manuel Casanueva,

159 *Travesía* to **Caleta Llico**, Arauco, Chile
1989, Tomás Browne

160 *Travesía* to **Usno**, Argentina
1989, Juan Purcell, Jorge Sánchez

161 **Juncal** *Travesía*, Chile
1989, Isabel M. Reyes, Miguel Eyquem

162 *Travesía* to **Churrecué, Chonos Archipelago**, Chile
1989, José Balcells, Salvador Zahr

163 *Travesía* to **Ritoque**, Chile
1989, Boris Ivelic

165 *Travesía* to **Errázuriz Bay**, Antofagasta, Chile
1990, Manuel Casanueva, José Balcells

166 *Travesía* to **Usno**, Argentina
1990, Juan Purcell, Jorge Sánchez, Patricio Cáraves, David Jolly

167 **Cochicó** *Travesía*, Argentina
1990, Fabio Cruz, Bruno Barla, Ricardo Lang, Silvia Arriagada, Isabel M. Reyes, Miguel Eyquem, Victor Boskovic, Jorge Ferrada

170 *Travesía* to **Mar Chiquita**, Argentina
1991, Juan Purcell, Jorge Sánchez, Claudio Girola, Ricardo Lang, Silvia Arriagada

171 *Travesía* to **Villa Mercedes**, Argentina
1991, Patricio Cáraves, David Jolly

172 **San Luis** *Travesía*, Argentina
1991, Isabel M. Reyes, Miguel Eyquem, Victor Boscovic

173 *Travesía* to **Ushuaia**, Patagonia Argentina
1991, Salvador Zahr, José Balcells

174 *Travesía* to **Ouro Preto**, Brazil
1991, Manuel Casanueva

175 *Travesía* to **La Dormida**, Chile
1991, Alberto Cruz, Bruno Barla

178 *Travesía* to **Santa Catalina**, Brazil
1992, Patricio Caraves, David Jolly

179 *Travesía* to **Santa Cruz de la Sierra**, Bolivia
1992, Juan Purcell, Jorge Sánchez, Silvia Arriagada

180 *Travesía* to **Puelches**, Argentina
1992, Isabel M. Reyes, Alejandro Garretón, Claudio Middleton

181 *Travesía* to **Huinay**, Chiloé Continental, Chile
1993, Fabio Cruz, Salvador Zahr, Boris Ivelic, Arturo Chicano, Ricardo Lang, José Balcells
See pages 130-133

184 *Travesía* to **Huinay**, *Amereida* vessel on *Travesía*
1994, Boris Ivelic
See pages 130-133

185 *Travesía* to **Concepción**, Chile
1994, Juan Purcell, Jorge Sánchez

186 *Travesía* to **Villa del Totoral**, Argentina
1994, Isabel M. Reyes, Miguel Eyquem, Claudio Middleton, Paz Undurraga

187 *Travesía* to **Puerto Sánchez**, Chile
1994, Fabio Cruz, Salvador Zahr, José Balcells, Ricardo Lang, Arturo Chicano, Carlos Covarrubias

188 *Travesía* to **Cajón del Maipo**, Chile
1994, Alberto Cruz, Bruno Barla, Alejandro Garretón, Silvia Arriagada

189 **Cuiabá** *Travesía,* Brazil
1994, Patricio Cáraves, David Jolly

190 *Travesía* to **Victoria**, Argentina
1994, Justo Uribe, Víctor Boskovic

192 *Travesía* to **Corral**, Chile
1995, Alejandro Garretón

193 *Travesía* to **Santa Rosa de Chena**, Chile
1995, Alberto Cruz, Bruno Barla

194 *Travesía* to **Peine**, Salar de Atacama, Chile
1995, Isabel M. Reyes, Miguel Eyquem

195 *Travesía* to **Cuenca**, Ecuador,
1995, Fabio Cruz, Salvador Zahr, José Balcells, Ricardo Lang, Silvia Arriagada *et al.*

196 *Travesía* to **Brasilia**, Brazil
1995, Justo Uribe, Víctor Boskovic, Claudio Middleton

197 *Travesía* to **Buenos Aires**, Argentina
1995, Juan Purcell, Jorge Sánchez, Andrés Garcés

198 *Travesía* to **Formoso do Araguaio**, Brazil
1995, Patricio Cáraves, David Jolly

199 *Travesía* to **Huinay**, Chiloé Continental, Chile
1995, Boris Ivelic

202 **Railway** *Travesía*, San Salvador de Jujuy, Rosario, Argentina
1996, Juan Purcell, Jorge Sánchez

203 *Travesía* to **Asunción**, Paraguay
1996, Patricio Cáraves, David Jolly

204 *Travesía* to **Puerto Saavedra**, Chile
1996, Fabio Cruz, Salvador Zahr, José Balcells, R. Lang, J. C. Jeldes, M. Wilkomirsky

205 *Travesía* to **Garca**, Brazil
1996, Arturo Chicano, Alejandro Garretón

206 *Travesía* to **Loa River**, Chile
1996, Isabel M. Reyes, Miguel Eyquem

207 *Travesía* to **Huinay**, Chiloé Continental, Chile.
1996, Boris Ivelic

208 *Travesía* to **Colchane**, Chile
1997, Juan Purcell

209 *Travesía* to **Nova Almeida Vitoria**, Brazil
1997, David Jolly, Patricio Cáraves, Mauricio Puentes, Rodrigo Saavedra, María Paz Larenas

210 *Travesía* to **Potosí**, Bolivia
1997, Fabio Cruz, Salvador Zahr

211 *Travesía* to **Juncal**, Chile
1997, Isabel M. Reyes, Miguel Eyquem

212 *Travesía* to **Huinay**, Chiloé Continental, Chile
1997, Boris Ivelic

213 *Travesía* to **Quito**, Ecuador
1997, José Balcells, Ricardo Lang, Marcelo Araya, Alejandro Garretón, Arturo Chicano, Carlos Covarrubias, Juan C. Jeldes, Michele Wilkomirsky, Silvia Arriagada, Jaime Reyes, Alejandra Rojas, Lois Cabezas

214 *Travesía* to **Quillota**, Chile
1997, Alberto Cruz, Justo Uribe

219 *Travesía* to **Iquitos**, Amazonas, Peru
1998, Juan Purcell, Jorge Sánchez

220 *Travesía* to **Coihue Estate**, Bio Bio, Chile
1998, Isabel M. Reyes, Miguel Eyquem

221 *Travesía* to **Arambaré, Lagoa dos Patos**, Brazil
1998, David Jolly, Patricio Cáraves, Mauricio Puentes, Rodrigo Saavedra, Jorge Ferrada

222 *Travesía* to **Puerto Cisnes**, Aisén, Chile
1998, Fabio Cruz, Salvador Zahr

223 *Travesía* to **Obstrucción Fjord**, Magallanes, Chile
1998, Iván Ivelic, David Luza

224 *Travesía* to **Buenos Aires**, Argentina,
1998, José Balcells, Ricardo Lang, Marcelo Araya, Alejandro Garretón, Arturo Chicano, Carlos Covarrubias, Juan C. Jeldes, Michele Wilkomirsky

225 *Travesía* to **Puerto Montt**, Chile
1998, Boris Ivelic

227 *Travesía* to **La Paz**, Bolivia
1999, José Balcells, Ricardo Lang, Silvia Arriagada, Alejandro Garretón, Arturo Chicano, Carlos Covarrubias, Juan C. Jeldes, Michele Wilkomirsky

228 *Travesía* to **Santa Cruz de la Sierra**, Bolivia
1999, Juan Purcell, Jorge Sánchez

229 **Central Littoral** *Travesía*, Chile
1999, Isabel M. Reyes, Miguel Eyquem, Giancarlo Mewe

230 *Travesía* to **Open City**, Ritoque, Chile
1999, Manuel Casanueva

231 *Travesía* to **Canudos,** Barra do Itarirí, Brazil
1999, Patricio Cáraves, David Jolly, Mauricio Puentes, Rodrigo Saavedra, Jorge Ferrada, Michele Wilkomirsky, Juan C. Jeldes, Marcelo Araya, Carolina Vignola

232 *Travesía* to **Caleta Tortel**, Chile
1999, Fabio Cruz, Salvador Zahr *et al.*

233 *Travesía* to **Puerto Montt**, Chile
1999, Boris Ivelic

236 *Travesía* to **Andacollo,** Chile
2000, Fabio Cruz, Salvador Zahr

237 *Travesía* to **Quingues**, Ecuador
2000, Ivan Ivelic, David Luza, Silvia Arriagada,

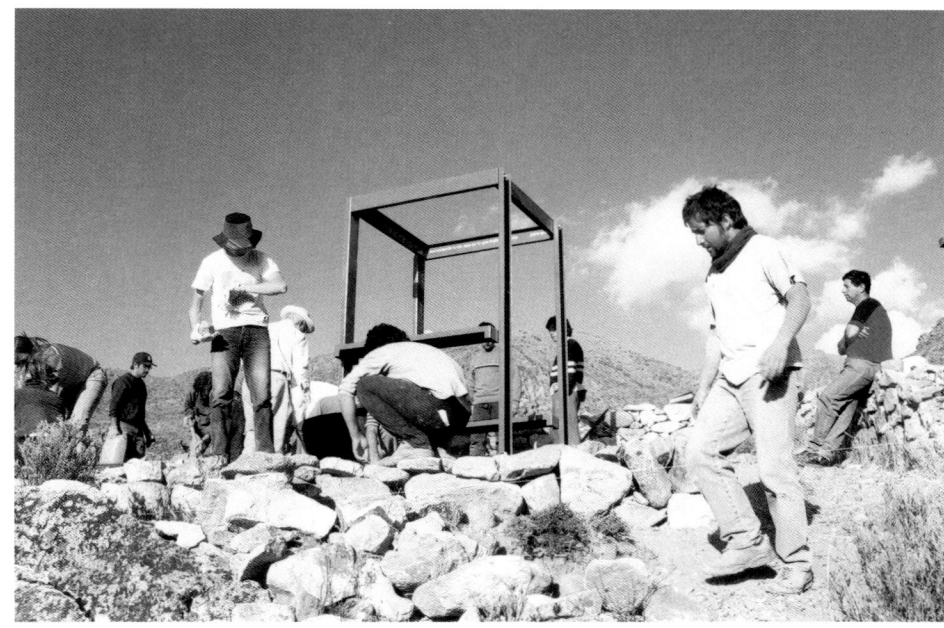

246

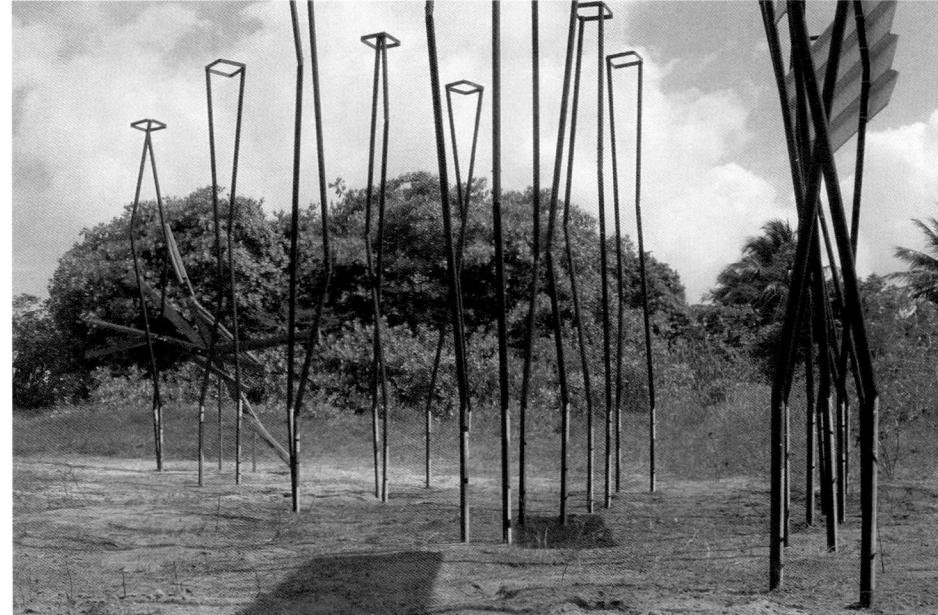

249

Alejandro Garretón, Ricardo Lang, Jaime Reyes, Arturo Chicano, Carlos Covarrubias, Dolores Andrade

238 *Travesía* to **Porto Seguro**, Bahía, Brazil
2000, Patricio Cáraves, David Jolly, Mauricio Puentes, Rodrigo Saavedra, Manuel Sanfuentes, Michele Wilkomirsky, Juan C. Jeldes, Marcelo Araya, Andrés Garcés

239 *Travesía* to **Paranal**, Antofagasta, Chile, 2000, Isabel M. Reyes, Miguel Eyquem

240 *Travesía* to **Puerto Montt**, Chile
2000, Boris Ivelic

241 **Edge** *Travesía,* Andes from Antofagasta to Bariloche, Argentina and Chile
2000, Jorge Ferrada, Giancarlo Mewe

242 *Travesía* to **Brasilia and Rio de Janeiro**, Brazil
2000, Jorge Sánchez, Juan Purcell

245 *Travesía* to **Portugal**
2001, Manuel Casanueva

246 **Continental Edge** *Travesía*
2001, Jorge Sánchez, Juan Purcell

247 *Travesía* to **Santa Cruz de la Sierra**, Bolivia
2001, Iván Ivelic, Mauricio Puentes, David Luza, Rodrigo Saavedra

248 *Travesía* to **Humahuaca**, Argentina
2001, Fabio Cruz, Salvador Zahr, José Balcells

249 **Joao Pessoa** *Travesía*, Brazil
2001, Patricio Cáraves, David Jolly, H. Spencer, Michelle Wilkomirsky, Marcelo Araya, Juan C. Jeldes

250 *Travesía* to **Puerto Montt, Amereida vessel**
2001, Boris Ivelic

251 **Athenea** *Travesía*, Santiago de Chile
2001, Isabel M. Reyes, Miguel Eyquem

252 **Land Opening** *Travesía* **in Open City**, Ritoque
2002, 12 teachers and around 280 students

253 **Design Party** *Travesía*, La Serena, Puerto Montt, Rancagua, Open City, Ritoque, Chile
2002, 8 teachers and 120 students

151

Biography and Chronology
Captions on page 160

SCHOOL OF ARCHITECTURE

Deans, Faculty of Architecture and Town Planning

Manuel Marchant Lyon	1950-1953
Carlos Bresciani	1953-1969
Hugo Rojas	1973-1984
Alberto Cruz Covarrubias	1984-1991
Juan Purcell Fricke	1991-1997
Salvador Zahr Maluk	1997...

Re-founding members, School of Architecture

Alberto Cruz Covarrubias	1952
Godofredo Iommi Marini	
Jame Bellalta Bello	
Miguel Eyquem Astorga	
Francisco Méndez Labbé	
Fabio Cruz Prieto	
José Vial Armstrong	
Arturo Baeza Donoso	
Claudio Girola Iommi	1956

Directors, School of Architecture

Arturo Baeza Donoso	1958-1967
José Vial Amstrong	1968-1976
Fabio Cruz Prieto	1976-1984
Justo Uribe Olmedo	1984-1988
Boris Ivelic Kusanovic	1988-1992
Jorge Sánchez Reyes	1992-1996
David Jolly Monge	1996-2002

Professors with a significant participation

Jorge Sánchez Reyes, Architect	1958...
Juan Purcell Fricke, Architect	1959...
Justo Uribe Olmedo, Architect	1959-1998
Victor Boskovic, Architect	1965-1997
Boris Ivelic Kusnovic, Architect	1969...
Manuel Casanueva González, Architect	1970...
Isabel Margarita Reyes Netle, Architect	1972...
Salvador Zahr Maluk, Architect	1974...
Bruno Barla, Architect	1977-1996
José Balcells Eyquem, Sculptor and Graphic Designer	1978...
David Jolly Monge	1978...
Ricardo Lang, Objects Designer	1978...
Patricio Cáraves Silva, Architect	1978...
Alejandro Garretón, Graphic Designer	1988...
Silvia Arriagada, Graphic Designer	1988...
Arturo Chicano, Objects Designer	1988...
Ivan Ivelic Yanes, Architect	1994...
David Luza Cornejo, Architect	1994...
Juan Carlos Jeldes Pontio, Designer	1994...
Jorge Ferrada, Architect	1996...
Rodrigo Saavedra Venegas, Architect	1996...
Mauricio Puentes Riffo, Architect	1996...
Michele Wilkomirsky, Designer	1997...

Other architect professors at the School

- Fernando Antequera
- Oscar Butazzoni
- Horacio Carmona
- James Chadwick Vergara
- Enrique Concha Gana
- Patricia Cruz
- Andrés MacDonald
- Mario Orfali Bejer
- Miguel Ossandon
- Herman Rojas
- Hugo Rojas
- Jaime Sepúlveda Buzovsky
- Rómulo Trebbi del Trebigiano
- Oscar Valenzuela
- Antonio Vicente Molina

OPEN CITY GROUP

Updated 14 February 2002

Active founding member	AF
Deceased founding member	DF
Inactive founding member	IF
Guest, lodge visitor	G
Active member	AM
Participant (occasional)	P

Arriagada Cordero, Silvia	Designer, AM
Baeza Donoso, Arturo	Architect, DF
Baixas Figueras, Juan	Architect, P
Balcells Eyquem, Ignacio	Poet, IF
Balcells Eyquem, José	Sculptor, Designer, AF, G
Barla Hidalgo, Bruno	Architect, P
Boskovic Boskovic, Víctor	Architect, IF
Browne Covarrubias, Tomás	Architect, AM
Buschmann De Santos, Walter	Architect, P
Cáraves Silva, Patricio	Architect, AM, G
Casanueva Carrasco, Manuel	Architect, AF
Chadwick Vergara, James	Architect, IF
Chicano Jiménez, Arturo	Designer, AM, G
Covarrubias Fernández, Carlos	Poet, AF
Cruz Covarrubias, Alberto	Architect, AF
Cruz Prieto, Fabio	Architect, AF
Emilfork, Leonidas	Poet, IF
Eyquem Astorga, Miguel	Architect, AF
Ferrada Herrera, Jorge	Architect, AM
Garcés Alzamora, Andrés	Architect, AM
Garretón Correa, Alejandro	Designer, AM
Girola Iommi, Claudio	Sculptor, DF
Hernández Flaño, Gustavo	Architect, P
Iommi Marini, Godofredo	Poet, DF
Ivelic Kusanovic, Boris	Architect, AF, G
Ivelic Yanes, Iván	Architect, AM, G
Jara Guarda, Jorge	Architect, P
Jeldes Pontio, Juan Carlos	Designer, AM, G
Jolly Monge, David	Architect, AM, G
Lang Viacava, Ricardo	Designer, AM, G
Lara Varennes, Iván	Philosopher, IF
Lorca Barros, Rodrigo	Architect, AM, G
Luza Cornejo, David	Architect, AM
Mastrantonio Freitas, Juan	Architect, IF
Méndez Labbe, Francisco	Painter, IF
Mewe Vianello, Giancarlo	Architect, P
Middleton Olguín, Claudio	Architect, P
Pedrina Rigonni, María	Architect, P
Prieto Ovalle, José	Architect, P
Puentes Riffo, Mauricio	Architect, AM, G
Purcell Fricke, Juan	Architect, AF
Reyes Gil, Jaime	Poet, AM
Reyes Nettle, Isabel	Architect, AF
Rodríguez Severín, Virgilio	Poet, IF
Saavedra Venegas, Rodrigo	Architect, AM, G
Sánchez Reyes, Jorge	Architect, AF, G
Sanfuentes Vío, Manuel	Poet, AM
Uribe Olmedo, Justo	Architect, IF
Vial Armstrong, Alberto	Mathematician, DF
Vial Armstrong, José	Architect, DF
Vicente Molina, Antonio	Architect, DF
Wilkomirsky Uribe, Michele	Designer, AM
Zahr Maluk, Salvador	Architect, AF

In 1540, the Spaniard, Pedro de Valdivia, starts colonizing the area. Over the next three centuries, this isolated province (General Captaincy) of the Viceroyalty of Peru is characterized by the crossbreeding of races and cultures, the creation of vast estates, and the rise to power of a Castilian-Basque aristocracy (the Larrain, Ovalle, and Covarrubias families). Bernardo O'Higgins leads the struggle for independence and the foundation of Chile (1810-30), a long (4,330 km) and narrow stretch of land between the Pacific and the Andes (peaks of up to 6,885 m), a land of telluric landscapes, earthquakes and volcanoes.

1917: Chile has 3,900,000 inhabitants, of whom 90% live in poverty and 0.5% form part of the aristocracy (with titles to 50% of the land); copper is the country's

16th-19th century
Quintero, Diego de Almagro's pilot (1536), names the town whose municipal area encompasses the beach and sand flats of Ritoque, 25 km north of Valparaíso (Valdivia's Puerto de Santiago). In the epic poem *La Araucana* (1569), Ercilla praises the Araucanians, the unyielding warriors who were granted autonomy by Charles III in 1769. In 1593, the Society of Jesus is established in Chile. Valparaíso, a free port since 1822, achieves its greatest splendour as the cultural and economic capital of the country until eclipsed by the opening of the Panama Canal (1914-20).
Adapting to the area's irregular topography of steep hills and cliffs that fall sharply to the sea, the streets and houses climb and turn in search of views, in a decadent Mediterranean setting. In 1874, the Viña del Mar residential neighbourhood and resort is developed on the site of the former estate of the same name, now joined to the city by the coastal highway that forms the Valparaíso-Viña del Mar conurbation.
In 1888, when the capital's population is over 150,000, the Archdiocese of Santiago sets up the Catholic University of Chile (PUCCh) and sees the publication of *Azul* [Blue], with which Ruben Darío introduces Modernism in poetry.

1917-1930
Birth of Alberto Cruz Covarrubias in Santiago, Chile in 1917. This year also sees the birth of the multifaceted and libertarian artist Violeta Parra, the publication of Neftalí Reyes's first book in Temuco, and the design of Alberto Cruz Montt's eclectic Club de la Unión and Palacio Ariztía buildings.

Hispanic contribution to 16th C humanism—Latin American cities are laid out along reticular, orthogonal grids following the City of God Renaissance ideal. Hundreds of settlements attempt to give concrete shape to the utopia of a New World. Over 30 towns or Jesuit missions are established in Paraguay (17th - 18th C). The forerunners and top exponents of symbolism in poetry include Baudelaire (1821-67), Verlaine (1844-96), Rimbaud (1854-91), and Mallarmé (1842-98). In 1916, Rubén Darío, who lived in Valpa-raíso, dies, Einstein publishes his *General Theory of Relativity* and Freud his *General Introduction to Psychoanalysis*.

1917: Russian revolution; Mondrian and De Stijl's Neoplasticism. 1919-28: Bauhaus, *Art Déco*, avant garde movements; Stalin rises to power; Fascism (Mussolini) and

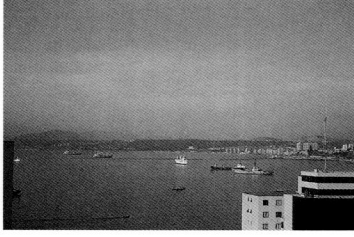
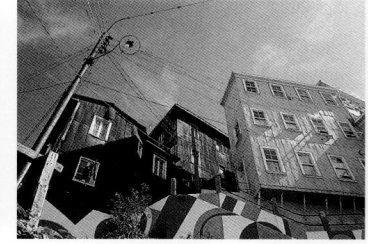

main export; birth of labour unions and strikes. 1920: Life expectancy is 30 years; the market for saltpetre (sodium nitrate, a natural fertilizer), the country's second natural resource, collapses. 1927-31: Ibáñez, the Chilean "Mussolini", is president.

Devastated by the Great Depression, the country lives through a period of crisis, social inequality and proletarian exodus to the cities. The Popular Front, the only party of its kind outside Europe, wins the elections. 1939: An earthquake devastates the South and Spanish refugees arrive. 1945: Gabriela Mistral is awarded the Nobel Prize for Literature. 1947: Copper demand falls.

Women gain the right to vote. Girola and Maldonado travel to Europe, the former working as a disciple of Georges

In 1920, Gabriela Mistral, director of the Temuco Lyceum, encourages the literary efforts of Neftalí Reyes Basoalto, who later adopts the *nom de plume* of Pablo Neruda [*Residence on Earth*, 1933] and writes jointly with Vicente Huidobro (*Poemas árticos*, 1918, *Altazor*, 1933), a sublime poetry of universal scope. In 1923, Claudio Girola is born in Rosario de Santa Fe, Argentina. In 1928, the Catholic University of Valparaíso (UCV) is founded. The architect and painter, Roberto Matta, works in Le Corbusier's atelier (1935-36).

1938-1947
In 1939, Girola joins the School of Fine Arts in Buenos Aires, which he leaves in 1943 after issuing a manifesto against its orientation. In 1940 Alberto Cruz graduates from the PUCCh School of Architecture in Santiago and, for five years, works with Fernando López and Jorge Elton on the design of single-family houses, until he joins the faculty of his former school in 1945. In that same year, following the 1944 *Concrete Art* exhibition organized by Max Bill in Basel, Claudio Girola, Tomás Maldonado (b. Rosario, Argentina, 1922), Alfredo Hilto and Ennio Iommi set up the Concrete Art Association in Argentina.

1949
Students of the PUCCh School of Architecture in Santiago rebel against the authorities and go on strike: They demand a move away from the classical methods and towards the adoption of the principles of contemporary architecture, and defend professor

Nazism (Hitler) take root. 1928: Freyssinet invents prestressed concrete. 1929-30: Mies van der Rohe designs the German Pavilion, Barcelona; Le Corbusier travels to Buenos Aires and designs the Errazuris House in Zapallar, Chile; the beginning of the Great Depression.

J. Huizinga writes *Homo Ludens*. 1939: The Spanish Civil War ends and Franco's dictatorship and mass exile begin; start of World War II. 1942: Niemeyer designs the Pampulha Restaurant. 1944: Villanueva designs the University Campus, Caracas. 1945: US drops the first atomic bombs; World War II ends; the United Nations is established; Barragán plans the El Pedregal project for Mexico City.

Mao proclaims the People's Republic of China. Germany is divided into two states. Simone de Beauvoir writes *The*

Vantongerloo and the latter taking a teaching position at the Polytechnic University in Milan. Over this decade, copper becomes Chile's main source of income.

Public deficit is high. Pablo Neruda writes *Canto general* [General Songs]. The Generation of the 50s—José Donoso and others—is formed.

Carlos Ibáñez defeats Salvador Allende (b. Valparaíso, 1908), the rising star of the Socialist Party, in the presidential elections.
Chile's population rises to 6,000,000. Emilio Duhart, Alberto Cruz's fellow student at the Catholic University of Chile in Santiago, works with Le Corbusier on his India projects.

Copper sales experience a sharp fall. Inflation: 50%.

Strikes in the mining industry, among others. A state of siege is declared. Nicanor Parra writes *Poemas y anti-poemas* [Poems and Antipoems]. Inflation: 58%.

Inflation: 88%.

Bresciani / Valdés / Castillo / Huidobro design the Portales Housing Estate in Santiago.

A group of young graduates from the PUCCh found the Christian Democratic Party, PDC.

Alberto Cruz Covarrubias and his first year course, Workshop of Plastic Arts. Students José Vial and Arturo Baeza, who come into contact with Godofredo Iommi, are among the leaders of the strike, which is backed by the University's Catholic Action movement and has the sympathy of the young faculty members. Sergio Larrain, who came into contact with the Bauhaus and Le Corbusier in the Twenties, directs the School.
1950
Taking up Jaime Bellalta and Miguel Eyquem's invitation, Alberto Cruz travels to Europe and remains there for a year, the same year in which Max Bill begins directing the Hochschule für Gestaltung in Ulm, the design school that followed in the footsteps of the Bauhaus.
1951
Claudio Girola holds an exhibition of his work at the Museum of Modern Art in Sao Paulo.

1952
Accepting an invitation from Father Jorge González Foster, the rector of the UCV, Alberto Cruz, Godofredo Iommi and a group of young architects trained at the PUCCh of Santiago—including the painter Francisco Méndez and the architects Arturo Baeza, Jaime Bellalta, Fabio Cruz, Miguel Eyquem and José Vial—travel to Valparaíso, where they take up teaching positions at the preexisting UCV School of Architecture. Hired as a group, they live with their families in houses on the Cerro Castillo, in Viña del Mar, where they develop a communal attitude to life and work, rejecting the conventional

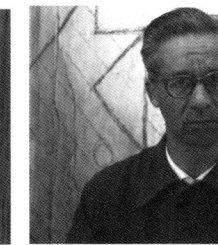 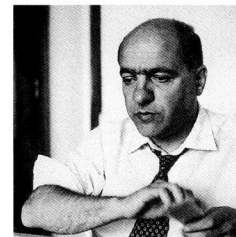 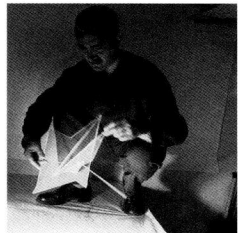

practice of their profession. At the same time, and following Iommi's initiative, the group creates the UCV Institute of Architecture to foster post-graduate studies.
1953
Alberto Cruz works in the Chapel on the Los Pajaritos country estate project.

1954
The urban development project for Achupallas, in Viña del Mar, whose "principles" will exert great influence over the future development of the School, is published.

1955
The sculptor Claudio Girola joins the group on a permanent basis.

1956
The Institute of Architecture participates in the Naval Academy of Valparaíso competition. The design submitted by the Institute is one of the four projects chosen.

1957
Guillermo Julián de la Fuente, one of the members of the first class to graduate from the School of Valparaíso, joins Le Corbusier's studio, later becoming its supervisor.

Second Sex. P. Johnson designs the House in New Canaan, Le Corbusier the Curuchet House in La Plata, Argentina.

The Korean War begins. The first Diner's club card appears. O'Gorman et al. design the University Library, Mexico City.

C. Tedeschi writes *Una introducción a la historia de la arquitectura* [An Introduction to the History of Architecture], Tucumán.

Eisenhower becomes president of the United States, and Paz Estensoro president of Bolivia (after a military coup). Elizabeth II becomes Queen of England. Aalto builds the Säynätsalo Town Hall, SOM the Lever House Building, New York. Jacobsen designs the Ant chair.

Hemingway writes *The Old Man and the Sea*. Picasso paints *War and Peace*.

Crick and Watson discover the double helix structure of DNA.

Le Corbusier builds the Chapel at Ronchamp. R. Banham writes *The New Brutalism*. T. Maldonado teaches at Ulm. Bill Haley gives birth to rock and roll.

Latin American Architecture since 1945 exhibition at the MOMA in New York.

Saarinen designs the TWA Terminal, New York. O. Paz writes *The Bow and the Lyre*.

The European Community is created; Sputnik launched; X CIAM Congress held; Team Ten formed. L. Costa plans Brasilia.

The conservative Alessandri defeats Allende, Eduardo Frei et al, by 33,000 votes, in the presidential elections.

1959
The DFL-2 Law increases social housing.

A strong earthquake takes place. E. Duhart designs the United Nations Building in Santiago.

Inflation rises and numerous strikes take place.

Agrarian reform and Electoral reform (increasing the voting population) are implemented. Inflation: 28%.

1958
Godofredo Iommi visits Tomás Maldonado in Ulm and has frequent contact with Juan Borchers and Guillermo Julián in Paris, where he is joined by Miguel Eyquem and Francisco Méndez. Jaime Bellalta leaves for London. Work starts on Cruz House in Calle Jean Mermoz, Santiago.

1960
Alberto Cruz, A. Baeza, J. Vial and the Institute of Architecture prepare a new draft design for the Benedictine Monastery of Las Condes in Santiago.

1961
Designs are drawn up and work is undertaken to rebuild the Southern churches destroyed by the earthquake of 1960: Candelaria Chapel in San Pedro (demolished), Corral Parish Church in Valdivia, Paillaco Church... Building work begins on the Parish Church of Santa Clara in Santiago.

1962
Engineers A. Vives, A. Pinto, A. Lamana, and architect S. Rojo join the School of Valparaíso. Design and building work begins on the Mother Church of Puerto Montt, and on the churches of Arauco (demolished), Caranilahue, Lebu, Florida (Concepción), and Carampangne (Concepción). 10th Anniversary Exhibition of the UCV School of Architecture is held. Girola exhibits his work at the XXXI Venice Biennial.

Giuseppe Roncalli becomes Pope John XXIII. Eladio Dieste designs the Atlántida Church in Uruguay.

1959
Castro assumes power in Cuba. Wright dies.

The birth control pill is put on the market. John F. Kennedy becomes president of the United States.

Kennedy's Alliance for Progress assigns 720 million dollars to Chile (until 1970). The Cold War intensifies. Gargarin is the first person to travel in space.

Amnesty International is founded. The U.S. Telstar is launched. Robert Venturi designs the Vanna Venturi House in Philadelphia, Alejandro de la Sota the Maravillas School Gymnasium in Madrid.

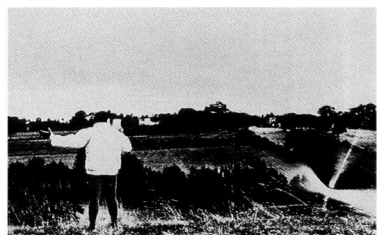 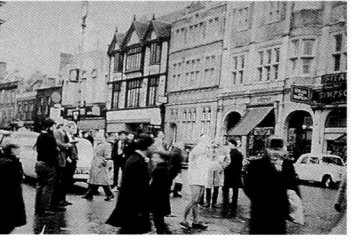 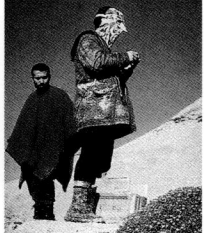 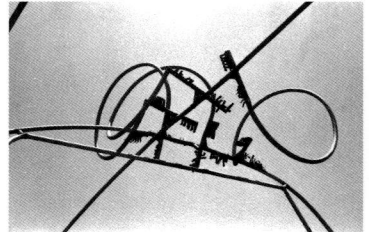

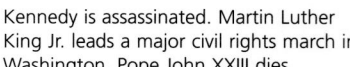

The Chilean copper industry supplies 15% of the world market.

Frei is elected president. His party of catholic social reformers (PDC) is the first of its kind to rise to power in Latin America.

The Frei administration sets up the Urban Improvement Corporation, CORMU, in which J. Bellalta works and for which Miguel Eyquem draws up two projects. Valparaíso-Viña del Mar has a population of 400,000.

1966
José Ricardo Morales writes *Arquitectónica*.

The folklore singer, Violeta Parra, leading figure of the *New Chilean Song*, dies.

1963
Crisis at the School of Architecture over the Domeyko case: Interventions by J. Borchers and Alberto Cruz. Claudio Girola exhibits his work at the National Museum of Fine Arts, Buenos Aires, wins the Georges Braque Award and travels to France.

1964
Godofredo Iommi, together with Girola (who exhibits his work in Paris and collaborates with the *Revue de Poésie*) and other poets and philosophers, participates in the *Phalènes*, the poetic acts held in different French cities, before returning to Valparaíso.

1965
First *Travesía Amereida* voyage across the continent, from Punta Arenas, in the south, to Santa Cruz de la Sierra, in Bolivia, where it is cut short by the guerrilla activities of Che Guevara. Participants include Alberto and Fabio Cruz (architects), Godofredo Iommi, Edison Simonds, Michel Deguy and Jonathan Boulting (poets), Henry Tronquoy and Claudio Girola (sculptors), François Fedier (philosopher), and Jorge Pérez Román (painter). Iommi transcribes and edits the writings of the *travesía*: *Amereida*.

1967
June 15 manifesto, endorsed by all the students of the School of Valparaíso. Gradually, not only other schools from the Catholic University of Valparaíso but

Kennedy is assassinated. Martin Luther King Jr. leads a major civil rights march in Washington. Pope John XXIII dies.

Krushchev falls. The Ulm School closes down. Hossdorf designs the Pavilion for the National Swiss Exhibition. Pop Art succeeds at the Venice Biennial.

Le Corbusier dies. R. Porro designs the School of Plastic Arts in Havana. Peter Collins publishes *Changing Ideals in Modern Architecture*. The U.S. invades the Dominican Republic.

1966
Rossi publishes *The Architecture of the City*. Yamasaki: World Trade Center, New York.

R. Buckminster Fuller designs the U.S. Pavilion for Expo 67, Montreal. Caveri

J. Borchers writes *Institución arquitectónica*. The journal *CA* appears.

Several left-wing parties unite to form the Popular Unity party. The *New Chilean Song*—groups such as Quilapayún or Inti-Illimani and singers such as Víctor Jara—r ses to fame.

Allende is elected president. The Popular Unity administration opens the way for socialism. Collective and popular arts proliferate.

Pablo Neruda receives the Nobel Prize for Literature. The copper industry is nationalized. Cultural initiatives proliferate. Leopoldo Castedo's *Historia del arte y*

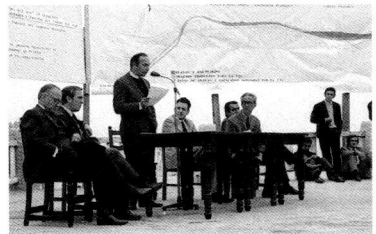

arquitectura latinoamericana [History of Latin American Art and Architecture] (1970) is disseminated.

The Agrarian reform movement gains speed. High inflation. Mass protest demonstrations. A state of siege in Santiago. Pawley and A. van Eyck participate in the housing exhibition.

Social coexistence is put to the test. The economy collapses. Allende's assassination, during a military coup, is followed by a wave of repression.

General Pinochet assumes the presidency.

The Peace Committee promoted by the Catholic Church is closed down.

Ultraliberal economic policies open the

from the rest of the country support the manifesto. University reform begins in Chile.

1968
The Bottegas, or professor and student workshops, are set up as a projection of what the Institute of Architecture had fostered up to that time.

1969
The School of Valparaíso expresses its strong opposition to the overpass project fostered by the Ministry of Public Works to link Valparaíso and Viña del Mar along the coast, and presents the Avenida del Mar project as an alternative proposal. Girola participates in the Amsterdam Biennial.

1970
After its establishment, the Cooperativa de Servicios Profesionales Amereida (co-operative of professional services) buys 270 Ha of land along a 3,030 m stretch of beach in Ritoque, 30 km N of Valparaíso, where the Open City is founded in part as an alternative to the failed University reform promoted by the School of Valparaíso in 1967.

1971
The book *Fundamentos de la Escuela de Arquitectura de la Universidad Católica de Valparaíso* [Principles of the UCV School of Architecture] is published. Work on the Open City begins with an Igloo, a collective work, forerunner to the team work that would later become known as "en ronda". The Graphic Design and Object Design

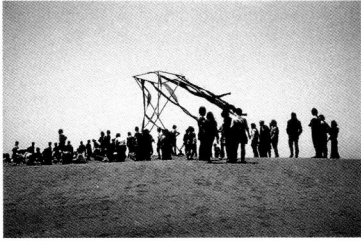
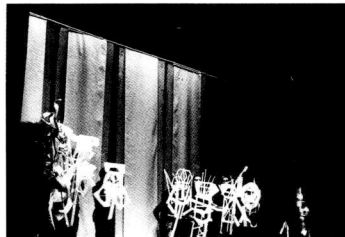

Schools are established: These, together with the School of Architecture and the pre-existing Institute of Art, form the UCV Faculty of Architecture. Miguel Eyquem receives the National Town Planning Award.

1972
The Music Room and the Tronquoy Agora, both in the Open City, are built. The Institute of Art stages three theatre performances based on Iommi's odes: *Nahuatl*, *América*, and *América sin patria*. The UCV School of Architecture 20th Anniversary Exhibition is held at the National Museum of Fine Arts in Santiago.

1973
Work begins on the Ancient Palace in the Open City. The School draws up urban development projects commissioned by the administration: Estero Marga Marga (Viña del Mar) and UCV-BID (Valparaíso).

1974
The Water Towers (first version), as well as the Double or Banquet Lodge are erected in the Open City.

1975
Alberto Cruz Covarrubias receives the National Architecture Award.

1976
Work begins on the Open City's Cemetery. Claudio Girola completes the sculpture El Pozo.

writes *El hombre a través de la arquitectura* [Man through Architecture], García Márquez *One Hundred Years of Solitude*.

Student protests take place in Paris. Martin Luther King is assassinated.

Armstrong is the first man to walk on the moon. 250,000 people demonstrate against the Vietnam War. Rossi designs the Gallaratese Apartment Building in Milan, Kahn the Kimbell Museum of Art in Fort Worth.

In the US, 50% of the female population works outside the home. Greenpeace is founded. SOM (B. Graham) designs the John Hancock Center in Chicago.

Communist China is admitted to the United Nations. Sáenz de Oiza designs the Banco de Bilbao in Madrid. H. Léfèvre publishes *La révolution urbaine*. Bacon is

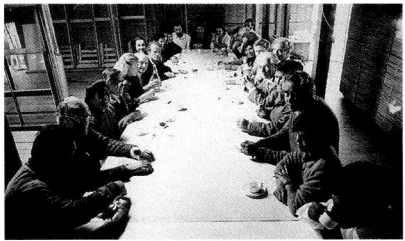

designated painter of the year. Girola participates in the XI Antwerp Biennial.

The Watergate scandal breaks. The Kassel Documenta brings Hyperrealism to the fore. Venturi / Scott Brown write *Learning from Las Vegas*. The Moscow Plan is drawn up.

OPEC's oil embargo causes a worldwide energy crisis. Pablo Picasso and Pablo Neruda die. I. M. Pei builds the Hancock Tower in Boston.

Richard Nixon resigns. Isozaki designs the Gunma Prefectural Museum of Art.

The Vietnam War ends. Juan Carlos I is crowned King of Spain.

Mao dies. G. De Carlo designs the Free

way for capitalism. C. Fernández Cox designs the Pontifical Seminary Building.

The first number of the journal *Ars*, (published until 1991) appears.

Chile issues its first credit card. Imported consumer products experience a rise in demand.

Pinochet wins the plebiscite for a new constitution and begins his eight-year presidency. The journal *ARQ* appears.

Sustained economic growth: GDP rises 7% per annum, on average, since 1976.

The Plaza Lyon Building, by Larrain, Mur-

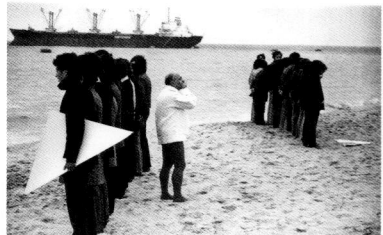

tinho & Assoc., is inaugurated in the middle of a marked economic recession.

Renewed economic growth. C. de Groote designs the Errazuris House.

Gigantic foreign debt: 143% of the GDP. New economic policy. National Agreement for Transition to Democracy is signed.

An attempt on Pinochet's life fails.

E. Browne designs the Caracola House.

1988
In the second plebiscite called by the dictator, the "No to Pinochet" wins.
1989
Mario Pérez de Arce receives the National Architecture Award.

Aylwin elected president. Pinochet, head of

1977
Work begins on the Design Lodge. Iommi writes *A un nadador* [To a Swimmer].
1978
Work begins on the Guest Agora and the Dormitory Lodge in the Open City. Godofredo Iommi writes *La Carta del Errante* [The Wanderer's Letter].
1979
The Children's Home in Valparaíso is designed. Luis Peña House in Colina, Santiago, designed by M. Eyquem, is built.

1980
The Nail Lodge is built in the Open City.

1981
The first version of the Wanderer's Lodge is built in the Open City.

1982
The Palace of Dawn and Dusk, the Entrance Lodge and the Bo Cenotaph Garden are

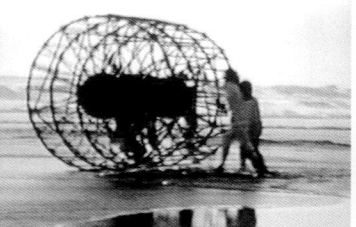

built. 30th Anniversary Exhibition of the UCV School of Architecture is held at the National Museum of Fine Arts in Santiago.
1984
The School of Valparaíso adopts the American *Travesías* as part of its pedagogical program, turning them into a regular annual event.
1985
Girola exhibits his work in Buenos Aires and Santiago de Chile.

1986
The second volume of *Amereida* is published.
1987
The Study Lodge is put up in the Open City.

1990
The Design Workshop is built in the Open City. One of Girola's paintings is chosen for

University in Urbino.

Pompidou Centre by Rogers and R. Piano.

Karol Wojtyla becomes Pope John Paul II. Spain has a new democratic constitution.

Sony develops the Walkman. Thatcher becomes the first female Prime Minister of Great Britain. Marcuse dies. Gehry designs the Gehry House, Santa Monica.

Ronald Reagan becomes president of the United States.

Mitterrand becomes president of France. J. Stirling, the Pritzker Prize Laureate.

Alejo Carpentier writes *La ciudad de las*

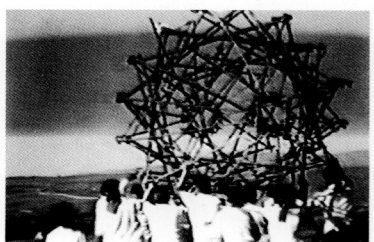

columnas [The City of Columns].

The AIDS virus is identified.

Navarro Baldeweg designs the Convention Centre and Exhibition Hall, Salamanca.

Nuclear disaster in Chernobyl, USSR.

Pope John Paul II visits Chile. R. Salmona designs the Casa de Huéspedes, Cartagena.
1988
An exhibition on Deconstructivism is held in London and New York.
1989
The Berlin Wall is torn down. Gehry wins Pritzker Prize, F. Castillo America Prize.

East and West Germany are reunited.

the Armed Forces. Browne/Huidobro design the Consorcio Vida Building.

J. Cruz Ovalle / G. del Sol design the Chilean Pavilion for Expo92 in Seville, F. Méndez the Open Air Museum in Valparaíso, with murals by Matta and Antúnez, and others.

Monument to the victims of Pinochet's repression lists over 4,000 names.

Architecture Centennial at the PUCCh in Santiago, for which Emilio Duhart receives a Doctor Honoris Causa.

C. Boza designs La Reina House, Totoralito, Los Vilos.

the *Art in Latin America* exhibition held in London, Stockholm and Madrid.

1992
On the 40th Anniversary of the School of Valparaíso, 600 local and foreign guests gather in the Open City for the inauguration of an exhibition on the 50 *Travesías* undertaken to that date. The House of Names pavilion and the main Road are prepared for the event. Girola organizes the *Escultura y Travesía* exhibition held at the Sculpture Park in Santiago. *Amereida – Travesías* is published.
1993
Alberto Cruz receives a Doctor Honoris Causa from the Catholic University of Valparaíso.

1994
B. Ivelic's project, the Travesía Amereida Vessel, is financed by the FONDECYT agency. Claudio Girola dies in Viña del Mar.
1995
The FONDECYT grants research funds for the New Wanderer's Lodge project in the Open City designed by M. Casanueva et al.

1996
The Interval Table, Open City, is designed. An exhibition on the Open City is held at the IAU (International Architect's Union) Congress in Barcelona.

Rossi, Pritzker Prize. Moneo designs the Kursaal Hall, San Sebastián.

The Earth Summit (conservation and sustained development) is held in Rio de Janeiro. Bill Clinton becomes president of the United States. Alvaro Siza becomes the Pritzker Prize Laureate.

Navarro Baldeweg wins the competition for the S. Allende Museum in Santiago.

Tadao Ando designs the Historical Museum in Minami-Kowachi.

Rem Koolhas designs the Congress Hall in Lille. Salmona receives the America Prize.

Moneo receives the Pritzker Prize and the commission to build Los Angeles Cathedral.

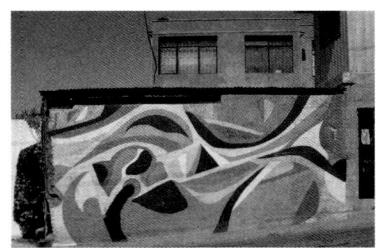 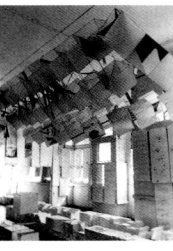 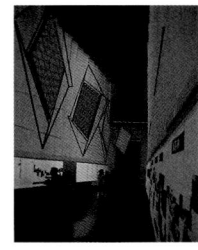 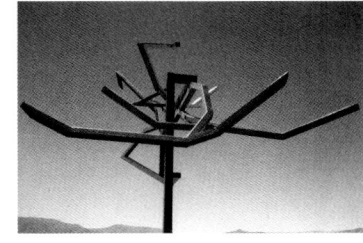 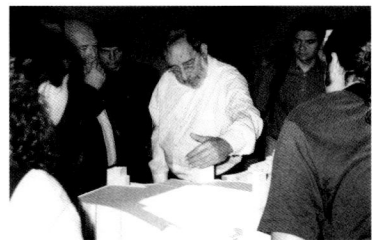

1998
The Water Towers and the Sculptor Workshop in the Open City are rebuilt. The Amereida co-operative is dissolved in order to establish the Corporación Cultural Amereida (cultural corporation). The FONDECYT grants more research funds for the New Wanderer's Lodge project in the Open City.
1999
The Cemetery Chapel in the Open City is built.
2000
The School begins work on the Avenida Brasil project (Valparaíso) commissioned by the Town Council. Trial launching of the Travesía Amereida Vessel.
2001
Godofredo Iommi, founder of the School of Valparaíso and the Open City, dies. His remains are laid to rest in the Open City Cemetery. Work begins on the Signs Lodge. The Museum of Fine Arts in Santiago organizes an exhibition in homage to C. Girola.

2002
The Royal Architectural Institute of Canada grants an Honorary Fellowship to the Open City team in recognition of the excellence of its architecture. The 50th Anniversary of the School of Valparaíso is celebrated at the National Museum of Fine Arts in Santiago.

The socialist, Lagos, is elected president.

USA and Spain are the main investors in Chile. Pinochet is prosecuted in Madrid.

Pinochet is prosecuted in Santiago de Chile.

A woman, the socialist Michelle Bachelet, becomes Minister of Defence. The III Ibero-American Architecture Biennal is held in Santiago de Chile.

Peter Eisenman designs the Aronoff Center in Cincinatti. Kohn, Pedersen Fox build the WFC, the tallest building in the world (460 m).

N. Foster, Pritzker Prize Laureate.

Manuel de Solá-Morales is the first European Town Planning Prize Laureate.

Madrid: the Reina Sofía Prize for Poetry to N. Parra, an exhibition on Huidobro and events commemorating Neruda. Attack on the Twin Towers (New York), designed by Yamasaki.

G. Murcutt, Pritzker Prize Laureate. The largest EU agreement is signed with Chile.

1   View to the north, as seen from the terrace of the Valparaíso School of Architecture, in Recreo
2   View of Valparaíso bay, as seen from the Atkinson promenade in the monumental quarter of the city
3   Partial view of the hills which descend to the sea and on which Valparaíso stands
4   Local architecture in Valparaíso
5   Detail of 19th C buildings erected on the broken topography of Cerro Concepción

6   Arturo Baeza, Claudio Girola, Alberto Cruz, José Vial
7   Alberto Cruz
8   Godofredo Iommi
9   Claudio Girola in his studio

10 Godofredo Iommi's *Phalène* in France
11 Godofredo Iommi's *Phalène* in England
12 Edison Simonds and Jonathan Boulting on the *Amereida I* voyage, 1965
13 Detail of the Atenea sculpture support, by Claudio Girola, in Costanera Río Mapocho, Santiago
14 Open City inaugural act, Ritoque, Quintero

15 Class of 1969 inaugural act: Arturo Baeza, José Vial, and Alberto Cruz
16 Opening ceremony of the Open City territory, 1970
17 *Nahuatl, América,* and *América sin patria,* Municipal Theatre, Viña del Mar, 1972
18 Weekly group meeting at the Music Room, Open City

19 Muelle Vergara *Phalène*, Viña del Mar, with Godofredo Iommi in the centre
20, 21 and 22   Game sequence in the Open City

23 Francisco Méndez's Mural at the Open Air Museum, Valparaíso, 1992
24 Spatial course, Comet Tournament, first year, 1999
25 Exhibition at the Museum of Fine Arts, partial view, Santiago de Chile, 2000
26 *Travesía* to Humahuaca sculpture, 2001
27 Alvaro Siza with students of the School of Architecture during the *Travesía* to Portugal, 2001

From right to left:
Three generations of members of the School of Valparaíso, the Open City group:
Alberto Cruz,
Juan Purcell,
Salvador Zahr;
Aula Viga [Beam Hall], School of Architecture,
Catholic University of Valparaíso,
Recreo, Viña del Mar, March 2000

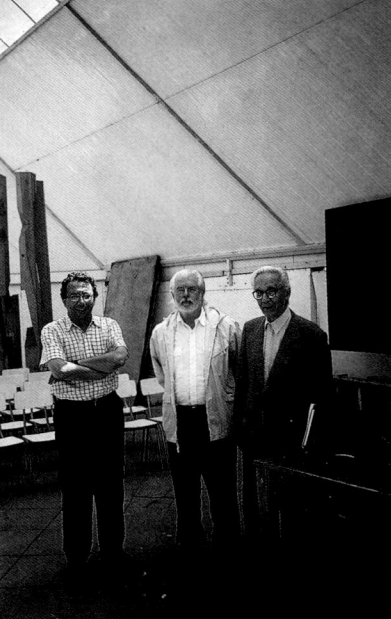

Bibliography

Abbreviations used in this bibliography:

UCV Universidad Católica de Valparaíso
(Catholic University of Valparaíso)
PUCC Pontificia Universidad Católica de Chile
E. de A. Escuela de Arquitectura
(School of Architecture)

AA.VV. "Análisis de las Arquitecturas de Iglesias en Puerto Montt" in *AA.VV: La Arquitectura Contemporánea de la madera en Chile. Un estudio de su desarrollo entre 1960 y 1990*. Santiago: Investigación Fondecyt no. 0655-91 (March 1993).
— *Arquitectura e Societá. L'America Latina nel XX Secolo*. Milan: Jaca Book, 1996, pp. 33, 39, 132, 185, 231, 304.
AA.VV (Gutierrez, Ramón: Coord.). *Arquitectura Latinoamericana en el siglo XX*. Barcelona: Lunwerg, 1998.
AA.VV. *Casas: Obra de Arquitectos Chilenos Contemporáneos*. Santiago: Ediciones ARQ, 1997.
ALFIERI, Massimo. *La Ciudad Abierta*. Santiago: Editrice Librerie Dedalo, 2000.
AMEREIDA, CORPORACIÓN CULTURAL. *Un trazo de veinte años, por la arquitectura recorrido por el Instituto de Arquitectura y más tarde por la Escuela de Arquitectura de la Universidad Católica de Valparaíso*, en CD-ROM. Valparaíso: Corporación Cultural Amereida, 1999.
— *Claudio Girola*. CD-ROM. Valparaíso: Corporación Cultural Amereida, 1999.
— *Amereida, travesías por América, UCV. Escuela de Arquitectura*. vol. III. Valparaíso: E. de A., UCV, 1992.
ARAYA CÉSPEDES, Olga. "Ciudad Imaginada." *YA* magazine, *El Mercurio*, Santiago, 29 September 1987, pp. 8-9.
ART D'AUJOURD'HUI. "L'art concret et la mer." *Art d'aujourd'hui*, Paris, 1953.
AUCA. "Una Lección Universitaria." *AUCA*, no. 9, Santiago, (June 1967), pp. 4-5.

BAEZA, Arturo; UCV, Instituto de Arquitectura. "Capilla de la Candelaria." *AUCA*, no. 13, Santiago, (February 1968), pp. 50-51.
BAIXAS, Juan. "Dos Aulas Neumáticas." *CA*, no. 54, Santiago, (October 1988), pp. 52-59.
— "Pisos y Mesa de Dibujo, Doblando un Tubo." *CA*, no. 99, Santiago (October 1999) p. 75.
BARLA, Bruno. "Casa de los Pinos." *Vivienda y Decoración*, *El Mercurio*, Santiago, 22 October 1994.
BENEVOLO, Leonardo. *Historia de la Arquitectura Moderna*. Barcelona: Gustavo Gili, 1974 (1st ed. Spanish).
BORCHERS, Juan. *Institución Arquitectónica*. Santiago: Andrés Bello, 1968.
BRESCIA, Maura. "La Otra Arquitectura." *La Epoca*, Santiago, 12 March 1989, p. 32.
— "Una escultura de regalo para Santiago." *La Epoca*, 16 December 1987, p. 25.

BROWNE, Enrique. "Arquitectura e poesía em Valparaíso." *Projeto* no. 65 (June 1984), pp. 96-99.
— "La Ciudad Abierta en Valparaíso." *Summa*, no. 214, Buenos Aires (July 1985), pp. 74-83.
— *Otra arquitectura en América Latina*. México: Gustavo Gili, 1988, pp. 149-152.
BROWNE, E. and R. PÉREZ DE ARCE. "Ciudad Abierta", in *Annals of the Architectural Association School of Architecture, AA Files,* no. 17, London, 1989, pp. 42-48.

CÁCERES, Osvaldo. *La Arquitectura de Chile Independiente. 1ª Parte*. Concepción: 1974, without printer's imprint, PUCC Library of Architecture, Santiago.
CASANUEVA, Manuel. *Desarrollo en el espacio constructivo de elementos técnico-arquitectónicos que gradúan las energías de la interperie*. Valparaíso: Proyecto Fondecyt, no. 1941189.
— "Habitar en Hospederias." *CA*, no. 84, Santiago (April 1996), pp. 34-39.
— "The errant's lodge: Reconstruction, Research, Teaching." *ARQ*, no. 2, vol. 2. London: Emap Business Publication (Winter 1996), pp. 40-49.
— "Hospedería del Errante." *Architectural Research Quarterly,* no. 2, vol. 2, 1996.
— "Cinco Torneos. Curso de cultura del cuerpo", *CA*, no. 48, Santiago (June 1987), pp. 58-61.
— "Trances del ocio: la fiesta y el juego." *Revista Universitaria*, no. 39, Santiago, 1993, pp. 36-39.
— *Tesis del Arquitecto Orfebre*. Santiago: Proyecto Fondecyt, no. 91-551.
— "Santiago, Pena Capital." *ARQ*, no. 25, Santiago (January 1994), pp. 2-7.
— "La Rueda Hélice, Ingenuidades para un Ingeniero." *ARQ*, no. 45, Santiago (July 2000), pp. 30-31.
CASANUEVA, M. and J. NEGRETE. "Potencial y desarrollo." *CA*, no. 61, Santiago (July 1990), pp. 60-67.
CASTILLO, Eduardo. *...de una trayectoria americana en la escultura moderna. Escritos, obras y dibujos de Claudio Girola*. Graphic Design Thesis, Valparaíso: E. de A., UCV, 1987.
CELEDÓN, Pedro. "Educación y Cultura." *La Epoca*, Santiago, 25 April 1995, p. 9.
COSTA, Lucio. "Raçoes de uma nova arquitectura." *Registro de uma vivencia*. Empresa das Artes, 1997.
CRISPIANI, A. and R. MOYA. *Claudio Girola. Vida y obra*. Investigación de la Dirección de Investigación y Postgrado. Santiago: PUCC, DIPUC. no. 2632017-05, 2001.

CRUZ, Fabio. "Casa Cruz", *ARQ*, no. 16, Santiago (March 1991), pp. 31-39.
CRUZ, Alberto. "Proyecto Achupallas y Capilla Pajaritos", *Anales de la U.C.V.*, no. 1, E. de A. UCV, Valparaíso, 1954.
— "Alberto Cruz, Cooperativa Amereida, Chile", *Zodiac*, no. 8, Milano (September 1992), pp. 188-199.
— "Ritoque, Ciudad Abierta", *Arquitectura Panamericana*, no. 1. Federación Panamericana de Asociaciones de Arquitectos, Santiago (December 1992), pp. 130-141.
— "Ciudad Abierta". *Summa*, no. 214, Buenos Aires (July 1985), pp. 82-83.
— "Exposición de 40 años de la Escuela de Arquitectura de la Universidad Católica de Valparaíso". *Diseño*, no. 18, Santiago (March 1993), pp. 90-93
— "Exposición 40 años Escuela de Arquitectura U.C.V.", *CA*, no. 71 (January-February-March 1993), p. 23.
— "Seminario de la Escuela", E. de A., UCV, Valparaíso (7 December 1970).
— *Estudios de Territorios Parroquiales*. Handwritten, Instituto de Arquitectura UCV, Ubic. 103, Valparaíso, 1960.
— "La libertad de formas". *Cuadernos de Arquitectura*, no. 6-7, Habitar el Norte, 1998, Facultad de Arquitectura, Construcción e Ingeniería Civil Universidad Católica del Norte, Antofagasta, pp. 4-8.
— "Opinión". *AUCA*, no. 28, Santiago, 1975, p. 27.
— "El arquitecto y la calidad de Vida". *AUCA*, no. 34, Santiago (June 1978), pp. 77-78.
— *Arquitectura Punto de Vista*. E. de A., UCV, Valparaíso.
— *Forma y Figura en la Arquitectura*. E. de A., UCV, Valparaíso.
— *Estudio acerca de la Observación en la Arquitectura*. E. de A., UCV, Valparaíso, w/d.
— *Travesías*, formulario de postulación proyectos Fondecyt, Biblioteca de E. de A., UCV, Valparaíso, 1986.
— "El Parque se vende", *AUCA*, no. 40, Santiago, October, pp. 55-58.
— "Premio nacional de Arquitectura 1975" to Alberto Cruz. *C.A.*, no. 68, Santiago (April 1992), pp. 78-81.
— *Amereida Palladio. Carta a los Arquitectos Europeos, Amereida Palladio. Lettera agli Architetti Europei*. CD-ROM, E. de A., UCV, Valparaíso, 1999.
— "Alberto Cruz Covarrubias". *CA*, no. 16, Santiago (July 1976).
— "Composición Pre-Arquitectónica". *Plinto*, no. 1 (October 1947), pp. 10-11.
— "Discurso Alberto Cruz al recibir el grado del D.H.C. 1993". Biblioteca E. de A., UCV, Valparaíso, pp. 1-4.
— "Premio de Honor al arquitecto Alberto Cruz C.", *El Mercurio*, Santiago, 2 April 1976.

— *Don Arquitectura*. Santiago de Chile: ARQ Ediciones, 2002, handcut thread-paper booklets.
CRUZ, Alberto; BROWNE, Tomás. "Acerca de los edificios en altura hoy". *ARQ*, no. 40, Santiago (November 1998), pp. 31-34.
CRUZ, Alberto; EYQUEM, Miguel. "Casa Olivetti en Santiago". *ARQ*, no. 47, Santiago (March 2001), pp. 16-21,
CRUZ, Alberto; IOMMI, Godofredo. "Ciudad Abierta: de la utopía al espejismo". *Revista Universitaria*, no. 9, Santiago (April 1983), PUCC.
CRUZ OVALLE, José. "El Inchubismo Cultural y la arquitectura". *El Mercurio*, Santiago, 28 January 1979, pp. E-7.

DAVIDS, Rene: "The City That is not a City", *By the Way - D.B.R. Design Book Review*, no. 39, 1997, pp. 45-47.
DE AMBROSINI, Silvia. "Viaje a Ciudad Abierta". *Artinif*, no. 31-32 (March-April 1982), pp. 45-46.
DE CARLO, Giancarlo. "L'utopia di Ritoque". *Spazio e Societá*, no. 66, Rome, 1994, pp. 24-25.
DE LA VEGA, Luz María. "Ritoque, 30 años de Ciudad Abierta". *Vivienda y Decoración* no. 194, *El Mercurio*, Santiago, 25 March 2000, pp. 24-38.
DI GIROLAMO, Vittorio. "Lo grande y lo bello de la pobreza voluntaria". Sunday supplement, *El Mercurio*, Santiago, 10 January 1993, p. E-8.
— "Los locos de Valparaíso". *Qué Pasa*, no. 80, Santiago (October 1972), pp. 48-50.
DURAN-COGAN, M.F.; GÓMEZ-MORIANA, A. (eds.). *National Identities and Sociopolitical Changes in Latin America*. New York: Routledge, 2001.

EL MERCURIO. "Acto en la Plaza de la Matriz". *El Mercurio*, Valparaíso, 6 April 1967, p. 3.
— "Hoy se celebra el día del urbanismo". *El Mercurio*, Valparaíso, 8 November 1979, p. 9.
— "La Arquitectura como Acto poético". *El Mercurio*, Santiago, 31 October 1982, p. E-5.
— "Poetas de la forma". *Vivienda y Decoración*, *El Mercurio*, Santiago, 6 April 1991.
— "Labor de 10 años de arquitectos en Exposición Ciudad Abierta". *El Mercurio*, Santiago, 11 September 1992.
— "Navegantes de la Poesía, del Arte, del Mar...". *El Mercurio*, Santiago, 29 January 1995, p. E-10.
— "Mañana partimos a recorrer América". *El Mercurio*, Santiago, 9 June 1996.
— "Una escultura para recorrer presenta C. Girola". *El Mercurio*, Santiago, 28 May 1987.
ELIASH, Humberto; MORENO, Manuel. *Arquitectura y Modernidad en Chile, 1925-1965*, PUCC, Santiago,1989.
— "Institucionalización de la modernidad", *Cuadernos Luxalón*, Santiago, 1985, pp. 17-18.

ESTILO: "Arquitectura Latinoamericana obra de la Cooperativa Amereida". *Estilo*, no. 18, pp. 57-61.
EYQUEM, Miguel: "Central de Adquisiciones Automotrices". *AUCA*, no. 34, Santiago (June 1978), p. 43.
— "Casa Luis Peña". *CA*, no. 31, Santiago (December 1981), pp. 24-28.
— "Casa Peña". *ARQ*, no. 6 (November 1981), po. 9-13.
— "La Casa Peña en la colina". *ARQ*, no. 41, Santiago (April 1999), pp. 42-49.
EYQUEM, Miguel; BAEZA, Arturo. "Estudio del Transporte Aéreo en Chile". *CA*, no. 103, Santiago (October-November-December 2000), pp. 25-31.
— "Centro oriente según la CORMU 1970-1974". *ARQ*, no. 40, Santiago (November 1998), pp. 42-49.
EYQUEM, Miguel; LANGLOIS, Vicuña. "Edificio Escalonado y en Terrazas". *CA*, no. 22, Santiago (December 1978), pp. 30-32.

FERNÁNDEZ, Roberto. "Cartografías del Tiempo". *Revista de Crítica Arquitectónica*, no. 2, Barcelona, Departamento de Composición Arquitectónica ETSAB-UPC, 1999, p. 25.
CRUICKSHANK, Dan et al. (eds.). *Sir Banister Fletcher's A History of Architecture*. Oxford: Architectural Press, 20th edition, 1996, p. 1,538.
FREEITELD, Abraham. "El realismo en la obra escultórica de Claudio Girola". Santiago: Ultramar, 1961.

GARCÉS, Andrés; IVELIC, Iván; JELDES, Juan Carlos; LUZA, David; PUENTES, Mauricio; REYES, Jaime; SAAVEDRA, Rodrigo; SANFUENTES, Manuel; WILKOMIRSKY, Michelle. "Une journée particulière à Ritoque". *L'Architecture d'Aujourd'hui*, no. 336 (September-October 2001), pp. 114-119
GIROLA, Claudio. *Reflexiones sobre la Representación del espacio en las Artes Plásticas*, E. de A. UCV, Valparaíso, w/d.
— *La escultura es un Arte Decepcionante*. E. de A. UCV, Valparaíso, w/d
— *Durante la Travesía a Chochi-co*, E. de A., UCV, Valparaíso, 1991.
— *Contemporaneidad en la Escultura*. E. de A., UCV, Valparaíso,1981.
— *Simetría y Lateralidad en las Artes Plásticas*. E. de A. UCV, Valparaíso, 1982.
— *Los nuevos campos Expandidos de la Escultura*. E. de A., UCV, 1988.
GLUSBERG, Jorge. "Claudio Girola, Escultura y Travesía". *Diseño*, no. 9, (September-October 1991), pp. 80-83.
GROSS, Patricio; VIAL, Enrique. *El Monasterio Benedictino de las Condes: Una Obra de Arquitectura Patrimonial*. Santiago: PUCC, 1988, pp. 36-40 / 46-51.

GUERRA, Ana María. "La vida diaria en la poética e incómada Ciudad Abierta de Ritoque". *La Segunda*, Santiago, 6 March 1987, pp. 41-42.

HALPERT, Marta. "La diferencia de la similitud". *Economía Hoy*, Caracas, 16 March 1991, p. 25.

IOMMI, Godofredo. *Estorninos*. Valparaíso: E. de A., UCV.
— *Carta del Errante*. Valparaíso: E. de A., UCV.
— *Tres Odas*. Valparaíso: Ediciones Universitarias, 1972.
— *La semejanza más sorda*. Valparaíso: E. de A., UCV, 1975.
— *El Paraíso*. Valparaíso: E. de A., UCV, 1976.
— *A un nadador*. Valparaíso: Omega, 1977.
— *El expediente*. Buenos Aires: Gabinete del Grabado Ediciones, 1978.
— *Semónides 8 ó el espejo de mujeres,* Valparaíso: E. de A., UCV, 1979.
— *Comentario y Cadencias*. Valparaíso: E. de A., UCV, 1980.
— *O purete purete*. Valparaíso: E. de A., UCV, 1981.
— *Los héroes*. Valparaíso: E. de A., UCV, 1981.
— *Hay que ser absolutamente moderno, Arthur Rimbaud*. Valparaíso: E. de A., UCV, 1981.
— *Cantata ciertos números a José Vial*. Valparaíso: E. de A., UCV, 1983.
— *Discursos de los secretos*. Valparaíso: E. de A., UCV, 1984.
— *El testamento de Rimbaud*. Valparaíso: E. de A., UCV, 1984.
— *X1, X2, X3*. Valparaíso: E. de A., UCV, 1984.
— *Fuese*. Valparaíso: E. de A., UCV, 1984.
— *Dos conversaciones de Godofredo Iommi*. Valparaíso: E. de A., UCV, 1984.
— "El azar como riesgo floreciente". *Artinif*, 1985.
— "Por qué, cómo y cuando existe arte". *Revista Universitaria*, no. 9, Santiago, 1986, pp. 8-13.
— *Sentido poético de la cólera*. Valparaíso: E. de A., UCV, 1986.
— *Los ascensos*. Valparaíso: E. de A., UCV, 1990.
— Poems published in successive bi-monthly numbers of *Ladeco América,* Santiago, between August 1990 and February 1995.
— *Tu forastero*. Valparaíso: E. de A., UCV, 1993.
— "La Ciudad Abierta: de la utopía al espejismo". *Revista Universitaria*, no. 9, Santiago, 1983, pp. 1-25.
— *A sol depuesto*. Valparaíso: E. de A., UCV, 1994.
IOMMI, Godofredo; GIROLA, Claudio. "La Eneida y América 4. Acto Poético de Rimbaud". *Artinif,* no. 31/32 (March-April 1992), pp. 40-44.
IVELIC, Boris. "Embarcación para la región Austral. Proyecto Fondecyt". *ARQ*, no. 29, Santiago (April 1995), pp. 40-47.
— "Embarcación experimental para la región austral". *2G*, no. 8, Gili, Barcelona, 1998, pp. 104-106.
— "Hospedería de los Diseños". *ARQ*, no. 17, Santiago (July 1991), pp. 32-35.
— "Embarcación para las travesías a la Patagonia Occidental: Teoría de las cualidades intrínsecas o peculiares de los objetos". *ARQ*, no. 49, Santiago (December 2001), pp. 30-35.

LA EPOCA. "Un dialogo entre arquitectura y poesía", *La Epoca*, Santiago, 10 January 1993, p. 28.
LA ESTRELLA. "Una manera diferente de aplicar la arquitectura". *La Estrella*, Valparaíso, 25 November 1991.
LABORDE D., Miguel. "Laboratorio de experimentos arquitectónicos". *Decoración y Diseño*, supplement of *El Mercurio*, Santiago, 11 September 1982.
— "El poeta Godofredo Iommi". *El Mercurio,* Santiago, 4 March 2001.
LAFOURCADE, Enrique. "Sobre encantadores y encantados". *El Mercurio*, Santiago, 28 January 1979, p. E-4.
LARRAIN, A. María. "Godofredo Iommi en el borde de los desconocido". *Carola, Santiago,* no. 117 (May 1987).
LARRETA, L. Alfredo. "El porqué de la Ciudad Abierta". *El Mercurio*, Santiago, 26 September 1982, p. 7.
LAS ULTIMAS NOTICIAS. " Artistas Concretos llaman la atención". *Ultimas Noticias*, Santiago, 11 November 1952.
LIERNUR, Francisco J. *Escritos de Arquitectura Latinoamericana en el siglo XX*. Sevilla-Madrid: Tanais Ediciones, 2002.
LÓPEZ A. Jorge. "Una metáfora en la obra de Claudio Girola". *El Economista*, Buenos Aires, 20 September 1985.

MACINNES, Katherine. "The Wise Man Built his House upon the Sand". *World Architecture*, no. 48, Cheeman, London (July-August 1996), pp. 60-61.
MACKAY, David. *La casa unifamiliar*. Barcelona: Gustavo Gili, 1984, casa Peña, pp. 58-61.
MELLO, Gerardo. "Viña del Mar hubo un poeta", *Artes y Letras,* supplement of *El Mercurio,* Santiago, 4 March 2001.
MORENO, Alex. "Casa Cruz. Comentario a la obra". *ARQ*, no. 16, Santiago (March 1991), p. 39.
MORGADO, Patricio A. *Reconstrucción de las Iglesias del Sur después del terremoto de 1960 por la Escuela de Arquitectura de la Universidad Católica de Valparaíso: el caso de Nuestra Señora de la Candelaria*, Thesis on Architecture. Santiago: E. de A., PUCC (Library code: TUC 1994 M847R), 1994.
MOYA, Rafael. *Del Curso del Espacio a la Travesía. Los talleres de enseñanza en la Escuela de Arquitectura de*

la Universidad Católica de Valparaíso. Thesis on Architecture, E. de A., PUCC (Library code: TUC 2000 M938T), Santiago, 2000.
MUÑOZ, María Dolores. *Premios Nacionales de Arquitectura, 1969-1985*. Concepción: Universidad de Bío-Bío, 1986.

NOVOA, Mariana. "Acto poético de Rimbaud". *Paula*, Santiago (October 1982), pp. 61-63.

PENDLETON-JULLIAN, Ann M. *The Road That Is Not a Road: And The Open City, Ritoque, Chile*. Cambridge, MA: Graham Foundation / The MIT Press, 1996.
— "La strada che non é una strada e la Cittá Aperta di Ritoque, Cile". *Spazio e Societá*, no. 66, Rome (April-June 1994), pp. 26-41.
PÉREZ DE ARCE, Mario. "Chili". *T.A.*, no. 334 (March 1981), p. 90.
PÉREZ DE ARCE, Rodrigo. "Ciudad Abierta". *Abitare*, nc. 353, Milano (July 1996), pp. 83-87.
— "Acerca de las Travesías", unpublished (June 1991).
— See Browne...
PÉREZ OYARZÚN, Fernando. "Ortodossia / eterodossia. Architettura moderna in Cile". *Casabella*, no. 650, Milano (November 1997), pp. 8-15.
— "The Valparaíso School". *The Harvard Architecture Review*, no. 9, 1993, pp. 82-101.
— "Alberto Cruz, entre la Observación y la Ofrenda", *CA*, no. 72, Santiago (April 1993), pp. 78-80.
PÉREZ OYARZÚN, Fernando; BANNEN, Pedro; RIESCO, Hernán; URREJOLA, Pilar. "El espacio como reto a la arquitectura moderna". *Arquitectura*, no. 30, Santiago, pp. 4-18.
PÉREZ OYARZÚN, Fernando et al. *Iglesias de la Modernidad en Chile. Precedentes europeos y americanos*, Santiago: Ediciones ARQ, 1997.
PÉREZ OYARZÚN, Fernando; TORRENT, Horacio. *La arquitectura que no fue: obras modernas no construidas en Chile 1950-1970. / Seminario de Investigación 1996*, Biblioteca de Arquitectura, PUCC, no. 720.983 P438a, 1996.
PURCELL, Juan; SANCHEZ, Jorge. "Travesía Iquitos-Amazonas". *CA*, no. 99, Santiago (October 1999), pp. 25-29.

REVISTA DO PATRIMONIO HISTORICO E ARTISTICO NACIONAL. "Cidade Aberta: primeira visita". *Revista do Patrimonio Historico e Artistico Nacional*, no. 23, 1994, pp. 204-213.
RÍOS, Oscar. "Ciudad Abierta de Ritoque". *Diseño*, no. 5 (December 1990), pp. 62-67.
RODRIGUEZ, León. "La vanguardia en Chile. Reforma de 1949 en la P. U. Católica". *CA*, no. 69, Santiago (July-August-September 1992), p. 61.

RODRIGUEZ SERRA, Ernesto: "Figura Poética de Godofredo Iommi". *Revista Universitaria*, no. 32, Santiago, 1991, pp. 1-25.
ROJAS, Hugo. "Rodelillo Valparaíso". *CA*, no. 53, Santiago (July 1988), pp. 60-61.

SÉGURET, Francois. "Ritoque ou l'utopie", "Une journée particulière à Ritoque". *L'Architecture d'Aujourd'hui*, no. 336 (September-October 2001), pp. 110-113.
SERRANO, Margarita. "Godofredo Iommi: La Vida Peligrosa". *Mundo*, no. 105 (August 1991).
SOLÀ-MORALES, Ignasi (main speaker) et al. *Present i futurs, Arquitectura a les Ciutats*. Barcelona: Colegio de Arquitectos de Cataluña - Centro de Cultura Contemporánea de Barcelona, catalogue of homonymous exhibit on the ocassion of the XIX UIA Congress, International Union of Achitects, Barcelona, 1996.
SPAZIO E SOCIETÁ. "Hospedería del Errante, la locanda del viandante". *Spazio e Societá*, no. 78, Rome, 1997.

UCV, ESCUELA DE ARQUITECTURA. "Arquitecturs", *Dilemas*, no. 2 (January 1967), p. 13.
— *Declaración del Consejo de Profesores de la Escuela de Arquitectura por la Reorigninación Universitaria*, text without printer's imprint, Library of the E. de A., UCV, Valparaíso, June 1968.
— *Voto al Senado Académico*, without printer's imprint, Library of the E. de A., UCV, Valparaíso, 1969.
— *Fundamentos de la Escuela de Arquitectura de la Universidad Católica de Valparaíso*, E. de A., UCV, Valparaíso, 1971.
— *Para una situación de América Latina en el Pacífico*. Valparaíso: E. de A., UCV, 1971.
— "La casa de lo Curro". *Revista del Domingo*, Santiago, 24 February 1974, pp. 4-5.
— "Exposición de los Fundamentos de la Escuela de Arquitectura UC.V. en el Museo de Bellas Artes de Santiago 1972", *AUCA*, no. 28, Santiago, 1975, pp. 39-45, and no. 30.
— "Plan seccional Estero Viña del Mar". *AUCA*, no. 26, Santiago (September 1974), pp. 38-41
— "Parroquia de Corral". *CA*, no. 32, Santiago (March 1982), pp. 28-33.
— "Muebles por el Diseño de Objetos UCV". *ARQ*, no. 7, Santiago (November 1982), pp. 24-31.
— "Iglesia Matriz de los Jesuitas de Pto. Montt". *CA*, no. 37, Santiago (April 1984), pp. 22-29.
— "Nuestra Latitud Patagonia". *CA*, no. 40, Santiago (June 1985), pp. 11-17
— "Proyecto Escuela Naval". *CA*, no. 43, Santiago, (March 1986), pp. 32-34.

— "Diseño de Objetos". *CA*, no. 47, Santiago (March 1987), pp. 52-57.
— "Travesía y obra en la Cordillera de los Andes". *CA*, no. 48, Santiago, (June 1987), pp. 46-51.
— "Una avenida de tres modos". *CA*, no. 51, Santiago (March 1988), pp. 38-43.
— "Nuevas Hospederias en la Ciudad Abierta. Cooperativa Amereida, Valparaíso 1981-89". *ARS, Revista Latinoamericana de Arquitectura*, no. 11, Santiago, 1989.
— "Obra travesía Monumento Athenea". *ARQ*, no. 14, Santiago (March 1990), pp. 36-43.
— "Proyecto Estero Marga - Marga". *CA*, no. 63, Santiago, 1991, pp. 34-39.
— "Casa de Los Nombres". *CA*, no. 87, Santiago, 1992, pp. 50-53.
— "Cubículo en Ritoque". *CA*, no. 89, Santiago (July 1997), pp. 68-73.
— "Open City Group - Cittá Aperta, Valparaíso, Cile". *Domus*, no. 789, Milano (January 1997), pp. 22-31.
UCV, ESCUELA DE ARQUITECTURA (G. Iommi, ed). *Amereida*, Lambda, Santiago, 1967; 3rd edition, E. de A., UCV, Valparaíso, 1997.
— *Amereida, volumen segundo*. Valparaíso: E. de A., UCV, 1986.
UGARTE, Juan José et al. *amereida poesía y arquitectura. godofredo iommi, alberto cruz*, investigación a partir del Seminario "amereida poesía y arquitectura". Santiago: Ediciones ARQ (December 1992).

VALDÉS, Cecilia. "Claudio Girola, Arte y Poesía". *El Mercurio*, 15 September 1991, pp. EB, EG.
— "Claudio Girola en la visión poética de Amereida". *El Mercurio*, Santiago, 26 June 1987, p. E-9.
— "Godo Dice la Palabra Poética con Voz Blanca", *Artes y Letras*, supplement of *El Mercurio*, Santiago 4 March 2001.
VEA. "El arte Concreto". *Vea*, Santiago (November 1952)
VIAL, José et al. "Quillota y El Aconcagua". *CA*, no. 46 (December 1986), pp. 44-49.

WARKEN, Cristián. "América llora la muerte de Godofredo Iommi". *Nor-Este*, Santiago, 17 March 2001.

ZAHR MALUK, Salvador. "Taller de un Escultor en Ritoque". *CA*, no. 97, Santiago (June 1999), pp. 40-43.
ZEGERS, Cazzú. "Iommi, el poeta de amereida". *Nor-Este*, no. 35, Santiago (April 2001).
ZUÑIGA, L. "Vida poética postula grupo de arquitectos". *El Mercurio*, Santiago, 11 September 1982.

Glossary

This brief glossary or word map has been drawn up by the Editor to help readers enter and find their way round the world of this highly unusual group of creators. It consists of merely a few notes for practical and informative purposes and lays no claim to academic rigour—for which we defer to the main body of the book—and, therefore, does not necessarily reflect the thoughts or opinions of the Valparaíso School / Open City group.

Agora
A physical site where the principal meetings of the group are held. The meetings themselves.
Pages 62-64, 72, 98

Amereida
Poem and books—the first in 1965—named after the contraction of America and *Eneida* (Spanish for the *Aeneid*), the account of the first *travesía* or crossing—see entry below. Poetic vision of America. Official name given to the first organization called Amereida Cooperative, later Corporation.
Pages 9, 13, 14, 16

Amereida Cooperative of Professional Services
Name adopted for the non-profit making association formed by the group after 1967 in order to purchase land and build the Open City.

Amereida Cultural Corporation
New legal form adopted in 1999 by the Amereida Cooperative of Professional Services.

Collective
Essential character of life, teaching and architectural research, management and ownership of land and *hospederías* or lodges in the Open City, design method, authorship of that design and of the work.

Ephemeral, temporary
Attribute reassessed by the group in the face of the *Vitruvian* firmitas, in line with their world view and manifesting itself in multiple aspects: fragility of structures, leaving nature to destroy what has been built, constant change in the design and the building, conception of the habitat (see Hospedería).

Hospedería
A multi-purpose dwelling—house, studio, workshop, etc.—where the member of the Open City who actively promoted it and contributed to its initial financing, is lodged provisionally, and which has been designed according to the collective method, subject to approval in an *agora* by the group, and owned by the latter (the Amereida Corporation, formerly Cooperative).
Pages 58, 86, 102, 144-147

Institute of Architecture
Upon arriving at the School of Architecture of the Valparaíso Catholic University in 1952, the group made up by Alberto Cruz, Iommi and other young people, created an Institute of Architecture, a university organisation for the purposes of research, project design and execution, etc. It tends to overlap and be confused with the School of Architecture.

Materials
Local, rough, reused, wood, brick, concrete, neither treated nor polished, in harmony with the ideas of austerity, stripping bare, nature.

Open City
Idea, utopia, city which is not a city (begun in 1970), cultural project undertaken by the architects and designers of the School of Architecture of the Catholic University of Valparaíso who sought another path after their relative failure in 1967 to transform the School, aimed at creating a community devoted to living, working and studying to promote crafts and freedom. See also Cooperative and Corporation.
Pages 9, 13, 15, 56-121, 142-147, 153

Phalène
Word given to the poetic acts.
Pages 8, 9, 12, 14-16, 80, 156, 158

Poetic act
No work is begun without a "founding act", says Alberto Cruz. For the group, poetry is their vital and intellectual principal. Thus, they will perform a whole series of public poetic acts, known as *phalènes*. Furthermore, each building is in itself a poetic act.
Pages 8, 9, 12, 14-16, 80, 156, 158

Poetry
The ultimate distillate of the word, poetry becomes the co-generating element of their Architecture. They start from the premise that the human condition is poetic. Pages 7, 11, 13, 14-16, 80, 156, 158

Poverty
Central value in the group's conception of the world, and hence affecting everything they do, ranging from the collective ownership of the land and *hospederías* of the Open City to the use of local resources and the technique of self-construction. The "splendour of poverty" is one of their key expressions.

Ronda: work *en ronda*, construction *en ronda*
A collective and changing way of working through which the group teaches, researches, designs and builds. Pages 11, 17, 60, 80, 102

School of Architecture
In its first definition, as a concrete institution, School of the Catholic University of Chile at Valparaíso, created in 1928. The group made up of Alberto Cruz, Iommi and others, hired in 1952, refounded it in an intellectual sense. Secondly, the Valparaíso School denotes the movement, group and line of thought and action centred around the School itself, sometimes vaguely and overlapping or becoming confused with other names and organisations, such as Institute of Architecture, Amereida, Open City, etc.
Pages 153, 159

Travesía
Journey undertaken by professors and students, architects, poets, sculptors, designers, etc. through the lands and waters of America, a voyage of initiation, a task forming part of the curriculum of the academic year, experience, appropriation and marking of territory through the performance of poetic acts and works of architecture, sculpture or land art.
Pages 9, 12-17, 80, 122-133, 146, 148-151

Utopia
Giancarlo De Carlo asked them, "Are you a utopian community?". They answered "Yes".

Valparaíso
A coastal and poetic city, a seaport on the shores of the Pacific, 120 km from the capital Santiago; given that name in 1536 by the Spaniard Juan de Saavedra.
Pages 12, 32, 154, 159

Word
"In the beginning was the Word" is more than just a quote. The power of the word is the basis of everything and impregnates everything. They write down everything, to the point of excess and a certain inaccessibility. See 'Amereida' and 'Poetry'.

TEAMS, CONTRIBUTORS, AUTHORS

The conception of a work and the creation of a book require the contributions of a large number and variety of people and organisations.
There is not enough space to name them all here and, furthermore, in many cases they have asked to remain anonymous.
The Publishers, however, would like to thank all of those whose work made this book possible, symbolically represented by those listed on the right and by the following:

Valparaíso School, Open City group
José Balcells, Sculptor
Sigris Cartagena, Secretary
Jorge Ferrada, Architect
Iván Ivelic, Architect
Juan Purcell Fricke, Architect
Pamela Zavala, Librarian

Santiago de Chile
Elizabeth Bennet D., Architect
Juan Purcell, Architect
Jubal Varas, Poet and Educator

Madrid, Seville and Tanais editorial team
Andrea Buchner, Architect
Laura Abril, Degree in Art
Nieves Acedo, Degree in Art
Isabel Fernández Hiraldo, Degree in Philology
Belén Gómez, Degree in Fine Arts
and
Guillermo Vázquez Consuegra, architect, who first proposed this book.

Illustration Credits

José Balcells 123b, 123c
Andrea Buchner 41a, 41b, 154d
Alberto Cruz 56b, 106a
Fabio Cruz 128a, 128b
Corporación Cultural Amereida 6, 56a, 58, 60a, 62a, 64b, 64c, 68-69, 70-73, 74b, 75b, 76a, 76c, 98-101, 104-107, 108a, 108b, 114-115, 117b, 119a, 119b, 120a, 142, 144b-144d, 145, 146c, 146d, 156-157, 157b, 158b-158d, 168
Escuela de Arquitectura de la Universidad Católica de Valparaíso 9b, 10, 11, 14-17, 25-27, 77, 86, 87, 89b, 90b, 90c, 91b, 92-93, 94, 96, 97a, 111c, 122, 123a, 123d, 124, 125, 127a, 127b, 128c, 128d, 128f, 128g, 131, 132b, 133, 137, 140a, 141, 143, 144a, 149, 151, 155-156, 157a, 157c-158a, 159
Escuela de Arquitectura de la Universidad Católica de Valparaíso / *ARQ* 132-133
Escuela de Arquitectura de la Universidad Católica de Valparaíso / *CA* 80a, 82b, 83b, 83c, 88, 89a, 89c, 92
Instituto de Arquitectura de la Universidad Católica de Valparaíso 20-23, 28-30, 31c, 32-40, 42-43, 44e, 45d, 46-55, 136, 140b
Instituto de Arquitectura de la Universidad Católica de Valparaíso / *ARQ* 42, 44a-44d, 45a-45c
Instituto de Arquitectura de la Universidad Católica de Valparaíso / *CA* 30-31a, 30-31b, 31
I.U.M. Munich 41c
Patricio Mardones 60b, 90a, 108c, 113a, 118b, 119c, 120b, 120c, 121a, 121b
Alfonso Noguera 126a, 127c, 127d, 127e, 128e
Rodrigo Pérez de Arce 62b, 109, 110b, 110c, 112a, 112d
Juan Purcell 12, 61, 66-67, 74a, 78-79, 80b, 81, 82a, 83a, 84, 85, 102-103, 146a, 146b-147
Raúl Rispa 9a, 57, 59a, 59b, 60c, 63, 64a, 65, 69, 75a, 76b, 89d, 91a, 91c, 95, 97b, 110a, 111a, 111b, 112b, 112c, 113b, 113c, 113d, 116, 117a, 147a, 154a, 154b, 154c, 154e, 160

School of Valparaíso, the Open City group

Protagonist team and author of the work featured in this book. Its members and references are summarized in page 153. The voice and face that has acted on behalf of the group, **Salvador Zahr** (Valparaíso, 1945) graduated from the UCV School of Architecture and did his postgraduate studies at the Milan Polytechnic. Professor, researcher, and lecturer—Universities of Barcelona, Berlin, Manitoba—he has designed some 20 houses.

Rodrigo Pérez de Arce
(Santiago de Chile, 1948) graduated from the PUCCh School of Architecture in Santiago and did his post-graduate studies at the AA in London. Since 1978, he has taught at the AA School in London, the University of Bath and Schools in Pennsylvania, Rome, Miami, Buenos Aires. In 1990 he joined the faculty of the PUCCh in Santiago, where he directs the Extension Program of the Faculty of Architecture, Design and Town Planning Studies. He has written several books—on Guillermo Julián and 19th C Santiago—and essays, published in journals such as *AA Files*, *A+U*, *Architectural Review*, *Lotus*. As a practising architect, he has been responsible for the design of the Cultural Centre of Santiago (1994, co-author) and the remodeling of the city's Plaza de Armas (2000).

Fernando Pérez Oyarzun
(Santiago de Chile, 1950) graduated from the PUCCh School of Architecture in Santiago and earned a doctorate from the Polytechnic University in Barcelona, where he worked with Moneo at the School of Architecture. He has been a guest lecturer at the Universities of Harvard, Cambridge and Terza in Rome, and a member of the faculty of the PUCCh, where he was Director of the School of Architecture (1987-90) and Dean of the Faculty of Architecture and Fine Arts (1990-2000). As a researcher, he has published several books—on Le Corbusier, C. de Groote, churches of Modernity, and as co-author, *Los hechos de la arquitectura*—and several articles in journals such as *Casabella*, *Harvard Architecture Review*.

Raúl Rispa
(Seville, 1945) publisher since 1968, with wide international experience, he has written several books and published many others, including *Expo'92 Seville: Architecture and Design*, *Barragán: The Complete Works*, *Architecture Guide: Spain 1920-2000*...

Valeria Varas
(Temuco, 1966) studied in Bologna and works as an editor specializing in visual arts, first from Modena and Vignola, and currently from Madrid.

Teresa Santiago
(Madrid, 1961) graduated in Hispanic Philology (Universidad Complutense, Madrid); Master of Publishing (Stanford University, Palo Alto, California). Editor since 1983.

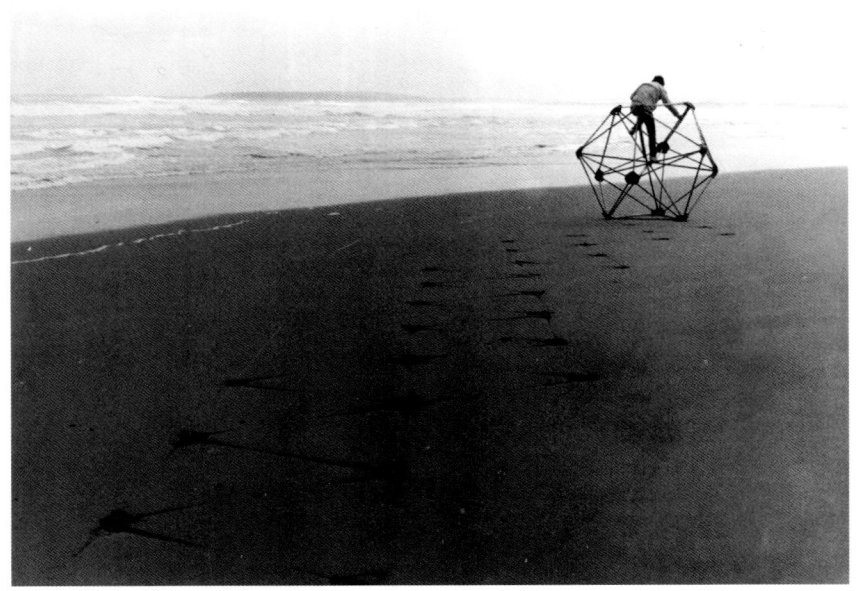